賴聲川

SELECTED PLAYS OF STAN LAI

Selected Plays of Stan Lai

Volume 2:

The Village and Other Plays

STAN LAI

Translated by the Playwright

Edited by Lissa Tyler Renaud

University of Michigan Press
Ann Arbor

Published in the United States of America
by the University of Michigan Press
Manufactured in the United States of America
Printed on acid-free paper
First published December 2021

A CIP catalog record for this book is available from the British Library.

ISBN 978-0-472-07508-9 (hardcover : alk. paper)
ISBN 978-0-472-05508-1 (paper : alk. paper)
ISBN 978-0-472-12956-0 (ebook)

Acknowledgments

Thanks to all who have worked so tirelessly to bring these plays to performance, and into print, particularly to all the actors who collaborated on the various works during the creative stage, and to all my colleagues at Performance Workshop in Taipei and Theatre Above in Shanghai. Thank you for your patience in the process, your dedication, and your artistry.

Thanks to Chang Hsiao-yen, for taking the challenge of the journey that became *Sand on a Distant Star*; to the Institute for Diversity in the Arts and the Department of Drama at Stanford University, and the Lark Play Development Center, New York, for their assistance in the creation of *Like Shadows*, particularly to Harry J. Elam Jr. and Michael Ramsaur at Stanford, and to David Henry Hwang for curating the Lark readings; to Wang Wei-chung for sharing his village stories and insisting that I write and direct the work that became *The Village*, to the Esplanade, Theatres on the Bay, Singapore, for its generous help in the initial production of the play; to the Hong Kong Repertory Theatre for its support in the creation of *Writing in Water*, and to the National Theatre, Taipei, which has generously hosted all of these plays on its stage, including the world premieres of the first four, and to all those who worked on this project at the University of Michigan Press, for their care and expertise in bringing the manuscript to print.

Contents

Digital materials related to this title can be found on the Fulcrum platform via the following citable URL: https://doi.org/10.3998/mpub.12103829

How I Wright Plays

In noting that the Chinese term for "playwriting" (*bianju*) means to "weave a play," as in weaving fabric or reeds, I am reminded that the English word "playwright" is spelled with "wright" and not "write." To "wright" is a whole different skill from putting pen to paper, as in "wrought iron," heating metal to a workable temperature and then shaping it into the desired beautiful form. The *Cambridge Dictionary* defines "wright" as "a person who makes or builds things." This more accurately reflects the way I create theatrical works, and makes me wonder: when did they start using what is to me the incorrect spelling for "playwrighting"? The *Oxford English Dictionary* tells us that in Shakespeare's times, the word was "play-wright," with a hyphen, and that in 1898, George Bernard Shaw referred to himself using the other word.

In performance, a play's script does not exist in text form. It is living onstage through the bodies, speech, and minds of the performers, and a complete performance combines the efforts of director, designers and various other collaborators in a grand team effort. A playscript may be a written guide on how to present a theatrical work. It may also be a record of a theatre piece after the work has been performed. To me, it is like a musical score, which represents the music, but is not the music *itself*. You can transcribe a Charlie Parker solo from a recording, but it is only a representation of the performance. For a novel, the words *are* the novel itself, so it is valid that it be created on paper (or device), to be read on paper (or device). For a theatrical work, thus, it is valid, and in my mind organic, to create a work using the same ecology as the actual performance—on a stage, or in a rehearsal space, with the performers and designers present. A preexisting text is not a prerequisite to this process, nor is the process designed to necessarily produce a text. Some theatre artists work this way, seeing work in the studio as a more organic and effective approach to theatrical creation than using paper and pen, or word processing software. It certainly is the standard way that choreographers work, and in many ways a play is choreography, a dance with life, between characters and actions and words and thoughts and emotions and—life. Many composers work with their musicians present, to hear what they are writing as they compose. There are even filmmakers who make films this way, but it is normally prohibitively expensive to do so, and that is why use of the prewritten script has become the dominant way of working in film, though the more economical way is not necessarily the more organic way.

I learned the art of "weaving" plays from Shireen Strooker of the Amsterdam Werkteater, one of the most inspiring theatre groups to come out of the 1970s. In their method, the "fabric" or "metal" is an idea, or an image, or a story, and the process of "weaving" is to do structured improvisations on designated topics to do with the fabric. Through these collective sessions, the contents and sometimes structure of a piece grow and blossom in an organic way. Though the person in charge of the piece is in effect the playwright and director, the title they use is not "playwright-director," but "stimulator." This is not an easily understood term, because so much of the work is intuitive. In this method, the work of playwrighting and directing is not a sequential operation, but one process: when the "wrighting" is done, so is the direction.

From this basic approach, my own method has evolved over the years. My earliest work, done in the then creative vacuum of Taiwan under martial law in the 1980s, attempted to emulate the Werkteater method as best I could. Working with actors who had little formal training in any acting style, and who had actually never experienced much modern theatre before, I would first set a "destination," an often obscure place, even to myself, and we would journey together, exploring topics through improvising on them, developing characters and scenes along the way. As scenes accumulated through improvisations, I tried to let the structure of the piece grow organically alongside, and though I would be the one who chose which scenes to discard, which to use, and in what order, the early works may be seen as more of a free approach to play-wrighting than later, and looking back, these plays became examples that showed how modern Asian plays could be created without copying the ready-made models of the West.

As my process developed over the years, improvisation in the studio became less prominent, though no less essential, but much more of my time would be devoted to developing the idea beforehand, and writing/editing/revising during the process. The free approach gave way to a structured process, which has evolved to this day.

Now my creative process normally begins with a personal incubation period, where I am inspired to do a work, and then have figured out how to do it, with confidence to proceed and actualize it onstage. Sometimes the inspiration is a quick spark (seeing the bans lifted on travel in November 1988, I started work on *The Island and the Other Shore* soon after, which premiered six months later), sometimes slow simmering (10 years for *Ago*). When I am ready to assemble a cast, I have usually written an outline, which includes characters, their descriptions, the story, and the structure of the work, with detailed scene-by-scene descriptions. Earlier in my career, these outlines were simpler, often explained orally to the actors, and would be revised by the ensuing work. Now they sometimes are very detailed (29 pages for *A Dream Like a Dream*, 18 for *Ago*, 16 for *The Village*). These outlines are usually presented to the actors at first rehearsal, in lieu of a finished script. Then perhaps one month of the two-month rehearsal period (longer for the longer plays) is devoted to developing the characters and improvising on the scenes as written in the outline. An assistant notates everything that goes on in such improvisational sessions. Outside of rehearsal, I have my quiet "writer's time" to edit, rework, rewrite whole scenes, or sometimes write in new scenes, and assemble everything together into the final whole. Ideally a month before performance, the final script is presented to the team by me, and we refine everything in what looks more like normal rehearsals, but the actors now have intimate knowledge of their roles, as well as where they need to be onstage. The play, finally, is "wrought."

The "stimulator" improvisational sessions are perhaps what intrigue people the most about my creative process. These, in particular, have evolved over time. Over the years I have moved from giving actors limitless space, to controlling more and more the area in which they are free to improvise. This happened naturally, for one, because as time went on, my main collaborators became less and less available due, happily, to growing fame and opportunities in film and television. *That Evening, We Performed Crosstalk*, for instance, had a total creative period of seven months in 1984–85, a luxury the actors could not afford again. Whereas we were sort of proud that we accumulated eight times the necessary material for that play, I was later forced to be much more efficient with improv material/actual material ratio. The second reason for the evolution of my method was simply me getting better at improvisation, no longer treating it with awe, as if it were some force of nature we were privileged to tap into once in a while. I began to understand it intimately, and was then able to use it to quickly see the truths of any given moment (setting up the structure of a scene), or the truth of the character in that moment (what the character will say or do). The key to mastering the use of this "force of nature" is in gradually acquiring a kind of intuitive vision to see how what is happening during an improv connects, within the improv itself, and without—how all that is happening somehow can connect to larger purposes, ideas, themes, structures.

And so when I work with improvisation these days, sometimes it all happens very quickly. Where the ratio in *That Evening* between improv and actual material was 8:1, for *A Dream Like a Dream* (2000) and *The Village* (2008), for instance, it was more like 1.1:1. For *Ago* (2019) it was more like 0.3:1, meaning that material coming from improv sessions was less than what came from my own writing, and also that my voice was dominating the improv sessions. I became the main improviser.

Improvisation in its simplest sense is spontaneously "living" in the moment. From loosely defining parameters of an improv when I started out, I learned that the stricter the definition of the borders were, the more fruitful the improvs became. I have worked with exceptional improvisers, like Lee Li-chun, Chin Shih-chieh, and Ismene Ting, to name a few. Their presence is strongly felt in works such as *Look Who's Crosstalking Tonight*, *The Island and the Other Shore*, and *I Me She Him*. When these artists "live" in the moment that is set up for them in the rehearsal studio, they bring their whole life experience and emotions to that moment, to the great enrichment of the work. Then, whatever comes from their inner souls interacts with my inner sense of the piece, and the piece evolves, day to day, until it reaches its final expression.

Even for beginners, like the many inexperienced students I have worked with at Taipei National University of the Arts, Berkeley, Stanford, and the Shanghai Theatre Academy, they can be productive in my system just by learning how to "be there"—adhering to the parameters, becoming the character, in the situation. That is the gist of my method, and to me the gist of play-wrighting. "Being there" is not unlike a meditation exercise, but to expect a beginning meditation student to immediately become proficient at it is asking too much, and so the parameters serve as a practice prop, if you will, asking you to focus on specific circumstances. By "being there," you act and react faithfully in the moment that has been laid out for you. Of course, the design of those circumstances is paramount to the success of the improv. This design comes from the essence of your creative endeavor, what you as leader set out to achieve in the piece. This is the guiding force for designing and conducting the improvs. The creative process, then, is like an extended meditation for me. To "be there," constantly inside the piece, keeps you connected with the truth of the work. The truth always leads the way. The truth of the inner urges of the artist leads to the shape of the story or stories to be told. The truth of the story leads to the truth of the characters and the design of the improvs; the truth of the character leads to the truth of his or her action during improvs, which circles back to the truth of the story.

Improvisation, when used effectively, cuts most quickly through the superfluous and reveals the essential. As Shireen taught me, as stimulator, you need to develop a sensitive inner "lie detector" to know when an actor in improvisation is faking it, for a fake improv can lead to false impulses and disastrous results. I have learned that you also need that lie detector to continually challenge yourself as to the decisions you yourself make, which are tightly tied to the goals of your work, what benefit it might bring for an audience, and whether what you are doing when "weaving" is wasting people's time or not. Therefore, when an improv is not yielding results, the problem may be not in the abilities of the actors, but in your design itself, and in the deeper motivations for setting out to create the piece. If there is something wrong at the source, the creative essence of the piece, no amount of improvising can embellish or make it right.

Strindberg once wrote on the role of chance in artistic creation, describing an ideal creative process as being "a charming mixture of the unconscious and conscious" urges on the part of the artist.[1] He was speaking of a spontaneous way of painting, though his later theatre works exemplify these thoughts. In dealing with a collective group as opposed to working alone, the role of chance magnifies not only in relation to the multiplied "conscious and unconscious urges," but more importantly, in relation to the skills and sensitivities of each individual actor. When I work with accomplished professionals who know the process, it is not unlike competent jazz musicians jamming. The difference is, these actors are improvising not for an audience en masse, but for one solitary "audience" member, me, and they fly to the heights of improvisational riffs while being tethered to the parameters of character and scene, anchored together in a common purpose. In turn, I attempt to "live" in the same moment as they, flying with them, occupying the different characters in turn, and I will shout out directives to them on the spot that change the path of that present moment even as they improvise. These directives are also improvised, appearing out of the moment of improvisation, and thus, are often deadly accurate.

More and more over the years, during improvs, it is often my voice that the assistant is notating. Perhaps this is because of the pressures of production—I do not have the luxury of developing a piece with no time frame—but I do believe it is also part of the evolution of the process. In these moments the work in the studio feels more to me like an artist painting, with his models before him, who provide the context and inspiration. Think of a playwright

1. August Strindberg, "The New Arts, or the Role of Chance in Artistic Creation," in *Inferno, Alone, and Other Writings*, trans. Albert Bermel (New York: Doubleday, 1968), p. 99.

with *characters* assembled before him, living in the moment of the scene. That is what it feels like when I have the opportunity to work with actors during the "wrighting" period now. You can also consider it as being like a conductor improvising with his musicians, toward the purpose of composing a new work.

Oxford defines "wright" as a "joiner." I guess that's what I do: join characters, through thoughts and emotions, to words, words to words, words to actions, characters to characters, characters to situations, situations to situations, scenes to scenes, acts to acts, early scenes to later acts, first-act characters to their later selves, meanings to actions, everything to life. The whole art of play-wrighting is a complex act of joining, connecting, and the final product must have everything joined together exactly properly in order to work, to release information and actions and emotions at proper moments, to create chemical reactions that blossom at the right time and place, to manifest whatever power a play may hold to the fullness of its potential.

The plays in this collection have been "wrought" through many different situations, over four decades, with actors of differing skill levels and life experience participating, in differing contexts. Some plays have been "written" wholly by me, on paper and device (*Ménage à 13, Sand on a Distant Star*). Others have used improvisation under lecture-demonstration workshop conditions (*A Dream Like a Dream, Like Shadows, Writing in Water, Ago*), or in professional situations with set performance dates and tickets already sold (*The Village*, and all others).

This simple explanation of my creative process may or may not affect how you approach my plays. But no matter how my plays are created, I often remind my audiences who watch them in performance, that how the chef prepares the meal in the kitchen is not at all important. When eating, the taste, and how that taste expands into time and space, into your life, that is what matters.

—Stan Lai, Taipei, in the time of virus, 2020

How I Translate My Own Plays

Translation is sometimes not so much the work of choosing words, but that of choosing cultural ideas. A "faithful" translation can either be an accurate rendition of the original words, which may make them inaccessible to a foreign reader, or a text faithful to the idea behind the words, which may make them culturally transmittable, though possibly literarily distorted.

When I began translating the plays in this collection, I asked myself: who are they for? Being the playwright and director of all these plays, I found my answer was: for performance. And so I have translated them primarily for performability onstage, and not for 100% literal accuracy. Instead of my keeping obscure allusions that need distracting footnotes to explain, the plays are meant to be understood culturally, as best as they may, in the context of the modern world at large. That said, they are all at least 95% literally accurate, in my estimation, the degree varying play to play.

Something that resonates to a Chinese ear may not mean anything to a Western ear. What I have tried to capture is not the actual words that resonate, but the "resonation" itself, whatever that may be. As my own translator, I am not bound to the original words, but am free to make certain choices that change words that may be doomed to obscurity in their original form, into something equivalent but understandable. This is helpful, particularly working on the two crosstalk plays in this collection, which have many lines that are culturally almost impossible to translate that I choose to either just let go without explanation, delete, or rewrite with different content. The alternative would be a literally "correct" text that would harbor a minefield of footnotes, impeding the reader at every phrase and severely limiting performability.

To give a simple example of how many different directions a translation can go, in "The Art of Language" in *Look Who's Crosstalking Tonight* (vol. 1), the common Chinese term *feihua* is up for translation. There is nothing in English equal to *feihua*, which literally reads "wasted talk," meaning words spoken that are unnecessary, excessive, and/or redundant. Its usage is, for instance, "Did you just get shot?" "Yes." "I'll bet that hurts." "*Feihua.*" Such a dialogue is quintessential Chinese-ness. If you translated it literally, you would say "That was wasted language" or "You wasted your words." A laid-back English translation would be "I'll say," or "Yeah, that's quite an observation." A dictionary will define *feihua* as "nonsense," and that is in the ballpark, but the ballpark is vast indeed. See my translation of the term, in parentheses:

> STERN: There are some basic requirements to be a crosstalk actor.
> CHAT: And what requirements would those be?
> STERN: First, one must be able to talk.
> CHAT: *Feihua*. (That's saying nothing.)
> STERN: And, one must be able to say *feihua* (nothing).
> *Chat is ticked off by Stern. Pause.*
> CHAT: Are you trying to tell me that you have gone through specialized *feihua* (nothing) training?
> STERN: At the highest level.
> CHAT: *(not getting it)* Does that even exist?
> STERN: Ever since I was a kid, I was picked to participate in speech contests. You tell me how good I am at *feihua* (saying nothing)!

In the next page or so, the word *feihua* appears eight times, so that's eight "nothing"s, or whatever word you have chosen to use. The consequences for the comedy are obvious. If you are tied to the literal words, you lose the humor, even if you keep explaining through footnotes.

In the original Chinese of the scene "The Pulse of a Laugh" in *Millennium Teahouse* (vol. 2), the final series of punch lines deals with "The 24 Paragons of Filial Piety" of traditional Confucian thought. The Chinese word for "filial piety," *xiao*, happens to be homonymous with "laugh," but this is impossible to replicate in English, because no homonym for "laugh" in English means "filial piety" or vice versa. So I have rewritten accordingly, willing to lose the pun but keep the structure of the joke, until the part about the last empress. In Chinese, she is "Empress Wu," *wuhou*, a pun on "with no descendants," which is part of the punch line that ends the scene. You can see the choice I have made, by necessity, to forsake the original lines, and to call her "Empress Last." By doing this, I lose the pun, but create a new play on words, to make a different yet equally potent punch line, in my mind, to end the scene. This fulfills the scene's original intent, but certainly it is not close to a literal translation.

Many of the plays have historical backgrounds that the audience MUST know in order to derive any meaning. I have taken the liberty of adding such essential information straight into the dialogue, thus avoiding footnotes or a whole section of explanation. For instance, for *Secret Love in Peach Blossom Land* (vol. 1) there are two essential pieces of information in my mind that a foreign reader or audience needs to know for the play to make sense, both of which are common knowledge to a Chinese audience: the events of 1949, when the Communists took over China and the Nationalists retreated to Taiwan, and the fact that "A Chronicle of the Peach Blossom Land" is a well-known classical text that tells of a utopian land. Though projecting footnotes onstage during performance may be an interesting staging option, that is not how I envision this play to work, and so I have taken the liberty of altering my own play in two places where these two points are explained, within a slightly expanded dialogue. The same goes for explanations of the traditional art of crosstalk, and how military dependents' villages came to be, for instance, in *Look Who's Crosstalking Tonight* and *Millennium Teahouse*, and in *The Village*. It is my hope that these additions help the reader/audience in a seamless way.

Another liberty I have taken is in character names. A scholar of Chinese may find it curious and inconsistent that in many cases I have chosen to stray from straight *pinyin* transliteration of character names. To understand the challenge, and my eventual choices, take the names of the Chao family children in *The Village* (vol. 2) as example. Transliterated, they are Damao, Ermao and Xiaomao. That works, but doesn't give you anything besides a sound. What do the names mean? They are affectionate nicknames that literally mean "Big Hair," "Second Hair," and "Little Hair," names that are misleading or meaningless in English. I decided on Bigs, Deuce, and Smalls. If they sound a little gangsterly—that's the point! That's the "village" culture. The names of their father and the other first-generation village dwellers created a unique challenge. They are named Zhao, Zhu, and Zhou in Chinese—if kept this way they might have proved maddeningly similar and difficult to differentiate for the non-Chinese reader, and so I changed them accordingly, to Hanbin, Chu, and Ning, to provide contrast and easy recognizability.

In other plays I have westernized the names, such as in *Writing in Water*, the background of which is the highly westernized city of Hong Kong, but in places like the Shanghai brothel in *A Dream Like a Dream*, I have chosen to keep names like Hsiang-lan and Tsui-chin, sparing the reader from "Fragrant Orchid," "Jade Zither," and the like. I have also chosen to mix the different Chinese transliteration systems, using the older Wade-Giles system in general for plays set in Taiwan in a time when Wade-Giles was the only system used, or in pre-Communist situations. But this is not rigid, and I have chosen not to be 100% consistent in system use. In all, you will find the rationale behind the choice of all the names is simply ease of recognition for a reader, ease of pronunciation and performability onstage. In many cases I feel I have found a comfortable place between Chinese and English that works onstage, like

Nightingale, Hawker, and Money in *Sand on a Distant Star* (vol. 2), names that reflect the Chinese and are easy to pronounce and recognize onstage, but that are not real English names. The important thing is, to me, they *feel* like the characters I wrote and, in reading, do not in my mind draw attention to themselves for any oddness.

The choice of the name "Hell" for the flunkey in *Millennium Teahouse* was perhaps the most difficult one, for it strays from the original's meaning, but it fulfills its dramaturgical purpose: the original Chinese name, "Wanyier," is not a name, but a Beijing colloquialism that means "small thing" or "gadget"; when "What" is added before it, as in the play, it becomes slang for "What the hell?" (*shenme wanyier?*) Though "gadget" and "hell" don't mean the same thing, "what the gadget" doesn't mean anything. My choice of words here allows the comedy and play on words to flow essentially the way they do in the original. To keep the name in its transliterated form, "Wanyier," would not be an option in this case. You would lose too much.

These are a few illustrations of the challenges inherent in the work. When in doubt, I have looked to the plays themselves for guidance, and they have shown me directions where the spirit of the plays, first and foremost, may be expressed, through whatever words are proper.

—S. L.

Introduction to Volume 2

Raymond Zhou

The five plays in this volume span the years from 2000 to 2016, a fertile period in Stan Lai's prolific career, during which he created 15 new theatre pieces, including what is considered to be one of his masterpieces, *The Village* of 2008. The works reflect diverse concerns, and the shifting of his creative base from Taipei to other places, including Beijing, California, Hong Kong, and Shanghai.

MILLENNIUM TEAHOUSE

Lai's reimagining of the traditional Chinese performing art of crosstalk (*xiang-sheng*) and its conventions can be seen in earlier plays of his, such as *That Evening, We Performed Crosstalk* of 1985, and *Look Who's Crosstalking Tonight* of 1989 (vol. 1 of this collection), in which the original stand-alone, 15-minute crosstalk routines are transformed into a grand theatrical dialogue lasting a whole evening. In Lai's crosstalk experiments, he accomplishes his purpose of dealing with serious subject matter within the confines of a comedic form, breaking away from what was then the widely accepted crosstalk tradition, but bringing the art form to a new level of significance.

Written in 2000 by Lai in collaboration with the original cast in Taipei, using Lai's creative system (see "How I Wright Plays"), *Millennium Teahouse* is the fifth play in the crosstalk genre that Lai initiated and developed. It can be argued that this play is the most complex of all of Lai's crosstalk plays, with a narrative structure that allows the different crosstalk scenes (routines) to shine independently, but in contrast and comparison to, and often in conversation with, parallel scenes. It has two contrasting acts, set 100 years apart to the day. One might think that the two-act structure superimposed on the usual crosstalk conventions would inhibit the players, but like a brilliant piece of ancient poetry, the play finds its freedom within these constraints.

Despite its modern form, *Millennium Teahouse* conforms to all the customs and intricacies of the traditional art it draws from. It pays homage by setting the first act on the last day of the 19th century, a heyday for this grassroots form of entertainment, and in old Beijing, its birthplace. If one could isolate all the crosstalk segments in the play, they would already be first-rate routines in themselves. But only when placed in the deceptively simple narrative structure do they achieve a transcendence that the term "crosstalk play" can hardly capture.

The play is a study in contrasts: past and present, the ruling and the ruled, an imperial system in decay and a democracy in chaos, highbrow and lowbrow—the list goes on and on. Unlike in many crosstalk routines that can be adapted for the one-person stand-up, the role of the "straight" here is equally as important as the "comic." This is illustrated by the Act One closer, when both actors describe what they did when foreign forces invaded Beijing—the aristocrat saving the Empress Dowager and the crosstalk performer meeting his courtesan lover—in a rapid step-by-step juxtaposition that creates an almost cinematic "split-screen" collage only achievable in the theatre. Crosstalk has never been taken this far, this high.

Underlying poignancy in the play suggests that history repeats itself in the cruelest and most ironic ways possible. Many lines in the year 1900 of Act One seem obliquely to comment on the present, while those in the year 2000 of Act Two force one to question the progress achieved in the intervening century. In a sense, crosstalk itself has been the cruelest target of this "progress": the Communist government elevated it from something little more than street entertainment to a respected art form, and in the process smothered it by forbidding it to lampoon the powers that be. Can you imagine a stand-up punch line that sings the praises of the establishment?

The second act's "Chicken Feather Party" scene is a tour de force that combines crosstalk, theatre, and Taiwan election politics performance, an unreal but accurate portrayal of the rowdy Taiwan campaign culture that continues to this day, including all the outrageous, undeliverable promises and absurd propositions. During the scene, the seemingly benign and ignorant M.P. grows to monstrous proportions, a caricature of the ultrasophisticated yet equally deadly menace of Act One, Lord Beile.

After its successful Taiwan premiere in December 2000, *Millennium Teahouse* became the second Stan Lai play to be brought to mainland China, after *Red Sky* in 1998, and the first with his Taiwanese acting troupe. Although not originally written with the intention of being performed in China, the play passed the censors and opened in November 2001 at the Chang'an Theatre in Beijing, a stronghold of traditionalism near Tiananmen Square, with front-row tables set up for tea service. The audience's initial skepticism was palpable. A Taiwanese group performing crosstalk in the cradle of crosstalk culture, Beijing? It was surely an act of blasphemy, a taunt. Lai remembers, "I seemed to hear the voices in their heads: 'What the . . . ? A Taiwanese group performing *xiangsheng*?'" However, they soon became invested in the action and were laughing along with the Taiwanese members of the audience.[1]

The critical response to *Millennium Teahouse* in Beijing was immediate and overwhelming. It was as if in crosstalk's stronghold, the audience was more acutely aware of how revolutionary Lai's creation was. The review in *Beijing Youth Daily* reflected what most were thinking:

> The revelations of this production are many: how to maintain and continue cultural traditions, how to bring together artistic creation and contemporary society, how to create a theatre that the public loves but that also has depth. . . . "As Stan Lai thinks, so we laugh." After we laugh, we begin to think along with him.[2]

The excitement created by *Millennium Teahouse* brought with it an invitation to perform an excerpt at the 2002 China Central Television (CCTV) New Year's Gala, an iconic event that annually draws hundreds of millions of Chinese viewers. Despite the good intentions of the television producers, who sought to overhaul the ultraconservative program, it exposed the fact that a 12-minute excerpt from even a well-structured and stylish play, playing to the broadest, most popular audience imaginable, was ill fit for such a platform.

SAND ON A DISTANT STAR

The second play in this volume is one of the few Stan Lai plays not created using his improvisational collaborative approach. It also has a straightforward narrative structure, which is not typical of Lai's oeuvre. The story came to Lai in a dream in July 2002, when he was on a trip to California and under mounting pressure to deliver a play promised to the television personality Chang Hsiao-yen, known as the "Oprah of Taiwan," a task he had brought on

---

1. Su Yushu, *Like a Dream, Like an Illusion: 30 Years of Performance Workshop* (Taipei: Performance Workshop, 2015), p. 85.

2. "After That Evening, the Media Crosstalks," *Beijing Youth Daily*, November 27, 2001.

himself as a compassionate exercise in dramatic therapy: he hoped to bring Chang out of a depression that she had fallen into after losing her husband to cancer.[3] These interesting circumstances laid the foundation for this charming and eccentric work that borders on science fiction.

In *Sand*, we find some of the ingredients that run through all of Stan Lai's plays: his interest in time, the question of memory, the motifs of abandonment and reunion, and the dreamlike, illusory quality of life. Time in this play is marked by abandonment, or the disappearance of a loved one. The character of Nightingale marks that disappearance in her own life as an anniversary, and she pores over it like a scientist as she optimistically calculates the time of reunion. The watch Nightingale sells on the street has two times, one regular and one of special significance. There is even something Einsteinian in the climactic scene, when the briefly returned husband says, "As long as we truly live, time doesn't exist." As if to illustrate this, all characters in the final scene become frozen in a simple but effective stage vignette.

The choice to hold on or let go, which assumes a more philosophical character in *A Dream Like a Dream* (vol. 3) and is more graphically explored in *Secret Love in Peach Blossom Land* (vol. 1), is here in *Sand* laid painfully bare. The leading female character is seen by those around her as delusional. It seems clear to them that her husband either died two decades ago or abandoned her for a new family, as rumors suggest. Morally, these are shifting sands, because whether he died or abandoned her or something else, her response tells us what to think about her: that her waiting for her husband is either till-death-do-us-part devotion or sacrifice for someone who has cheated on her. The play refuses to clarify, thus leaving untied ends that fill the space around it. The scene when Nightingale is finally reunited with her husband for a few minutes after a separation of 20 years is crafted in ambiguity: it is either dream or waking, or perhaps both or neither.

The mysterious disappearance of a major character seems to hold special interest for Lai. Death would be tragic; abandonment is too soapy; amnesia is for a 1940s Hollywood romantic tearjerker. A science fiction tale, by definition, has to be innovative. Leaving the matter open at least provides room for the audience's imagination, pointing to faith as the ultimate salvation, even if the faith is delusional.

Nightingale's story is complemented by two parallel examples of abandonment: the character named Money left his wife on her deathbed, and Hawker was left by his Vietnamese wife. It is worth noting that the Vietnamese wife's watch not only marks that moment when she left him, but also the

---

3. Su, *Like a Dream, Like an Illusion*, p. 95.

earlier time when she left her hometown to marry and live in Taiwan. That leaving is also a form of abandonment, and probably one that leaves a deeper scar.

The Vietnamese wife reminds us of a recurring figure who walks around in the landscapes of Stan Lai's plays. The Mysterious Woman in *Secret Love in Peach Blossom Land* and Granny Lu in *The Village* are other obvious examples. These characters usually stand out from the rest of the dramatis personae because we don't know anything about their backgrounds, and because they behave in inexplicable ways. They are the X factor in these plays, a bit "off," detached from the mise-en-scène. But the imbalances they create always seem to contribute to a different, more random kind of balance that fits with the quirky nature of the plays themselves.

Sand on a Distant Star premiered at Taipei's National Theatre at the height of the SARS epidemic in 2003. A well-known photo of the audience, all in masks, made its way into Eugenio Barba's *The Five Continents of Theatre*, his book on the anthropology of the theatrical event, as an example of an audience's determination to watch live theatre.[4] A new production was chosen to open Lai's own Theatre Above in Shanghai in 2015.

LIKE SHADOWS

It is difficult to imagine that Stan Lai used collective input in the shaping of the intricate plotting and the delicate flow of the third play in this volume. It was incubated at Stanford University in 2006, in English, when Lai was invited to teach his creative methods and create a new work. Lai's central question to the workshop participants, intended to drive the theme of the new work, was: "Do you know anyone who died recently, who won't be able to get where he or she thinks he or she is going?"[5] Lai, who had never before written a murder play, received the narrative spark from a student who had witnessed the death of his neighbor's wife at the hands of his neighbor, who then fled and eventually killed himself. Students at Stanford floated observational and narrative thought bubbles that contributed to the idiosyncratic quality of the work.

Like Shadows is Lai's first play written in English. It was first called *Stories for the Dead*, and later translated into Chinese for productions in the Chi-

---

4. Eugenio Barba and Nicola Savarese, *The Five Continents of Theatre: Facts and Legends about the Material Culture of the Actor* (Leiden: Brill Sense, 2019), p. 238.

5. Su, *Like a Dream, Like an Illusion*, p. 119.

nese world with the name *Like Shadows Following Along* (《如影隨行》). It was again incarnated into English in 2016, when it received two readings at the Lark Play Development Center in New York. The English and Chinese versions have different character names and locations, but the structure remains the same. A comparison of the two versions shows an ease with which Lai shifts from one set of cultural images to another: he can place a scene in a Denny's eatery (in later versions a dim sum restaurant) in the English version, and in the Chinese version involve a shamanistic ghostbuster in the same sequence.

The play is anchored in the Vajrayana Buddhist notion of the Bardo, the "between" state, usually taken to mean the state after death, but which includes all states of betweenness. At the end of scene 5, the narrator, a character named V, locates the Bardo here:

> Between sleeping and waking, between imagining and being imagined, between abandoning and being abandoned, between the constant oscillations of day and night, springs summers autumns winters, life and death, death and rebirth, rebirth and more life, between a breath and another breath, and more betweens, and more breaths, and more lives, and more deaths.

The state between death and life is a source of fascination for everyone of any religious stripe. Lai's inspiration is obviously *The Tibetan Book of the Dead*, which the character Boss reads from in the play, and which has been read for centuries to the bodies of the recently deceased, as a guide for them in the Bardo state.

Lai's signature "dream" can be found here in the floating and fragmented narrative of the play. A full discussion of the narrative inventiveness in *Like Shadows* runs the risk of spoiling the layers of suspense built into it. *Like Shadows* takes off where films such as *The Sixth Sense* end, and it contains characters in its universe that are not simply deceased but are different degrees of imaginary, like V, or the abandoned soul of a saxophone player. It is as if Lai is crafting in four dimensions, running angels through a motorcycle shop that the police suspect to be a front for drugs, and in the end revealing that the crucial character leading to Penelope's murder exists only in the realm of her own imagination.

It is rare in this genre to have revelations in the very first scene that might otherwise be saved for the final plot twist. But *Like Shadows* is abundant in narrative material, and it has viewers in its grip until the last moment, when the emotional climax is reached and the existential puzzle is solved. In Lai's plays, narrative technique always serves something larger and deeper, whether it is emotional connection or soul-searching, and his technique is on full display in this eccentric work.

THE VILLAGE

After the Communists defeated the Nationalist Army in the Chinese Civil War in 1949, around 800 clusters of simple housing were built for military personnel and their dependents retreating to Taiwan from China. They were meant to be temporary; they were small and cheap. But as time went on, the hoped-for counterattack by the Nationalist Army that would defeat the Communists and recover the mainland never materialized. The villages became permanent, crowded homes to these displaced families. Today, most have been demolished, replaced by modern housing projects.

Many prominent people in all fields have come from these villages, including movie stars, pop artists, politicians, businessmen, and gangsters. Over the years, they have injected their special talents and mentality into the kaleidoscope of Taiwan society.

A main feature of these villages was diversity. People from all provinces of China were packed into these crowded refugee centers, speaking different dialects, cooking different foods with whatever improvised ingredients they could come by in Taiwan. Thus, a village was a place where one could hear all dialects and smell different foods from all over China. Within this diversity, the inhabitants had one thing in common: the desire to go home. That wish was denied them for almost four decades. Outside the village was the original world of the Taiwanese themselves, whose native dialect could not be understood by a mainlander. How to adjust, get along, communicate—these were challenges for these displaced people.

The Village is a 60-year panorama of the bleak history of a Taiwan military dependents' village. It unfurls with humor and compassion, based on stories from Wang Wei-chung, a guru of Taiwan's television variety shows. It also includes many stories and characters from Lai's own coming of age in Taipei in the 1960s and 1970s. His observations on the displaced generation of his parents also informs other plays in this collection, such as *Secret Love in Peach Blossom Land*. The wealth of material for *The Village* almost threatens to overwhelm the three-generation, three-family tapestry. But it is the first generation, the one that endured the most suffering, that provides the focus, and that has over the years endeared the play to its audiences.

The Village was an instant success on its 2008 premiere at the National Theatre in Taipei. Theatregoers, including many who had been villagers themselves, were seeing their own recent history onstage. The cast consisted of many accomplished actors who had grown up in such villages, and they volunteered their services before even knowing what Lai was going to write.[6] In 2010, the play first toured mainland China, where the image of the routed Kuomintang soldier had previously been nothing but a retreating silhouette, or a caricature in period dramas. The play passed censors with only superficial changes in wording, and the deep response stirred by the performances of Lai's own troupe speaks volumes. Its annual tours of Chinese cities, which transcend both political factions and the generational gap, are a must-see for young theatregoers, who form the bulk of today's audiences in China. Despite their not being familiar with the "village" world, they are often hungry for art that holds genuine power, rather than the praise-singing propaganda pieces spoon-fed to them when they were growing up.

The richness of the characters is a throwback to the age of the great Lao She, whose 1957 play *Teahouse* is populated by a phalanx of meticulously crafted characters that represent different strata of society. In fact, under Lai's direction, *The Village* has drawn comparisons to the Beijing People's Art Theatre premiere production of *Teahouse* (1958), one of the most iconic ensemble acting performances in modern Chinese history. But the particular blending of mirth and woe in the three-and-a-half-hour *The Village* is uniquely Stan Lai's.

The Village is rooted in the traditional ethics and aesthetics that most Chinese people would use to evaluate a masterwork. It is Confucian in its unabashed embrace of the collective good; the fate of the individual is linked to the vicissitudes of history. Still, against the backdrop of a nation torn apart by war, the individuals' fight for survival reinforces the resilience of the Chinese people, a theme frequently handled in some of the finest works of modern Chinese literature and cinema. In the theatre, *The Village* stands alone.

Two bittersweet scenes rank among the best in Chinese-language theatre. In one, a village elder has died and the poverty-stricken villagers attempt to buy a coffin at an impossibly low price. In another, we see the return-home visit when the retired soldiers are allowed, in the late 1980s, to travel back to their mainland homes after 40 years in exile. Lai's work is noted for its fre-

---

6. Su, p. 126. "They didn't even ask what role they were to play, including Chu Chung-heng, Feng Yi-gang, Ann Lang, Sung Shao-ching, etc."

quent juxtaposition of tragedy and comedy, and this scene has both. In one of three parallel visits, Chu visits his first wife in China, accompanied by his longtime Taiwanese wife, whom he has left in the dark about where they are going. It dawns at the same time on the audience and on his Taiwanese wife that Chu has actually had a wife all along in his Chinese hometown, and the subsequent scene is an unalloyed fusion of tragedy and farce.

More importantly, these scenes touch on the thorny issue of provincial ethnic conflicts, the Chinese version of racism within the Han ethnicity. China was a vast country with limited mobility in the old days, and people not only spoke dialects that were often incomprehensible to others, but also carried with them customs and stigmas that were frequent causes for rupture. A village of such ethnic diversity was a tinderbox, and even more so in its relations with those outside it. These are rifts that have continued to run through Taiwan politics for decades. Stan Lai's masterpiece looks past the simmering tensions and reaches the deeper layer of humanity common to all. Beyond the vast human suffering, it is a celebration of love and compassion, conceived and written with artistic polish of the highest order.

WRITING IN WATER

Originally written in Hong Kong, the last play in this volume is Stan Lai's second play set in the Fragrant Harbor (see *I Me She Him*, vol. 1). Several sources for this play converged for Lai in Hong Kong, where he was invited to create a new work in early 2009, at the height of the global recession. So, to start with, he sensed the gloom that gripped this formerly vibrant city. Not long before this, Lai had translated a book on the nature of happiness, written by his friend, the Buddhist monk and writer Matthieu Ricard. Added to these two was a story in the news that an Austrian man had imprisoned his whole family in a dungeon for 24 years.[7]

These diverse elements formed a wistful, offbeat play that was given 20 performances by the Hong Kong Repertory Theatre, a company Lai has worked with many times. A later permutation of the play, presented in Taiwan, changed all the characters and locations to Taiwan. The version in this collection premiered at Theatre Above in Shanghai in 2016, with the gender of the protagonist changed from female to male, and with the popular television

---

7. Su, p. 133.

star He Jiong in the lead role. Over time, the play took on new elements and shed others, and, according to Lai, the version in this collection is "the most complete expression" of the play.[8]

The concept of "writing in water" derives from the Tibetan school of Buddhism, where, in the Great Perfection, or Dzogchen teachings, an advanced stage of mind training brings the practitioner to a state in which thoughts arise naturally in the mind and, through "nonclinging," immediately dissolve, like writing in water. Compared with these states of mind, the thoughts that most people have bring nothing but an endless series of entanglements to their lives.

We might associate this play with magic realism or time travel, but unlike most setups in those genres, the protagonist Frank does not have a vision of his younger self, or of a twin brother living a rustic, carefree life far from the maddening crowd. The time-bending experience Frank has is in his present, adult state.

The central story of a character's confinement, melodramatic as it may be, can be read at a symbolic level. If a whole village, or even a country, is isolated from the rest of the world, just subsisting will force one to focus on the most essential things in life. While the Austrian man holding his family captive was a psychopath, the play steers in another direction, focusing on the relationship between Frank and Enji, a seemingly random and brief encounter that will be life defining.

The nature of success by today's standards—the bank accounts, stocks, and properties one must own to show for it—has skewed the general notion of happiness and convulsed the whole nation of China in a relentless chase that obscures everything else. In its lyrical style, this play hints at joy in the purest form.

The plays in this volume give the reader a unique window onto Chinese-language theatre. More importantly, they shed light on the modern Chinese mind. They paint a vivid and complex picture of the contemporary Chinese experience, which, for a variety of reasons, tends to be seen either as mysterious or reduced to cartoonish representations abroad. The plays are also dynamic works that should find their true home on stages anywhere in the world. Today, in the new century of the new millennium, Stan Lai remains as prolific as ever, his plays always gaining more scope and depth, delving

---

8. "Stan Lai: This Version of Writing in Water is Finally Complete," Sina.com, May 19, 2016, http://ent.sina.com.cn/j/drama/2016-05-19/doc-ifxsktkp8950979.shtml

deeper into the history across the Taiwan Strait and the psyche on both sides. Like the proverbial "celestial horse soaring through the skies," a reference to an artist who seems to be able to conjure up whatever he or she wishes, Lai is in peak form. His plays may tickle your funny bone or break your heart, sometimes concurrently. There is always tenderness behind his themes and ideas, and a caring for the human condition that is transmitted to all who come into Lai's orbit.

Millennium Teahouse

CHARACTERS

Beijing, 1900

SKY HIGH, stage name of a performer of crosstalk (*xiangsheng*), the traditional Chinese stand-up comedy, in Beijing in the late Qing Dynasty (early 20th century)
SKIN DON'T LAUGH, his stage partner, with revolutionary sentiments
LORD BEILE, pronounced BAY-LUH, an aristocrat in the Qing Dynasty court, aficionado of Peking Opera and crosstalk, lover of all sophisticated things of Chinese culture
HELL, his underling
OLD STAGEHAND

Taipei, 2000

KICKS, stage name of a crosstalk performer in early 21st-century Taipei, Taiwan
THICK SKIN, his stage partner
M.P. REAL, a parliamentary hopeful
CAMPAIGN MANAGER, his backer

Sky High and Kicks are played by the same actor.
Skin Don't Laugh and Thick Skin are played by the same actor.
Lord Beile and M.P. Real are played by the same actor.
Hell and the Campaign Manager are played by the same actor.

SETTING

Act One: December 31, 1900, Thousand Year Teahouse, a traditional teahouse theatre in Beijing, backstage and on the stage proper. It is the day the theatres and teahouses have reopened after months of closure due to the attack of united foreign armies on Beijing.

Act Two: December 31, 2000, on the same teahouse stage, now antique, transported to Taipei, Taiwan, and backstage. It is Millennium Eve.

Millennium Teahouse was first performed on December 29, 2000, at the National Theatre, Taipei, Taiwan, written by Stan Lai in collaboration with the original cast, directed by Stan Lai, produced by Performance Workshop:

Cast:
Chin Shih-chieh as Skin Don't Laugh and Thick Skin
Zhao Zi-qiang as Sky High and Kicks
Ni Minran as Lord Beile and M.P. Real
Lee Chien-chang as the Old Stagehand, Hell, and the Campaign Manager

Scenic Design by Stan Lai
Lighting Design by Michael Lee-zen Chien
Costume Design by Christine and Lei Suzuka
Music by Chi-chi Hung

Produced by Nai-chu Ding

Photo: *Millennium Teahouse.* Taipei, National Theatre, Taipei, Taiwan, 2000, Act One, Scene 2. *Standing, from left*: Sky High (Zhao Zi-qiang), Skin Don't Laugh (Chin Shih-chieh); *Sitting*: Lord Beile (Ni Minran). Photo by Franco Wang.

ACT ONE

Prologue: Today Is the Last Day of the Last Year

Backstage at an old Beijing teahouse theatre, December 31, 1900, in the later years of the Qing Dynasty (1644–1911, the last Chinese monarchial dynasty, overthrown by the Republic of China in 1911). A table and chair, traditional props, and costumes scattered backstage. A long ladder leads to an unseen attic above.

Skin Don't Laugh, a performer of traditional crosstalk, sits at the table, writing. The Old Stagehand is cleaning up. All of the men wear their hair in a long pigtail queue, standard for all Qing men.

In the background, sounds of a Peking Opera performance coming from the stage proper.

Sky High, Skin's stage sidekick, enters. He is upbeat, energetic, excited.

SKY HIGH *(abbreviated below as "HIGH")*: We're a hit! We're a hit! Did you see? Our first day after reopening, the audience is pouring in! What a great day!

SKIN DON'T LAUGH *(abbreviated below as "SKIN")*: What a terrible year.

HIGH: Absolutely! That's why now that the theatres have reopened, everyone is coming out to see some crosstalk! *(to the Old Stagehand)* Hey you—you . . . Didn't I tell you to hang the stage couplet plaques on the pillars, one left, one right?

OLD STAGEHAND: I did.

HIGH: Yeah, really. You got them backwards!

OLD STAGEHAND: Backwards, forward, reads pretty much the same to me . . .

The Old Stagehand exits.

HIGH: My oh my! What a year! Finally we are allowed to perform, and the heavens pour down rain!

High grabs what Skin is writing.

(reading) "Today is the last day of the last year . . ." Are you crazy? Have you joined the revolution? Are you part of some radical party?

SKIN: Do you care?

HIGH: Then . . . ?

SKIN: It's a new script I've been writing. I'll perform it when we have a chance.

HIGH: Well, I hope I don't have to see it. Skin Don't Laugh, you listen to me, the theatres have been closed since summer. We entertainers have been left to starve. Now, finally, we are allowed to perform opera and crosstalk again. Our audience is just dying to see some of our classic stand-up comedy routines. All we have to do now is dust off the old scripts, deliver them properly, and everybody will be happy! To hell with your new scripts! You'll get our heads chopped off! What a year!

SKIN: What year?

HIGH: What?

SKIN: I'm asking you.

HIGH: No, I'm asking you! No, I'm not asking you, I'm asking the heavens, I mean, it's a rhetorical question, okay?

SKIN: Not okay. What year and month is it now?

HIGH: What do you mean?

SKIN: What month and what day?

HIGH: *(counting)* It's the 11th. So?

SKIN: The 11th day of the 11th moon. What year?

HIGH: What do you mean what year? It's this year! Now!

SKIN: According to the Western calendar, today is December 31, 1900. Tomorrow is the start of a new century!

HIGH: What are you talking about?

SKIN: We are about to pass through a gateway. That's what I'm talking about.

HIGH: Listen, Skin Don't Laugh, you want to know what year this is? The year our country was invaded by the armies of the Eight Nations Alliance—that's the German Empire, Japan, Russia, Britain, France, the United States, Italy, and Austria-Hungary combined! Enough for you? The year the Boxer Rebellion collapsed, the year the Empress Dowager fled the palace, the year Beijing was sacked, the year corpses were scattered all over the city, and in the end, WE are going to have to pay reparations to the foreign devils, and apologize to THEM for their kicking OUR ass! It's the Gengzi Year of the lunar calendar, the 26th year of the Emperor Guangxu of the great Qing Dynasty, okay?

Skin laughs.

Skin Don't Laugh, I warn you, don't you laugh! You should count your blessings just to be alive. We don't need your naïveté around here. Political reform is not your job. We're just poor actors, who peddle our emotions for a living.

SKIN: You have a problem with peddling emotions for a living?

HIGH: I warn you, tonight Lord Beile from the imperial court is coming to grace our theatre. Don't even think of trying any new tricks onstage!

SKIN: You think I give a damn about Lord anybody?

HIGH: You'd better! If you say one thing that rubs him the wrong way, one thing that touches a nerve, our theatre gets shut down immediately, and we disappear.

SKIN: Oh, you're scared?

HIGH: Are you kidding? Me? Of course I'm scared!

SKIN: What a corrupt old geezer. "Now is the time for the voice of the people to be heard!"

HIGH: You can't be serious!

SKIN: Don't worry, I'm just rehearsing my lines.

Thunder and lightning. Rain starts falling inside.

HIGH: So stop writing that . . . *(feeling the rain)* Are you kidding? The roof is leaking. *(to the Old Stagehand)* Hey you . . . hey you . . .

SKIN: "Hey you" went onstage to fix the couplets.

HIGH: Oh. Then . . . *(pointing to Skin)* Hey you . . .

SKIN: So now I'm "Hey you"?

HIGH: Please, go up and fix it. It's just some roofing that blew off. All you have to do is put it back in place. Please . . .

SKIN: *(standing up)* My God, "the last day of the last year . . ." It's the proverbial "leaking roof that meets the torrential rain!"

Skin climbs the tall ladder. High peeks at the stage proper. The sounds of the performance onstage continue.
Thunder and lightning. The Old Stagehand enters and stands beneath the ladder, looking up.

OLD STAGEHAND: . . . Hey Skin, to the left. Right. You almost got it . . . To the left . . .

Fierce lightning and thunder. Tremendous explosion and shout.

SKIN: *(offstage voice)* Ahhh——!!

High rushes over and looks up.

HIGH: What happened? Why is he hanging there?

OLD STAGEHAND: Lightning! He got struck by lightning . . .

HIGH: Hurry, bring him down!

The Old Stagehand climbs the ladder. Lights fade out.
Lights fade in. The sounds of the performance onstage continue. Skin lies motionless on the ground. High and the Old Stagehand stand beside him. Silence.

HIGH: What hellish year is this? What stupid idiot told him to go up there? I thought our luck had turned, and now I'm going to have to scrape up the dough to buy him a coffin. What the hell happened, exactly?

OLD STAGEHAND: I don't know. I just heard this huge sound, and then everything was so bright! The roof had been slashed open. I just heard this loud sound, and I saw . . . How can I put it? Everything was . . .

Skin opens his eyes.

SKIN: So bright!

OLD STAGEHAND: Right, so bright!

SKIN: Like the sky had opened . . .

OLD STAGEHAND: Right, like the sky had . . . ?

Pause. High and the Old Stagehand realize that Skin is alive.

HIGH: What?

SKIN: And then . . . So quickly, so many images flew past my eyes.

HIGH: *(shouting toward offstage)* HOLD THE COFFIN, HE AIN'T DEAD YET!

SKIN: Where am I?

HIGH: Backstage.

SKIN: What day is it?

HIGH: What day is it? The day of our reopening!

Lightning. Loud thunder. Skin starts to repeat everything that High says, like a parrot.

SKIN: The day of our reopening!

HIGH: The performance has already started.

SKIN: The performance has already started.

HIGH: We're up next.

SKIN: We're up next.

HIGH: What's wrong with you?

SKIN: What's wrong with you?

HIGH: How come you keep repeating me?

SKIN: How come you keep repeating me?

Lightning again, and loud thunder again.

So many images.

HIGH: So many images?

SKIN: How profound . . .

HIGH: How profound?

SKIN: How come you keep repeating what I say? Are you a parrot?

HIGH: Come on! Tell me, what was so profound?

SKIN: I just saw so many things I never dreamed of. How amazingly beautiful!

HIGH: How amazingly beautiful?

SKIN: How incredibly frightening!

HIGH: How incredibly frightening?

SKIN: The two of us were onstage performing crosstalk.

HIGH: How incredibly . . . What's so frightening about that? Don't we do that every day?

SKIN: But everything was different. Flashing lights, in different colors.

Skin feels for his long pigtail.

Our hair—the pigtails were gone.

HIGH: What?

SKIN: I saw . . .

Skin gazes into empty space. A long moment.

HIGH: Skin, what's going on?

Pause.

SKIN: Astonishing! Let's perform!

HIGH: Perform? You can't go onstage like this!

Skin sees that his gown has a big hole burned into it.

SKIN: I'm good.

HIGH: You're good?

SKIN: I feel great all over! Gentlemen, today is a special day. Even if there's no tomorrow, tonight we'll put on one heck of a show! Shall we?

High and the Old Stagehand look at each other. Skin exits to go onstage. High follows.

Scene 1: The Pulse of a Laugh

A classic Qing Dynasty teahouse stage, with columns, wood carved railings, and an ornate roof. The traditional plaque hanging over the main playing space has the words "Thousand Year Teahouse" carved in wood on it. A Chinese couplet, carved in calligraphy on two long vertical plaques, hangs on the right and left pillars. It reads: "A hundred lifetimes like a moment—just a springtime dream; / Ten thousand threads all waiting for an ending—the human condition."

High and Skin stand onstage, facing the audience. They are dressed in traditional Chinese gowns and caps, standard for crosstalk performers. Skin's gown is damaged from the lightning accident. They hold fans, which are used expressively throughout the performance.

A standard red Peking Opera table is set stage center in crosstalk style. The two actors stand in traditional positions for crosstalk, with the comic to the right of the table, giving him the mobility to move around the stage, and the straight man behind.

The duo greets the audience with a stock opening, announcing their names.

HIGH: Sky High,

SKIN: and Skin Don't Laugh . . .

HIGH AND SKIN: *(in unison)* Ascend the stage with a bow!

They bow to the audience.

HIGH: *(energetically)* Today marks the reopening of our Thousand Year Teahouse Theatre! It's truly a great honor to be able to stand up here onstage and greet all of you!

SKIN: That's right. This whole year can be described as *(ironically)* "Auspicious winds and gentle rains. A year of great peace, the people enjoy life like the gods!"

HIGH: You don't have to bend that far.

SKIN: Sorry, let me try again. This whole year can be described as "The fortunate ones starved to death!"

HIGH: *(warning him)* Hey, you . . .

SKIN: Sorry, I meant "It's fortunate no one starved to death!"

HIGH: And more fortunate to come in to see us perform crosstalk, right?

SKIN: Well said!

HIGH: *(to himself)* That was close!

High continues the routine in a formal way.

> For a crosstalk performer, the biggest kick is to be able to deliver some funny lines, and then listen to the laughter that comes from the audience.

SKIN: I would call that an addiction. Are you saying you're a performer because you always need to be sky high?

HIGH: I'm not in it for any addiction. I AM Sky High, and I'm here to do research.

SKIN: Oh, so you are conducting research as you deliver punch lines?

HIGH: That is correct.

SKIN: And what is this research about?

HIGH: Laughter.

SKIN: Are you saying you are doing a study on audience laughter?

HIGH: Correct. Every human being has a different laugh. From the sound of an individual's laughter, we can understand the native's physical condition.

SKIN: Are you kidding me?

High points at the audience.

HIGH: I kid thee not. Take that esteemed gentleman over there for instance. One listen to his laughter, and I can tell you his physical condition.

SKIN: Well?

HIGH: He's overweight.

SKIN: No need to listen, just look.

HIGH: No, listen. His laugh went "Kekeke . . ." and you could see all of the fat on his body trembling!

SKIN: That's still looking.

HIGH: You don't get it.

SKIN: I guess I don't.

High points toward another direction.

HIGH: Let's take that young madam over there. One listen and I can tell . . . congratulations, you are expecting!

SKIN: And how would you know?

HIGH: Her dainty laugh went *(hand covering mouth)* "Haha . . . *(nauseous)* Ugh . . ." You can even tell how far along she is!

SKIN: You're full of it!

HIGH: There's a name for this. It's called "taking the pulse of a laugh."

SKIN: "Taking the pulse of a laugh"?

HIGH: I'm sure you've heard of Chinese doctors taking a person's pulse.

SKIN: Of course. Through the pulse, the patient's general condition can be diagnosed.

HIGH: It's the same with "the pulse of a laugh." May I trouble you to laugh once for me?

SKIN: Me?

HIGH: I'd like to take the pulse of your laugh. Relax. Just laugh.

Pause. Skin struggles to work up a laugh.

SKIN: *(very unnaturally)* HA! HA! HA!

Pause.

HIGH: Did you just sit on a firecracker?

SKIN: You told me to laugh.

HIGH: How fake can you get! Come on. Relax. Again, please.

SKIN: Okay. Hold it.

HIGH: Hold what?

SKIN: I need to work it up.

HIGH: You don't need to work it up. Just laugh.

SKIN: Without context?

HIGH: Does a pulse have context?

SKIN: Okay. Then ... *(laughing)* Ha ha ha ha hey hey ho ho hoo hoo hoo!

High listens intently, like a doctor conducting a test on a patient.

    Well?

HIGH: Not very good.

SKIN: Why?

HIGH: You have chronically weak kidneys.

SKIN: Gimme a break! You got that from my laughter?

HIGH: Your laugh contains more "ha"s than "ho"s. That indicates more breath going out than coming in.

SKIN: So?

HIGH: We Chinese have studied in depth the "Five Elements" of the universe—"metal, wood, water, fire, and earth," which in the body correspond respectively to "lung, liver, heart, kidney, and spleen," which in one's laughter correspond respectively to "Ha, hey, ho, hee, and hoo." In your laughter just now, I didn't detect a single "hee," a strong indicator that your kidneys are weak, and may I say, extremely so, to the point where I wonder if they even exist! Are times so hard that you went and sold them?

SKIN: *(holding his temper)* You say my laughter lacks "hees"?

HIGH: Right.

SKIN: "Hee-hee" is a figure of speech. Have you ever actually heard any-one laugh with the sound "hee-hee"?

HIGH: Are you kidding? Haven't you ever noticed Master Wang, who owns the opium den near the brothels? Every day, when he comes out of the brothel and passes our theatre, you can hear him going *(while nodding left and right)* "Hee-hee-hee-hee-hee . . ." All you need is to hear his laughter and you know . . .

SKIN: His kidneys are strong.

HIGH: Very strong.

SKIN: Good for him.

HIGH: But all of his other organs are shot.

SKIN: What?

HIGH: That's why his laughter has been reduced to one sound—"hee."
He does so many good deeds every day, he's proved he has strong
kidneys, but he's ruined everything else. As for you, I have a
prescription.

SKIN: A medical prescription?

HIGH: Of course. Stand straight. *(gesturing)* Fold your hands together and
go: "hee hee hee" . . .

SKIN: *(mimicking him)* "Hee hee hee . . ."

HIGH: Three times a day, after every meal, I guarantee within a fortnight
your kidney problems will improve.

SKIN: So now you're a medical physician?

HIGH: "Taking the pulse of a laugh" not only reveals one's physical condition, but can also determine one's character.

SKIN: That's a little much.

HIGH: Since you don't believe me, I would like you to laugh for me again.
This time I need a long one.

SKIN: What for?

HIGH: To take the pulse of your character. Hold on . . .

High takes out a stopwatch.

SKIN: And what is this gadget?

HIGH: It's foreign. You're not into the latest trends. They call it a horse
watch.

SKIN: For horses?

HIGH: Now when I say go, you start laughing as loudly as you can, for as long as you can.

SKIN: You mean just laugh?

HIGH: Yes. Go!

High presses the stopwatch.

SKIN: Hreeeehreehreehreehreehreehreeeeeee . . .

Pause. High stares at Skin.

What's wrong?

HIGH: Are you human?

SKIN: What happened!

HIGH: Don't laugh like a horse just because I'm using a horse watch.

SKIN: Sorry. You've made me quite nervous.

HIGH: About what? Take it easy! Just laugh naturally. Don't we laugh every day? And in that laughter we reveal our character. So just go like . . . *(laughing with piglike sounds)* Snort—hum—snort—hum . . .

Pause. Skin stares at High.

SKIN: I need a pig watch to time you.

HIGH: Enough nonsense. Again, please, laugh as long as you can, till your breath runs out. And go!

High presses the stopwatch.

SKIN: *(a long laugh)* Hahahahahahahahaaaaaaaaaa . . .

Pause. High checks the stopwatch.

Well?

HIGH: Good.

SKIN: *(pleased)* Really?

HIGH: Yours is a heroic character.

SKIN: How do you get that?

HIGH: Because you're short of breath.

SKIN: Wait! How did you get that?

High shows Skin the stopwatch.

HIGH: Look. Your laugh only lasted 4.6 seconds. That fits in perfectly with the classical saying "Heroes have short breath." On the other hand, villains have long breath, they can laugh for more than 40 seconds without stopping! *(quick laughter without stopping)* Hahahahahahahahahahahahahahahahaha . . .

SKIN: Villain you are!

HIGH: Just giving you an example.

SKIN: But the saying you quote refers to heroes who lose their will! It's not literally "breath."

HIGH: *(ignoring him)* Then there is another kind of laugh, most inauspicious. When you hear this laugh, you know not only that the person has a poor constitution, but that his spirits are in sad shape, too.

SKIN: How terrible. And what kind of laugh would that be?

HIGH: A laugh that sounds like crying.

SKIN: Is there such a thing?

High's voice trembles while he laughs, sounding like crying. His face is contorted, as if he is in anguish.

HIGH: *(face contorted)* "Uh uh uh . . ."

SKIN: Hold it. Are you crying?

HIGH: I'm laughing! *(face contorted)* "Uh uh uh . . ."

SKIN: What happened to you?

HIGH: My daughter's getting married. *(face contorted)* " Uh uh uh . . ."

SKIN: Congratulations! Why are you in such anguish?

HIGH: I'm not in anguish! That was a laugh!

SKIN: Oh, then, in that case . . . Congratulations!

HIGH: She's getting married to an aristocrat from the court. *(face contorted)* " Uh uh uh . . ."

SKIN: What great fortune!

HIGH: My son-in-law is filthy rich! . . . *(face contorted)* "Uh uh uh . . ."

SKIN: Wealth and prosperity for all their years. That's really something to laugh about!

HIGH: My son-in-law is the head eunuch in the court! My daughter's life is ruined! *(face contorted)* "Uh uh uh . . ."

SKIN: Your daughter's life is ruined, why are you so happy?

HIGH: I'm crying! *(angry)* CAN'T YOU TELL THAT I'M CRYING NOW? WHAT'S WRONG WITH YOU, CAN'T YOU EVEN TELL THE DIFFERENCE BETWEEN CRYING AND LAUGHING? *(face contorted)* "Uh uh uh . . ." She's going to be a married widow! *(face contorted)* "Uh uh uh . . ."

SKIN: Who could tell the difference?

HIGH: In all, such a person's physical condition is terrible, his mind is in chaos, his emotions are all tied in a knot.

SKIN: That's what the ancients would call "Appropriate neither for laughter nor tears."

HIGH: Wrong phrase, my man. You need to bone up on your classics. The phrase "Unable to laugh or cry" would be more appropriate.

SKIN: I disagree. "There's no longer any right or wrong" hits the bull's-eye.

HIGH: What?

SKIN: "Wishing to cry but lacking tears" says it even better.

HIGH: What?

SKIN: Look at what's happened to our great Qing Dynasty. It seems this kind of laughter is most suited to the times.

High realizes that Skin is going off book.

HIGH: *(softly)* Where are you going with this?

SKIN: *(ignoring him)* Now I understand. When you take the pulse of a

laugh, not only can you understand an individual's physical condition, but you can also see the state of a whole era.

HIGH: *(trying to pull him back)* Wait a minute. Are you leading or am I
leading?

*Skin takes over the position of the comic, right of the table, subtly nudging High
to the position of the "straight," behind the table.*

SKIN: No one's leading. In these times, aside from a laugh that sounds
like crying, there's only one other type of laugh that can sustain one's
survival.

High is forced to go along.

HIGH: And what might that be?

SKIN: The official's laugh.

HIGH: What?

SKIN: The laughter of court officials. That's something you have to learn.

HIGH: Forgive me for never having been to the imperial court. What does
the laughter of court officials sound like?

*Skin keeps his mouth shut, laughing wryly, suppressing his laughter inside his
mouth.*

SKIN: "Hmm hmm hmm . . ."

HIGH: Why's your mouth shut, your eyes squinting, and your laugh
smothered? Where's the joy in such a laugh?

SKIN: Are you kidding? How can you show joy if you are an official? Let's
say you're at court, sitting high up on the bench, looking down at the
quivering bandit kneeling before you.

*Skin plays the official, who speaks authoritatively, referring to High as the
bandit.*

"You! *(suddenly laughing uninhibitedly)* HAHAHAHA, have you ever
seen such a goofy-looking bandit? HAHAHAHA, take him out and
behead him!" Is that any way for an official to behave?

HIGH: That does seem to lack authority.

SKIN: Therefore, since ancient times, all officials have practiced the same laugh. So whoever you meet, whatever the circumstances, the first thing you do is laugh: *(smothering the laughter)* "Hmm hmm hmm . . ."

HIGH: The first thing? Just laugh?

SKIN: At the same time that you *(smothering the laugh)* "Hmm hmm hmm," you take the opportunity to observe what's going on. In that moment, you evaluate all the pros and cons of the situation and the individual you are confronting, and once you have figured it all out, you finish your laugh, and you talk.

HIGH: You can do that much in one instant of laughter?

SKIN: Hey, that's the basic skill of being a court official! Only by employing this kind of laugh will you be able to survive. If you don't believe me, give it a try.

HIGH: What?

SKIN: Let's pretend that we are court officials.

HIGH: Me? I get to be an official?

SKIN: You have the perfect face for an official.

HIGH: So what kind of official do you have in mind for me?

SKIN: Let's say . . . Admiral of the Northern Seas.

High is so happy he runs around the stage.

HIGH: Dad, Mom, I've become a great official, ha ha ha . . . !

SKIN: *(stopping him)* Act like one!

High stops.

Come.

They stand close to each other, face-to-face, mouths shut. Skin keeps his mouth shut and smothers his laugh.

Hmm hmm hmm . . . Congratulations, congratulations . . .

HIGH: *(stepping out of character)* Hold on a moment. For what?

SKIN: Don't ask. Didn't I say? Just laugh.

HIGH: Oh.

High mimes the smothered laugh.

> Hmm hmm hmm . . . Thank you, thank you . . . *(to himself)* For what?

SKIN: *(smothered laugh)* Hmm hmm hmm . . . His Majesty is brilliant indeed!

HIGH: *(smothered laugh)* Hmm hmm hmm . . . Indeed, Long live His Majesty! . . .

SKIN: *(smothered laugh)* Hmm hmm hmm . . . His Majesty is so brilliant to send you to negotiate the purchase of battleships from the French!

HIGH: Is that what happened?

SKIN: Laugh.

HIGH: *(smothered laugh)* Hmm hmm hmm . . . Those foreigners have all the latest Western technology, so we've got to have some, too!

SKIN: *(smothered laugh)* Hmm hmm hmm . . . That battleship you purchased is so pretty!

HIGH: *(smothered laugh)* Hmm hmm hmm . . . *(with exaggerated humility)* Not so, not so, it's just an ugly little boat . . .

SKIN: *(smothered laugh)* Hmm hmm hmm . . . I heard you scored a fortune as the middleman!

High suddenly breaks into a hearty laugh.

HIGH: OH HA HA HA!!

SKIN: Wait. Why are you laughing like that?

HIGH: Don't you wait all your life for an opportunity like this? DAD, MOM, I'M RICH! I SCORED A FORTUNE! *(laughing heartily)* HA HA HA . . .

SKIN: *(sternly)* Act like an official!

High comes back to his place and settles down.

HIGH: *(smothered laugh)* Hmm hmm hmm . . . Wind blowing through an empty cave—no such thing! . . .

SKIN: *(smothered laugh)* Hmm hmm hmm . . . I hear a document leaked . . .

HIGH: *(smothered laugh)* Hmm hmm hmm . . . The true gentleman doesn't make accusations that cannot be substantiated . . .

SKIN: *(smothered laugh)* Hmm hmm hmm . . . I have the document right here . . .

Pause. High starts to cry.

HIGH: *(crying)* Waahh . . . !!

SKIN: Wait. What are you crying for?

HIGH: MERCY, MY LORD, I HAVE AN 80-YEAR-OLD MOTHER, PLUS CHILDREN . . . !

SKIN: *(sternly)* ACT LIKE AN OFFICIAL!

HIGH: *(smothered laugh)* Hmm hmm hmm . . . I hear that all of the charitable funds for the flooding in the South went into your pocket . . .

SKIN: *(smothered laugh)* Hmm hmm hmm . . . If only I were so capable! . . .

HIGH: *(smothered laugh)* Hmm hmm hmm . . . To be frank, I have here a little piece of incriminating evidence . . .

He takes out a document.

SKIN: *(smothered laugh)* Hmm hmm hmm . . .

He also takes out a document.

Not as incriminating as mine . . .

They mime showing each other the evidence, threatening each other, and then stealthily exchanging their documents. They finally laugh together, a smothered laugh of mutual understanding.

SKIN AND HIGH: *(in unison)* Hmm hmm hmm . . .

They nod to each other, then split up and circle back to the table.

HIGH: Jeez! I swear if I had to laugh like that every day, my eyes would get crooked and my mouth would grow sideways!

SKIN: That's what I'm saying. During times like these, the laughter of neither officials nor the people sounds like laughter. This makes me

think back to a golden age in Chinese history, when laughter provided the foundation of life.

HIGH: What age was that?

SKIN: You don't know? All the ancient books praise that era.

HIGH: What books? Quote something.

SKIN: "In the beginning, man's character was laughter; laughs were all
the same, but laughing habits would differ."

HIGH: I swear that sounds like a rip-off of the opening of the "Three-Word
Classic." "In the beginning, man's nature was benign . . ."

SKIN: That shows the extent of your learning.

HIGH: So what was it? Enlighten me.

SKIN: "The Book of Laughter."

HIGH: "The Book of Laughter." Sure. And what dynasty would that have
been written in?

SKIN: The Laugh Dynasty.

HIGH: The Laugh Dynasty? That's a good one. Never heard of it.

SKIN: Never heard of it? Any schoolchild can count the dynasties of
China, from ancient times onward: *(counting the dynasties on his
fingers)* "The Yellow Emperor; Emperors Yao, Shun, Yu, Tang; the Qin,
the Han, the Sui, the Tang, and the Laugh." See?

HIGH: *(suspicious)* Are you sure?

SKIN: Emperor Wen founded the Laugh Dynasty; Emperor Wu expanded
its territory.

HIGH: Emperors of the Laugh Dynasty?

SKIN: All 24 of them.

HIGH: Like the "24 Paragons of Filial Piety"? Come on, I can see where
the Laugh Dynasty might have "24 Gaffes," but "24 Laughs"?
That's—laughable.

SKIN: That's the exact word the historians used. You know how magnif-
icent the Laugh Dynasty was? I tell you, not only did people laugh,
even animals laughed.

HIGH: Animals laugh?

SKIN: Haven't you heard the phrase "doggedly on one's last legs"?

HIGH: That refers to a person so tired he is running on fumes.

SKIN: That refers to a dog that has laughed so hard he is running on fumes.

HIGH: What?!

SKIN: Haven't you ever seen a dog laughing while propped up on his legs—*(miming a dog laughing)* Ha ha ha ha ha ha ha ha . . . *(out of breath)* "Doggedly on one's last legs"!

HIGH: Why would a dog laugh like that?

SKIN: Because he's happy!

HIGH: Bull!

SKIN: Precisely! Not only did dogs laugh, but bulls and chickens and goats and birds all laughed, too.

HIGH: No way.

SKIN: Haven't you heard of "fowl laughter"?

HIGH: "Foul laughter" refers to a very disgusting laugh.

SKIN: On the contrary! "Fowl laughter" is very soothing:

Skin mimes a chicken laughing.

"Googoogoogoo . . ."

HIGH: Why would a fowl be "Googling"?

SKIN: Someone answered the fowl, too.

HIGH: Who?

SKIN: A goat.

HIGH: And what did the goat say?

Skin mimes a goat call.

SKIN: "Yahooooo . . ."

HIGH: Please!

Skin mimes the sounds of chickens, goats, and birds.

SKIN: " Googoogoogoo . . ." "Yahoooo . . ." *(miming a bird)* "Twitter twitter . . ."

HIGH: And what the hell was that?

SKIN: That's called chickens, goats, and birds "inter-mating."

HIGH: Inter-mate?

SKIN: Once they've introduced themselves, they consider themselves inter-met.

HIGH: What?

SKIN: I tell you, during the Laugh Dynasty, not only did animals laugh, even the elements laughed!

HIGH: *(scoffing)* Elements of nature, laughing?

SKIN: Haven't you ever heard of a "giggling brook"?

HIGH: It's "babbling brook."

SKIN: No, in those days they "giggled." *(miming a "giggling" brook)* "Hehe-hehe . . . hehehehe . . ." Pay attention. That's different from a "roaring tide."

HIGH: A "roaring tide" refers to high waves.

SKIN: Which are high because they are roaring with laughter.

Skin mimes waves laughing.

"HAhahaHAhahaHAAAA~~~!!" Then there's the "Sky breaking up."

HIGH: That refers to the clouds parting.

SKIN: That refers to the sky breaking up in laughter. "A-HA!"

High is going nuts.

I tell you, during the Laugh Dynasty, even when someone died, everyone at the funeral laughed.

HIGH: I get it. It's called "Rolling in the aisles."

SKIN: Not bad. I thought you would say "Laughing all the way to the grave."

HIGH: Okay. So, can you explain to me why everything under heaven was so happy in the Laugh Dynasty?

SKIN: The reason was actually very simple.

HIGH: Tell me.

SKIN: Because nothing much was going on.

HIGH: Nothing much was going on?

SKIN: Nothing.

HIGH: Don't try to pull one on me. You describe a golden utopian age as "nothing going on"?

SKIN: Precisely because it was a golden utopian age, there was nothing going on. Precisely because there was nothing going on, everyone had the time to laugh. Otherwise everyone gets so busy, there's no time, there's no mood to laugh. And what a pity, this golden age faded into oblivion.

HIGH: It faded?

SKIN: It crumbled in the hands of the last empress.

HIGH: Really?

SKIN: Historians don't know what kind of adversity she went through, but all her life she refused to laugh, and put out an edict barring people from laughing.

HIGH: No laughing? Then how did they take the pulse of their laugh?

SKIN: Exactly! What are you going to take when there's no pulse? And no laugh?

HIGH: What if I feel like laughing?

SKIN: You've got to hold it.

HIGH: And what if I can't hold it?

SKIN: Then you're dead.

HIGH: Really?

SKIN: Are you kidding? That's how the phrase "die laughing" came into being.

HIGH: "Die laughing"? That's a figurative way to say you die of laughter.

SKIN: Precisely. In the day the phrase was inverted. Then when people started using the incorrect phrase, no one corrected them. And that's how you get the phrase in its current form.

HIGH: So what was it originally?

SKIN: "Laughing?" *(gesturing: you will be beheaded)* "DIE!" You see how powerful the inversion makes it?

HIGH: Awesome.

SKIN: After some time, not just the animals, but all of nature ceased to laugh. The harvest was barren, the forests silent. Very quickly, the Laugh Dynasty came to its end.

HIGH: Too bad. Did this empress have a name?

SKIN: Of course.

HIGH: And her name was . . . ?

SKIN: Empress Last.

HIGH: That's too easy.

SKIN: You never heard of Empress Last? She really lived up to her name. She strived to be last in everything.

HIGH: Quite ambitious.

SKIN: Damn right. She was always last in her one-on-one private tutoring.

HIGH: That's an accomplishment.

SKIN: At any rate, she was a big proponent of "Last man, or woman, standing."

HIGH: But what does that have to do with a ban on laughter?

SKIN: Don't you know? She coined the famous phrase.

HIGH: What famous phrase?

SKIN: By banning all laughter, she was the only one in the whole country who could laugh.

HIGH: So?

SKIN: "She who laughs, Last, laughs best."

HIGH: Get the heck out of here!

They announce their names in a crosstalk stock ending.

SKIN: Skin Don't Laugh . . .

HIGH: Sky High . . .

SKIN AND HIGH: *(in unison)* Signing off with a bow!

They bow.

Scene 2: Lord Beile Ascends the Stage

SKIN: *(to the audience)* Thank you, everybody!

HIGH: *(reprimanding Skin)* What's with you? *(to the audience)* Ah . . . That little dialogue was just some light entertainment to bring a chuckle to your day. There is no deeper meaning. I hope nobody is offended! *(to Skin)* Don't get smart with me again! *(to the audience)* And now, we have prepared for you a charming little dialogue which . . .

Commotion in the audience. One individual in the back of the house is suddenly applauding loudly.

LORD BEILE: Bravo . . . bravo . . .

Skin and High peer into the audience. Lord Beile, an aristocrat from the imperial court, enters the audience from the back and makes his way toward the stage, carrying a covered birdcage. He is fully decked out in official splendor. He is pompous and haughty, with exaggerated gestures and manner.

Behind Lord Beile is his flunkey, "Hell," an expressionless menial who labors to carry a surreally large assortment of props on his shoulder in the service of Lord Beile. He is like an overburdened laborer carrying a long pole with all sorts of things hanging on each side: an umbrella, a hot pot, a teapot, towels, a fan, a spittoon, a kite, etc. A small wooden slab is tied to his head. He follows behind Lord Beile, and looks like a walking hardware store.

HIGH: *(to Skin)* We're finished!

SKIN: What?

HIGH: Lord Beile!

SKIN: He's here?

HIGH: He's coming onstage!

Lord Beile ascends the stage, followed by Hell. High immediately kneels down. Skin surveys the situation and then also kneels down, but doesn't salute him.

HIGH: Hail to Lord Beile! May your prosperity be like the East Sea!

Lord Beile walks around onstage.

LORD BEILE: Outstanding . . .

HIGH: *(pointing at the audience)* Lord Beile, um, seating for our valued guests is over there.

LORD BEILE: Here is quite fine.

SKIN: But Lord Beile, this is the stage.

Lord Beile stoops down to examine the boards. Hell parks his elaborate load upstage.

LORD BEILE: What a beautiful rosewood stage.

SKIN: Rosewood?

LORD BEILE: Exquisite! Look at the quality, the construction. I would guess it was built during the reign of the Emperor Xianfeng.

HIGH: Right, right, it's old . . .

SKIN: A beat-up old stage, our apologies.

Lord Beile reads the poetic couplet on the two pillars.

LORD BEILE: *"A hundred lifetimes like a moment—just a springtime dream;*

Ten thousand threads all waiting for an ending—the human condition."

How lovely! But don't let me interrupt. Continue, continue.

Lord Beile gives the birdcage to Hell, who hangs it up.

(to the birdcage) Be good.

HIGH: *(to the audience)* My dear spectators, let's have a round of applause for Lord Beile from the imperial court, who has personally come tonight to grace our stage! Can we move you folks first row center for our honored guest? . . .

LORD BEILE: No need to stand on ceremony. Why have them give up their seats? *(pointing to the stage)* It's quite nice right here. What the—?

HELL: Hell.

High and Skin are stupefied. This is Lord Beile's way of calling his attendant to attention.
Lord Beile points to a spot. Hell immediately positions a stool for him to sit. Lord Beile sits down without even looking, and the stool is there waiting for him, on cue.

SKIN: *(to High)* He's sitting there? Hell, that's my place!

LORD BEILE: Don't call his name. He won't respond to you.

SKIN: What?

They don't get it.

HIGH: Shh. *(to Lord Beile)* Lord Beile, so sorry, we haven't even served you your tea.

LORD BEILE: Shh. *(to Hell)* Hey you, what the—?

HELL: Hell.

LORD BEILE: Did you hear that? They consider you slow.

HIGH: Not at all.

Hell rushes to his props and starts making tea. Lord Beile stands up and walks around the stage, looking around.

LORD BEILE: Outstanding. The theatres are open again! Superb . . .

As Hell makes tea, he carries the stool in his hand, following Lord Beile around, anticipating where he is planning to sit. Lord Beile walks around and seamlessly ascends the central table, with Hell placing the stool in the exact right spot at the right moment, so that Lord Beile can step up to the table without missing a beat. Lord Beile stands on the table. Hell places the stool behind him, right at the moment when he sits down.

Pause. The two actors watch in wonder at Lord Beile sitting on top of the table. He sticks out his right hand, without looking at Hell.

Yeah?

On cue, Hell hands him a hot towel. Lord Beile wipes his face with the towel. Lord Beile holds out the towel with his left hand.

Nay!

On cue, Hell takes away the towel. Lord Beile sticks out his right hand.

Yeah?

Hell quickly pours out a cup of tea from the teapot in his props and gives it to him. Lord Beile enjoys his tea, on top of the table, at his own pace.
High and Skin are speechless.

HIGH: Smells like good tea.

LORD BEILE: This season's is not up to par. Bit strong on the gunpowder. Foreign invasions and the like. We make do. Carry on, please. Don't worry about me, perform! Perform crosstalk!

HIGH: Right right . . .

SKIN: *(to High)* Don't worry about him? He's sitting right smack in the center, on our table, how are we going to perform?

HIGH: Shh.

SKIN: And that guy next to him? What the Hell?

HELL: Here!

Skin and High are startled.

LORD BEILE: What do you mean "here"? WHAT THE—

HELL: HELL!

LORD BEILE: They are using your name in a colorful figure of speech. They are addressing each other, not you. *(to Skin and High)* His name is Hell.

HELL: Here!

Skin and High are dumbfounded.

SKIN: I get it. The gentleman's name is "Hell."

HELL: Here!

HIGH: Master "Hell."

Lord Beile spits in contempt. Hell catches the spit seamlessly with a spittoon he grabs quickly from his props.

LORD BEILE: Please! "Master"? Him? He's a flunkey! What a headache flunkies are these days.

Hell is confused and afraid, and he brings out a fan to fan Lord Beile.

In the winter, they fan me; in the summer, they give me a big blanket.

Hell is confused and opens an umbrella over Lord Beile, who grows furious.

NOW I'M INDOORS, AND HE OPENS UP AN UMBRELLA? WHAT THE . . .

HELL AND HIGH AND SKIN: *(in unison)* HELL!

HELL: HERE!

LORD BEILE: OH HOW I SUFFER! Let me ask you two, how many do you see behind me?

HIGH: What? How many?

Pause. High and Skin look and look.

One . . .

LORD BEILE: Eight!

HIGH: Oh, you mean he has to serve eight masters?

LORD BEILE: What?

Lord Beile uses his fingers to signify "five." Hell adds "three," on the same beat.

Out of eight flunkies, only one remains.

Lord Beile descends from the table, with Hell bringing the stool down on cue so he can step down seamlessly. Lord Beile walks around. Hell follows with the stool nervously, anticipating his possible sitting down.

What a year! Ever since the reign of His Majesty Shunzhi of our great Qing Dynasty, whenever any single lord of my rank came out in public, was there anyone who didn't bring *(using his fingers to signify "three," Hell adding "five")* eight?!

Lord Beile starts speaking faster and faster, like the rapid "guankou" passages of an accomplished crosstalk master.

One step forward, eight feet follow, two steps forward, sixteen feet behind, carrying lanterns, opening umbrellas, holding the teapot, wielding the spittoon, *(accelerating)* preparing the charcoal, heating the hot pot, dipping the tripe slices and mutton shavings, all this while providing the tools for calligraphy, music and chess, flower painting, pots, pans, sticks and stones, everything that can be eaten, worn, used, carried, slept on, napped on, plus a little container for crickets, a big kite, even with eight old hands, *(using his fingers to signify "four," Hell adding "four")* IT WASN'T NECESSARILY ENOUGH TO GET BY, AND NOW AFTER MY RESOURCES HAVE BEEN COMPROMISED, ALL THAT'S LEFT IS ONE!

Hell raises his finger.

AND IT TURNS OUT TO BE THIS ONE!

Hell points at himself.

YOU TELL ME, HOW CAN I GET BY?! WHAT THE—

HELL AND HIGH AND SKIN: *(in unison)* HELL!

HELL: HERE!

LORD BEILE: Oh, how I suffer!

Lord Beile sits down, Hell providing the stool at the right moment.

After downsizing, I, the noble Sparrow in the Cloud, have been subjected to such an inhumane existence. *(sigh)* You tell me, is there anyone whose days are more miserable than mine?

Pause. No one answers.

What?

HIGH: *(quickly answering)* Sorry, sir, you are definitely the worst.

LORD BEILE: What?

HIGH: I mean, you are the best.

LORD BEILE: What?

HIGH: I mean, I am the worst.

LORD BEILE: What?

HIGH: You are the worst.

LORD BEILE: *(shaking his head, sighing)* Ah! I say, you! What the—

Hell forgets to answer.

Huh?

HELL: *(hastily answering)* Hell!

LORD BEILE: He missed a beat! Alas! That makes me SO ANGRY! SO ANGRY! SO ANGRY!

Lord Beile stands up and in rapid succession sits and stands three times, moving forward each time, forcing Hell into rapid movement to catch up each time with the stool.
Sitting, Lord Beile props his legs up on the carved stage railing. He sticks out his right hand. Hell, propping up his back against Lord Beile's back to keep Lord Beile in balance, hands Lord Beile two iron balls to play with in his palm.

SKIN: How true, Lord Beile. These are not good times. When we the people have nothing to eat, that's perfectly normal. But to see you, Lord Beile, suffering so, that really breaks my heart.

High is apprehensive. Lord Beile stands and starts walking around the stage.

LORD BEILE: *(poetically)* Everything is in the state of degeneration. All things in regression, all beauty, all sophistication, gradually fading away, toward the inevitable oblivion.

Lord Beile gestures for Hell to place his stool down center. He then sits on the stool with his back to the audience.

But you must stop listening to me blathering on, interrupting your performance. Come, perform for us!

HIGH: Us?

LORD BEILE: Aren't you doing crosstalk?

HIGH: So you want us to . . . ?

LORD BEILE: Give us some sophisticated passages! We long for something with artistic finesse!

Hell brings the birdcage over next to Lord Beile. High and Skin stand behind the table. The audience's sight lines have been obstructed by Lord Beile.

SKIN: Something sophisticated . . .

Lord Beile strokes the birdcage.

LORD BEILE: *(to the birdcage)* Good girl, we're going to listen to crosstalk. Last time it was the opera, tonight it's crosstalk.

Pause. The two performers attempt to restart, under the new and stressful conditions.

HIGH: *(without confidence)* I say . . .

SKIN: Yes?

HIGH: What would we call "artistic sophistication"?

Lord Beile turns his left shoulder and looks at the audience.

LORD BEILE: Wait a second. *(pointing to the audience)* Look! All of them are sitting over there, *(pointing at the two performers)* and you two are standing here. How do you expect them to see you?

Pause.

HIGH: That's true. There is a sight-line problem.

LORD BEILE: Then find a solution!

Pause.

You need to get taller.

SKIN: That's not so easy after a certain age.

LORD BEILE: UP! On the table!

Hell pats the table.

(irritated) How come these people have no problem-solving capabilities?

High and Skin climb onto the table.

SKIN: *(while climbing)* Only heard of Peking Opera gymnasts bounding onto the table in "Three Way Crossroads." First time I ever heard of crosstalk actors climbing onto a table . . .

Lord Beile turns his head to the spectators and encourages them to applaud.

LORD BEILE: Bravo! Bravo!

The two performers stand tall on the table. Reluctantly, they continue their performance.

HIGH: I say . . . "The heights bring on loneliness . . ."

SKIN: On the other hand, "If the tune is lofty, why must it inevitably go unappreciated"?

Lord Beile sticks out his hand while focusing on the performers. Hell hands him the spittoon by mistake. Without thinking, Lord Beile takes it to be a cup of tea, and tries to drink from it, immediately realizing his mistake. He throws down the spittoon.

LORD BEILE: *(clearing his mouth)* PTOOEY!—WHAT WAS THAT?!

Hell quickly puts away the spittoon.

HIGH: *(continuing)* So what can we call "sophisticated"?

SKIN: What is sophisticated?

HIGH: Shall we . . . stage a cricket duel?

Hell brings the whole steaming hot pot to Lord Beile. Without looking, Lord Beile sticks his hand out and holds the hot pot. It is too hot for him.

LORD BEILE: *(leaping up)* Oh, my God! Hot hot hot!

Hell quickly takes back the hot pot.

SKIN: Now that's damn sophisticated.

HIGH: And then we can sit down together, have tea, and write poetry . . .

LORD BEILE: Stop.

Pause. Lord Beile gestures to the two actors.

Come down, down! What are you guys blathering about?

The two performers come down from the table. Hell puts the birdcage on the table.

HIGH: I'm afraid we are lacking in this area.

LORD BEILE: Lacking? Can truth be spit out of a dog's mouth? Who are you to understand the true meaning of "lacking"?

SKIN: Of course we can't understand the meaning of "lacking." Because we lack everything! We lack rice, we lack bowls, we lack soup to warm our souls, we lack dads and we lack mums, we lack blankets to warm our bums!

High quickly grabs Skin and pushes him offstage. He decides to deal with Lord Beile himself.
High kneels in front of Lord Beile in fear.

HIGH: Lord Beile, that sidekick of mine, he lacks morals and he lacks brains. Whatever your needs, your humble servant is here to oblige.

Pause. Lord Beile sticks out his right hand to Hell.

LORD BEILE: Yeah?

Hell hands a beautiful fan to Lord Beile. Lord Beile opens the fan, then points at High.

(to Hell) Yeah?

Hell does not understand. Lord Beile gazes at High. Hell produces a very, very small fan for High. Hell retreats to his prop area.

Scene 3: Listen to the Flower

Lord Beile and High stand facing the audience. They announce their names in the stock opening and then start performing. Lord Beile leads. High does not know what to expect.

LORD BEILE: Sparrow in the Cloud . . .

Pause.

HIGH: *(nervous)* Your humble servant Sky High . . .

LORD BEILE: Ascend the stage with a bow . . .

They bow to the audience. High suddenly kneels down.

Stand up.

HIGH: Your humble servant doesn't dare!

LORD BEILE: In crosstalk, there is no high or low. We perform as equals onstage. Don't treat me like aristocracy, and I won't treat you like a sycophant, okay?

High stands up.

HIGH: Yes, sir.

LORD BEILE: Good.

Pause.

Let's talk about sophistication. About "beauty."

HIGH: *(very nervous)* Let's talk about "beauty."

LORD BEILE: Tell me what you think of as "beautiful."

HIGH: "Beautiful."

LORD BEILE: Don't give me that pretentious crap that you just did on the table. Tell me, the most beautiful thing you can think of now.

High is forced to talk.

HIGH: The most beautiful thing I can think of now is—a big bowl of hot, fragrant, rice with no pebbles or wood shavings, no rice worms, and it's all mine!

LORD BEILE: *(not at all impressed)* So you just described "beauty"?

HIGH: "Beauty."

LORD BEILE: Ptooey! That's called "hunger."

HIGH: Please don't spit into my bowl.

LORD BEILE: Try again!

HIGH: "Beauty" is when your clothes have few patches, your roof doesn't leak when it drizzles, your house doesn't flood when it pours!

LORD BEILE: You call this . . .

HIGH: "Beauty."

LORD BEILE: Ptooey! That's called "poverty."

HIGH: Please don't spit on my clothes.

LORD BEILE: How strange, people these days no longer understand beauty. I say, when people don't know beauty, this era is coming to an end!

HIGH: *(to himself)* What's "beauty" without food and clothes?

LORD BEILE: On the contrary, if you have "beauty," who cares about food and clothes?

HIGH: You heard me?

LORD BEILE: You're standing next to me. How could I not hear you?

HIGH: But . . .

LORD BEILE: That bowl of rice in front of you? All you do is eat it, then you are full, then you defecate, then you are hungry again. You call that "beauty"?

HIGH: But I'm so happy to see that bowl of rice.

LORD BEILE: See? I have discovered the problem.

HIGH: What?

LORD BEILE: Is "beauty" meant to be "seen"?

HIGH: If beauty isn't meant to be seen, are you telling me it's meant to be . . . smelled?

LORD BEILE: Ptooey! Open your ears.

HIGH: Use my ears to eat?

LORD BEILE: To listen!

HIGH: Listen to the rice? Is it going to talk to me?

LORD BEILE: If it doesn't, how are you going to hear?

HIGH: *(getting worked up)* So let me ask you, how does rice talk?

LORD BEILE: Look, a big bowl of rice, nice and hot . . .

High suddenly grabs the imagined bowl of rice.

HIGH: I'm eating it! I'm eating it! . . .

LORD BEILE: Back!

High stands back in place.

> Listen carefully. At the moment the vapor ascends, there is a sound . . .

HIGH: And what is that sound?

LORD BEILE: "Fragrance!"

HIGH: The rice is saying that it's fragrant?

LORD BEILE: Come on, that's the *sound* of the rice! Why would rice refer to itself as fragrant? Rice *is* fragrant! And if you can hear that, that's beauty.

HIGH: That's not very convincing.

LORD BEILE: Look. Autumn. *(gesturing)* A hillside full of red leaves. What do you say about that?

HIGH: A hillside full of red leaves in autumn, of course that looks very beautiful.

LORD BEILE: Jeez! If I forced someone like you to open your eyes all the way, you still wouldn't be able to understand the beauty of a hillside full of red leaves in autumn.

HIGH: So you can't look.

LORD BEILE: You have to listen.

HIGH: Listen to the sound of the autumn leaves.

LORD BEILE: Right.

HIGH: I've done that.

LORD BEILE: And . . . ?

HIGH: *(making the sound of leaves)* "Rustle . . . rustle . . ."

LORD BEILE: Come on, you can do better than that! That's the sound of the autumn wind kicking up the fallen leaves.

HIGH: Right, that's what I just described.

LORD BEILE: That is not the sound of the leaves themselves. You can't describe it unless you really hear what the red leaves themselves are saying!

HIGH: And so the sound of the red leaves is . . . ?

LORD BEILE: "Reddd . . ."

HIGH: Hold on. If that's true, then when spring comes, and the hillside is full of red, yellow, blue, white, and violet flowers, then we have a problem, because when I get home, I tell everyone that the flowers outside are so beautiful, their sound is "redyellowbluewhiteviolet"!

LORD BEILE: *(shaking his head)* That shows you didn't really hear it.

HIGH: Damn right I didn't.

LORD BEILE: How can that be the sound of the red yellow blue white and violet flowers blooming in springtime?

HIGH: Then please tell me, what is the sound?

LORD BEILE: Listen. *(pause)* "Springggg . . ."

HIGH: I knew it. Spring awakening.

LORD BEILE: Spring isn't awakening, spring IS spring!

HIGH: Not very convincing.

LORD BEILE: Isn't that beautiful?

HIGH: But . . .

LORD BEILE: *(forcing him)* Isn't it?

HIGH: *(kneeling down)* You're damn right it's beautiful!

LORD BEILE: *(kneeling down beside High)* So I say, people today do not understand beauty because they do not understand how to listen.

HIGH: That's pretty hard to understand.

LORD BEILE: Even you, a crosstalk performer, don't know how to listen. No wonder you are such a lousy performer!

HIGH: I take your criticism to heart.

High discovers that Lord Beile is kneeling beside him.

Whoops! What are you doing, Lord Beile . . . ?

LORD BEILE: Don't you know you can't perform crosstalk kneeling?

High quickly helps Lord Beile up.

Come, let me teach you how to listen. Listen.

HIGH: To what?

Lord Beile suddenly kneels down again, head to the floor. High also kneels down. He is very nervous.

LORD BEILE: *(pointing at the stage)* The stage.

Lord Beile puts his ear next to the stage floor.

HIGH: The stage?

LORD BEILE: Listen to what the stage has to say. Do you hear it?

High is forced to go along with it.

HIGH: Yes, yes! I do!

LORD BEILE: You do?

HIGH: Loud and clear!

LORD BEILE: Great. Tell me.

HIGH: It says . . .

LORD BEILE: Yes?

HIGH: "STAGE!"

Lord Beile shakes his head in disgust.

(correcting himself) Sorry. Wrong. It was *(making a sound)* "BOARDS! . . ."

LORD BEILE: Getting closer.

HIGH: Getting closer? How about "PLANKS"?

Lord Beile leads him to repeat the sound, springily.

Planks? Plank . . . plank . . .
"plankplankplankplankplankplankplank . . ."

High starts sounding like Peking Opera percussion. As if on cue, Hell immediately takes out a drumstick and uses the board bound to his head to pound out a rhythm while occasionally banging on a gong that he holds in his hand, becoming a surreal one-man Peking Opera band.

To this percussion, Lord Beile sings an aria from The Yang Family Generals.

LORD BEILE: *(singing) Drops of tears spill forth,*
   defeated at the battle on the beach,
   our Yang family sons were slaughtered,
   your big brother's chest was pierced by a spear,
   your second brother lost his life on the sunny platform to a sword,
   your third brother was trampled by horses into pieces of mud,
   most pathetic, your seventh brother was bound to a banana tree by Pan
      Hong,
   where arrows pierced through his body, and he died with no burial,
   Yanhui, my son,
   what wind has brought you
   back to me?

High applauds with fervor.

HIGH: Bravo!

Lord Beile takes a bow. High thinks about it.

   Lord Beile, are you trying to tell me that this stage can sing?

LORD BEILE: How could a stage sing? It's reminiscing.

HIGH: The stage is reminiscing?

LORD BEILE: It's reminiscing about the most "beauty" it had ever seen in a day. That was during the reign of the Emperor Tongzhi. Master Qiu Wanlin performed the Old Matriarch here at Thousand Year Teahouse.

HIGH: Must have sold out the house.

LORD BEILE: On the day before the performance, his little son had waded into the river to gather fish, and drowned. What grand sorrow! So after this famous passage in *The Yang Family Generals*, after the old lady recounts how she lost her sons, after he finished this passage, nobody onstage or in the audience dared to shout bravo. Total silence!

HIGH: How truly sad.

LORD BEILE: How truly beautiful!

HIGH: Wait a minute, how can you call that beautiful?

LORD BEILE: It's called "melancholic beauty." My God, you can drag a cow to Beijing, but it's still a cow. How do you expect me to teach you? Come here!

They stand next to the birdcage, by the table. Lord Beile points at the birdcage.

Tell me. What is this?

HIGH: A birdcage.

LORD BEILE: You are still using your eyes!

HIGH: But . . .

LORD BEILE: All right. Then let's for convenience's sake call it a "birdcage." Inside it is . . . ?

HIGH: A bird. *(pause)* I guess.

LORD BEILE: You guess! *(shaking his head)* OK, let's for convenience's sake call it a bird! Listen! What is the bird saying?

HIGH: *(making a chirping sound)* "Dikdik . . ."

LORD BEILE: Again? Is that what you hear?

HIGH: "Dikdikdikdikdikdikdik . . ."

LORD BEILE: How many "dick"s?

HIGH: Two.

LORD BEILE: What?

HIGH: One.

LORD BEILE: What?

HIGH: Maybe none.

LORD BEILE: *(sighing)* Alas, if you really knew how to listen, you would hear a story with melancholic beauty.

HIGH: A melancholy bird.

Pause.

LORD BEILE: What's wrong with people these days? Come here . . .

Lord Beile opens up the cloth around the birdcage, revealing not a bird inside, but a flower in a pot.

HIGH: *(instinctively using the stock go-to line)* Get the heck out of here!

High hits Lord Beile on the head with his fan, as is tradition when saying this line.

LORD BEILE: What?

High is in horror at his performer's instincts.

HIGH: *(correcting himself)* Nothing! I'm scolding myself.

High hits himself over his head with the fan, and kneels down again in subservience.

LORD BEILE: Get up. This is . . . ?

HIGH: A flowerpot in a birdcage.

LORD BEILE: Didn't you just say it was a bird?

HIGH: It's a flower.

LORD BEILE: These days people always judge things by their appearances.

HIGH: Right, right, I judged by appearances, and mistook a bird for a flower.

LORD BEILE: But if you insist that it is a flower, let's then, for convenience's sake, call it a flower.

HIGH: *(mystified)* Convenience or not, it IS a flower.

LORD BEILE: Okay. Now we come to the crux. What is it saying to you?

HIGH: It?

LORD BEILE: Listen!

HIGH: To the flower?

LORD BEILE: LISTEN!

High does not know how best to please Lord Beile. He "listens."

HIGH: *(frightened)* Yes, yes, I hear it!

LORD BEILE: And what does it say?

HIGH: *(guessing)* "To be or not to be a bird . . ."

Pause. Lord Beile is silent.

LORD BEILE: Did it also say "A rose by any other name . . ."?

HIGH: No.

LORD BEILE: Listen!

High is even more frightened, and "listens" more intently to the flower.

HIGH: Got it!

LORD BEILE: And what is it?

HIGH: I heard it say . . . "I'm growing."

LORD BEILE: Does it say that every day? Does a child tell you that it's growing up?

HIGH: But . . .

LORD BEILE: Listen! *(ordering him)* Come on! What is it telling you? Listen . . .

HIGH: Okay, Okay, I'm listening! Jeez . . .

High is out of ideas, so he starts saying random things.

Such a beautiful flower, why would it be captive in this tiny little birdcage?

Pause.

LORD BEILE: You heard it?

HIGH: I . . .

LORD BEILE: You understand what it's feeling?

HIGH: Well . . . *(realizing he is saved)* I can sort of grasp the dilemma.

LORD BEILE: Good. Now I can return to the story.

HIGH: My ears are bathed in respectful anticipation.

High breathes a sigh of relief.

> LORD BEILE: There used to be the most amazing bird living in this cage. Deep within this bird's eyes were stored all of the beautiful memories from the past. *(shaking his head)* Hard to believe, his master was so good to Me. Why did Me have to fly away?

High cannot understand what Lord Beile is saying.

> HIGH: What?

> LORD BEILE: One day, Me flew away. He wasn't used to seeing an empty birdcage, so He went and chose a pretty flowerpot and put it in as a replacement. Sometimes, He could still imagine that Me was still there.

> HIGH: Hey, wait a minute. I don't get it. What are you saying? Who flew away?

> LORD BEILE: "Me."

> HIGH: You?

> LORD BEILE: No, "Me."

> HIGH: You flew away?

> LORD BEILE: The bird! The bird flew away!

> HIGH: Didn't you say "Me"?

> LORD BEILE: The bird's name was "Me"!

High is dumbfounded. Pause.

> Come on, what don't you understand?

> HIGH: The bird's name was . . . ?! Okay, I get it. So what happened to Me?

> LORD BEILE: Who gives a damn what happened to you?

> HIGH: Sorry, that came out wrong. Actually, that came out right. But— Okay, let me phrase it again: please tell the story of "Me."

> LORD BEILE: For that, you'll need to go home and ask your mama. Now I'm going to tell the bird's story.

> HIGH: The story of "Me"?

LORD BEILE: HOW DARE YOU COMPARE YOURSELF TO THE BIRD? You think you're in that league?

HIGH: *(pointing at the birdcage)* I mean it! It!

LORD BEILE: "ITS" NAME IS "ME"! ITS MASTER IS "HE"!

HIGH: Fine, Okay, I got it, so . . .

High points at himself, imitating Lord Beile's grunts.

> "Nay" wants to listen to . . . *(pointing at the birdcage)* "Yeah's" story. Please, *(pointing at Lord Beile)* "Yeah," can you tell it to *(pointing at himself)* "Nay"?

LORD BEILE: What happened to you?

HIGH: Can you please just continue?

LORD BEILE: The bird's story?

HIGH: Yes.

LORD BEILE: Why didn't you just ask?

HIGH: I've been asking all along.

Order is restored. Lord Beile continues the story.

LORD BEILE: The master cared lovingly for Me. Me sang to He every day, the most beautiful sound. Every day He had to attend to duties in the court, with nothing to say to anybody. He could only talk to Me.

HIGH: He was downtrodden?

LORD BEILE: Yes.

HIGH: For once I got it right!

LORD BEILE: The court is just a gang of lackey yes-men. The only sound you hear when anyone speaks is—"Yes sir." "Yes sir yes sir yes sir yes sir yes sir . . ."

HIGH: A bunch of yes men.

Lord Beile stares at High.

> Yes sir.

LORD BEILE: Such a collection of sycophants. Anyone with the slightest ideas of their own would inevitably have been smothered in there long ago. The only time that He felt some comfort was when He came back to the room and talked to Me.

HIGH: Life is tough.

LORD BEILE: One day, He said to Me, "Cute little Soul, if I opened the little door of this birdcage, would Little Soul want to come outside and take a look?"

HIGH: *(interrupting)* Hold it. I'm lost. Who is "Little Soul"?

LORD BEILE: Pet name, pet name.

HIGH: Sorry. Whose pet's name?

LORD BEILE: *(very frustrated, slowly)* THE PET NAME OF THE LITTLE BIRD WAS "LITTLE SOUL"!

HIGH: Got it.

LORD BEILE: Is it that difficult?

HIGH: Yes sir. I mean no sir. I mean . . . Forget I said anything. So the nickname of the little bird was "Little Soul." May I ask if there was anyone called "Big Soul"?

LORD BEILE: *(emotional)* In all of the Qing Dynasty, there are no Big Souls, only Little Souls, THERE ISN'T A SINGLE GODDAM BIG SOUL IN THE QING DYNASTY, ONLY VERY VERY VERY MANY LITTLE SOULS, EVERYWHERE, EVERY SPACE IS FILLED WITH LITTLE SOULS!!

Pause.

HIGH: Got it. *(recapping)* So, if the little door of the birdcage is opened, will Little Me seek to come out and have a look?

LORD BEILE: "Little Me" said: "Yes, thank you!" He said: "Then when Me comes out, and has seen enough, will Me obediently fly back in?" Me said: "Of course." And so He opened the door of the birdcage . . .

HIGH: And?

LORD BEILE: *(suddenly emotional)* Goddam moron went "WHOOSH—!" and flew far the dickens away, never to return!

Pause. Lord Beile looks at the distance. High is moved.

HIGH: *(with spiritual longing)* "Me" flew away!

LORD BEILE: You couldn't fly anywhere! Flap your arms as hard as you can, you wouldn't get past the first row before you plummeted to the floor! What are you trying to do to me? I almost made it to the denouement, and you pulled me back down! How do you expect me to start up again?

HIGH: Sorry.

LORD BEILE: Where were we?

HIGH: "Yeah" flew away. The little bird.

LORD BEILE: Oh yes.

Lord Beile calms down.

So to memorialize his bird, He wrote a poem in the four-line five-character style.

HIGH: A Tang Dynasty–styled poem? About Me?

LORD BEILE: Get out of here! Who would write a poem about you?!

HIGH: True, true. So would it behoove you to let everyone listen to this classical verse?

LORD BEILE: It's written in a very obscure style. I'm afraid you wouldn't appreciate it.

HIGH: My ears are bathed in respectful anticipation.

Lord Beile thinks, then starts to recite poetry.

LORD BEILE: "The country is ravished, but mountains and rivers remain . . ."

HIGH: What? Are you sure this poem was written by you?

LORD BEILE: "Spring in the city, the trees and flowers grow deep . . ."

HIGH: Isn't that Du Fu's most famous poem?

LORD BEILE: *(very softly)* "In an emotional moment, Me shed tears . . ."

HIGH: Wait. The original is "even the flowers shed tears."

LORD BEILE: "Fearing separation, Me is fearful at heart"!

HIGH: No! It's "Birds are fearful!" It's . . . Get the heck . . . *(raising his fan at Lord Beile)* out of . . . *(realizing he is saying the wrong thing)* HE better get . . . *(turning sharply)* ME BETTER GET THE HECK OUT OF HERE!

Lord Beile announces his name in a stock crosstalk sign-off.

LORD BEILE: Sparrow in the Cloud!

HIGH: *(catching up)* Your humble servant Sky High!

BEILE AND HIGH: *(in unison)* Sign off with a bow!

They bow to the audience.
High immediately kneels down again.

Scene 4: Change Partners

HIGH: *(pleading while kneeling)* Lord Beile, have mercy! It's a stock response, every time any crosstalk actor gets to this point in a scene, the stock line is always "Get the heck out of here!" I wasn't scolding you, please have mercy!

LORD BEILE: How come you keep kneeling down during performance? What the—!

Hell, who has been standing in the back throughout, suddenly answers.

HELL: HELL!

LORD BEILE: *(to Hell)* Dammit, none of your business, don't interrupt us. *(to High)* Stand up please.

High stands up.

I truly hate lackey yes-men.

HIGH: Yes sir.

LORD BEILE: Tell me, what is a lackey?

HIGH: What is a lackey?

LORD BEILE: Someone who keeps repeating what others say.

HIGH: *(agreeing)* Someone who keeps repeating what others say.

LORD BEILE: Someone who keeps copying what others do.

HIGH: Someone who keeps copying what others . . .

High realizes that he is repeating everything, and kneels down again.

LORD BEILE: Look at you, soft bones, no guts. Can we find somebody tougher? Change!

HIGH: Change? To who?

Skin enters.

LORD BEILE: Isn't there that other guy over there? I'll take him!

HIGH: What? *(frightened)* He . . . He can't do it. Lord Beile, his noggin is screwed on wrong!

LORD BEILE: Out of the way!

SKIN: Are you calling me?

HIGH: No . . . Get out of here! He wasn't calling you.

Hell suddenly speaks.

HELL: Out.

High exits, reluctantly, shown out by Hell.

Scene 5: The Old Budda and Little Foxy Red

Pause. Lord Beile stares at Skin, who is still defiant.

LORD BEILE: So, are you always the sidekick?

SKIN: I have my moments.

LORD BEILE: Let's perform.

SKIN: After you.

They stand together. Lord Beile starts in the standard crosstalk style. Skin replies, using stock interjections.

LORD BEILE: I say . . .

SKIN: Uh-huh.

LORD BEILE: Yesterday . . .

SKIN: Mm-hmm . . .

LORD BEILE: Afternoon . . .

SKIN: Ah.

LORD BEILE: Before dinner . . .

SKIN: Righty-O . . .

Pause. Lord Beile stares at Skin.

LORD BEILE: *(critical of his replies)* Is that all you've got?

SKIN: There's plenty more. The stock interjections of the art of crosstalk include "Yoho!" "Yahei!" "Ahh~~right!" "Ahh~~Ughh!" "Get the heck out of here!" . . .

LORD BEILE: So you are still a lackey! Can I hear the sidekick having some ideas of his own? Let's try it again. One more time, trash the old stuff.

SKIN: Trash the old stuff?

LORD BEILE: I don't want any of that standard "Uh-huh mm-hmm righty-o," okay?

SKIN: Fine with me.

LORD BEILE: Keep "Get the heck out of here!" That's got character.

SKIN: Understood.

LORD BEILE: Ready?

SKIN: No.

Pause. Lord Beile starts up again.

LORD BEILE: I say . . .

SKIN: Get the heck out of here!

LORD BEILE: *(immediately stepping out of character)* That was way too fast! It lacked logic! Before I've said anything, you tell me to get the heck out of here. Doesn't make sense. Let's try it again! Whatever I say, don't go along with me!

SKIN: Whatever you say, don't go along with you?

LORD BEILE: Right!

SKIN: You said it.

LORD BEILE: I said it.

SKIN: *(to himself)* That's called "The ruling class forces the people to revolt."

LORD BEILE: Ready?

SKIN: Shoot.

Pause. Lord Beile starts up again.

LORD BEILE: I say . . .

SKIN: I'm not interested.

LORD BEILE: *(immediately stepping out of character)* Nice! That shows character.

Pause.

   Yesterday . . .

Skin says the opposite of everything on purpose.

SKIN: Today . . .

LORD BEILE: In the afternoon . . .

SKIN: In the morning . . .

LORD BEILE: The Empress Dowager sent an order to see me.

SKIN: Little Foxy Red had a note sent to me.

LORD BEILE: I say . . . *(stepping out)* Hold it. Who is "Little Foxy Red"?

SKIN: None of your business.

LORD BEILE: Good!

SKIN: Bad! *(aside)* All of this is going public.

LORD BEILE: *(continuing)* Alas, my heart was heavy . . .

SKIN: Hooray, I was so lighthearted . . .

LORD BEILE: I didn't know how to report to the Empress Dowager.

SKIN: I had it all figured out.

LORD BEILE: So I went straight into the Forbidden City . . .

SKIN: So I strolled slowly along Red Lantern Lane . . .

LORD BEILE: On the street I looked up . . . how come there were so many people?

SKIN: When I got into the alley . . . how come I didn't see a single brothelgoer?

LORD BEILE: How come they're all running?

SKIN: How come everything's so quiet?

LORD BEILE: When I got into the Warm Winter Chamber, I was so shocked when I saw the Empress Dowager!

SKIN: When I got to Sumptuous Spring Garden, I was so elated to see Little Foxy Red.

LORD BEILE: The old lady's hair was all white, face totally pale, eyes unfocused . . .

SKIN: The young woman's hair was neatly combed, her gown red, a red flower in her tresses . . .

LORD BEILE: I immediately knelt down to the Empress Dowager and said, "Old Buddha, long life, long life, long long life . . ."

SKIN: Little Foxy Red took me in her arms and said, "Man oh man oh man oh man . . ."

LORD BEILE: "Your Majesty, your lackey has urgent news for you."

SKIN: "Little Foxy Red, your man has something to tell you."

LORD BEILE: "Your Majesty, do you want the good news first or the bad news first?"

SKIN: "Hey Red, do you want the bad news first or the good news first?"

LORD BEILE: *(in the voice of the empress)* "Let me hear the good news first."

SKIN: *(in the voice of Little Foxy Red)* "Let me hear the bad news first."

LORD BEILE: "My report to Your Majesty: the weather is beautiful today, perfect for an outdoor excursion."

SKIN: "The bad news is that my family has gone bankrupt. I have nothing to my name."

LORD BEILE: *(in the voice of the empress)* "Then what's the bad news?"

SKIN: *(in the voice of Red)* "And what is the good news?"

LORD BEILE: "Your Majesty, the foreign devils of the Eight Nations Alliance have advanced into the city. We have no choice but to evacuate!"

SKIN: "Hey Red, the good news is that I have decided to buy out your contract. I'm not going anywhere without you."

LORD BEILE: I . . . *(stepping out of character to argue)* Hold it. You just contradicted yourself. You say you have nothing left to your name, then how are you going to buy out her contract?

SKIN: My plan was to take her out of the brothel, and then we would . . . Hey, what do you care about my lines? Mind your own business!

LORD BEILE: Sorry. Continue.

They get back into role.

SKIN: "Hey Red, though your man is flat broke, I have decided to elope with you! Let's go, far away from the brothel district!"

LORD BEILE: "Your Majesty, though we have everything, we must leave the palace to save your precious life!"

SKIN: *(miming giving two slaps)* "Bing-bang," Little Foxy Red delivered two pot stickers to my face.

LORD BEILE: "Meow meow . . ." something flew above the Old Buddha's head.

SKIN: *(stepping out)* Hold on. How come there was the "Meow meow" sound of a cat?

LORD BEILE: Don't get it, right? She also asked me: *(in the voice of the empress)* "How come a cat flew over my head?"

SKIN: *(asking the same question for himself)* How come a cat flew over her head?

LORD BEILE: *(stepping out)* Damn! What do you care about that? Mind your own lines! I'm in the process of reporting to the Boss Lady!

SKIN: Oh.

They get back into role.

LORD BEILE: "My report to Your Majesty: That's the sound of a bullet."

SKIN: *(in the voice of Red)* "You silly boy, Sumptuous Spring Garden is like an enormous cage. No one simply steps out of it."

LORD BEILE: "Your Majesty, the foreign devils are closing in on us. You need to run for your life."

SKIN: "Red, the gate is wide open, I say we get out of here right now!"

LORD BEILE: "Your Majesty, your humble lackey will guard the royal palace for you!"

SKIN: *(in the voice of Red)* "Even if we get past the gate, the madam will send someone to drag us back."

LORD BEILE: *(kneeling)* "Your Majesty, please get on the sedan chair and let us go!"

SKIN: "Where's the madam? There's no one here!"

LORD BEILE: "Your Majesty, hurry!"

SKIN: I grabbed Red's hands, and thought, how in the world could there be a pair of such soft and tender hands?

LORD BEILE: I grabbed the Old Buddha's feet, and thought, how in the world could there be a pair of such small and stinky feet?

SKIN: We wandered out of Sumptuous Spring Garden, she turned back to have a look . . .

LORD BEILE: We came out of the Hall of Spiritual Cultivation, crossed through the Nine-Dragon Wall . . .

SKIN: *(in the voice of Red)* "Wait. I forgot to bring the ring you gave me."

LORD BEILE: *(in the voice of the empress)* "Wait. I forgot to toss the consort Zhen into the well."

SKIN: *(aside)* Forgot that piece of history. *(back to his narrative)* I said, "Red, we have to hurry."

LORD BEILE: "Your Majesty, please hurry and shove her in."

SKIN: *(in the voice of Red)* "Oh, the ring is in my pouch. Come, hurry and put it on my finger."

LORD BEILE: *(in a rush)* "The consort Zhen is standing there next to the well, please just shove her in!"

SKIN: "Let's hurry and put it on your finger."

LORD BEILE: "Let's hurry and shove her in."

SKIN: I was thinking, how come her fingers are so short?

LORD BEILE: I was fuming, how come the consort Zhen was so big? The Old Buddha kept shoving . . .

SKIN: I kept pushing . . .

LORD BEILE: She shoved shoved shoved . . .

SKIN: I pushed pushed pushed . . .

LORD BEILE: Shove shove shove . . .

SKIN: Push push push . . .

LORD BEILE: Then I heard the sound "Boom"!

SKIN: Then I heard the sound "Zip"!

LORD BEILE: Down she went.

SKIN: On it was.

LORD BEILE: Dead.

SKIN: Done.

LORD BEILE: So we carried on.

SKIN: So we held each other's hands, and gazed into each other's eyes.

LORD BEILE: There was a sound from behind.

SKIN: Everything around us was so quiet.

LORD BEILE: "Help! . . ."

SKIN: *(to Beile)* Consort Zhen was still alive?

LORD BEILE: No! It was a huge mob of people behind us who were shouting!

SKIN: Who?

LORD BEILE: The foreign devils had forced their way into the city!

SKIN: Run for your life!

LORD BEILE: *(politely, but in a hurry)* Then forgive me for not attending to you further.

They get back into role.

SKIN: *(getting back to his narrative)* Just at this time . . .

LORD BEILE: There was an earth-shattering sound . . .

SKIN: Sand flying, rocks falling . . .

LORD BEILE: *(making a sound)* Honglonhhualaaa~~!!

SKIN: *(likewise)* Pilipalaaa~~!!

LORD BEILE: Kwanglangshiliii~~!!

SKIN: Kongdongkualaa~~!!

LORD BEILE: Whoosh!

SKIN: Bang!

LORD BEILE: Boom!

SKIN: Crack!

LORD BEILE: A cannonball flew in and demolished half the Pavilion of Longevity!

SKIN: A gust of sandy wind blew in, everything became murky, you couldn't even see the fingers on your hand!

LORD BEILE: Kwanglanglang, kwanglanglang, the footsteps of the foreign devils drew near.

SKIN: Pilipa, pilipa, I grabbed Little Foxy Red and we ran across the Heavenly Bridge.

LORD BEILE: I watched as the Old Buddha's sedan chair and entourage disappeared into the distance.

SKIN: I stood at the head of the alley and gazed out. There was nobody to be seen.

LORD BEILE: *(kneeling to the empress)* "Your Majesty, may you be blessed with peace and prosperity. Your lackey vows to hold his position till death."

SKIN: *(voice of Red)* "My man, I can't see the way, where are we coming from? Where are we going?"

LORD BEILE: Damn! I forgot something.

SKIN: "Don't be afraid, your man has thought of a good place to go."

LORD BEILE: Without hesitation, I turned back and sprinted toward the Hall of Spiritual Cultivation.

SKIN: Without a word, I grabbed Little Foxy Red and we rushed straight to the Thousand Year Teahouse.

LORD BEILE: I thought, these foreign devils are coming straight into the palace. What are we going to do about all the treasures?

SKIN: "In this day and age, a man's life is worth nothing. But on the old stage, that's where our life force is."

LORD BEILE: So I had to get there before the foreigners, to grab the treasures.

SKIN: And so we . . . *(to Beile)* Wait a minute. You became a looter amidst the chaos, pilfering the palace of treasures?

LORD BEILE: *(explaining)* No, no, I was trying to save the treasures! If I save one that means they get one less, if I save two, then they lose a pair. Don't worry about me, take care of that old stage of yours. I haven't any time, go, go!!

SKIN: "Hey Red, back to the stage, hurry!"

LORD BEILE: So I came to the Hall of Spiritual Cultivation. I took one look, *(shaking his head)* what a devastating sight.

Skin acts like he is seeing ruins.

SKIN: Oh my God, the old stage has collapsed!

LORD BEILE: All sorts of things, broken and smashed . . .

SKIN: For a thousand years, warriors and maidens took their turns on this stage, spouting their wisdom, singing their songs. How could it just cease to exist?

LORD BEILE: I thought, this doesn't look good, but there are still a lot of things I can loot, *(correcting himself)* I mean save!

SKIN: *(voice of Red)* "I say, my man, this is all junk from the past, nothing to get attached to. Let's go."

LORD BEILE: I rolled up my sleeves, and thought . . . It's time to start gathering things.

SKIN: "No, Red, this is our home, we have to reconstruct it."

Lord Beile mimes picking up many things. The two men walk and run around the stage freely, their language going at breakneck speed.

LORD BEILE: I carried stuff on my shoulder, in my hand, I saw things on the ground, and thought of things on the wall. Beneath my right armpit I squeezed Wang Xizhi's masterpiece "Clearing after Quick Snow," plus "A City of Cathay"—the version collected by the Emperor Qianlong . . .

SKIN: I picked up the carved railing, bricks, and eaves, together in one pile . . .

LORD BEILE: *(gathering more and more)* . . . Under my left armpit I stashed the "Embroidered Plum and Bamboo Mountain Scene" scroll, the foreigner Matthieu Ricci's white jade crucifix, the 24 "Buddhas of Ecstasy in gold and copper and eight precious jewels" from Emperor Shun of the Yuan Dynasty . . .

SKIN: . . . I looked down and saw that I was standing on top of a large wooden plaque. On it was carved the four words: "Thousand Year Teahouse Theatre." . . .

LORD BEILE: *(carrying things with increasing difficulty)* . . . I came to the Hall of Heavenly Peace, and added the ancient Tripod Container from the West Zhou Dynasty, the great bell from the Eastern Zhou, the precious plate of the San clan, all around my neck, and between my shoulders I placed Guan Yunchang's Green Dragon Crescent Sword . . .

SKIN: . . . I carried the great plaque in my hand, but slipped and fell, sitting within a big six-sided lantern . . .

Lord Beile is to the point of being crushed by all the things that he is carrying.

LORD BEILE: . . . I then rushed to the Military Strategy Department on my right, put on the unbreakable armor from Xue Rengui, the iron jacket of the King of Chu, and then I locked everything together with a great five-colored Dragon and Phoenix plate from the Wanli period! . . .

SKIN: . . . I removed the curtains from the stage where generals roamed, and dusted them off. And then I stood up the fallen table, by which thousands and thousands of crosstalk scenes had been performed . . .

LORD BEILE: . . . Up and down, I ran and raced, I pulled and crawled, until finally I had dragged all of these treasures out of the Forbidden City . . .

SKIN: . . . I stood up tall and shouted, "Little Foxy Red, come here, let's greet the audience with a bow!" . . .

LORD BEILE: . . . "Someone, come! Help!"

Pause. They slow down.

SKIN: . . . No one answered. "Where is everybody?"

LORD BEILE: . . . What happened to my eight flunkies?

SKIN: ". . . Red, my girl . . ."

LORD BEILE: "Come back, you lackeys . . ."

SKIN: "Where have you gone? . . ."

LORD BEILE: How come they all disappeared?

SKIN: I went through every street of the whole town, but I couldn't find her. The whole city was empty.

LORD BEILE: My arms were so full, so full! I hovered around the Avenue of Eternal Peace . . .

SKIN: . . . I was empty, floating emptily down the streets of the city . . .

LORD BEILE: There was a narrow bridge ahead of me, and I thought, all these treasures would be safe once I made my way across the bridge.

SKIN: Red must be on the other side of the bridge.

They cross to opposite sides of the stage. Lord Beile wobbles ahead with great difficulty.

LORD BEILE: . . . I stopped somewhere to catch my breath . . . *(gazing ahead)* My God, hellish smoke everywhere . . .

SKIN: . . . In the smoke, the haze, before me there stood . . .

Skin stops in his tracks, and gazes ahead at Lord Beile.

What is this crazy-looking thing?

LORD BEILE: I looked out with squinted eye, hey . . .

Lord Beile stops in his tracks and looks at Skin.

. . . this silhouette, far away . . .

SKIN: Oh my God, what's a big antique display cabinet doing in the middle of the road?

LORD BEILE: Forget about him, I forged ahead toward the bridge . . .

Lord Beile continues to forge ahead, miming carrying everything.

SKIN: Wait. That antique cabinet can walk?

LORD BEILE: *(making an effort to move ahead)* I moved ahead step-by-step, and I got onto the bridge . . . I thought, "Look at that raggedy guy, must be a bandit."

SKIN: I thought, "This guy has got treasures stashed all over him. He's got to be a foreign mercenary."

LORD BEILE: I looked across the bridge . . .

The two men stand on either side of the stage, gazing toward each other.

SKIN: What's that up ahead?

LORD BEILE: Drizzly rain . . .

SKIN: Misty fog . . .

LORD BEILE: The autumn wind swirls . . .

SKIN: The fallen leaves fly . . .

LORD BEILE: Is there anything out there?

SKIN: Is the bridge destroyed?

LORD BEILE: *(with gesture)* With my left foot, I forged ahead one step . . .

SKIN: *(with gesture)* With my right foot, I took one step forward . . .

Their legs lock together.

LORD BEILE: Oh no, I'm stuck . . .

SKIN: Oh my God, I've sprained an ankle . . .

LORD BEILE: *(to Skin)* Sir Bandit, may I bother you to let me pass?

SKIN: *(to Beile)* Sir Foreign Mercenary, can you please move away that large blade? It's almost sticking into my back!

LORD BEILE: I can't, I am not my own master!

Skin suddenly notices something on Lord Beile's body.

SKIN: Don't move.

LORD BEILE: What happened?

SKIN: Is that a cricket container around your neck?

LORD BEILE: Yes.

SKIN: Well the cricket has crawled out, and is now on the underside of your jaw . . .

LORD BEILE: No!

SKIN: Now it is crawling up to your nostril . . .

Lord Beile starts to get nervous.

LORD BEILE: *(working up a sneeze)* Ah . . . ah . . .

SKIN: It went in. Don't sneeze. Please . . . Hold it. If you sneeze, all of the treasures of Chinese civilization will crash to the ground!

Lord Beile cannot hold back, and lets out a grand sneeze.

LORD BEILE: ACHOOOO~~!

Silence. They survey all of the imagined treasures that now lie broken and scattered on the ground.
They look at each other.

Skin turns toward the audience, and softly states his name, in the standard crosstalk sign-off.

SKIN: Skin Don't Laugh . . .

LORD BEILE: *(following)* Sparrow in the Cloud . . .

BEILE AND SKIN: *(in unison)* Sign off with a bow!

They bow to the audience.

Scene 6: Bringing Down the House

Hell brings the stool to the right of the table, where Lord Beile sits down in delight.

LORD BEILE: That was great! I haven't heard dialogue with such character in a long, long time.

Suddenly, loud lightning and thunder. This triggers Skin into becoming a "parrot" again, repeating everything that he hears.

You did a good job, kid.

SKIN: *(repeating)* You did a good job, kid.

LORD BEILE: You have your own unique style.

SKIN: You have your own unique style.

LORD BEILE: You don't follow blindly.

SKIN: You don't follow blindly.

LORD BEILE: You aren't just copying the old stuff.

SKIN: You aren't just copying the old stuff.

LORD BEILE: Just like me.

SKIN: Just like me.

Pause. Lord Beile stares at Skin. High comes in through the upstage entrance, terrified at what is happening..

LORD BEILE: What happened to you?

SKIN: What happened to you?

LORD BEILE: How come you're repeating what I say?

SKIN: How come you're repeating what I say?

LORD BEILE: I was just saying that you are special, so how come you are suddenly acting like a parrot?

SKIN: I was just saying that you are special, so how come you are suddenly acting like a parrot?

LORD BEILE: How come you've become my echo?

SKIN: How come you've become my echo?

LORD BEILE: Echo echo echo echo . . .

SKIN: Echo echo echo echo . . .

LORD BEILE: *(angrily)* Lackey!

SKIN: Lackey!

LORD BEILE: Enough!

SKIN: Enough!

LORD BEILE: *(almost hysterically)* Stop!

SKIN: Stop!

HIGH: Stop!

LORD BEILE: How dare you order me to stop?

SKIN: How dare you order me to stop?

LORD BEILE: It's because of parrots like you that the great Qing Dynasty has nothing left but dark clouds, cold winds, and bitter rain.

SKIN: It's because of parrots like you that the great Qing Dynasty has nothing . . .

HIGH: Don't say it!

Suddenly, lightning and thunder. Skin has returned to normal.
    A great noise. A part of the roof above them has been blown away. Rain starts coming in onto the stage.

SKIN: *(slowly)* . . . It's because of parrots like you that the great Qing Dynasty has nothing left but desolate landscapes and displaced families. It's time for a change!

Pause. Lord Beile stares at Skin.

HIGH: Have mercy, Lord Beile! He was hit by lightning! He has no idea what he's saying!

LORD BEILE: *(angrily)* Enough! I now proclaim, starting now, the Thousand Year Teahouse Theatre is hereby shut down. No more performances here!

Lord Beile gestures to Hell, to take away Skin and High. Hell grabs the two of them by their collars, and takes them toward the upstage exit.

SKIN: Hold on a moment.

LORD BEILE: What?

Pause.

(to Hell) Let go of him.

Hell lets go of Skin.

SKIN: Don't you have anything new?

LORD BEILE: What?

SKIN: Can I repeat what you said, and can you NOT give me the axe? You lackey!

LORD BEILE: How dare you!

SKIN: You call me daring because you are scared! All these years, you've been exploiting we the people, for no reason other than that you have the power! When the armies of the Eight Nations Alliance pushed into the city, all your sort could do was grasp at the old, without ever thinking of what is new! You and your kind, you can't let go of yesterday, you can't handle today, and you can't see tomorrow. But starting tomorrow, everything changes! Starting tomorrow, your kind is going to be chosen by our kind! I AM THE ONE WHO WILL DECIDE WHICH UNREMARKABLE, INCAPABLE, STINKING OFFICIAL I AM GOING TO ABANDON!

Pause. Lord Beile stares at Skin. High is so frightened he trembles on the ground.

LORD BEILE: What gall! You who take up the cause of the revolution, how can you not be axed? You've got some pretty big dog's guts. You know what day it is?

SKIN: What day is it?

LORD BEILE: Don't repeat my words!

SKIN: I'm not repeating your words, I'm asking you!

LORD BEILE: What?

SKIN: What day and what year? The last day of the last month of the last year, do you get it?

LORD BEILE: What?

SKIN: No matter how crazy it is today, starting tomorrow, everything changes. When the time comes, you can't behead me because I'm a lackey! I say what I like, and you can't axe me! When that day comes, you'll hear the callous laughter of lackeys everywhere!

Pause.

LORD BEILE: So you stomp on my nose to step on my face?

SKIN: Let me stomp a step further!

Skin stands directly on top of the table.

HIGH: *(extremely frightened)* Will you stop already, stop talking!

SKIN: *Once that Old Buddha of yours flees to Xi'an, that's about the end of her story!*

Pause. Lord Beile stares at Skin in astonishment.

It won't be more than 11 years before the great Qing Dynasty is no more!

LORD BEILE: How do you know these things?

SKIN: Just before the performance, in the wind and the rain, in the lightning and the thunder, I saw it all!

LORD BEILE: Demonic rumors, rabble-rouser!

SKIN: That braid hanging down your back will be cut off! There'll be nothing beside you, beneath you, or behind you!

LORD BEILE: *(feeling the back of his head)* Is that even human?

SKIN: It's been a long time since you were human! Your birdcage is empty, You flew away a long time ago! An empty birdcage swaying back and forth, I am surprised you haven't fallen flat on your face!

Pause.

LORD BEILE: *(softly)* Announce your names and make your exit.

Hell grabs the two of them by their collars. He presses their heads very low.

SKIN: *(defiantly)* Skin Don't Laugh!

HIGH: Sky High . . .

LORD BEILE: Yeah?

SKIN AND HIGH: *(in unison, stock ending)* Sign off with a bow!

Lord Beile gestures to Hell to take them away. Hell takes them away.

LORD BEILE: *(shouting the proclamation)* THIS HOUSE IS HEREBY CLOSED!

Dirgelike music comes from far away.
Lights fade out.

ACT TWO

Prologue: Today Is the Last Day of the Last Year

Sounds of contemporary popular music.
Lights fade in. The afternoon of December 31, 2000. Taipei. Backstage. Everything looks the same as Act 1, except that there are many more modern items. Sounds of construction from the stage.
Thick Skin, a contemporary crosstalk performer, has fallen asleep on the table.
Kicks, his stage partner, enters.

KICKS: . . . Millennium Eve, December 31, we're ready to go! . . . *(shouting to the stage proper)* Hey kid, be careful, this stage is two or three or four centuries old! You're not allowed to put nails in it!

Sound of a stagehand hammering nails.

Yeah, I guess you heard me. Oh, and that poetic couplet, be careful not to get it backwards! *(to Thick Skin)* Hey, Thick, what are you writing? I tell you, you better behave yourself tonight. A potential sponsor is coming. He'll give us funding if he likes us! Hey! Wake up! Do you have any clue what month and what year it is? Hey!

Thick Skin wakes up. He starts writing on a laptop computer at breakneck speed.

THICK SKIN *(abbreviated below as "THICK")*: Today is the last day of the last month of the last year! Tomorrow marks the beginning of a new millennium! And look what we're doing?!

KICKS: What are you talking about? *(reading from the computer screen)* "Hell places the stool beneath Lord Beile. Lord Beile: 'Oh how I suffer!' . . ." Which script is this?

THICK: This is not a script. It's a dream I had.

KICKS: A dream? *(reading)* "The 26th year of the Emperor Guangxu . . ." That's a pretty long dream if you ask me.

THICK: I stood here, gazing at this old stage, fell asleep, and had a dream. A stream of images flashed by before my eyes.

Thick gazes into the empty space for a long moment.

"It's because of parrots like you that the great Qing Dynasty has nothing left but desolate landscapes and scattered families."

KICKS: What?

THICK: Pure genius!

KICKS: Huh?

THICK: Alright, let's get ready!

KICKS: *(surprised)* What?

THICK: Get ready to perform. Today is a special day. Even if there's no tomorrow, we'll put on a hell of a show tonight! So, shall we?

KICKS: What the . . . ?

Kicks and Thick exit.

Scene 1: The Futility of Language

Popular music. Lights up. The same stage as Act 1, but it has been "modernized"—kitschified—with lots of colorful fluorescent betel nut stand lights hanging on the side, which flash frenetically.

Fanfare. Thick and Kicks enter from the two upstage entrances, and stand in position. They wear modernized traditional Chinese shirts unbuttoned over flashy tees. They open with the stock crosstalk opening.

KICKS: Kicks!

THICK: And Thick Skin!

THICK AND KICKS: *(in unison, bowing)* Ascend the stage with a bow!

KICKS: It's Millennium Eve.

THICK: Let's crosstalk!

KICKS: Cool! Just look at our stage, pink hot!

THICK: We're rockin'!

KICKS: Tonight our producers have gone overboard, with no regard to budget! They have brought over this National Treasure artifact of a stage, with every piece intact, from mainland China. Every single board and carving from this elaborate "Thousand Year Teahouse Theatre" has been airfreighted to Taiwan.

THICK: They say that this 300-year-old stage has not been performed on for 100 years. So this is the first time in 100 years that it is hosting a performance!

KICKS: What a beauty!

Lights flash all over.

THICK: Right! And so what are we going to talk about on this beautiful stage tonight?

KICKS: Whatever we want! This is the age of democracy, where nothing goes unsaid. If you like someone, you scream it out; if you hate someone, you kick him down.

THICK: Then if you change your mind, who cares?

KICKS: If you are a genius, I can choose to ignore you; if I am a lackey, there's nothing you can do about it!

THICK: This is an era of pundits. Turn on the TV, you will see a row of them sitting there analyzing current affairs. Switch channels, another row of them are sitting there doing the same thing. Turn off the TV, another row of them are sitting on your sofa doing the same thing. Everywhere, you say what you like, he says what he likes, I say what I like . . . Wait a minute . . . Where am I?

KICKS: What happened?

THICK: Who are you? What is this place?

KICKS: You're confused, aren't you? You don't know where you are? Today is December 31, 1900. It's the turn of the century, we are in Beijing!

THICK: What?!

KICKS: Confusion! Confusion! We are in Taiwan! It's Millennium Eve! Just one look and you will agree, only in Taiwan would we have such creative lighting!

Kicks points to the colorful flashing betel nut lamps attached to the old stage.

THICK: Right, right! Can I get some betel nut? Sorry for being incoherent, I'm back!

KICKS: Don't apologize. In this day and age, very few people know what they are saying.

THICK: What?

KICKS: At this moment, as we enter into a new millennium, language has very little efficacy left. When we get to the new age, there won't even be a need for crosstalk.

THICK: Why not?

KICKS: You have to be more attentive to the fashions of the times. People today either say a lot and mean little, or say things that mean a lot, but no one listens.

THICK: Is that how it is?

KICKS: Let me give you a random example. A few days ago, I was watching cable news, I was so pissed off that I decided to call in.

THICK: You had an opinion about the state of the nation.

KICKS: They only gave me 20 seconds.

THICK: You were lucky even to get through.

Kicks mimes a talk show anchor.

KICKS: "Mr. Kicks on a cell phone, 20 seconds." "... Uh ... Greetings to the host host host, greetings to the esteemed guests esteemed guests esteemed guests, all of the all of the national national audience audience every every body body, greetings greetings greetings ..."

THICK: What the hell is wrong with you?

KICKS: "Please lower the volume of your television set."

Thick shakes his head.

"... Oh, so sorry. Well, I mean to say ... that um ... I have an important comment on the state of our nation ..." *(voice of moderator)* "Thank you. Next!"

THICK: You didn't present your point, so no one wanted to listen.

KICKS: I couldn't say it in time.

THICK: If you're calling in to a talk show, you have to have everything prepared, and then once your call gets through, say it all.

KICKS: That's what I thought. The second day, I got through again.

THICK: Not easy.

KICKS: *(voice and manner of moderator)* "Mr. Kicks on a cell phone, 20 seconds . . ." I was prepared.

THICK: The clock is ticking. Go!

Kicks speaks extremely rapidly, suggesting the guankou style of rapid-fire talking in crosstalk.

KICKS: "In truth, all of our problems are because in this day and age there is nobody who can teach us how to LIVE. When traditional values dissolve, the social paradigm shifts, the family structure disintegrates, the global village rises, the internet becomes king, the only thing that can teach us how to live is the MEDIA, *(accelerating)* and if you believe in the media and what it teaches us, the only information it gives is 'BUY BUY BUY! BUY AS MUCH AS YOU CAN, AS FAST AS YOU CAN!' This has become the highest guiding principle in our lives. THERE IS NO HIGHER GUIDING PRINCIPLE FOR THESE SPIRITUALLY BANKRUPT TIMES."

THICK: *(applause)* Bravo!

KICKS: Everyone was in shock!

THICK: You were shocking.

KICKS: No one understood a thing.

THICK: Neither did I.

KICKS: So they acted like I hadn't said anything. *(voice and manner of moderator)* "Thank you! We appreciate! Next . . ."

THICK: They treated it like so much air.

KICKS: These days, most people have no idea what they are talking about, but their mouths keep moving.

THICK: True.

KICKS: It's called evolution.

THICK: Not knowing what you're talking about is called evolution?

KICKS: Sure. In Parliament, they say one thing here, lie about something there, you attack me, I assault you, everything is in total chaos, and suddenly a new law is passed.

THICK: True.

KICKS: So I say, in this new millennium, we as crosstalk performers need to learn the art of saying meaningless things.

THICK: Learn what?

KICKS: You think it's easy? You have to train for this in everyday life. A while back I stumbled across such a learning opportunity. It was great. It's given me the sense that I'm now well equipped to enter the next millennium.

THICK: Tell me about it.

KICKS: The other day, I was walking on the street. A stranger came from the opposite direction. I did not know him at all. But for some reason, we made eye contact . . .

Kicks mimes walking on the road, then plays the other person, raising his hand in greeting.

"Hey . . ."

Kicks turns around and plays himself. He doesn't know the other person, but greets him anyway.

"Hey . . ."

THICK: How come you "Hey"-ed each other?

KICKS: *(playing the other)* "How's it goin', man?" *(playing himself)* "Hey how's it goin'?"

THICK: You recognized him!

KICKS: Totally no idea who he was.

Kicks mimes turning pages in his mind.

THICK: What are you doing?

KICKS: I'm turning pages in my Rolodex. In those short few seconds, I processed all the people, from my elementary school to college graduation yearbooks and mailing lists, to see if I could find this guy. My search engine failed to produce anyone.

THICK: Not good.

KICKS: No need to panic. I have some more good moves. "Wow . . . You lost weight."

THICK: How could you say that?

KICKS: It's a valid topic, and you have a 50/50 chance of guessing right.

THICK: So you were guessing.

KICKS: "Me? Naw, I gained! But YOU, man . . . You've definitely lost weight!"

THICK: He definitely guessed wrong.

KICKS: "I . . . Yes, actually, quite a lot."

THICK: How could you lie to him?

KICKS: I didn't feel like explaining. *(himself)* "Hey it's so cool to meet you here."

THICK: Not saying much.

KICKS: *(playing the other)* "Cool, cool, man."

THICK: More bull.

KICKS: *(himself)* "How are things?" *(the other)* "Not bad." "Okay then I'll see you." "Bye." He left.

THICK: So who was this gentleman?

KICKS: I wanted to know, too!

THICK: Well, forget it. Just a random occurrence.

KICKS: A few days later, when I was having lunch at a restaurant, I met him again!

THICK: Again!

KICKS: *(himself)* "Oh my . . ." *(the other)* "What a coincidence!" "You are eating here . . . ?" "Right, right, I'm eating here."

THICK: Can you say something slightly original?

KICKS: *(himself)* "It's pretty cold, you're wearing short sleeves?"

THICK: Now that's creative.

KICKS: *(the other)* "Doesn't feel hot to me."

THICK: So he answered.

KICKS: *(slapping him on the back)* "That's so you!"

THICK: You even slapped him on the back.

KICKS: *(the other slaps Kicks)* "You're still the way you always were!"

THICK: As if you knew.

KICKS: At this moment he said: "Wait a minute . . . my class was two years ahead of yours, right?"

THICK: Aha! So he was a classmate!

KICKS: I had no impression whatsoever. *(himself)* "I think it was one."

THICK: But you went ahead and answered him.

KICKS: *(himself)* "Right, you and whatshisface were in the same class!"

THICK: *(the other)* "What's his face?"

KICKS: *(himself)* "Uh . . ."

THICK: What are you "Uh"-ing about?

Kicks mimes grabbing the bill.

What are you doing?

KICKS: I'm grabbing his bill.

THICK: Changing the subject.

KICKS: The conversation had dried up.

Kicks mimes two men fighting for the bill.

(the other) "What are you doing?" *(himself)* "This one's on me." "No way! It's mine!" "Upperclassman, no need to be this way!"

THICK: You called him "upperclassman."

KICKS: *(the other)* "No, no . . ." *(himself)* "I got this, I got this . . ."

Kicks plays the other, successfully grabbing the bill.

"Come on, man! You know how I am when it comes to fighting for the bill!"

THICK: So he paid.

KICKS: So I got a free meal.

THICK: So you got a free meal.

KICKS: "Well then, upperclassman, thanks, and . . ."

Kicks raises his hand in parting.

THICK: Bye-bye.

KICKS: *(playing himself)* "Oh, excuse me, upperclassman, could you give me your business card?"

THICK: That's something you should have asked for a long time ago.

KICKS: *(the other)* "What do you and I need to exchange business cards for?"

THICK: He wouldn't give one to you?

KICKS: *(himself)* "Right! Oh, so your phone number . . . ?"

THICK: Right, ask for his phone number.

KICKS: *(the other)* "Hasn't changed. Call me. On my cell."

THICK: Call who on who's cell?

KICKS: How would I know?

THICK: No problem, you'll never see him again.

KICKS: The next day I went to a sauna, and there he was.

THICK: You guys must have been a couple in your past life!

Kicks mimes wading into a hot pool.

KICKS: I had just gotten into the big Turkish bath when . . . *(pointing at the other)* "Yo!" *(pointing at himself)* "Yo!"

THICK: So this time you "Yo"-ed each other.

KICKS: *(playing himself)* "Upperclassman . . ."

THICK: I'm anxious to hear what you said next.

KICKS: *(himself)* "I had no idea you had such a . . . pale complexion."

THICK: What the hell was that?

KICKS: What else could I have said? "Upperclassman, your towel is a very pale shade of white"?

THICK: Was he really your upperclassman?

KICKS: I desperately needed to know. I decided to deepen the dialogue.

THICK: How do you "deepen" a dialogue?

KICKS: "Wow, the water's quite hot."

THICK: You call that "deepening"?

KICKS: Look, I lowered myself into the pool, the pool was deep, I couldn't think of anything else to say.

THICK: Jeez. And what did he say?

KICKS: *(the other)* "You're right. My little bird is already cooked."

THICK: I dare not listen anymore.

KICKS: *(the other)* "Man this place has gone to the pits." *(himself)* "Right, it's gone straight downhill since last we were here." Uh-oh!

THICK: So you guys had come here before?

KICKS: That just came out of my mouth.

THICK: And what did he say?

KICKS: *(the other)* "What did you just say?" *(himself)* "Um . . . nothing . . ." "Last time?" "Ah . . . uh . . ."

Awkward moment. Kicks suddenly mimes grabbing the bill.

THICK: What are you doing now?

KICKS: Grabbing the bill!

THICK: Changing the subject again.

KICKS: That's right.

THICK: Wait a minute, how would there be a bill in the water?

KICKS: You're right.

Kicks suddenly stops his hand in midair.

THICK: So what were you grabbing?

KICKS: "SO SORRY, UPPERCLASSMAN!!!"

THICK: You grabbed his—?

KICKS: Towel.

THICK: That was close.

KICKS: "Goddamnit, upperclassman, you are not paying today."

THICK: Successful shift of topic.

KICKS: *(the other)* "No no no, you know how I feel about these things." *(himself, heroically)* "Upperclassman, you are making a big mistake if you don't let me pay this time!" "Underclassman, if that's what you think . . ."

THICK: What?

KICKS: *(the other)* "Okay, you pay!"

THICK: That's fair. Last time he paid.

KICKS: No problem, I pay. I was thinking, how much could it possibly cost for a dip in the bath?

THICK: So go pay.

KICKS: So I dressed, and went to the counter.

THICK: No problem, 300 New Taiwan dollars.

KICKS: Thirteen thousand three hundred!!

THICK: What?

KICKS: He had a whole set of shiatsu and essential oils massages and called two girls for "special services."

THICK: He did what?

KICKS: How would I know? But I paid for it. By the time he had put on his pants and walked out, I asked him, "Upperclassman, where are you headed?" "Nowhere." "Then let's go out for a drink."

THICK: You don't even know the guy, what are you going out for a drink for?

KICKS: For revenge! I needed to drink that 13,300 into 37,500 worth!

THICK: That's a lot to drink.

KICKS: So we went to the lounge next door. Once we downed a few, our inner emotions started pouring out.

THICK: Hear hear..

KICKS: "Damn, underclassman, wasn't it great back when we were in school?" "Damn right, upperclassman, that was the life!"

THICK: Which school?

KICKS: He didn't say. He was going to sing the school fight song, but before he started, he began to tear up.

THICK: Listen carefully, there may be a clue somewhere.

KICKS: "Underclassman, our campus was so beautiful." *(testing for clues)* "Right, upperclassman, but tell me what was so beautiful about the campus?"

THICK: Here it comes.

KICKS: *(the other, slightly drunk, tearing up)* "The big tree, the tall building . . ."

THICK: Every campus has a big tree and a tall building.

KICKS: Right, suddenly he says, "Goddamnit, underclassman, let's go back to school!"

THICK: Which one?

KICKS: *(the other)* "Let's go find our teacher!"

THICK: Which one?

KICKS: He stood himself up!

THICK: So you're going to find out!

KICKS: And then he sat himself back down.

THICK: Guess not.

KICKS: *(the other)* "No! No! How can I go back? We can never go back! Look at what's happened to me ever since I graduated! Our teacher won't recognize me! The big tree won't recognize me! The tall building won't recognize me! . . ."

THICK: How would you respond to that?

KICKS: *(himself)* "You say our teacher won't recognize you? Well, let me tell you, I'M THE ONE WHO DOESN'T RECOGNIZE YOU!"

THICK: You were that explicit?

KICKS: I was that pissed. *(himself)* "Goddamnit, tell me! WHO THE HELL ARE YOU, REALLY?"

THICK: That'll get an answer.

KICKS: "Thank you, underclassman. Only someone who really cares would ask a question like that."

THICK: True. Finally we can get an answer.

KICKS: *(the other)* "WHO THE HELL AM I, REALLY? IF I KNEW, I WOULDN'T BE WASTING MY TIME FOOLING AROUND WITH YOU EVERY DAY!"

THICK: Straight from the heart.

KICKS: I grabbed him, pushed him to the wall, and said: "Goddamnit, do you really know who I am?"

THICK: Couldn't have stated it more clearly.

KICKS: "Underclassman, does anybody in this world really know who anyone is?"

THICK: So now he's a philosopher.

KICKS: I pinched his neck and asked him, "YOUR NAME! All I want to know is YOUR NAME!"

THICK: Couldn't be more direct.

KICKS: "I'VE LET DOWN EVERYONE IN THIS WORLD WHO HAS EVER CALLED MY NAME . . . !!"

THICK: Stubborn.

KICKS: I wouldn't let him off. "TELL ME YOUR NAME!" "Underclassman, you are relentless. OK! I'LL TELL YOU WHO I AM!"

THICK: So finally we get the answer.

Thick waits for the answer.

KICKS: *(the other, slowly)* "I'M A STUPID PIG!"

THICK: No!

KICKS: "SMASH!"

THICK: What was that?

KICKS: He threw the bottle of Suntory whiskey on the ground, and it smashed into a million pieces.

THICK: Drunken rage.

KICKS: "BOOM!"

THICK: What did he smash next?

KICKS: That was me. I threw the bottle of Johnnie Walker straight at the wall.

THICK: On your way to 37,500!

KICKS: *(the other)* "WAITRESS! MORE BOOZE!"

THICK: More?

Kicks mimes trashing all sorts of liquor.

KICKS: As soon as they brought it, we'd go "SMASH!" Napoleon on the ground . . . "BOOM!" XO on the wall . . . "WHOOSH!" Six bottles of 21-year-old Courvoisier on the ceiling . . .

THICK: Enough!

KICKS: "BANG!" The imported table lamp . . . "KIANG QIANG!" The crystal screen . . . "ZZZZ . . ." The leather sofa . . .

THICK: Looks like more than 37. You probably couldn't get out of there without paying 37 hundred thousand.

KICKS: "THUMP!!" . . .

THICK: And what did you smash now?

KICKS: Nothing. He tripped and fell on the floor! "THUMP" . . .

THICK: You tripped and fell, too?

KICKS: Nope, that was me kicking him.

THICK: What was the benefit of that?!

KICKS: That's a drunken rage! "THUMP" . . .

THICK: What's it now?

KICKS: I didn't know what was going on. I didn't see anything, only heard these sounds . . . *(sound diminishing)* "thump" . . . "thump" . . . "thump" . . .

Things finally quiet down for a brief moment.

THICK: What happened?

KICKS: I fell asleep. *(mimicking birds chirping)* Chirp chirp . . . tweet tweet . . .

THICK: And what was that?

KICKS: Day has broken. "Thump" . . .

THICK: What was that?

KICKS: I woke up. What time is it? *(looking at his watch)* Hey, somebody had given me a new watch! Wait. How come this watch doesn't have a face? What are those diamonds on the band?

THICK: Sounds fancy.

KICKS: Wait a minute, those are screws. Wait a minute. How come the watch is connected to the wall?

Pause.

THICK: That's called a handcuff.

KICKS: What was I doing in handcuffs? I raised my head, what's going on? How come there are so many video cameras out there?

THICK: You are in the precinct. Keep your head down. What happened?

KICKS: I don't know what happened. All I could hear was the media outside, already reporting the news via SNG connection.

Kicks plays a media reporter, reporting from the scene.

"Early this morning there was an arson attack at a drinking lounge in Taipei City. The two suspects have already been apprehended . . ."

THICK: You guys what?

KICKS: ". . . After chasing away all of the customers and staff, the two suspects burned the place to the ground."

THICK: My God, you guys sure had a great time! What about the other gentleman?

KICKS: He also had on his new watch, and was right next to me. He stank of booze. *(laughing)* What a pig.

THICK: Look who's talking.

KICKS: *(sound of a fist on the table)* BOOM!

THICK: What was that?

KICKS: *(policeman's voice)* "Awake? Then fill out these forms. ID number, name . . ." Ha!

THICK: What was there to laugh about?

KICKS: This was my chance! I could take a peek at his form and finally get to know who he was!

THICK: The benefits of getting arrested.

KICKS: So we slowly filled out our forms . . .

Kicks mimes glancing at his neighbor's form.

BOOM!

THICK: What happened?

KICKS: *(Policeman's voice)* "What are you peeking at? Don't you know how to write your own name?" *(himself)* "Sorry sir, I'm used to cheating on exams."

THICK: What a disgrace.

KICKS: So I persevered, and I kept peeking, and I saw it! His "Occupation" blank said "Actor."

THICK: Same as us. What was his name?

KICKS: I saw his last name—Shen.

THICK: *(thinking)* Would we know anyone named "Shen"?

KICKS: Wait a minute. It wasn't Shen. It was "Skin."

THICK: What?

KICKS: Stage name: Thick Skin.

Pause.

That was you?

THICK: What the hell are you talking about? *(thinking)* Wait a minute. You . . . ?

KICKS: YOU? How could you not recognize me?

THICK: Speak for yourself! How come you didn't know it was me?

KICKS: Is there anybody in this world these days who really knows anybody else?

THICK: Get the heck out of here!

They announce their names in stock sign-off.

KICKS: Kicks . . .

THICK: Thick Skin . . .

KICKS AND THICK: *(in unison)* Sign off with a bow.

They bow to the audience.

Scene 2: The Chicken Feather Party

Lights onstage flash, forcing a lively atmosphere.

KICKS: Just look at the scene we just did.

THICK: Even this centuries-old stage is jumping for joy!

KICKS: Now, before our eyes, is a bridge!

THICK: A bridge to the future!

KICKS: The New Millennium!

THICK: Who will take us across this bridge?

A blast of Taiwan election campaign-style music, whic is melodramatic, used as a background to shout emotional grievances or slogans. A commotion in the house. A parliamentary election candidate, M.P. Real, enters the auditorium from the back, and progresses toward the stage. Behind him is his Campaign Manager. M.P. wears a tacky suit, and a diagonal red sash with his name embroidered on it—typical Taiwanese election garb. The Campaign Manager holds a boom box, with megaphone, plus a folded camping chair. Though the performance is ongoing, they shake hands with the audience, and hand out promotional flyers. This surreal image seems quite normal in Taiwan's election scene, which is notorious for its lack of restraint.

M.P. REAL *(abbreviated below as "M.P."):* Thank you! I beg of you! Your sacred vote! . . .

Kicks and Thick make an effort to continue.

KICKS: So as we stand on this bridge . . .

M.P. and the Campaign Manager walk directly onto the stage, without any hesitation.

M.P.: *(to the two performers)* Thank you, I beg of you, your sacred vote!

KICKS: Wait a minute. May I ask who . . . ?

M.P. addresses the audience, with no regard for the performance or performers. He uses a very emotional and high-pitched tone, and intense campaign rhetoric, which is standard for many Taiwan politicians.

M.P.: Tonight is Millennium Eve! Let us all join our hands and our hearts together, for the benefit of our 23 million compatriots! . . .

Pause. M.P. now realizes that Kicks and Thick are onstage.

May I ask what you are doing?

KICKS: We are in the middle of a crosstalk performance.

M.P.: Crosstalk? *(to the Campaign Manager)* Wasn't this supposed to be a striptease show for the senior citizens?

The Campaign Manager speaks in M.P.'s ear.

> Oh ... *(high-pitched rhetoric again)* Culture! YES! Great! We are so happy you are using our stage to perform crosstalk!

THICK: Your stage?

Kicks and Thick are surprised.

> M.P.: Carry on. We will allow you to use this stage until midnight tonight, after which the "M.P. Real Campaign Headquarters" will be established here. At that moment, we will be taking down this beautiful stage!

> THICK: Take it down? But our performance ... ?

> M.P.: Don't worry. We will exercise utmost caution, because we are going to reassemble it on an enchanting electronic campaign float that will drive through all the streets and alleys of our beautiful land!

M.P. gives his name card to Kicks and Thick. Their performance has been disrupted, and they don't know what to do.

> Thank you for your kind support!

> KICKS: *(reading the name card)* "M.P. Real ..."

> THICK: *(to Kicks)* So he's the meal ticket?

> M.P.: Let me introduce you. This is my kid brother-in-law!

The Campaign Manager shakes hands with Thick and Kicks.

> KICKS: Oh. Ladies and gentlemen, he is our sponsor for this evening.

> THICK: So the chairman of the board and the CEO are both here.

> M.P.: How kind of you to say that. *(pointing at the Campaign Manager)* He's the gold mine. If I didn't have his support, there would be no way that I could enter the election, and therefore no way to help sponsor you guys. Thank you!

> CAMPAIGN MANAGER *(abbreviated below as "MANAGER")*: And now let us give him some encouragement:

> *(shouting)* M.P. FOR PARLIAMENT!

> M.P. FOR PARLIAMENT! ...

The Campaign Manager plays canned applause from his boom box.

KICKS: Excuse me, boss, but we were halfway through our
performance . . .

M.P.: No problem! Continue performing crosstalk,
(continuing with slogans) To share joy with the people!
To let the land yield its greatest benefits,
To let each person yield his greatest talent,
To let each object yield its greatest worth,
To let all merchandise yield its greatest flow!

THICK: He's quoting Dr. Sun Yat-sen?

M.P.: Wait a minute, I never said I wanted to be father of the country!
(laughing bawdily) Ha ha! That's what I call humor! To be a political
figure, you have to have a sense of humor!

KICKS: So, boss, you are a member of Parliament?

M.P.: No no no. My dad wanted me to aspire to become a great person,
so he named me "M.P." That is why on election day you must give me
your vote, so that not only is my name "M.P.," I will also truly become
a REAL member of Parliament! *(laughing loudly)* Ha ha ha . . . Get it?
How's that for a sense of humor?

The Campaign Manager plays canned applause from his boom box.

KICKS: *(trying to appease him)* Ha ha, that's pretty funny. Kind of.

M.P. instructs the Campaign Manager to unfold his camping chair onstage.

M.P.: Carry on, please, pay no attention to me.

M.P. sits down onstage.
Kicks and Thick are at a loss.

KICKS: Boss, we would like to restart our performance. And so may we
ask you to . . .

M.P.: Right, right. *(pointing at the audience)* I don't want to be in their
way. *(pointing at the two performers)* And I don't want to be in your
way. So I'll sit right here, in my own way! Perform, perform . . . *(to the
audience)* Here we go now! The crosstalk performance is revving up!
Culture is kicking off! APPLAUSE PLEASE!

The Campaign Manager plays applause from the boom box.
Kicks and Thick are speechless.

>What are you guys standing there for? I tell you, I'm an expert on crosstalk. When you start, first you announce your names! So go ahead and announce your names! Crosstalk always starts by announcing names! Ready? AND GO!

Faced with such an abomination, Kicks and Thick do not know what to do.
They decide to start from the top.

>THICK: Thick Skin . . .

>KICKS: Kicks . . .

>KICKS AND THICK: *(in unison)* Greet you with a bow!

M.P. laughs like crazy, interrupting the performance.

>M.P.: HA HA HA HA, THAT'S SO FUNNY! One has Thick Skin and the other gets his Kicks! That's hilarious! Continue, continue! READY, SET . . . GO!!

Kicks and Thick persevere.

>KICKS: However you say it, before our eyes there is a bridge!

>THICK: And what kind of a bridge is it?

>KICKS: A bridge that leads us to the future!

>THICK: And who is going to lead us across this bridge?

M.P. suddenly interrupts.

>M.P.: Who cares?

The two performers look at M.P. He remains sitting on his chair, with no particular reaction.
They continue.

>KICKS: How many actions of ours have been barbaric and harmful? Let us leave them behind us.

>M.P.: No way!

Pause.

THICK: All of the kind, the good, the warm, the positives, we bring to the other side of the bridge.

M.P.: *(very loudly interjecting)* Man, that's going to screw up everything!

M.P. stands up and starts walking around in front of the two performers, shaking his head as he walks. They continue carefully.

THICK: *(persevering)* Mankind's genetic code is already in our hands!

M.P.: *(nodding)* That's good . . .

THICK: But we don't even know how to process nuclear waste.

M.P.: If that's how you really feel, okay, let me think of a way.

KICKS: *(to M.P.)* And your way is . . . ?

M.P. stands at the far side of the stage.

M.P.: Just drive your truck over, and we'll take it from there.

KICKS: What? Drive the truck over the bridge?

M.P. hits his ear.

M.P.: Goddammit, this Bluetooth crap is worthless! *(moving around)* Hello? Hello?

M.P. taps his wireless earphone.

Got it! Now I can hear you! . . . If you need the railing, then take it first. Oh, and the betel nut lamps are also yours . . .

THICK: Might as well take the table, too.

M.P.: . . . Oh, right, there is a table here that you might as well take. But it's so noisy here, there're these two guys here who are . . . well, talk later . . . Bye.

M.P. looks at the two performers.

So, are you guys about done? If so, then I'll take over and say a few things to everyone.

THICK: It's your stage!

M.P.: No, we should do this together! It's so important to be together in moments like these!

M.P. pulls the two performers close to the audience. Kicks and Thick can only go along with him, but Thick's reluctance shows on his face.

> This is an age of democracy! Every individual has the right to take the podium!

THICK: Democracy!

KICKS AND M.P.: *(shouting in unison)* DEMOCRACY!

THICK: PEOPLE POWER!

KICKS AND M.P.: *(shouting in unison)* PEOPLE POWER!

THICK: PUT THE PEOPLE IN A COOKING POT AND TURN ON THE POWER!

M.P.: PUT THE PEOPLE IN A . . . What?

Pause.

THICK: My regards to your mother! Talk all you want, but do it yourself.

M.P.: What?

KICKS: *(to Thick)* Don't, please, our sponsorship for next year . . .

Kicks cannot restrain Thick. Thick exits.

> Boss, so sorry. My friend isn't feeling so good. He's been in the zoo too long.

M.P.: He lives in the zoo?

KICKS: It's called the bear market.

M.P.: *(laughing loudly)* How humorous! May I say something now?

KICKS: Of course.

M.P. steps forward, preparing to make a speech consisting entirely of Taiwan election campaign rhetoric: high pitched, exaggerated, dramatic, cheesy.

M.P.: My dear townsfolk, my dear elders, tonight is Millennium Eve. With so many voters congregated together in this auditorium, we can say that this is the biggest vote warehouse in the land! Therefore, tonight I would like to humbly share with everyone our party's strategy for ruling the country.

KICKS: A strategy to rule the country?

M.P.: My strategy is the only true strategy. No one else's strategy is strategy!

KICKS: How humble.

M.P.: I strive to be the humblest!

KICKS: That's good, boss, but you haven't revealed to us which party you are from?

M.P.: What a great question! What party am I from? Now I shall tell you. I am from . . . *(miming the sound of trumpets)* Da daaa!! . . .

The Campaign Manager brings out a multicolored feather duster and hands it to M.P. M.P. holds it high.

> The Chicken Feather Party!

Pause. Kicks is stupefied.

KICKS: A feather duster?

M.P.: The Chicken Feather Duster is the party flag of our Chicken Feather Party!

KICKS: The Chicken Feather Duster is your Chicken Feather Party's . . . flag?

M.P. AND MANAGER: *(in unison)* Clemency for all past wrongs!

> Out with the old, in with the new! . . .

M.P.: *(keeping up the rhythm)* Out with everything of the past,
Let's be transparent about everything!
Let the rainbow appear,
Let your lives change from black and white to color! . . .
APPLAUSE PLEASE!

The Campaign Manager uses his air horn to make a tremendous rabble-rousing noise. The Campaign Manager and M.P. shout in a frenzy, while holding their rainbow feather dusters high.

M.P. AND MANAGER: *(in unison)* M.P. FOR PARLIAMENT! M.P. FOR PAR-LIAMENT! . . .

They sing to the tune of a popular song.

> *Have you any chicken feathers to sell?...*
> *Have you any chicken feathers to sell?...*

They jump around onstage like madmen.

KICKS: Ha ha, truly the politician! You really know how to joke around!

M.P.: Who's joking? All the other parties are the ones that are joking! *(seriously)* Let me ask you, when you were a kid, what was the one thing that made you remember something forever and never forget?

KICKS: What?

M.P. raises the feather duster as if to give Kicks a beating on the bottom.

M.P.: It's every mom's greatest disciplinary tool! The fearful FEATHER DUSTER! When we are the opposition, we must use our feather dusters to SUPERVISE THE GOVERNMENT. After we are voted into office, then we must use our feather dusters to BEAT—THE—PEOPLE!!

KICKS: What?

M.P.: Wrong!... slip of the tongue!

KICKS: Slip of the tongue... *(to the audience)* He made a mistake!

M.P.: *(trying again)* TO SUPERVISE—OURSELVES!

M.P. gives the feather duster to Kicks.

> Now you can cane me 10 times.

KICKS: Why should I cane you?

M.P.: No problem, I can cane myself!

M.P. uses the feather duster to pat himself lightly on the rear.

> 12345, 678 9 10, finished!

KICKS: Why are you hitting yourself?

M.P.: It's called "self-discipline"! Our feather duster is designed to discipline the government! After we come into office, we will give one feather duster to every citizen. If the government does something wrong, that's okay, no need to force us out of office, all you have to do is use your feather duster to DISCIPLINE THEM! Next, I would like to take the opportunity to explain what the Chicken Feather Patty's policy is.

KICKS: You must have a pretty big patty to have a party.

M.P.: We have a very small party.

KICKS: And how small is your party?

M.P.: Just we two. But that's okay, the party policy of the Chicken Feather Patty is: "Loyalty to the patty! Be true to your patty!" Our patty . . .

KICKS: Party . . . ?

M.P.: *(trying hard to correct himself)* Party . . . patty . . . PARTY . . . *(raising the feather duster)* symbolizes true racial harmony and political bipartisanship! Blue, green, red, yellow, all of the colors of ALL of the political parties are contained within!

M.P. shows off all of the colors of his feather duster.

> *(not at all humbly)* How great am I? Secondly, *(raising the feather duster)* our patty . . . party stands on high moral ground. We vow to clean up all of the dust, all of the special privilege, all of the illicit funds . . .

KICKS: Is that possible?

M.P.: Of course not. Because everything has already decayed to shit!

KICKS: Right! But you still have to have a platform, right?

M.P.: The platform of the Chicken Feather Party is: everything that has happened over the last few decades, all of the corruption, all of the darkness, all of the illegality, all of the mudslides, flooding, contamination of the rivers, illegal harvesting of the forests, even after 100, 200, even 300 years, there still will be no solution! Today is Millennium Eve. Starting from tomorrow, we will dust off the whole lot, and reset all accounts to zero! APPLAUSE PLEASE!

The Campaign Manager makes a blast on his air horn.

KICKS: What?

M.P.: Aren't I great?!

KICKS: What did you say? Did I hear right?

M.P.: You heard right!

KICKS: What?

M.P.: *(screaming in a frenzy)* WE WILL LET ALL CRIMINALS OUT OF ALL JAILS!

MANAGER: *(repeating)* OUT OF ALL JAILS!

M.P.: WE WILL RESET THE STOCK MARKET INDEX TO ZERO!

MANAGER: RESET TO ZERO!

M.P.: WE WILL DISSOLVE THE CABINET! DISBAND THE PARLIAMENT! DISCHARGE THE JUDICIAL COURT! DISMISS THE WATCHDOG AGENCY! DISMANTLE THE EXAMINATION BUREAU!

KICKS: What?

M.P.: I'm too great! *(in rhyme)* Military, go take a long furlough!

Policeman, go get a hair blow!

Workers, no need to punch your time card!

Hey Mr. President, go mow your backyard!

KICKS: What are you saying?

The performance has evolved into a crazed surrealistic state. Kicks listens, more and more frightened.

M.P.: STUDENTS MAY ATTEND CLASS WHENEVER THEY LIKE!

KICKS: What about the teachers?

M.P.: TEACHERS MAY ATTEND WHENEVER THEY LIKE, TOO!

KICKS: Then how do they give grades?

M.P.: THE STUDENTS WILL GRADE THEMSELVES!

KICKS: So what happens if the students and the teachers never meet?

M.P.: THEN YOU CAN USE YOUR FEATHER DUSTER TO DISCIPLINE THE TEACHER! And so, this is the greatest present that we, the Chicken Feather Party, can give to everybody on Millennium Eve: WE WILL RESET EVERYTHING TO ZERO!

KICKS: But that's not possible. Just take traffic, for instance, how can you reset to zero?

M.P.: WE WILL ABOLISH ALL FREEWAY TOLLS!

KICKS: Not a bad idea.

M.P.: WE WILL CEASE MAINTENANCE OF ALL ROADS!

KICKS: Not good.

M.P.: WE WILL CUT POWER TO ALL TRAFFIC LIGHTS!

KICKS: Then everything goes back to zero.

M.P.: BANKS MAY LOAN FREELY, NO NEED FOR COLLATERAL, AND NO UPPER LIMIT!

KICKS: What the . . . ?

M.P.: LET THE LAND YIELD ITS GREATEST BENEFITS,

LET EACH PERSON YIELD HIS GREATEST TALENT,

LET EACH OBJECT YIELD ITS GREATEST WORTH,

LET ALL MERCHANDISE YIELD ITS GREATEST FLOW!

WE WILL REZONE ALL AGRICULTURAL LAND INTO LUXURY VILLAS!

KICKS: So what happens to the luxury villas that are already there?

M.P.: WE WILL TRANSFORM ALL LUXURY VILLAS INTO HIGH-RISES!

KICKS: And what about the current high-rises?

M.P.: WE WILL TEAR DOWN ALL OF THE CURRENT HIGH-RISES AND LET THEM BECOME AGRICULTURAL LAND!

KICKS: So we're back to where we started?

M.P.: LET THE LAND YIELD ITS GREATEST BENEFITS,

LET EACH PERSON YIELD HIS GREATEST TALENT,

LET EACH OBJECT YIELD ITS GREATEST WORTH,

LET ALL MERCHANDISE YIELD ITS GREATEST FLOW!

KICKS: You're like a broken record.

M.P.: LET THE MUDSLIDES SLIDE ON,

LET THE HIGH MOUNTAINS DISSOLVE INTO THE PLAINS,

LET TAIWAN DOUBLE ITS AREA IN SIZE!

The Campaign Manager makes a blast on his air horn.

Aren't I amazing?

KICKS: What kind of a vision is that?

M.P.: Have you ever seen a slim guy gain weight?

KICKS: I have experienced that.

M.P.: That's the vision!

KICKS: No!

M.P.: LET THE GARBAGE KEEP PILING UP,

LET TAIWAN STAND TALLER THAN THEM ALL!

KICKS: What kind of a vision is that?

M.P.: Have you ever seen a child grow up?

KICKS: I've also experienced that.

M.P.: That's the vision!

KICKS: No!

M.P.: Then after Taiwan continues to grow larger and taller, IT WILL NATURALLY BECOME CONNECTED TO MAINLAND CHINA! THERE WILL BE NO DEBATE ON UNITY OR INDEPENDENCE! THERE'S NO WAY YOU COULD SPLIT US APART!!

KICKS: What kind of a vision is that?

M.P.: Have you ever had a taco wrapped in a burrito?

KICKS: Not sure.

M.P.: That's the idea!

KICKS: No!

M.P.: Isn't that great? Did you know that our Chicken Feather patty . . . *(correcting himself)* party . . . party's central maxim for the recent devastating earthquake is: We will never redevelop the disaster area!

KICKS: Then what happens to all of the disaster funds?

M.P.: Give them all to me!

KICKS: To you?

M.P.: I will spend it all voraciously!

KICKS: Damn right, anyone would spend it all voraciously!

M.P.: This is what the ancients called "Merchandise is not produced from one's body, and need not be hidden on oneself . . ."

KICKS: "That is the definition of the Great Harmony." Right?

M.P.: That is the definition of the great patty.

KICKS: What?

M.P.: *(correcting himself)* Great "party." "Chicken Feather Party." Everything starts anew, and our country is blessed with prosperity! Let's have a great round of applause!

The Campaign Manager presses down on his gas horn to make a tremendous rabble-rousing noise.

M.P. AND MANAGER: *(in unison, loudly)* M.P. FOR PARLIAMENT! M.P. FOR PARLIAMENT! . . .

(singing in unison) Have you any chicken feathers to sell? . . .

> *Have you any chicken feathers to sell? . . .*

They jump around the stage like madmen.

KICKS: Right, good . . . But hold on. To use a feather duster as your party flag, wouldn't you say that's a little far fetched?

M.P.: Do I hear a condescending tone from you? Wait until our feather duster is attached to the top of the Presidential Mansion, and you will know how great we are!

KICKS: So you're planning on making it the country's flag, too?

M.P.: Picture the feather duster on top of the Presidential Mansion. What authority! What grace! One rod shooting up into the skies, unshakable! One stick, above them all! The most creative flag on Earth!

KICKS: Creative?

M.P.: All of the flags of the over 200 countries in the world sway, right?

KICKS: It's only natural.

M.P.: "Swaying in the wind, with no will of one's own," what an inauspicious omen! Feather dusters do not sway! On National Day you will see, all government buildings will have feather dusters attached to them. All of the taxicabs will have feather dusters attached to them! All businesses and offices will have feather dusters attached to them! What an auspicious sight!

KICKS: How joyous.

M.P.: There's only one group of constituents who won't be so happy.

KICKS: Who?

M.P.: Chickens. All of their feathers will have been plucked. And so the government, in appreciation of the patriotic deeds done in the name of the country by the chicken, will erect a special monument to commemorate the chickens, opposite the great Buddha statue of the Paokung Temple, and it will be forever known as the "Kung Pao Chicken." When all of the elementary school students go to pay their respects, they will all bring fresh . . .

KICKS: Flowers.

M.P.: Chili peppers and peanuts! And then we will experience gentle wind and tender rain, peace and prosperity, five generations of growth, 66 makes a royal straight . . .

He switches to drinking lingo and shouts out a drinking game's lingo.

SEVEN SKILLS, EIGHT IMMORTALS, NINE DEMONS . . . ROYAL FLUSH . . . GRAND SLAM . . . !!

KICKS: Are you OK?

M.P. realizes his folly and apologizes.

M.P.: Sorry! Wrong place! I thought I was still at a banquet drinking with the lobbyists! But let me tell you, when the time comes, in all of the school auditoriums, in all of the conference rooms of government offices, everywhere, you will see it displayed!

KICKS: See what displayed?

M.P. turns his back to the audience, and gestures.

M.P.: Here . . . A framed photo of the Father of the Nation . . .

KICKS: Right.

M.P.: *(turning to his right)* Here . . . the president . . .

KICKS: Right.

M.P.: *(turning to his left)* Here . . . the vice president . . .

KICKS: Whatever . . .

M.P.: *(turning to the audience)* Here . . . the chicken!

KICKS: No!

M.P.: For its sacrifice for the country!

KICKS: *(stock ending phrase)* Get the heck out of here!

They state their names in stock sign-off.

M.P.: M.P.!

KICKS: Kicks!

KICKS AND M.P.: *(in unison)* Sign off with a bow!

They bow to the audience.
Workers enter, as does Thick. The workers start to take apart the stage.

M.P.: Oh, you're here? Good, good, take it apart. *(to Thick and Kicks)* Continue performing crosstalk, don't worry!

KICKS: Wait! What are you doing?

M.P.: Ladies and gentlemen, we will meet again soon! My "electronic cultural float" will soon start its voyage up and down all of the streets of our great land. We will bring culture straight to your home! I leave you tonight with the solemn thought: "ASK NOT WHAT THE CHICKEN CAN DO FOR YOU; ASK WHAT YOU CAN DO FOR THE CHICKEN!" Good night!

M.P. descends into the audience, followed by the Campaign Manager.

M.P. AND MANAGER: *(in unison)* M.P. for Parliament! M.P. for Parliament! . . .

(singing in unison) Have you any chicken feathers to sell? . . .

Have you any chicken feathers to sell? . . .

M.P.'s campaign theme music strikes up. M.P. and the Campaign Manager exit through the audience.

Scene 3: Endology

The workers continue to take the stage apart. The two performers settle down to continue.

KICKS: Millennium Eve! *(listlessly)* Yay! Well, we're approaching the end of our evening, which is also the end of the past thousand years. We stand at the head of a bridge that leads us to the future. Tell me, what are you feeling now?

THICK: I'm actually quite excited.

KICKS: The new millennium will soon begin. You should feel excited.

THICK: I don't care about beginnings. I'm more interested in endings.

KICKS: You're more interested in endings?

THICK: I specialize in the study of endings.

KICKS: What does that mean, "the study of endings"?

THICK: Haven't you heard of a new branch of learning called "Endology"?

KICKS: What?

THICK: As we enter the new millennium, Endology has become the most important branch of knowledge.

KICKS: *(cynically)* So tell me what kind of research does Endology do?

THICK: Endology is the study of the end of things.

KICKS: Fine. What about how things evolve, the process?

THICK: It doesn't care about the process. In the history of mankind, only endings are important. At this moment, as we see the ending of the millennium coming up, today becomes the most important day. The past thousand years end here.

KICKS: You say that process, the path, how we got here, that's not important?

THICK: Don't get worked up. Listen to me. The new millennium is all about speed and efficiency, who cares about process? All you have to worry about is the ending!

KICKS: It seems you have quite a grasp of it.

THICK: Are you kidding? I studied at the Graduate School of Endology.

KICKS: So Endology has a graduate school? What kind of people study there?

THICK: Only people who have demonstrated a talent in the field since they were young are allowed to study there.

KICKS: You need talent to study Endology?

THICK: I guess you don't get it. When you were a kid, and you received a new book from your elders, what would you do?

KICKS: You open it up, and start from chapter 1.

THICK: That's why you aren't cut out to study Endology.

KICKS: Otherwise?

THICK: Flip straight to the last page, to see the ending. Then you know immediately if the main character lives or dies, and you gain instant satisfaction.

KICKS: How deficient!

THICK: How efficient!

KICKS: May I ask what exactly one studies in Endology?

THICK: A very broad palette: history, science, literature, art; everything to do with food, clothing, travel, birth, old age, sickness, and death, this all falls within the range of our research.

KICKS: So you guys study literature?

THICK: Of course.

KICKS: May I ask a question?

THICK: Please.

KICKS: Shakespeare.

THICK: Yes?

KICKS: Have you ever read *Hamlet*?

THICK: Of course.

KICKS: Your opinion?

THICK: Not very high. The ending is a whole bunch of corpses lying there. Lots of plays end that way.

KICKS: How could you say that? What's important is how it all came to be that way, the relationship between a person's destiny and his actions, WHY there are a whole bunch of corpses lying there in the end!

THICK: To know that you have to read what happens before.

KICKS: And what happens before is . . .

THICK: None of my business. We only study endings.

KICKS: You don't care about the beginning?

THICK: Listen. It's called "Endology"!

KICKS: All right. Have you ever read *Journey to the West*?

THICK: Of course.

KICKS: And your opinion?

THICK: Dull.

KICKS: Why?

THICK: In the end the monk character lugs a lot of scriptures back home, job accomplished. Doesn't everyone go home after work? Aren't you going home after work tonight?

KICKS: What are you saying? What about what happens in the middle? The whole adventure? The comrades on the path, the demons and the monsters? He risked his life for the scriptures!

THICK: *(getting irritated)* I already told you, I only study endings!

KICKS: Okay. Have you read *Dream of the Red Chamber*?

THICK: That's a good one! Very moving! In the end the hero Jia Baoyu sees through the emptiness of existence, and decides to become a monk!

KICKS: What do you think about the heroine, Lin Daiyu?

THICK: Who?

KICKS: *(stupefied)* You say you read *Dream of the Red Chamber*, and you don't know who Lin Daiyu is?

THICK: I don't care what happens in front! I don't care if there is a Wang Daiyu or a Chen Daiyu or a Li Daiyu! You are being so unreasonable!

KICKS: Me?

THICK: I tell you, we worked hard at grad school! Every class was really tough!

KICKS: How tough?

THICK: We had to time it precisely so that we got into the classroom two minutes before the end of class.

KICKS: Why two minutes before the end of class?

THICK: To listen to the ending!

KICKS: I pity your teacher.

THICK: No need. She would always come in one minute after us.

KICKS: One minute later?!

THICK: She really taught by example. In all of her lectures, she never spoke of beginnings, only endings. And the ending would be limited to one choice word.

KICKS: What one word?

THICK: "Dismissed."

KICKS: What?

THICK: We would very respectfully reply with a shorter word.

KICKS: Which was . . . ?

THICK: "Bye."

KICKS: What kind of stupid class was that?

THICK: Stupid for you! I tell you, our community of Endology scholars share great principles. For one, we never attend friends' weddings.

KICKS: Why?

THICK: We prefer to witness the divorce.

KICKS: May I inform you that there are marriages that do not end in divorce?

THICK: Those people are not friends of ours.

KICKS: What?!

THICK: When friends open a business, we never go to the ribbon-cutting ceremony.

KICKS: Why not?

THICK: We prefer the bankruptcy litigation.

KICKS: No! There are companies that don't go bankrupt, mind you!

THICK: They aren't friends of ours either!

KICKS: Again!

THICK: I tell you, we're very principled. We are prohibited from going to baby showers.

KICKS: What's the problem? A baby is born, such a beautiful thing, the ending is . . .

Kicks scares himself, and shuts up.

I guess there are zero social events your classmates can attend.

THICK: We never miss a funeral.

KICKS: I knew it! Okay. So how does Endology apply to everyday life? Oh, I get it, say I plan to run a 10K, so I dash out of the house and come right back in the back door.

THICK: You've mastered an important concept.

KICKS: So if the two of us both studied Endology, and we come and perform crosstalk. Here's how we start—"Kicks, Thick Skin, signing off with a bow!" And we exit the stage.

THICK: Now you're talking.

KICKS: So how do you eat?

THICK: That's a problem. Most of our alumni are in poor health.

KICKS: Why?

THICK: Whenever we dine in a Western restaurant, we only eat the last dish.

KICKS: Which is . . . ?

THICK: Dessert. We all struggle with diabetes.

KICKS: You can choose to have Chinese food.

THICK: That's even worse!

KICKS: I get it. You go directly to the soup.

THICK: No, you go directly to the fortune cookie.

KICKS: That fast!

THICK: After I graduated, I opened a restaurant, following our guiding principles.

KICKS: So you started by serving fortune cookies to the customers when they sat down?

THICK: Wrong. I immediately presented them with the check.

KICKS: But they hadn't even ordered anything, how could you give them a check?

THICK: And so my business closed on opening day.

KICKS: What?

THICK: I was beaten up and sent to the hospital.

KICKS: For good reason!

THICK: Man, that was beautiful!

KICKS: Why?

THICK: That day all of my classmates came and gathered around my hospital bed. They lifted their thumbs in praise: "You are our role model. Your business plan was simple, beautiful, the opening was the ending."

KICKS: Not bad, you became a role model of Endology.

THICK: Our professor put my example into his classic *Fundamentals of Endology*.

KICKS: That's quite impressive.

THICK: Not really. It was inserted into the middle of the book, so nobody read it.

KICKS: You guys only read the ending.

THICK: You get it!

KICKS: I should have caught on by now. So you tell me you studied literature. How about cinema?

THICK: I love going to movies! But in order to study movie endings, you have to be very skillful.

KICKS: In what way?

THICK: If you are reading a book, all you have to do is turn to the last page, which isn't difficult. But if you want to see the ending of a film, you have to enter at the right moment, and if you get it wrong . . .

KICKS: What happens?

THICK: It's a disaster! You see the middle!

KICKS: Is that so awful?

THICK: I've studied 500 foreign films and 200 Chinese films, and developed a theory.

KICKS: Shoot.

THICK: The endings of most films are very similar.

KICKS: In what way?

THICK: They always finish with "The End."

KICKS: How can you say "most are very similar"? In this way aren't they all exactly the same?

THICK: Gibberish!

KICKS: Then you tell me what is different.

THICK: The font is usually different.

KICKS: That's it?

THICK: Despite my taste for literature and cinema, we students of Endology place our main emphasis on the study of history.

KICKS: History.

THICK: To study history, we have devised an important theory.

KICKS: And that is?

THICK: The ending is what's most important.

KICKS: You don't say!

THICK: Not only that, but the one who comes after always beats the one who comes before.

KICKS: Meaning?

THICK: Let me ask you, the Qin Dynasty and Han Dynasty, which came first?

KICKS: The Qin.

THICK: Which lost to the Han.

KICKS: That's so obvious.

THICK: What did I say? The one who comes AFTER always beats the one before. Between the Sui Dynasty and the Tang Dynasty, which came first?

KICKS: Of course it was the Sui.

THICK: Which lost to the Tang.

KICKS: Otherwise the pair would be nicknamed "Tang Sui" and not "Sui Tang."

THICK: It seems that you don't quite comprehend. Let me use some novels as example. Have you ever read *Red Rose, White Rose* by Eileen Chang?

KICKS: A classic of modern Chinese literature. I have.

THICK: Who won?

KICKS: Who won? I guess White Rose won.

THICK: Correct. Why?

KICKS: Because in the end the guy went back to White Rose, so White Rose won.

THICK: Wrong! It's because White Rose's name was placed AFTER, and so White Rose won. If Red Rose had been placed after, the guy would have run off with Red Rose. The one who comes AFTER always beats the one who comes before! If Eileen Chang had put an onion, or a piece of garlic, after Red Rose, it would have won!

KICKS: What the . . . ?

THICK: Hemingway's *The Old Man and the Sea.* Who won?

KICKS: Nobody won. In the end, the old man, tired as hell, dragged this big fish carcass, and came back to shore.

THICK: Both parties devastated.

KICKS: I agree.

THICK: The sea won.

KICKS: What?

THICK: The one who comes AFTER always beats the one who comes before!

KICKS: Is that how you work it out?

THICK: Here's an easy one: *Gone with the Wind.*

KICKS: Who won? You could argue that Scarlett O'Hara . . . The Wind won.

THICK: You're getting it.

KICKS: It's not theoretically easy to grasp.

THICK: A hint of arrogance. Okay. *Pride and Prejudice.* Who won?

KICKS: Prejudice won!

THICK: Obviously, but why?

KICKS: Why? Because it came after.

THICK: Wrong. Because I'm prejudiced. The theory allows for a subjective factor within the objective equation.

Kicks is almost going nuts.

KICKS: You call that a theory? Okay, so according to your logic, then, in *Romeo and Juliet,* Juliet wins.

THICK: One hundred percent correct!

KICKS: Aha! They both died, how could anyone have won?

THICK: Aha! Juliet stuck around a little longer. Romeo died first.

KICKS: Noooo!

THICK: Let me ask you the simplest question: in *The King and I,* who won?

KICKS: Who won?

THICK: It's self-explanatory! Of course I won!

KICKS: Why did you win?

THICK: If I hadn't won, how could I be standing here performing crosstalk?

KICKS: Enough!

THICK: Now you get it?

KICKS: I get it.

THICK: Then let's return to history. Let me ask you: in the Sino-Japanese War, who won?

KICKS: Well, according to your theory, the one listed later, Japan, won.

THICK: Wrong. War won.

KICKS: What?

THICK: Get it straight. What comes after always beats what comes before.

KICKS: So?

THICK: The First World War. Who won?

KICKS: Wow, there were so many countries, let me think . . .

THICK: War won.

KICKS: War . . . ?

THICK: The Second World War. Who won?

KICKS: War.

THICK: The Chinese Civil War?

KICKS: War.

THICK: The Korean War?

KICKS: War.

THICK: The Vietnam War?

KICKS: War won.

THICK: The Feishui Battle?

KICKS: Battle won.

THICK: The Red Cliff Showdown?

KICKS: Showdown won.

THICK: The Zhuolu Conflict?

KICKS: Conflict won.

THICK: Today's Fourth Nuclear Power Plant controversy?

KICKS: Controversy won.

THICK: The presidential recall fight?

KICKS: Fight won.

THICK: The television variety show ratings wars?

KICKS: Wars won. Enough already! What kind of absurd theory is this?

THICK: This is no absurd theory. In all battles, conflicts, and war, there is only one winner—war.

KICKS: I guess I've learned something today.

THICK: To be honest with you, there's a crucial purpose for Endology.

KICKS: Which is?

THICK: To study the end of mankind.

KICKS: The end of mankind?

THICK: Right.

KICKS: How could you possibly draw any conclusions about that?

THICK: This is a secret:

KICKS: Glad to know everyone's listening.

THICK: Because the new millennium is coming, a while back, all of the countries of the world organized a secret international research center for the purpose of this study. I was chosen to be one of the research members. Included were all of the most brilliant talents in the field of Endology. We gathered the most complete data from all these years of research, and, with a generous budget, worked in a secret location to draw up a conclusion, to serve as reference for all of the world's leaders in the new millennium.

KICKS: Must have taken quite a long time.

THICK: Not really. We all showed up at the end.

KICKS: Sticking to principles!

THICK: To tell you the truth, my emotions caught up with me at the time.

KICKS: Why?

THICK: When I started going through all the research materials, I suddenly became transfixed by a word.

KICKS: What word?

THICK: "The beginning."

KICKS: Challenging the taboo!

THICK: One day, I made a grave mistake, and arrived early to a meeting.

KICKS: How could you do that?

THICK: There was nobody in the room.

KICKS: Hurry up and leave!

THICK: But I didn't. In the room was a file cabinet labeled "Top Secret. Only for the Boss" No one ever dared touch it. But I couldn't resist, so I opened it.

KICKS: You did what?

THICK: There was only one file stored in there. I went through it. Wow, I saw some photographs that made me blush. My heart was pounding!

KICKS: That's what happened to me when I saw such photographs as an adolescent.

THICK: Not those kind of photographs.

KICKS: Then?

THICK: I saw rivers that were pure and clean, forests in their entirety, an infinite array of stars in the evening sky, some species of birds flying in the sky that I had never seen before, some unknown animals running on the ground. I thought to myself, What kind of file is this? I kept on turning the pages. I saw people living a simple existence, not having much, but not needing much. At peace, at ease. It was as if there was no beginning and no end, no you, no me, everything was one.

KICKS: What kind of file had you stumbled on?

THICK: I stood there for a while, numb, thinking, how come I'm like everyone else, so forcefully charging ahead, without looking right, left or behind, pushing myself to the utmost, without pause, without thought, toward the ending? That day, in the conference room, I studied those photos till my eyes were red . . .

KICKS: Good thing no one saw.

THICK: I looked up, my superior and all my colleagues were standing around me!

KICKS: Meeting time.

THICK: I was a mess. They looked at me . . .

KICKS: And came over to console you.

THICK: Who consoles anybody these days? Our superior addressed us.

KICKS: What did he say?

THICK: "Dismissed!"

KICKS: In the same tradition as your teacher.

The workers have removed all the decorations and trimmings from the stage, including the railings and prop table, and exited, leaving the stage bare.

Wait. With the methodology you guys use, how could you have possibly come to a conclusion about the end of the human race?

THICK: You have no idea!

KICKS: I don't!

THICK: In the end, we wrote a very important and very substantial report.

KICKS: Can you reveal a bit of the contents?

THICK: Sure.

KICKS: Straight to the end, please.

THICK: Now you're qualified to join us in the field of Endology.

KICKS: No thanks. I just want to know what's there on the last page of your report.

THICK: At the end, we wrote a poem, in couplets, and translated it into all the languages of the world.

KICKS: A couplet. How poetic. So, the first line was ... ?

THICK: "All rights reserved."

KICKS: And the second line was ... ?

THICK: "Unauthorized copying will be prosecuted."

KICKS: No!

THICK: What are you "no"-ing about? Of course we also had the bridging line that goes between.

KICKS: And the bridging line for the couplet was ... ?

THICK: "Price: $3.50."

KICKS: That's a pretty cheap conclusion, if you ask me.

THICK: That's not the conclusion! That's the last page! If you want the conclusion, you have to turn to the page before that!

KICKS: And the page before says ... ?

THICK: "The End."

KICKS: No! Are you trying to tell me that the human race ends with "The End"?!

THICK: Oh, so you want to know about the end of the human race?

KICKS: Of course!

THICK: Then you have to turn back to the previous page.

KICKS: One more page before. You guys wouldn't have written another couplet, would you?

THICK: You got it. The most important conclusion.

KICKS: Shoot.

THICK: "A hundred lifetimes like a moment, just a springtime dream ..."

KICKS: What?

Kicks looks for the couplets onstage. They are gone.

And?

THICK: "Ten thousand threads all waiting for an ending, the human condition."

KICKS: And the bridging line?

Pause. Thick thinks.

THICK: I forget.

KICKS: Get the heck out of here!

THICK: Wait! Yes, that's it!

KICKS: "Get the heck out of here"?

THICK: Thick Skin.

KICKS: And Kicks.

KICKS AND THICK: *(in unison)* We sign off with a bow.

They look at the bare stage.
  They take a bow.
  Lights fade out.

Epilogue

Lights fade in. Backstage, December 31, 1900, again. The moment when Skin wakes up after having been struck by lightning.
  Skin gazes into empty space. A long moment.

SKY HIGH: Skin, what's going on? . . .

Pause. Skin regains his senses.

SKIN DON'T LAUGH: Astonishing! Let's perform!

HIGH: *(shocked)* Perform? You can't go onstage like this!

Skin sees that his gown has a big hole in it.

SKIN: I'm good.

HIGH: You're good?

SKIN: I feel good all over! Gentlemen, today is a special day. Even if there's no tomorrow, tonight we'll put on one heck of a show! Shall we?

High and the Old Stagehand look at each other. Skin exits to go onstage. High follows.

Lights shift. We can see silhouettes of their backs through the small windows backstage.

HIGH: Sky High,

SKIN: . . . and Skin Don't Laugh . . .

HIGH AND SKIN: *(in unison)* Ascend the stage with a bow!

They bow to the audience.

HIGH: *(energetically)* Today marks the reopening of our Thousand Year Teahouse Theatre! It's truly a great honor to be able to stand up here onstage and greet all of you!

SKIN: That's right. This whole year can be described as "Auspicious winds and gentle rains. A year of great peace, the people enjoy life like the gods!"

HIGH: You don't have to bend that far.

SKIN: Sorry, I made a mistake. This whole year can be described as "The fortunate ones starved to death!"

Their voices drift away.
Lights fade out.

The End

Sand on a Distant Star

CHARACTERS

NIGHTINGALE: A middle-aged street vendor in Taipei, whose husband disappeared 20 years ago; an expert on astronomy and extraterrestrials
STRANGER: Nightingale's daughter, rebellious film school student
STRANGIE: A lovely, caring daughter in Nightingale's imagination, played by the same actor as STRANGER
HAWKER: Nightingale's fellow street vendor, who sells his often-changing goods next to her, whose wife, a Vietnamese mail-order bride, left him
HIGH: Stranger's boyfriend, a wannabe film director
MONEY: Dapper, wealthy middle-aged man who drifts around Taipei
MYSTERY LADY: Has a Vietnamese accent
DAVID: Nightingale's husband, abducted by aliens 20 years ago

Pedestrians and Customers on the street

SETTING

The play takes place in recent Taipei, Taiwan.

Sand on a Distant Star was first performed on May 9, 2003, at the National Theatre, Taipei, Taiwan, directed by Stan Lai, produced by Performance Workshop:

Cast:
Chang Hsiao-yen as Nightingale
Chin Shih-chieh as Money and David
Bright Pu as Hawker
Aya Liu as Stranger/Strangie
Lee Chien-chang as High
Ismene Ting as Mystery Lady
Stephanie Lai as Stranger's double

Scenic and Lighting Design by Alan Kwang-yen Nieh
Costume Design by Liu Lung and Pun Dailee
Music courtesy of Forward Music

Produced by Nai-chu Ding

Photo: *Sand on a Distant Star*, National Theatre, Taipei, Taiwan, 2003, Scene 7. Stranger (Aya Liu) and Nightingale (Chang Hsiao-yen). Photo by Liu Chen-hsiang.

Scene 1

Mysterious, distant sound. Stranger appears in a pool of light downstage, talking directly to the audience. She is an edgy film student.

> STRANGER: Hey. I'm talking to you. Are you ready to be beamed up? Where's your implant? You don't have one? Then tough, when they come for us, you don't get to go.

She points to her left wrist.

> Mine's here. That's what I've been told since I was a kid, but to prove it, I had to slash it open. I did, but couldn't find it. Anyway, don't doubt it. They're coming. When and where, only she knows.

Nightingale appears in another pool of light. She is a middle-aged woman, vending goods in the street. She sells a special kind of watch. When there are no customers, she peers at the sky through a telescope.

> Right. This woman's name is Nightingale. She lives for the night skies—a nocturnal, star-gazing Nightingale. And yet, when was the last time you saw stars in the city?

Stranger suddenly steps out of her narration.

> Cut.

High, Stranger's boyfriend, a young wannabe film director, enters and adjusts a video camera that has been placed on the ground in front of Stranger.

> STRANGER: *(to High)* How's that for an opening?

> HIGH: Stuck up. Stranger, you're sounding like an investigative reporter.

> STRANGER: But isn't that what I'm trying to do?

They take the camera and exit.
A street scene in Taipei. Pedestrians walk to and fro. Next to Nightingale's stall, Hawker, a street vendor, is selling toy aliens. They pitch their goods to pedestrians passing by.

> NIGHTINGALE: Time comes in two forms! Have a look!

> HAWKER: Hey aliens! Factory closeout on aliens! Get a cute new alien for your kid!

Nightingale notices Hawker's merchandise.

NIGHTINGALE: Hey Hawker, what's this you're hawking tonight? What happened to the scarves you were selling yesterday?

HAWKER: Scarves? What scarves?

CUSTOMER 1: How much for this one?

HAWKER: One hundred.

CUSTOMER 1: I'll give you 60.

HAWKER: That's an insult!

The Customer walks away.

Wait. I love to be insulted!

The Customer comes back. Hawker wraps an alien toy for the Customer while taking his money.

Don't leave him on the windowsill, or a spaceship might come to beam him up in the night! Ha ha!

Nightingale inspects Hawker's toys as the Customer leaves.

NIGHTINGALE: I don't get it. You didn't even finish selling your old inventory and now you've switched to something new again? How inconsistent! No wonder your wife left you.

HAWKER: *(furious)* DON'T MENTION MY WIFE! As for you, Nightingale, that stupid watch, that's the only thing you sell. You're sooo consistent, that's why your husband got kidnapped by aliens! *(to passersby)* Aliens, aliens, get your cute little aliens!

NIGHTINGALE: How shameless! You don't even believe in aliens!

HAWKER: *(shouting)* Shameless super sale! Step right up and insult me with an offer! *(to Nightingale)* Hey Nightingale, you have a customer . . .

Nightingale attends to her customer, who is looking at a watch.

CUSTOMER 2: This watch is defective.

NIGHTINGALE: No, Miss, our watches aren't defective. Let me explain: time comes in two forms, so this watch has two sets of hands. One goes forward. That's general time that applies to everyone. The other set doesn't move. That's your private moment, the time that belongs to you alone. With this watch, you can make time stand still at the most memorable moment of your life.

HAWKER: *(taking over fluidly)* Confused? Allow me to explain, Miss: *(melodiously and fluidly, like a jewelry commercial)* In every lifetime, there is one moment that stands out as unique, sacred, and by wearing this watch, you can carry that moment in your everyday life, forever . . .

The Customer tosses down the watch and walks away.

Dammit! If you don't want it you don't have to throw it! You're not good enough for this watch! *(like a gangster, pointing)* Don't let me catch you here again!!

Other pedestrians gather around the shouting Hawker.

(to pedestrians) What are you gawkin' at! Never seen a bad guy before?

NIGHTINGALE: Control yourself, Hawker! You should sign up for some anger management classes.

HAWKER: *(suddenly calm)* Did I come off as angry? Great, that's the angry guy character I created!

NIGHTINGALE: Really?

HAWKER: Honing my acting skills. I, Hawker, am the true diamond in the rough. Just wait till a talent scout finds me, and you'll see how far I go.

NIGHTINGALE: You don't need to create an angry guy. You ARE him. *(turning to pedestrians)* Time comes in two forms, have a look!

HAWKER: Aliens, aliens, factory closeout! . . .

Nightingale looks into the sky with a telescope. Hawker looks around the street. The pedestrians seem to be walking in slow motion.

(to himself) Look at all these people. Somehow, they don't look like people. They all just stare straight ahead, or at their phones, *(looking at Nightingale)* or at the sky. They've all been shut down. In moments like these, I feel like I'm the only person in the entire universe who's alive.

NIGHTINGALE: Not possible.

HAWKER: What?

NIGHTINGALE: Take the 250 billion planets in our galaxy alone. You know how many zeros that is? That's 2-5-0-0-0-0-0-0-0-0-0! Subtract all the stars that are too small, too cold, too big, or whose orbits are non-heat-sustainable, which basically includes most of them, and there are still a billion or so that will do.

HAWKER: That will do what?

NIGHTINGALE: Support life as we know it! And how many forms of life do we know of? So don't think you're so special.

HAWKER: Maybe I didn't phrase it quite right . . .

NIGHTINGALE: And don't make yourself out to be so lonely either.

HAWKER: Hey, I'm just complaining about how slow business is tonight! No need to give me the full lecture on the universe!

The street reverts to normal. Money, a middle-aged man, is wandering around nearby. He is dressed dapperly, like a Casanova who is past his prime. He holds an open liquor flask. He looks at Hawker's aliens, then at Nightingale's watches. A boy with his mother approaches Nightingale's stand.

BOY: *(inspecting a watch)* How come the dial doesn't move?

NIGHTINGALE: Because it's not supposed to. That way you can set it to the most important moment in your life and keep it there forever. Look. I wear one myself . . . *(showing the watch to the boy)* My watch shows 11:42. That was the night of the 15th of May, twenty years ago. It was the moment that . . . *(drifting into her own thoughts)* you could say it records the moment when my life stopped.

The boy tosses the watch back to the stand.

BOY: Loony!

NIGHTINGALE: Wait, son, that's not nice. Lunatics are people, too.

BOY: Alien!

NIGHTINGALE: Wow, even worse. Aliens are also beings, with rights, just like loonies.

MOTHER: Let's go.

The mother leads the boy away.

NIGHTINGALE: Um, you're his mother, I take it? Well you should know that if you let your son disrespect aliens, then he will not respect all the different life-forms in the universe, all the suns and the moons and the stars! If you don't respect all forms of life, then in the future we won't have any suns and moons and birds and . . .

They have exited.

You're welcome. *(to Hawker)* That does it. I'm done for the night.

Nightingale starts packing up. Money approaches her.

MONEY: Excuse me, miss. Did you say this watch could stop time?

NIGHTINGALE: Well, in an abstract sense, yes.

Money checks the watch carefully, then shakes his head and laughs.

MONEY: *(mumbling to himself)* Two kinds of time . . . one going forward and the other frozen. Forever! How much?

NIGHTINGALE: Three hundred fifty.

MONEY: That cheap?

NIGHTINGALE: *(not getting it)* No, sir, you don't understand. This is a unique design that you can't buy anywhere else, so . . . wait, what did you just say?

MONEY: I said, that cheap?

NIGHTINGALE: Huh?

MONEY: Can you sell it for more?

NIGHTINGALE: Um . . . can I sell it for more? I . . .

Hawker intervenes, having not gotten it, increasingly unsure as he speaks.

HAWKER: Listen, Sir, our prices are very reasonable. How can it be expensive? Look, it's the end of the day, she's giving you her best price, and . . . *(pause)* what?

Money has already put on the watch, taken out his wallet, and handed a US 100-dollar bill to Nightingale.

NIGHTINGALE: What's this?

HAWKER: US dollars?

NIGHTINGALE: Sir, I don't have change for 100 US dollars.

Money gives her another 100-dollar bill.

Sir, I have even less change for 200 US dollars!

HAWKER: Hey, you're putting her in a tough spot. She just runs a small business, we have no idea of the exchange rates, so . . .

Money gives Hawker another 100-dollar bill, tosses another bill in the air, and leaves. Nightingale and Hawker watch, speechless.
Police whistles.

HAWKER: Cops! Split!

Hawker grabs the bill on the ground. They quickly collect their belongings and scurry away, pushing their carts.

Scene 2

Nightingale's apartment. A window, next to which are her telescope and an armchair. A table with two chairs, a baby's cradle, and a bookshelf with a cassette player and books about outer space and UFOs. Books are also scattered all around the room. On the wall is a clock that is stopped at 11:42.
Nightingale and Strangie are arranging flowers. Nightingale cuts the flower stems with scissors. Strangie is Nightingale's imagined projection of her daughter, gentle and obedient. She has an unreal quality about her, like a doll, or a character out of a Japanese manga.

NIGHTINGALE: Strangie, dear, where are Daddy's slippers . . . ?

STRANGIE: I put them on the windowsill, Mommy, for when he arrives.

NIGHTINGALE: We should also put Daddy's favorite newspapers and magazines next to the bed.

STRANGIE: I'll get those ready as soon as we're done here, Mommy.

NIGHTINGALE: Good. Daddy's been away so long, and it's such a long way home. Everything needs to be perfect.

STRANGIE: When is Daddy coming home?

STRANGIE AND NIGHTINGALE: *(in unison)* The 15th of May!

They both laugh. It seems awkwardly unreal.
The sound of keys opening the door.

NIGHTINGALE: She's back.

STRANGIE: I'll go check.

Obedient Strangie exits. Nightingale continues to arrange flowers. Rebellious Stranger enters. Stranger and Nightingale glare at each other for a long moment. Stranger takes a pack of cigarettes from her bag and attempts to light up. Nightingale grabs the cigarette and cuts it in half with her scissors.

NIGHTINGALE: If everyone in the world lit up at the same time, do you know how much carbon monoxide, formaldehyde, and crotonaldehyde would be released into the ozone layer? Our planet would choke!

Nightingale continues to arrange flowers.

STRANGER: So what's this? Who are these flowers for?

NIGHTINGALE: You know very well what day is coming up.

STRANGER: Oh, for sure. Next week the "Third Window of the Universe" will open! Or something like that. Man, that's been old ever since I was a kid.

Stranger lights a cigarette and exits.
Nightingale waves the smoke away. Strangie enters again, carrying a stack of newspapers. She is a good girl again.

STRANGIE: Mommy, I got all the newspapers and magazines that Daddy likes. He can catch up on everything!

NIGHTINGALE: Good girl, just leave them there.

Strangie puts the newspapers on the bed.

You know how much your Daddy loved you?

STRANGIE: Of course! Every day when he came home, he would pick me up and hold me.

NIGHTINGALE: If you'd fallen asleep, he'd let you sleep on his shoulder.

STRANGIE: Really?! So why am I called "Stranger"?

NIGHTINGALE: Because the moment you were born, your Daddy held you in his arms and said, "Stranger than fiction! How amazing is life!" And so we called you "Stranger"!

STRANGIE: Mommy, I've heard that story so many times, but it never gets old!

NIGHTINGALE: Your Daddy was such a kind soul. *(pointing to the chair by the window)* He liked to sit here, look out, and think about the world, the universe . . .

Strangie exits with the bucket. Stranger reenters with a video camera and films Nightingale as she speaks.

One day as he was sitting right here, he said to me, "Night, the first time we met, you smiled at me. That one smile changed my life. Just think. If such a simple, spontaneous gesture can affect a person's life in such a profound way, then you must believe that the movement of a single grain of sand can affect a very distant planet."

Nightingale is lost in thought, but suddenly notices Stranger filming her.

Stop.

STRANGER: No. Keep going. It's crazy, it's great.

NIGHTINGALE: What I just said is none of your business.

STRANGER: What I'm filming is none of your business either.

NIGHTINGALE: *(pushing the camera aside)* Then stop it.

STRANGER: If it weren't for my senior project, I wouldn't be wasting my time on you in the first place.

NIGHTINGALE: Oh, so now I'm the subject of your senior project? Great! I get it! Film a lunatic, show how traumatic it is being a lunatic's daughter, right? You grew up at the corner breakfast stand because your mom never made you breakfast, right?

STRANGER: Not just the breakfast stand. I just interviewed that noodle shop lady because she's under the impression that SHE's the one who brought me up! I guess I should call her "Mom"?

NIGHTINGALE: Keep going. Say all you want. When the 15th of May rolls around next week, you'll see.

STRANGER: So what happens when May 15th rolls around? At 11:42 p.m. Dad is beamed back. *(pointing)* He comes in from that window. Then what? And what do you do if he doesn't show? Wake up, Mom! *(pointing at the cradle)* Look at this. Why do you still have this cradle? Haven't I grown up?

NIGHTINGALE: Stranger, how can you say such things? Have you no memory of what happened? Twenty years ago, on the 15th of May, at 11:42 p.m., we all went up together! It was you, Daddy, and me, the three of us together! We all have implants to prove it!

STRANGER: Of course we do!

NIGHTINGALE: The reason I had to come back was because of the C-section when I had you, which disqualified me for galactic travel!

STRANGER: Mom, can you lower your voice, please? The neighbors will hear.

NIGHTINGALE: You had to come back because I was breastfeeding you. Don't you remember? Of course not! Because you were only eight months old. You are my only witness, but you were too young to remember!

STRANGER: Mom, whatever you're high on, it sure beats anything my friends have. Can I get some?

Pause.

Okay, so your husband's coming back next week. Then what? You live happy ever after! Fine. Let me tell you something that will happen even sooner, and this at least is for certain: I'm moving out.

NIGHTINGALE: To move in with that good-for-nothing film director?

STRANGER: It doesn't matter with who.

NIGHTINGALE: He's playing you.

STRANGER: Get it straight. I'm playing him.

NIGHTINGALE: Listen, Stranger, Mom's not crazy. Mom has a good eye for men. One look at that guy High and I knew that he's the unreliable type.

STRANGER: Right, I definitely trust your "good eye" for men, especially since you found the most reliable one.

NIGHTINGALE: Your father IS the most reliable!

STRANGER: Of course, since he abandoned us 20 years ago. Before that he lost his job, had substance problems, and beat us. Indeed, a very nice and reliable man.

NIGHTINGALE: Where did you get that? The noodle lady? She never even knew your dad! And the breakfast stand didn't even open here until after your dad left! Stranger, you don't understand relationships, you don't understand how your father and I shared such deep happiness! You don't understand love, and you don't understand why two people need to be together.

STRANGER: As long as it feels good.

NIGHTINGALE: Well, you don't look like you feel good.

STRANGER: Then as long as it doesn't feel good.

NIGHTINGALE: You're wasting your life.

STRANGER: I learned from the best.

NIGHTINGALE: Well, you didn't get it right!

Nightingale sits down by the window.

STRANGER: Mom, wake up! That guy you claim to have been happy with lives in Shanghai. High has some paparazzi friends, and they've been investigating for me. They tell me he has a wife and kids, one is eight years old, and the other is . . .

NIGHTINGALE: That's total bull! What could the paparazzi find out about your Daddy? He isn't a movie star! If they wanted a real scoop, they would go to planet Penefere. That'd be the only way to get your Daddy's true story.

Pause.

>   STRANGER: Mom, can we please stop this? You've lied to me for 20 years.
>   I'm grown up now.

Stranger lights a cigarette and exits.
Nightingale turns on the cassette to listen to an old pop song. She sits back at the window.
Strangie enters from the other side, holding a cup of tea.

>   STRANGIE: Mommy, I made you some oolong tea, best of the season. I
>   picked the tea myself! *(pause)* Just kidding! How could that be possi-
>   ble? But I did go to the mountains to buy it!

Nightingale stares out the window.

Scene 3

A different street. The location is quieter. Hawker is selling pirated DVDs.

>   CUSTOMER 3: You got *Avengers 6*?

>   HAWKER: C'mon, they haven't even started shooting that yet. We special-
>   ize in pirated DVDs, not bootlegs.

>   CUSTOMER 3: I'll take these.

>   HAWKER: Thank you.

Customer pays, takes the DVDs, and leaves.
Nightingale enters, pushing her cart next to Hawker's spot. She flips through the DVDs. Another Customer approaches to browse.

>   NIGHTINGALE: Hawker, what's the matter with you? I can't even remem-
>   ber what you were selling yesterday!

Nightingale grabs a DVD from the Customer.

>   *(to the Customer)* Get lost! Don't buy these!

>   HAWKER: What are you doing, Nightingale? You're ruining my business!
>   Go away, I don't know you! *(to the Customer)* Hey lady, good price for
>   you . . .

The Customer leaves.

NIGHTINGALE: So tell me, how did you get this merchandise?

HAWKER: Yesterday, I heard about a bunch of mail-order Vietnamese brides working at an underground DVD factory.

NIGHTINGALE: And?

HAWKER: First thing I learned was, an "underground" factory is not necessarily underground. This one was on the 25th floor of a big building. I figured I'd catch her this time, my wife, and right there I'd show her who's boss! I broke in to find—all these old ladies, packing DVDs. These tough guys came over, but I acted like I knew what I was doing. I told them I was there to pick up a shipment, and they believed me because I definitely looked the part! That's how I ended up with this nice batch of merchandise.

NIGHTINGALE: Okay, I get it. The aliens you were selling—you got a tip that a toy factory had hired Vietnamese brides? Hawker, you can't change your merchandise every time you get a tip on your wife!

HAWKER: You're damn right! That's why tomorrow, we put an end to all this guesswork! Nightingale, tomorrow you and I set up our stalls on Linsen Road!

NIGHTINGALE: That's the red-light district.

HAWKER: Precisely why I've been avoiding that area. My wife is so pretty, I know that the only way her story ends is with her selling herself over there. Let's set up there, we find her, and I stab a knife right through her heart!

NIGHTINGALE: Fine. I'll go with you to Linsen tomorrow, if you come with me tonight to that building across the street *(pointing)*.

HAWKER: What for?

NIGHTINGALE: According to my calculations, there should be signs tonight.

HAWKER: Oh, so you came to this spot tonight with an agenda? What signs?

NIGHTINGALE: There will be flashing red lights in the sky tonight. The advance guard.

HAWKER: From?

NIGHTINGALE: The mother ship that is bringing my husband back.

HAWKER: That's absolutely wild! That's why I love working with you, Nightingale, because I get to hear such phenomenal stories. May I ask where this mother ship is coming from?

NIGHTINGALE: Planet Penefere, of course.

HAWKER: Hold it, you changed the name again!

NIGHTINGALE: Changed what?

HAWKER: You used to call it "Pefenere!"

NIGHTINGALE: Hawker, how many times have I told you: It's "Pe-ne-fe-re."

HAWKER: Okay, okay, whatever. So where is this "Pefenere"?

NIGHTINGALE: PENEFERE is 7,627 light-years away, in the northeast corner of our galaxy. It has three moons, and it rotates around this star called AG1142.

HAWKER: Aha! New details! Three moons? Then Pefenere must be super bright at night! When the Moon Festival comes around, which one are they supposed to look at?

NIGHTINGALE: It's "PE-NE-FE-RE"!

Hawker goes back to his stall to attend to a Customer.

HAWKER: Yeah, yeah, whatever . . .

NIGHTINGALE: Go ahead and laugh. The Third Window of the Universe will be open next week.

HAWKER: Sure thing. *(to himself)* As if I care about which window to where will open.

NIGHTINGALE: *(overhearing)* You don't get it, Hawker. Not only will they bring my husband back, but possibly your wife, too!

HAWKER: *(suddenly furious)* Hey we were just having fun! Why did you bring up my wife? Listen closely, Ms. Nightingale. My wife was not abducted by aliens. Neither was your husband. Behind every sad story, we long for a romantic explanation. But the truth is, NOT

EVERY MISSING PERSON WAS ABDUCTED BY ALIENS! Face it! We share the same sorry narrative! We were dumped, ditched, abandoned! *(to the Customer, angrily)* I'm closed! And did you know it's against the law to buy pirated DVDs?

The Customer walks off, puzzled. Hawker packs up his stall angrily.

NIGHTINGALE: Hey, Hawker, I was just joking! Why would the Peneferians need so many specimens? There's no reason to kidnap your wife!

HAWKER: DON'T MENTION MY WIFE!

Pause.

NIGHTINGALE: I just wanted to instill some hope in you, get it? Hope!! People need hope in order to go on, you know?

Pause. Police whistles.

HAWKER: WHISTLE WHISTLE WHISTLE I HEARD YOU ALREADY! We were just about to leave!

Nightingale and Hawker rush off with their goods.

Scene 4

Sound of the wind. The roof of a skyscraper. A parapet. Money slowly climbs onto the parapet and looks over the edge, intending to jump. He takes a drink from his flask.
His emotions fluctuate from nonchalance to deep despair.

MONEY: *(mumbling to himself)* "Time comes in two forms . . ." *(looking at his watch)* Soon both will cease to exist, and we will experience the third kind of time!

He braces to jump, but stops. He gathers himself. He takes off his shoes and places them neatly on the ledge, as is done in Japanese television dramas.
Nightingale enters and surveys the skies with her telescope, not noticing Money.
Money looks down at the street from the ledge. Nightingale circles around near him. Money takes a deep breath and braces to jump again, at which moment, Nightingale accidentally backs into him.

MONEY AND NIGHTINGALE: *(in unison)* AHHH—!!!

Money almost falls off the ledge, but pulls back just in time.
Pause. Nightingale stares at Money.

NIGHTINGALE: Sorry, Sir, but if I may, that's my spot.

Pause. Money is in shock.

MONEY: Excuse me?

NIGHTINGALE: You're in my spot.

MONEY: Your what?

NIGHTINGALE: A real savant! Not many people know about this spot. But it's the best. Now may I?

MONEY: May you . . . ?

NIGHTINGALE: Sorry. I have to be fair. First come, first served. After you, then!

MONEY: *(getting scared)* After me?

NIGHTINGALE: Do you mind if I watch?

MONEY: You want to watch?

Nightingale notices Money's shoes on the parapet.

NIGHTINGALE: I beg to ask: Why did you take off your shoes? Is it to do with the magnetic field?

MONEY: Magnetic field . . . ?

NIGHTINGALE: Sir, I've been doing this for 20 years. I've learned something new today!

MONEY: You've been doing this for 20 years, and you're still standing there?

Nightingale takes off her shoes, and places them next to his.

NIGHTINGALE: Is that the correct procedure?

MONEY: *(feebly)* That's how they do it in Japanese TV serials.

NIGHTINGALE: You look like a seasoned pro. I take it you've been up there before.

MONEY: Up where?

NIGHTINGALE: Whoosh! You take flight! There's no sense of gravity! You're floating . . . you're floating . . . The light . . . the light . . .

MONEY: *(terrified)* What light?

Nightingale checks her watch, steps up onto the parapet, and pulls Money up after her.

NIGHTINGALE: I'm sorry I'm being so talkative this evening. It's just that I can't wait, and . . . *(checking her watch)* Enough senseless banter! It's time! We can do this together!

MONEY: Do what together?

NIGHTINGALE: Share the experience!

MONEY: You can share this experience?!

NIGHTINGALE: *(spreading her arms wide)* Spread out your arms, and embrace the vastness of the universe!! YES!!

MONEY: NO!!

Money gets off the parapet and steps aside in fear.

NIGHTINGALE: *(looking at her watch)* The time has come!

MONEY: My time hasn't come!

NIGHTINGALE: Nine forty-three fifty-two . . . Which is NOW! READY!

MONEY: I'M NOT READY!

NIGHTINGALE: *(looking at watch)* On your mark, get set . . .

MONEY: NOOO~~!

The loud sound of an airplane passing over.
Pause. Nightingale is puzzled.

NIGHTINGALE: Did you see anything?

MONEY: Looked like a 737 to me.

Nightingale steps down. She is distraught. Money follows.

NIGHTINGALE: I guess that means he's not coming.

MONEY: Who?

NIGHTINGALE: My husband.

MONEY: You're waiting for your husband?

NIGHTINGALE: A sign of him. Aren't you waiting for signs of your family as well?

MONEY: What? I . . .

NIGHTINGALE: I've waited for 20 years. Today was supposed to be the same as that time, flashing red lights—the advance guard, but . . .

Pause. Nightingale goes back onto the parapet, looking down. Money watches with apprehension.

MONEY: Well, so what. Things have a way of working out . . .

NIGHTINGALE: You're right. If he's not back on the 15th of May, on May 16th, I'm going straight to him! Penefere isn't as far away as you think!

Nightingale extends her foot over the edge.

MONEY: Hey! Careful, come down, come down . . .

Money rushes to stop her and bring her down.

NIGHTINGALE: *(laughing)* Haha! I was just kidding. I'll bet you my math was off. We'll find out next week! Bless you! All you need is a little hope!

Nightingale starts to leave with her telescope, then looks back.

Sir, have I seen you before?

Nightingale exits. Money pauses, then extends his wrist, trying to show her his watch, but Nightingale has left already. He goes to get his shoes, and sees Nightingale's shoes.

MONEY: Wait! Hey, Time Lady, you forgot your shoes!

Scene 5

Nightingale's bedroom. High and Stranger are in the room. High is installing a hidden camera on the shelf by the tape player.

HIGH: This 1080HD wide angle is awesome. I got it all.

STRANGER: Are you done?

High looks at the cassettes on the shelf.

HIGH: Holy cow! Your mom listens to these?

STRANGER: That's all she listens to. Her whole life is stuck in those old songs.

HIGH: *(with a sense of awe)* Unbelievable. This is the place.

STRANGER: Huh?

HIGH: The scene of the event.

STRANGER: What scene of what event?

HIGH: Your old man was taken away from THIS room, and you were in THAT crib! You floated out THAT window! Man, how cool is that?

STRANGER: You believe the crazy things my mom says?

HIGH: Don't you remember? Don't you ever get the feeling of floating away? Wait . . . I'm starting to feel it.

STRANGER: If your camera is set, let's go.

HIGH: It's perfect! If aliens really bring your dad back next week, your dad will be sitting *(pointing)* here, the aliens will be standing over there, your mom and dad will be reunited, and my 1080HD will record everything! The Loch Ness Monster is shit! Aliens are the real deal!

STRANGER: Your 1080HD won't record anything, because what you described will not happen.

HIGH: That's okay, too. If the aliens don't show up next week, the least we'll get is your mom sitting on that chair, alone, defeated. The unquenchable thirst of a woman whose dreams have been obliterated by relentless fate. Like a solitary orange that's rolled off a container truck onto the merciless freeway of life, she disintegrates into pieces as she is squashed out of existence, juice squirting all over, trampled, dried . . . ! *(pointing to the floor)* Your mom. THEN! My paparazzi pals in Shanghai get footage of your dad and his woman doing it in their bedroom, and we edit this as a split screen: left screen, steamy sex; right screen, the torture of waiting; left screen, the pinnacle of bliss; right screen, the torment of suffering; left screen, the cigarette; right screen, the tears! It's a wrap! It's an Oscar!

STRANGER: Are you done?

HIGH: But only a nomination. It doesn't have a chance. Because it's the truth. People don't want the truth. People only want the modified truth.

STRANGER: What's the modified truth?

HIGH: Come next week, we'll MAKE it happen.

STRANGER: Come next week, nothing will happen.

HIGH: We'll employ two actors. One plays the alien, the other your dad. The only audience will be: your mom. It goes viral! Twenty million hits!

STRANGER: This is just a senior project.

HIGH: Senior projects are shit! The Cannes Film Festival is the real deal!

STRANGER: Cannes?

HIGH: I mean "drama therapy" is the real deal!

STRANGER: "Drama therapy"?

HIGH: You don't get it? I'm setting up a drama therapy session for your mom! Through dramatic role-playing, a crushed orange sees the truth!

STRANGER: But this truth comes from fabricated lies.

HIGH: Truth oozes through the lies! Next week: Strong backlight fades in through the window. Two actors. The alien brings your dad back. Your parents reunite. They pour out their hearts to each other, then your dad gets taken away again by the aliens. Exit. Strong backlight fades out. Scene! Amazing! Heart-rending! The Golden Palm Award!

Stranger pushes High away, and looks out the window.

STRANGER: Two actors? "Drama therapy?" . . .

Sound of a key opening the door, shocking Stranger and High. There is nowhere

to hide, so they stand still. Nightingale enters from outside, barefoot, with her
telescope, mumbling.

> NIGHTINGALE: *(to herself)* I need to recalculate. If this is true, there may
> be problems on the 15th . . . *(notices that things have been moved)*
> What's the chair doing here?

Nightingale looks back and sees High and Stranger standing still. Pause.

> HIGH: *(awkwardly)* Hi. I'm High.

> NIGHTINGALE: What are you doing in my apartment?

> HIGH: Stranger brought me here to check out the scene where her dad
> was kidnapped.

> NIGHTINGALE: So you're kidnapping my daughter?

> HIGH: Kidnapping?

> STRANGER: He's not taking me anywhere, Mom. I'm the one who wants to
> leave. Everything in here is fake. I'm suffocating! Mom, please. Don't
> blame everything on aliens. Face the truth! Face your failure!

> NIGHTINGALE: You face your failure! Ever since you were a kid, you've
> always done the opposite of whatever I asked you. All I could do was
> hope that after you'd been sufficiently bruised and battered outside,
> the impact would wake you up!

> STRANGER: Right. No matter how loud you yell at me, I can't wake up,
> and I can't disappear. So Mom, take a close look at your biggest fail-
> ure—ME! Face it! I date a totally unreliable jerk, in a relationship that
> is bound to fail, you have to accept it! Just like you have to accept the
> fact of your failed marriage. You failed! YOU ARE FAILURE!

High drags Stranger out, and they exit.
Pause.
Nightingale turns to the cassette player. She plays an oldie.
Strangie enters from the other side, smiling.

> STRANGIE: Mommy, don't be sad. Daddy will be back next week!

> NIGHTINGALE: *(shaking her head)* But what if . . .

> STRANGIE: There won't be any what-ifs, Mommy. You can't lose faith now!

High enters stealthily to get some equipment he left on the table.

NIGHTINGALE: My child, why are you always so optimistic? Mommy might have miscalculated this time.

High is startled.

STRANGIE: I don't think so. Mommy, your calculations have always been so accurate! So when the Third Window opens up next week, the wormhole will be filled with enough negative energy to bring Daddy back!

NIGHTINGALE: Even so, both space and time are dilated in galactic travel. So it means the 20 days Daddy spent on Penefere equals around 20 years on Earth. He'll be a young man. And look at how old Mommy is . . .

Pause.

STRANGIE: It's all just theories, Mommy! No one has proven anything yet! What's more important is that love goes beyond everything, right?

Strangie giggles. High doesn't know who Nightingale is talking to. He quietly gets his things and exits.
Nightingale turns to look at where High was.

Scene 6

The streets. A lonely, rainy night. Hawker has switched merchandise again, selling sausages in the traditional Taiwan street vendor style, on a parked bike with a grill and sausages attached to the back, and a large bowl for dice to gamble with customers. There is a stool on his left.

CUSTOMER 4: Come on! Boxcars! . . .

The Customer throws the dice into the bowl with flair.

HAWKER: *(pointing at the spinning dice)* Snake eyes! *(seeing the result)* Wow! Snake eyes again! You lose!

Hawker takes one of the sausages on the grill and offers it to the Customer.

Sorry, you didn't win a single sausage, so this one's on me. Help yourself to the chili and garlic . . .

Money enters with an umbrella, holding his flask of booze and Nightingale's shoes. He stares at Hawker. Customer exits.

MONEY: Hey, boss, remember me?

HAWKER: Oh, "Yankee dollar"! Sure.

Money extends his left arm and shows Hawker his watch.

> "Time comes in two forms." You're wearing it?

MONEY: Where's the time lady?

HAWKER: Nightingale? Funny, she's not here yet. Why are you looking for her?

MONEY: To give her back her shoes.

Money gives the shoes to Hawker.

HAWKER: *(taking the shoes)* How did you end up with her shoes?

MONEY: I just wanted to drop by and thank her. I owe her.

HAWKER: For what? She owes you. Heck, I owe you, too. Let me grill two sausages for you. Fresh! My treat, my treat!

Hawker prepares the sausages. Money reaches for his wallet.

MONEY: No no, I pay, I pay.

HAWKER: No no, my treat, my treat!

Money offers his flask to Hawker.

MONEY: Drink! Drink!

HAWKER: *(pointing to the stool)* Sit! Sit!

Money sits on the stool next to the bike.

MONEY: So, where are your alien toys?

Hawker has to think hard.

HAWKER: Oh, that was a long time ago.

MONEY: Bullshit, the day before yesterday!

HAWKER: Really?

MONEY: *(offering the flask)* Drink! Drink!

Hawker gives the sausages to Money.

> HAWKER: You want to know how I got this sausage cart? It's actually
> a weird story: last night after work I went to Linsen Road, to look
> for my wi—a wise old friend. I heard that she'd fallen on hard times
> and was working at one of the clubs there. *(angry)* I took one look
> at that club, and knew it was definitely a front for an underground
> escort service! *(calm)* But the person I was waiting for is decent, so
> she probably was doing dishes in the kitchen. I waited and waited,
> thinking that she had to get off work sooner or later, and I would
> catch her there!

> MONEY: And she ended up coming out in the arms of some macho tour-
> ist drunk, right?

> HAWKER: Drunk?

> MONEY: Man, those chauvinists, they pay for a chick, and treat them like
> dirt!

> HAWKER: *(very angry)* No way! *(burns his hand on the grill)* Ouch!

> MONEY: Boss, to be frank, I used to frequent those establishments.

> HAWKER: You??

> MONEY: A long time ago!

Hawker calms down.

> Tell me how your wife ended up working there?

> HAWKER: I just heard a rumor that she went there to . . . Wait, when did I
> say it was my wife?

> MONEY: Didn't you?

> HAWKER: Did I?

Pause.

> Okay, I admit it, I was waiting for my wife! I was watching from the
> other side of the street. There was a street vendor selling sausages
> nearby, so I thought, what the heck, I'll gamble on sausages while I
> waited. And just as you said, I saw the customers leaving one by one,

fondling and kissing the girls. It wasn't pretty. The more I watched, the angrier I got, the angrier I got, the bolder my betting got. One sausage became two, two became four, four became eight. I won 10 straight bets, doubling down each time! That's over a thousand sausages, more than I can eat in 10 years! The owner surrendered his whole stall to me. Dude, this is what you call "Lucky at dice, unlucky in love!"

MONEY: Boss, you're a man, right? Well, a real man, whose woman has left him to seek her fortunes in the red-light district, would simply make a clean break. Get it? Stop thinking about the past and make a clean break! Be a real man!

HAWKER: A clean break? No problem! *(heroically)* The moment I find her, I stab her through the heart! If there's a guy involved, he dies too! That's what I call a clean break!

MONEY: How childish!

HAWKER: Hey, I spent 10,000 US dollars to bring her over here! That's a lot of money! I had to travel abroad twice to make all the arrangements!

MONEY: I could never figure out why a real man would need to buy a mail-order wife. Can't get it on your own?

HAWKER: That's why I'm giving them one stab each, right through the heart!

Hawker walks into the rain and falls into his own thoughts.

(softly, to himself) And what good does that do? I just want to find her, to beg her for another chance. I know I did her wrong. She was stuck with this poor guy with a bad temper. But I couldn't understand anything she said. I admit it. I hit her. Sometimes. But it wasn't on purpose. If I hadn't, she was so beautiful she'd surely have run off with another man! But the more violent I became, the more she wanted to run away; the more she wanted to run away, the more afraid I got; and the more afraid I got, the angrier I got; and the more violent I got, until finally . . . she ran away.

MONEY: Hey, boss man. You're all wet.

Hawker realizes that he's in the rain and walks back to the bike. He takes his towel to wipe off the rain.

HAWKER: Bro, we've been talking for a while, but I still don't know your name.

MONEY: Call me Money.

HAWKER: Well, Mr. Money, you never met my wife. She was a real looker. For sure, our relationship had its serious shortcomings, but if I said I knew what love was, I'd say that we loved each other. Then how can you just make a clean break? *(showing Money his watch)* Look, 2:30 a.m. Approximately. The time she left me, the most important moment in my life, and what was I doing? Sleeping! The most important moment of my life, and I was unconscious!! Two thirty, two thirty . . .

Hawker absentmindedly throws the dice.

Even snake eyes beats two thirty!

Money suddenly speaks up.

MONEY: Four twenty-seven.

HAWKER: *(to himself)* Two thirty . . .

MONEY: The big clock in the hospital lobby read 4:27.

HAWKER: Huh?

MONEY: There's no winter in California. I walked through a long, dark hallway into the cold, white, rays of the sun.

Hawker listens intently.

HAWKER: America?

Pause.

MONEY: I was blinded by that ray of light. I stepped out and never looked back.

HAWKER: Your wife was in the hospital?

MONEY: Stomach cancer, stage 4. *(pause)* Wait. Did I say it was my wife?

HAWKER: Didn't you?

Money takes a big gulp of alcohol.

Wait. You left her in the hospital?

MONEY: No, no, I hired professional help! The best I could find! There were three of them, taking shifts 24/7, professionals!

HAWKER: No kidding?

Money stands up and throws the dice.

MONEY: How long should I have stayed by her side? Four, five, six months passed, enough? Every day, helping with the piss and shit . . . the stench . . . She wanted to wash her hair . . . she hadn't washed it in weeks . . .

He takes out his wallet to show a picture.

Look at her! A year before she got sick. A 50-year-old woman, hell, she could still be Miss China! And now, she . . . she . . . *(sighs)* We had all these plans, to see the world, to cruise the Aegean . . .

HAWKER: Wait a minute, Mr. Money. For any other person, that may be too much to take, but you're her husband, and you left her all alone in the hospital? You just got up and left?

MONEY: That's what a real man does, you understand?

HAWKER: *(to himself)* That's what a real jerk does, you understand?

MONEY: Make a clean break! Be a man! A real man! Make your decision and don't look back. I went straight to the airport.

HAWKER: Where to?

MONEY: Greece! Hellas! *(throws the dice onto the street)* HELL-ASS!!

Hawker hurries to pick up the dice.

HAWKER: Dude, don't throw the dice into the rain!

MONEY: Not a day of rain in Greece. The deep blue Aegean on a luxury cruise ship.

HAWKER: By yourself?

MONEY: Who goes on a cruise all by himself? I have this old flame in London that I called, and she came. Young, beautiful, hot! You should have seen her in her evening gown. There wasn't a single person on board who didn't turn their head till their neck snapped! At sunset, that chick stood on the deck, the sun kissing the curves on her perfect backside. What an absolute masterpiece! We were on that ship for a month, passing countless islands in the Aegean, each one more sensuous than the one before! But you know, see it and move on! No need to linger! Make a clean break!

HAWKER: With an island?

MONEY: With everything! That first day on board, I chucked my cell phone into the deep blue sea. So deep. So blue, it's probably still going down now! No more petty distractions! A clean break! And when the cruise was over, it was fare-thee-well. No afterthoughts, a clean break! Like a real man! Then this real man . . . *(quieting down a bit)* came back to his hometown, like a migrating goose, here to Taipei.

Money walks in from the rain. Hawker passes his towel to him to wipe off the rain.

HAWKER: Like a migrating ghost.

MONEY: That month, I had such a . . .

Money buries his face in the towel. He is howling, as if in triumph, but more crying out in pain.

. . . SUCH A GREAT TIME!

Hawker looks at Money, who has broken down.

HAWKER: Hey, Mr. Money, why did you do it if it made you so miserable?

MONEY: Did I say I was miserable? *(heroic again)* Let me tell you something, boss, man to man. You need to make a clean break with that Vietnamese mail-order bride on Linsen Road. Easy call. Just do it!

HAWKER: Wait. Did I say she was Vietnamese?

MONEY: Didn't you?

Pause. Hawker drinks from Money's flask.

Let her go! Life is too shitty to waste your time looking back on it! Tell the lady who sells watches, she saved my worthless life. I owe her one. Make sure she gets my message. All right, boss, I'm out of here . . .

HAWKER: Take it slowly, Mr. Money.

MONEY: No way! I'm out of here fast and furious! Clean break with you! Like a real man! That's how you do it!

Money runs off.

HAWKER: A real man!?

Hawker sees that Money has left his umbrella on the ground.

Hey! Hey! Mr. Money, your umbrella!

Hawker finds Money's wallet on the cart.

Your wallet!

Money is nowhere in sight. Hawker opens the wallet to look for ID. A passerby stops to gamble.

(to the Customer) Highs or lows?

CUSTOMER 5: Highs!

The Customer rolls the dice.

HAWKER: Snake eyes!

Stranger and High enter. High is filming Stranger, who talks into a handheld microphone.

STRANGER: This is where my mom normally sets up her stall. She's usually here around this time, lecturing others on how many planets in the 51 stellar systems within 16 light-years of us might have a chance to support life. I don't know what she's up to today. This further illustrates her total unreliability. *(looking around)* Sometimes I come here. From a secret vantage point, I watch her peddling her goods. I say to myself: My mother has spent her entire life on this street. This is her reality. No wonder she stares into the sky nightly, *(pointing up)* peering into the infinite stars in her fantasized yearning for happiness, in search of some imagined sense of emotional support. But tonight the heavens answer: rain. *(to High)* Okay, cut.

HIGH: Not OK! You sound so la-di-da, like a news anchor.

STRANGER: Shoot some of the surroundings.

HIGH: *(shooting)* Hey, your mom is really something. I saw her talking to thin air.

STRANGER: You saw that?

High nods.

>   She wasn't talking to thin air. She was talking to me.

HIGH: You?

STRANGER: I didn't pass QC, so my mom invented another me.

HIGH: An ideal you?

STRANGER: Right, an ideal me, made to her specifications.

HIGH: An ideal you . . . I'd like to meet her, too. Hook us up sometime?

STRANGER: You wouldn't have a chance with an ideal me!

HIGH: I'd settle for a one-night stand.

STRANGER: Shut up, just get an establishing shot.

At Hawker's sausage stand, the Customer leaves.

HAWKER: *(to the Customer)* Hey, that's pretty lousy luck. Come again!

Stranger walks to Hawker's sausage stand, and lets out her frustration by throwing the dice.

STRANGER: Come on! Wow! Boxcars! I won, boss!

Hawker and Stranger see each other.

HAWKER: Hey, Stranger, I was going to treat you to a sausage, but it's too late. You won already!

STRANGER: Hawker? How come you're selling sausages?

HAWKER: It's a long story.

STRANGER: Where's my mom?

HAWKER: Not here yet. Hey Stranger, your mom's been acting weird lately. She seems to have a lot on her mind. You better watch out for her.

High starts filming Hawker. Stranger holds the mic in front of Hawker.

> *(to High)* Are you filming? I'm actually quite photogenic, you know.

High continues to film.

> STRANGER: So Hawker, have you noticed any . . . irregular behavior in
> Nightingale recently?

*Hawker straightens his shirt and looks seriously at the camera. High moves the
camera around when filming, with sudden jerks in motion.*

> HAWKER: Hi everybody, my name is Hawker. I'm a friend of Nightingale's.
> I set up my cart every night next to her. We've been working side by
> side for about a year, and she looks out for me. Hey cameraman, I
> can't focus with you jerking around like that.

> STRANGER: Hawker, don't mind him. That's the style I want. Don't look at
> the camera.

> HAWKER: Don't look at the camera?

> STRANGER: Just look at me.

*High moves to film Hawker's profile. Hawker starts talking but turns reflexively
toward High.*

> HAWKER: Nightingale often talks about how her husband was kidnapped
> by aliens. I figure there's no harm in that. Everyone needs a dream,
> and her dream is really out there! This interview is getting boring, so
> I'll throw in some entertainment. Nightingale's favorite song. Here is
> the chorus:

Hawker clears his throat and searches for the opening note.

> *(singing) It's the same moonlight . . . the same smile . . . the same you
> and the same me . . .*

> HIGH: Cut, cut!

> STRANGER: Thanks Hawker, we're done.

> HAWKER: But I didn't finish.

> STRANGER: No problem, it's a wrap.

> HAWKER: No wait, I'm the original diamond in the rough! I grew up on
> *TV Guide.*

Pause. High's eyes light up.

> HIGH: Actually, Hawker, Stranger and I have a very interesting project that I think would be very suitable for you.

Stranger is puzzled, but starts to get what High is up to.

> HAWKER: High, you should have contacted me 800 years ago, man! My friends say that I should have gone into the entertainment business long ago. I actually train on my own, want to see? Okay, "Camera test: Hawker"! Now I shall perform the four foundational expressions: "Joy, Anger, Sorrow, and Bliss." One, Joy.

He acts "joy."

> Two, Anger . . .

He acts "anger."

> HIGH: Uh, that's okay. We don't need . . .

> HAWKER: And here's my signature trick. I can shed tears within five seconds. Time me.

Hawker makes a sad expression, approaching tears. His eyes well up.

> STRANGER: Okay, okay, I believe you! I am totally touched . . . I see a tear!

> HAWKER: Now, I'll play a dead person, I can do that better than anyone! My friends all say once they've seen me die, they want to see it again! Get the joke? Haha! Okay watch. Ahh!!!

> HIGH: Don't die in the rain!

Hawker writhes in pain, falls to the ground, plays dead. He gets up.

> HAWKER: That was "death from poisoning." This next one is totally different. Ahh!!!

Hawker writhes in pain and falls to the floor again the same way. He gets up.

> That was sudden death. And then there's death from assorted kinds of gunfire. It's perfect for a rainy day like this, which gives it a sense of heroic tragedy. I'll show you in slow motion. *(playing a gangster)* "I'll get you, I will!!" Ahh—!!!

Hawker rushes into the rain, and in slow motion gets gunned down by an imaginary machine gun. Stranger and High stop him.

HIGH: Don't die, don't die. We believe you! Really! We're very touched!

HAWKER: How did you like that? Did you feel the blood streaming down in the pouring rain? Did you know there are 28 kinds of death? I've practiced the first 27. You can't practice the 28th.

STRANGER: Why not?

HAWKER: Because the 28th is real death. *(pause)* Hahaha! That's called black humor! I'm great at comedy, too! Name any character type, and I can do it. I've practiced them all. Romantic lead, action hero, comic, the villain, you name it, I can do them all! Tell me now, what's the character type you want me to play?

HIGH: An alien.

Pause.

HAWKER: An . . . alien?

HIGH: Do I detect a slight reluctance?

HAWKER: Oh no, no. "There are no small roles, just small actors." Jackie Chan said that, I believe, referring to when he was an extra for Bruce Lee.

HIGH: It doesn't matter who said it. It's the concept that counts.

HAWKER: So this alien . . . does it have . . . emotional layering?

HIGH: Of course.

HAWKER: Good, 'cause the character has to be emotional for me to show my full range.

STRANGER: Of course, of course. This is a complex, multilayered alien!

HAWKER: So tell me what kind of script this is. What's the plot?

STRANGER: You know that my Mom fantasizes that my Dad will come back from outer space next week, right?

HAWKER: No way is that happening.

STRANGER: Right. No way. So High and I came up with this idea: we stage the scene for my mom, and maybe through this use of drama therapy, she sees the light and comes back to the real world.

HAWKER: Would that count on a résumé?

HIGH: You bet! It's a fully-budgeted production!

HAWKER: Stranger, I'm absolutely moved. I always thought you didn't give a damn about your mom, but now I see that you truly care.

STRANGER: Well then, are you going to help us?

HAWKER: You bet. I consider this a significant project. This will be my screen debut! Who plays the father?

STRANGER: Well . . . we want to use a fresh face, and he has to look like my dad. We've been searching all over, even checking out people on the street.

HAWKER: C'mon, kids, that's not the way to go! You've gotta put out a casting call in order to find an actor. Otherwise you're trying to find a needle in the sea of humanity!

Hawker gestures emphatically while holding Money's wallet in his hand. Stranger sees the wallet and takes it from him for a closer look at the ID inside.

STRANGER: *(pointing to the photo)* Wait. Who's this guy?

All three look at Money's wallet.

Scene 7

Nightingale's room. Nightingale is cleaning the telescope. Strangie enters with a man's old suit in hand. Nightingale's attitude has changed. She acts cold toward Strangie.

STRANGIE: *(obediently)* Mommy, is this suit for Daddy?

NIGHTINGALE: *(quietly)* Yes.

STRANGIE: I get it! After Daddy comes back, he'll need a suit for all the dinner parties, right?

Nightingale is silent and continues to clean the telescope.

Mommy, this is the suit Daddy married you in! Yes, I recognize it from the picture. Mommy, you were so pretty, and Daddy was so handsome!

NIGHTINGALE: Child, this isn't some fancy suit. Daddy bought it second-hand. I borrowed my wedding gown.

STRANGIE: I know! But what counts is all the memories contained within and all the happiness that was brought forth! Right?

Strangie giggles in a silly way.

NIGHTINGALE: Enough. Don't giggle at things you don't understand.

Strangie freezes.

STRANGIE: Mommy, you've never talked to me like that before.

NIGHTINGALE: I hate how you're always the same.

STRANGIE: *(uneasy)* What is it, Mommy? Tell me what you want me to do, I'll work hard at it!

Nightingale shakes her head and sighs.

NIGHTINGALE: I can't hide it. I don't want you anymore.

STRANGIE: What? Why? *(desperate)* This can't be. Mommy, I'm the only one that believes in you! I'm the only one you can talk to about Penefere!

Nightingale looks out the window.
There is a shadow at the door. It's Stranger back from the sausage cart. She stays there, watching.

"Penefere was once a place like our Earth, full of the beauty of life, but after 20 million years, a serious crisis befell them." Right? "All life on Penefere started coming apart, disintegrating slowly into the atmosphere. So they came to our planet to ask for our help." Right? Right?

NIGHTINGALE: Stop it. Not another word. Listen to me, child. After the 15th of May, the day after tomorrow, no matter what happens, I will never see you again.

STRANGIE: *(desperate)* Why? Mommy, why?

NIGHTINGALE: I need to make some changes. I need to journey to a distant planet. It's called "Reality."

STRANGIE: Mommy, you're joking, right? I must have done something wrong. I promise I'll be good, I promise. Please don't send me away. I can do household chores for you, I can dance for you, I can . . .

Strangie dances around in desperation.

NIGHTINGALE: *(agitated)* My child, I'm sorry. Please go now!

Strangie struggles to work this out. Stranger listens intently at the door.

STRANGIE: *(resigned)* Mommy, can you tell it one more time, please?

NIGHTINGALE: What?

STRANGIE: The story of Penefere. Let me hear it again. It's such a beautiful story. Please let me hear it one more time.

Pause.

NIGHTINGALE: *(slowly)* On a distant planet, one day, all forms of life started to fracture, then disintegrate, like sand dissolving into the air. They didn't know why. They went all over the universe to find a solution, but no one could help them. Then they came to our planet, and observed that though we were faced with all sorts of difficult problems, behind everything was a mysterious force unknown to them that seemed to hold everything together.

Strangie packs up her things into a bundle on a stick, curtsies courteously, and leaves the apartment quietly, in tears.
Stranger enters to replace her, listening intently.

They discovered that most of the people on our planet led unfulfilling and discontented lives, and this led to separation. But there were a few people who were different. Those few had this amazing, special force that created boundless connections to everything else. This was the energy that most solidly connected life together. And so they attempted to create this element as a means to save their planet. But no matter how advanced their chemistry was, they failed to build it. They rationalized that it might be easier to target someone who had this thing inside, and extract it from that one special person.

Pause. Nightingale senses that the obedient Strangie has left, so she stops.

STRANGER: Dad?

Nightingale glances at Stranger. The two lock eyes. Nightingale knows it is Stranger she is dealing with, not Strangie.

NIGHTINGALE: Your dad was a regular joe.

STRANGER: Then why did they choose him?

NIGHTINGALE: Honest to goodness, I don't know. For the past 20 years, I've tried to form my own hypothesis.

STRANGER: So tell me.

NIGHTINGALE: I thought of the time right before your dad was taken. You were born not too long before. It was a special time. A simple time, but a time of wonder. We didn't have much money, and since your father was between jobs, he had time to spend at home. Every afternoon we would go to the riverside, with you in our arms. On the levee, we watched the afternoon sun transform the city into gold. There was no need for words. We just looked at each other. We filled ourselves with each other, with you, with the river, with the sunlight, until it got dark, and the moon rose. Then we would go home.

STRANGER: "The same moon, the same you, the same me . . ."

NIGHTINGALE: One day, by the river, it started to pour. We scurried for shelter, with you in our arms, but there was nowhere to go! I was laughing so hard, and so was your father. We ran, soaking wet, to this street vendor who had just cooked a batch of green onion pancakes. Those were the best green onion pancakes we ever had. The vendor kept telling us to get out of the rain, but we didn't want to!

Pause.

We became one with the rain. Me, David, the rain, and you. Then the sun came back out, and we became one with the sun. The moon rose, and we became one with the night.

Pause.

That was the night. I was looking out our window and saw several strange red spots flashing in the sky over the levee. The advance guard was already observing us. A week later, they came, and took us up. They were researching us, our family, trying to analyze what it was we had, what it was that melded the three of us together so that we became one, and what it was we had that connected us to the world, to the universe, to each moment. This is what they were searching for. They wanted to download that special something we had. That is why they took your dad.

I don't know. The rest of my life after that, I seem to be trying to find back the feeling of those days, that special state we were in. Maybe "happiness" is the word, but it doesn't say enough.

Pause.

STRANGER: So you say they're "downloading" that "special something" from Dad?

NIGHTINGALE: They're trying to.

STRANGER: From what part of him?

NIGHTINGALE: I have no idea. Maybe that's why it's taking so long.

They are quiet.

STRANGER: Is this what the aliens told you when you were up there?

NIGHTINGALE: You don't remember anything?

STRANGER: Remember?

NIGHTINGALE: That yellow-green ray of light from the window ... gravity was suddenly suspended! We just went up! *(reliving the moment)* HOW BRIGHT! How could it be so bright? I thought to myself, what kind of light bulb is that?

STRANGER: Yellow-green ... ?

Stranger seems to have a flash of memory, but she wonders whether it's just her imagination.

NIGHTINGALE: Stranger, do you believe me?

Stranger suddenly starts, as if "waking up," and realizes that she shouldn't be there. She heads out the door and exits.

Scene 8

An empty apartment near Nightingale's house. It is High's temporary studio for his "staged reality" video production. Money sits on a chair, wearing a standard astronaut's suit. Hawker, High, and Stranger stare at his costume.

The room is empty, apart from a chair and a clothes rack. Money's street clothes hang on the rack.
Money tries to stand up but falls over. High and Hawker go to help him.

HIGH AND HAWKER: Mr. Money . . .

MONEY: *(sitting back down)* It's so damn heavy.

HAWKER: Just bear with it, Money. It looks real cool.

HIGH: Oh, let's not forget the headgear.

Hawker gets a fishbowl-like astronaut's helmet from the rack. High and Hawker put the helmet over Money's head.

HAWKER: That's classic.

Money looks uncomfortable.

STRANGER: High, what the . . . ? He's suffocating! He can't breathe!

HAWKER: It's fogging up. Can't see his face.

High removes the helmet, and Money can finally breathe.

MONEY: I can't do this!

Money tries to take off his costume and head out. Hawker and High grab him and try to convince him to stay.

HIGH: Money!

HAWKER: Money! You're a real man!

Money returns reluctantly. Stranger vents her frustrations on High.

STRANGER: What the hell is this? Is your costume designer some amateur just fooling around with us? Well, he's seen *Toy Story* one time too many! And what's with the fish bowl?

HAWKER: Stranger, that's what anyone coming back from intergalactic space travel looks like!

STRANGER: Look. My mom's crazy, but she's not an idiot. You couldn't fool a child with this crap.

HIGH: You don't know what you're talking about! If he isn't wearing the helmet, she'll see his face, and that'll ruin everything!

MONEY: Look, money isn't an issue. If it's money you need, I got it. But you don't get it. I can't do this.

Money tries to take off his costume and head out, but is stopped by Hawker and High.

HAWKER: Hey, Money! Don't forget that Nightingale saved your life! You owe her!

MONEY: I'll find a way to repay her, but I can't pretend to be her husband coming from outer space to reunite with her!

Money gets up to leave. Hawker restrains him.

STRANGER: High, you've got to change this costume.

HIGH: *(thinking)* Hang on a second. When he comes back, should he be older or younger?

STRANGER: Younger, of course! Ever heard of "time dilation"? Ever read Einstein?

HAWKER: That's impressive, Stranger!

HIGH: Wrong! You're totally wrong! I heard Doggie say there's another possibility in the wormhole theory, that coming back from galactic travel, you actually get older.

STRANGER: Are you even thinking? He's accelerating, so time is being condensed! You dumbass!

HIGH: Who are you calling a dumbass? He's going through time dilation, right?

STRANGER: Right, so . . .

HIGH: So . . . so . . . anyhow, Doggie told me if the energy in the wormhole is reversed, then you get older! And that's where we have a chance to make the costume work!

HAWKER: Brilliant! Nobody knows what her father looks like now, so it's going to work! Mr. Director, weren't you going to hand out scripts?

HIGH: Right, let's go over the script. If we just follow the script, there shouldn't be any problems.

High hands out a one page script, which they all start to read.

STRANGER: Who's "Dud"?

HIGH: Where?

STRANGER: The second line. "Dud."

HIGH: Oh, typo. It's supposed to be "Dad."

STRANGER: My dad's a dud?

MONEY: I play a dud?

HIGH: My computer keyboard is crap, okay?

HAWKER: Typo, typo.

STRANGER: Typo? I thought you were professional! We're shooting
tomorrow, and now you give us a typo . . .

HAWKER: That's enough, Stranger. Let's listen to the director. Mr. Director, please summarize the script.

STRANGER: *(to High)* Hurry it up!

High pushes over the clothes rack.

HIGH: It fell by itself.

High picks up the rack.

>*(pointing to the corner)* Door to Nightingale's room. *(gesturing to
>clothes rack)* Windowsill. My hidden camera is right over there.

HAWKER: *(to Money)* Listen closely. We're talking camera angles.

HIGH: *(pointing to in front of the rack)* Remember this spot! When the
time comes, that's your place. Do you need a spike?

STRANGER: Spike my ass! That's my mother's living room!

HAWKER: No need for a spike. I can handle it.

MONEY: What's a spike?

HAWKER: Come on, Money, get into it! It's a duct tape mark so you know
where to stand!

MONEY: So where am I going to stand?

HAWKER: *(pointing to the ground)* Here!

MONEY: Okay.

HIGH: Okay?

MONEY: But how am I going to get there?

HIGH: Don't worry. My boys have already scouted the location.

HAWKER: As long as they've scouted the location, there's nothing to worry about!

STRANGER: Right. Nothing to worry about! Just fly in from the window! Right, High? Hey, start teaching them the proper technique right now! Spread your arms wide, flap, and jump! Jump!

HIGH: Just keep quiet if you don't know what you're talking about.

STRANGER: I don't know what I'm talking about? You didn't even think this through. How the heck are you going to get to my mom's window on the fourth floor? I get it. Your boys erect a scaffold from street level, without being seen or heard, and then pretend they're cleaning the windows and climb up to my mother's windowsill. Then . . . they just jump in! Simple! Just train them in rock climbing first!

HIGH: Actors, don't worry about tech! I have everything set up—my boys are working on a film shoot that has a lot of night scenes, and my boys can, uh, borrow a 5K instrument that is brighter than daylight!

MONEY: So what's the deal? We ride those light beams into the room? You're all crazy! Nobody in this room is sober!

Money gets up to leave. Hawker restrains him.

HAWKER: Hey Money! Please! High, settle down and talk about the script, please!

Money gets pulled back again. Hawker signals to High, telling him to continue explaining the script.

HIGH: Okay. To do a good job on this script, you have to understand the behavioral patterns of aliens. According to Stranger's mom, before they arrived, there was a strong ray of light from the window. Then, without any transition, they just appeared.

HAWKER: Without any transition?

HIGH: Which means her mom didn't see how they came in, they just did. According to results compiled by my research team, 80% of extraterrestrial contacts of the so-called ET3 type occur this way.

HAWKER: Very impressive.

STRANGER: What he means by his "research team" is that he read this little booklet called "I Met an Alien" that he bought online.

HIGH: Shit, do you guys want to do this or not?! We can stop right here. I can jump jump jump the hell off the building and be splattered into a thousand little pieces!

High rushes through the clothes rack, as if he is jumping off the building, and writhes on the floor.

MONEY: ENOUGH!

Pause. Everyone is shocked. Money stands.

Be a real man, High! Do it the right way! We have a serious morale problem here. We lack something essential: SPIRIT! Let's go get something to drink and start over. Damn!

All exit, following Money.

Scene 9

On the street. Nightingale is selling watches to a Customer.

NIGHTINGALE: *(to Customer)* It's like this, Miss. Time comes in two forms. Once in your life, you must have felt . . .

CUSTOMER 6: *(answering her cell phone)* Hello . . . ? Oh, hi . . .

The Customer leaves. Nightingale continues talking, to the air, to herself.

NIGHTINGALE: *(finishing her sentence)* . . . the cessation of time, when your soul is shattered to pieces and lying on the ground . . . Right?

Enter the Mystery Lady. She is fashionably dressed, but with heavy makeup and a trace of the hard life in the red-light district. She picks up a watch at Nightingale's stall. She speaks with a Vietnamese accent.

MYSTERY LADY: Miss . . . This watch . . . how come the hands aren't moving?

NIGHTINGALE: *(rapidly and annoyed)* Time comes in two forms, one goes forward, and the other is stopped, frozen. I'm guessing you probably aren't interested. Goodbye.

Nightingale tries to take the watch back, but the Mystery Lady insists.

MYSTERY LADY: Wait. *(looking at the watch)* What did you say about . . . a shattered soul?

NIGHTINGALE: Huh?

MYSTERY LADY: Who would have thought? I always dreamed of a watch like this, but never thought someone would actually make one. Taiwanese businessmen are so clever!

NIGHTINGALE: Miss, are you from abroad?

Mystery Lady is a bit uneasy.

Take it easy, Miss, don't worry about me. What I'm doing isn't exactly legal, either.

MYSTERY LADY: Not legal? I'm legal! I'm . . . I once was legal.

Mystery Lady grows sad.

Are there three?

NIGHTINGALE: Three?

MYSTERY LADY: Time coming in three modes?

NIGHTINGALE: One that goes forward, and two that are in limbo?

MYSTERY LADY: "Lim-bo"?

NIGHTINGALE: It means stopped.

MYSTERY LADY: *(nods)* Yes. Stopped.

NIGHTINGALE: So the second is . . .

MYSTERY LADY: When I left my home. Eight thirty-one. The car drove around the bend, and I lost sight of my home.

NIGHTINGALE: And the third?

MYSTERY LADY: Two twenty-nine.

NIGHTINGALE: A.M.? In the middle of the night? You left home again?

MYSTERY LADY: I left the last family I had in the world. Since then I've been a wanderer, wandering around the universe.

Silence. The Mystery Lady suddenly starts, as if "waking up" from her reverie.

Sorry, miss, I'm standing on the street, rambling away, and you are actually listening to me! Thank you! You're a good person.

Mystery Lady turns to leave.

NIGHTINGALE: Wait, miss! We do carry it.

MYSTERY LADY: Carry what?

NIGHTINGALE: A watch with three kinds of time.

MYSTERY LADY: Really?

NIGHTINGALE: Yes! I rarely display it, but I have some in storage.

MYSTERY LADY: Really?

NIGHTINGALE: Usually it takes long enough to explain two. Very few customers need three.

MYSTERY LADY: Can I order one?

NIGHTINGALE: Of course.

MYSTERY LADY: *(reaching for her purse)* How much is it?

NIGHTINGALE: No need to pay now. Give me your phone number, I'll call you when I find it and you can come pick it up.

The Mystery Lady writes her phone number on a piece of paper.
Police whistles.

MYSTERY LADY: *(instinctively)* Cops! Quick! Run!

Nightingale and Mystery Lady start running in different directions.

Scene 10

The production apartment. Everyone has script in hand. Money drinks from a bottle of booze. Hawker enters in his costume: a shiny silver plastic short skirt.

HAWKER: Uh . . . Mr. Director, I'm not one to voice strong opinions, but this costume . . .

HIGH: Oh, it's not done yet. Doggie mentioned there was a special way to wear it.

HAWKER: So everything is all right?

HIGH: Don't worry. I'll tell you the details when I find out. Let's go. Places . . .

Everyone in their places, ready for rehearsal. High points to Hawker. Hawker reads from the script in a heightened theatrical fashion.

HAWKER: ATTENTION! HUMANS! I COME FROM A FARAWAY PLANET! A FARAWAY PLANET! I!

HIGH: Uh, Hawker, can you just read the lines, please?

HAWKER: Huh?

STRANGER: Don't repeat anything. Thank you.

HIGH: Just read what's on the page.

HAWKER: You didn't think that was good?

HIGH: No, look, you're just the pro—*(stops before finishing the word "prologue")* profound herald who sets the tone for the whole piece. You're very important.

HAWKER: Very important.

STRANGER: So it has to be short and sweet.

HAWKER: Short and sweet. So you're saying I was overly emotional just now?

HIGH: Somewhat.

HAWKER: Well, I am an emotional person. But that's okay, I can make adjustments. *(thinking it over)* Got it! I think I know what you want.

HIGH: Please then. Action!

Hawker takes a moment to gather himself, like an experienced actor entering a role.

HAWKER: *(in a monotonous drone)* Attention humans I come from a faraway planet on this day 20 years ago we took your husband to our distant planet Pefenere . . .

High buries his head in his hands.

STRANGER: *(correcting him)* "Penefere."

HAWKER: Huh?

STRANGER: The name of the planet is "Penefere."

HAWKER: Look, if it's just a small detail, don't stop me, OK? I was just getting into it, and now . . . How am I going to rechannel that?

HIGH: Sorry, continue.

HAWKER: *(continuing in a monotone)* On this day 20 years ago we took your husband to our distant planet . . .

HIGH: Uh, Hawker, can you insert a bit more emotion?

HAWKER: Are you talking about one bit or two bits? You have to be specific.

HIGH: *(with his thumb and forefinger)* Just this much, OK?

HAWKER: You got it!

Hawker continues. He adds a touch of punctuation and pitch to his robotic delivery.

We thank you for your patience. Today, we bring him back to reunite with you for a short while.

HIGH: Good. Now the lights intensify! Brighter than daylight! *(pointing)* Point in that direction!

HAWKER: *(pointing)* Humans! Cherish this short reunion! *(jumping out of character)* Can I add that sentence? It just came to me.

STRANGER: Sure, whatever.

HAWKER: I felt this sense of heroic tragedy!

HIGH: Fine, fine. Money, you're up!

Money is totally disoriented.

HAWKER: Money, you can do it!

MONEY: I still don't know how I'm supposed to get here.

HIGH: The lights will be so bright, Hawker will distract her, and you'll just walk in the door without her noticing. She'll look up and you'll just "be there."

MONEY: Does that make sense?

HIGH: Completely. I assure you it'll be totally believable. Let's do it.

High plays a science fiction sound effect from his phone to underscore the scene. Money is in position, script in hand. Pause.

HAWKER: Oh my god, I'm tearing up . . . !

HIGH: Shhh!

Money just stands there.

STRANGER: Say something!

MONEY: Wait a second . . . where is she going to be?

HIGH: What? Her? She's wherever she is.

MONEY: What do you mean: "She's wherever she is"?

HAWKER: Money, get into it! Look!

Hawker pulls up a chair and extends his fist to show where Nightingale's head would be.

Say your lines!

MONEY: To . . . ?

HAWKER: *(waving his fist)* This is Nightingale's head. That's how the pros do it. *(to Stranger)* It's called "establishing the sight line." You've got to read *TV Guide*, man!

Stranger shakes her head. High instructs her to sit on the chair.

HIGH: Stranger, take the place of your mom. Okay, Money, enter on sound.

Stranger sits down in the chair with her script. Money looks at Stranger, and then the script. Sound effects again.

Pause. Money stops the action again.

MONEY: Sorry. What should I call her?

HIGH: What do you mean what should you call her?

MONEY: It doesn't say in the script. I can't just make something up. Couples have pet names, nicknames . . . if I don't know, I could say the wrong thing!

HAWKER: Impressive!

HIGH: *(to Stranger)* What did your dad call your mom?

STRANGER: How would I know?

HAWKER: Don't panic. Allow me to conjecture: *(thinking out loud)* Nightingale. Nightie. Gale. Honey, Darling. Sweetie. Mommy . . . *(pause)* I recommend just mumbling "Hey." That's what most couples call each other.

MONEY: So I should just call her—"Hey"?

HIGH: That's why we don't have it in the script. Just don't call her anything.

MONEY: The real problem is, even if you had it written down I couldn't remember it. I can't remember all these lines.

HAWKER: Look, Money, I've heard that if pros have trouble with their lines, they write them down on their palms.

MONEY: I couldn't sink that low.

HAWKER: Just write down the key points! Don't you know that's why Jackie Chan does this all the time?

Hawker strikes a kung fu pose, palm facing his face.

HIGH: Don't you worry! I've got a plan, in case, I mean in case there's a problem or anything, just smile and say "Happy Anniversary!" Then you have a chance to get your bearings. Look, Money, the script is only a general idea, something to refer to, but you can improvise at any point and say what you want!

MONEY: I can what?

HAWKER: Come on, Money, don't you know what improvisation is? It's extemporaneous, spontaneous expression! Just say what you feel! Walk around the room, gather inspiration. What's happening in your mind? She hasn't seen you in 20 long years! Now you're back after passage through black holes and meteor rings and all that, so you feel all sorts of things! Jeez! This is the good stuff, and you don't get it! And they don't want me to do it!

Money drinks from his bottle.

HIGH: Stop it. Come on, one more time!

Sound effects again. Money settles down and starts reading from his script.

MONEY: *(reading)* "I'm back."

STRANGER: *(reading)* "You're back."

Stranger gestures to High what a stupid script it is. High gestures back.

MONEY: *(reading)* "I couldn't wait to see you."

STRANGER: *(reading)* "I can feel it."

MONEY: *(reading)* "I can feel it too. Your emotions . . . your waiting. . . . so many years, nobody ever believed you, nobody ever understood you. I know it's been difficult for you, so difficult . . ."

Stranger listens carefully and, despite herself, is drawn in.

STRANGER: Yes, it's been so difficult . . .

MONEY: *(reading)* "It's been 20 years. Are you well?"

Silence. All look at Stranger.

STRANGER: You ask: am I well?

Pause. She is not looking at the script.

That planet you're on, why is it so distant? Why can't I see you when I want to? Whisper to you? Talk about my feelings? Dad, I'm grown up, and I never knew you.

All are surprised. Money is very confused.

And what did you teach me? Why have you taught me that life is wandering? Why am I following in your footsteps, wandering, wan-

dering around Taipei, wandering to Shanghai . . . ? Is Shanghai any
closer to Penefere?

Money disconnects.

MONEY: Happy Anniversary! What am I supposed to say to that?

HAWKER: Improvise! Improvise!

Stranger throws the script down and stands to leave.

STRANGER: We've all gone mad! As long as we're all mad, we'll be fine!
Tomorrow at 11:42 we'll do just this. Bring it!

Stranger rushes off. High drinks Money's booze.

Scene 11

*The night of May 15. Nightingale has changed into a nice but simple dress after
making all the preparations, and is waiting quietly at the window. The table is
set for dinner for two.*
Stranger stands at the door, watching Nightingale.
Nightingale sees Stranger.

NIGHTINGALE: Good girl.

Stranger doesn't speak.

You knew to be home early today.

Stranger is still silent.

Actually child, you don't need to be here with me. Of course, it's best
if your father can see you when he comes back, but if . . . you know
what I mean. If he doesn't . . . *(pause)* I think it's better I handle this
alone.

STRANGER: Mom, it's me.

NIGHTINGALE: I know.

STRANGER: Then don't call me "child."

NIGHTINGALE: Why can't I call you "child"? Aren't you my child?

STRANGER: I'm not "her," OK? Can't you tell the difference? I'm not "her" and never will be! Mom! Wake up! Face the world! Stop hiding in your fantasies! Look clearly at who you're talking to! It's me! ME!

NIGHTINGALE: Of course I know it's you! Don't you think I know the difference? But YOU look at ME, look at my life. Don't I have the right to some fantasy?

STRANGER: But you can't live in a total illusion!

NIGHTINGALE: I know perfectly well what is and what isn't. I created "her." She appears when I want her to, and leaves when I don't want to see her. She's not like you, she never just shows up randomly on a whim!

STRANGER: "On a whim"?

NIGHTINGALE: You're never there when I need you the most. Naturally every time you show up it's on a whim!

STRANGER: You're the one who's never been there for me when I needed you the most. But even so, I didn't create another "you"!

NIGHTINGALE: That's because you're too lazy!

STRANGER: Okay, so now you need "her," where is she? Is her name Strangie? Call her! Where are you? Are you in the cradle? Come out! Come out! Oh, here she comes! *(cartoonlike)* "Mommy, I'm here for you. Mommy, I love you. Mommy, the whole world loves you." Where is she? At the most crucial moment she has abandoned you! And who's here? Me! The real me!

Nightingale controls herself. Stranger tries to calm down.

Mom, let's not do this. I'm here for you. This is an important day.

A cell phone rings. In the production apartment, High answers the phone. He is alone.

HIGH: *(to the phone)* Hello? Doggie? Yea, no problem . . . they're all in place. It's going to be great . . . What? The director changed his shooting schedule for tonight? . . . He needs the 5K at 11:30? How can you do this to me? I haven't even bitched at you for the crappy costume you made! We had to go online to fix it! . . . What? You want me to start early? Dude, don't mess with my masterpiece now! No, I am not nervous. What? . . . It's now or never? Then . . . OK! I'll start now! Nice going, Doggie. What a pal!

High hangs up. He is at a loss.

> *(into his walkie-talkie)* Attention all units. Due to circumstances beyond our control, Project AG1142 will start ahead of schedule. Everyone, standby. Now. Ready? Go.

In Nightingale's apartment, weird sound effects suddenly arise. A strong ray of light shoots in from the window. Nightingale and Stranger react to the light, which grows stronger and stronger.

NIGHTINGALE: It's happening!

STRANGER: *(embarrassed)* Mom, it's all . . .

NIGHTINGALE: Hush, child!

Smoke pours in. Hawker appears, wearing an alien helmet that hides his face. He looks like a child, actually kneeling so the short skirt he was wearing in rehearsal touches the ground, and his height is compromised. He gets into position laboriously.

HAWKER: *(robotic, with slight emotion)* Attention! Humans! I come from a faraway planet, a distant star. On this day 20 years ago, we took your husband to our faraway planet Pe—*(thinking hard)*—NEfere! . . . *(sighing in relief)* Whew! *(robotic again)* We thank you for your patience. Today, we bring him back for a short reunion. *(solemnly)* Humans! Cherish this short reunion!

Lights flash. Hawker "steps" aside, almost forgetting he should be kneeling. The light grows brighter. The silhouette of a man: Money stands by the window. He has on a long wig and clothes that look like they were borrowed from a Greek tragedy or a Gandalf costume bought online.

NIGHTINGALE: *(navigating the fog)* David, is that you?

MONEY: I'm back.

NIGHTINGALE: Is that really you? I can't see.

MONEY: *(delivering his lines faithfully)* I . . . couldn't wait to see you.

Nightingale looks at her watch.

NIGHTINGALE: You're early.

Pause. This is unexpected. Money stays faithful to the script.

MONEY: I can feel it, too.

Nightingale moves closer to Money.

NIGHTINGALE: Your looks have changed . . .

MONEY: What?

Pause.

Money struggles to look at the lines written on his hand.

Your emotions . . . your waiting . . . so many years, nobody believed you, nobody understood you. I know it's been difficult for you, so difficult . . .

Silence. Nightingale gazes out the window.

You're not saying anything? Then . . . Happy Anniversary!

No reaction from Nightingale. Money checks his palm again.

It's been 20 years. Are you well?

NIGHTINGALE: Me? Look. See for yourself.

MONEY: I'll look . . . around the room . . . I'll walk around the room and gather inspiration . . .

Money takes his flask from his pocket and drinks. He walks around, looking at the surroundings. He sees the clock.

That clock . . . it really stopped.

NIGHTINGALE: Right at that moment.

MONEY: I thought time had only stopped for me.

NIGHTINGALE: Eleven forty-two . . .

Money falls deep into his own thoughts.

MONEY: Four twenty-seven . . .

Pause.

I didn't dare think about you.

NIGHTINGALE: *(to herself)* No matter how far away you are, I think about you.

MONEY: Physical distance is nothing compared to how far apart our hearts are. What can I say? I'm so sorry. I just left . . . just left.

NIGHTINGALE: Don't be so hard on yourself. There are so many things in life that we have no control over.

MONEY: I know that nothing I say can help, but, what else can I say? I'M SORRY.

Nightingale seems to have figured out what's going on, but she chooses to be silent. She looks out the window. The bright light is still shining in. Money looks at Nightingale's silhouette.

How are you doing over there?

NIGHTINGALE: Over where?

Money is completely caught up in his own emotions. It is as if he sees his wife in silhouette.

MONEY: Over there. Where you are is such a distant place. Farther than any map can show. Farther than time! Farther than space! I just left you . . . over there. I MADE A CLEAN BREAK, LIKE A REAL MAN, AND LEFT!

Pause. Hawker is nervous. He thinks of interfering, but refrains.

It's so cold. Over there.

Nightingale looks at Money sympathetically.

NO! OVER HERE! IT'S COLDER HERE! It's so cold! So distant! I'M IN THE MOST DISTANT PLACE IN THE UNIVERSE! OUTSIDE OF TIME AND SPACE, I AM A WANDERER IN THE VOID! TIME HAS STOPPED! TIME HAS DIED! I CAN NEVER GO BACK! NEVER!

Money breaks down and sobs. Nightingale comes over to comfort him.

NIGHTINGALE: Hush, hush now.

Nightingale cuddles Money, who falls into her arms like a baby. Money grabs Nightingale's hand.

MONEY: Lillian . . .

NIGHTINGALE: What?

MONEY: I'm sorry. Other than that, there's nothing else to say. I can die a million deaths but still won't be able to take this back. Can you forgive me?

Nightingale pats Money on the head.

NIGHTINGALE: Yes, I can. You should take it easy. Just go home. And hold off on the booze.

Hawker sees that the situation has gotten out of hand and signals. Music and strong ray of light come in. Hawker "walks" on his knees, wobbling into the spotlight.

HAWKER: *(improvising)* ATTENTION! HUMANS! THE THIRD WINDOW OF THE UNIVERSE IS CLOSING! WE MUST RETURN WHILE WE STILL HAVE THE WINDS OF THE UNIVERSE IN OUR SAILS! FARE THEE WELL! FARE THEE WELL!

Smoke. Hawker grabs Money. The bright light grows brighter, and Nightingale covers her face with her hand.
Bright light out. Hawker and Money are nowhere to be seen. The room is back to normal. Nightingale looks out the window and at the clock, and then at her watch.

STRANGER: Mom . . .

NIGHTINGALE: Shh . . . , don't say a word.

STRANGER: I need to explain something to you.

NIGHTINGALE: No need.

STRANGER: We had good intentions. That guy, he . . .

NIGHTINGALE: He looked like he was in pain. It was good for him to let that out.

STRANGER: What?

NIGHTINGALE: I hope he's okay.

Pause. Nightingale hugs Stranger.

STRANGER: Mom, will I ever have the chance to talk to you like that?

NIGHTINGALE: Anytime, child . . . but not now. Child, what time do you have?

STRANGER: Eleven thirty-seven.

NIGHTINGALE: Five more minutes. Can you stay here with me?

STRANGER: I'm here.

Nightingale hugs Stranger.

Scene 12

The production apartment. High sits in front of his video monitor, rewinding the tape. Hawker enters in street clothes. He breathes a sigh of relief.

HAWKER: How was it?

HIGH: Not bad.

HAWKER: Got it all?

HIGH: Check it out!

High plays the tape for Hawker.

HAWKER'S RECORDED VOICE: Attention! Humans! I come from a faraway planet . . .

HAWKER: *(pleased)* Look! I remembered to face the camera.

HIGH: Good.

HAWKER: That last part, man, that took some sort of inspiration!

HIGH: Exactly, spontaneity!

HAWKER: Did you see? Mr. Money, man, he screwed up. Did you see? It was getting real good, real moving, and then he digressed into some shit that I couldn't follow. And then he called her "Lillian," and I thought, man, we're done for! I almost shouted "Happy Anniversary!"

HIGH: That's the nature of art. It's live, cutting, bleeding, exposing all of our naked scars, leading us to suffering and pain. What you saw was life—cut up and served to us! The only problem is: I thought it was Nightingale who was supposed to break down, not Money!

HAWKER: What's the problem?

HIGH: She's the lead! How the hell am I going to edit the scene? Let me show you the live feed.

High switches the video source input. Hawker looks at the monitor.

HAWKER: You're still shooting?

HIGH: You bet I am. Now comes the good stuff: Now they break out into their ugly real selves, and start to claw at each other's wounds.

HAWKER: What?

HIGH: If Stranger were smart enough, what she'd do now is become hysterical and start smashing things up. That would be perfect.

In Nightingale's room, it is as if Stranger can hear High talking. She approaches the cassette player, where the camera is hidden.

NIGHTINGALE: What are you doing, child?

In the apartment, Hawker and High watch Stranger approach the lens with growing trepidation.

HIGH: Stranger, what the hell . . . ?

STRANGER: High, I'm out. From here on in, you can play with yourself!

Stranger grabs the hidden lens and rips it out.

HIGH AND HAWKER: *(in unison)* Damn! . . .

Hawker and High stumble over each other as they scramble out of the production apartment.

NIGHTINGALE: Stranger!

STRANGER: It's nothing, Mom. You were right. I don't understand men. I don't understand a lot of things.

NIGHTINGALE: *(suddenly)* Child . . . what time is it?

Stranger checks her watch.

STRANGER: Eleven forty-one.

NIGHTINGALE: Wrong. My watch has 11:44 already. It's over.

STRANGER: Mom . . .

Nightingale looks intently out the window. Then she sits in the chair and despairs.

NIGHTINGALE: It's over. Gone. Forever. Your dad's not coming back.

Stranger tries to comfort Nightingale.

STRANGER: Mom, just forget it.

NIGHTINGALE: *(calmly)* Child, good girl. Remember what your mom tells you: Happiness isn't something you sit around waiting for. You have to work to find it. Mom never worked hard enough.

STRANGER: Mom . . .

Nightingale stops Stranger gently.

NIGHTINGALE: Child, can you please let your mom be alone?

STRANGER: No, I'm here. I'm right here for you.

NIGHTINGALE: There are some things in life that you have to face by yourself.

STRANGER: I understand, Mom.

Stranger exits.
Nightingale lingers by the window.
She takes a bedsheet and covers the telescope.
She turns on the cassette player and listens to music. She sits and, in torment, closes her eyes.
Lights fade out.

Scene 13

Through the darkness, a yellow-green light shines into the window.
In the semidarkness, David, Nightingale's husband, appears in the room. He is still in his 20s, dressed like the day he was taken. Nightingale is asleep at the table.
David gazes at the sleeping Nightingale. He looks around the room. He sees the telescope, clock, and cradle. He pulls a blanket from the cradle and drapes it over Nightingale.

Nightingale wakes. They gaze at each other. It is quiet, so quiet, like a dream.

DAVID: Night.

NIGHTINGALE: David.

DAVID: I'm back, as promised.

NIGHTINGALE: But how is this possible? Were my calculations wrong?

DAVID: It's good to be back, Night. Everything here's the same. You're the same. The room is the same.

NIGHTINGALE: It's all different. The world has changed.

DAVID: Let me have a good look at you, Night.

NIGHTINGALE: My face. It's all wrinkles.

DAVID: I don't care.

David turns Nightingale to face him.

NIGHTINGALE: David . . .

She touches his face. They gaze at each other a long moment.

DAVID: How have you been all these years?

NIGHTINGALE: All right. I sell things at a stall.

DAVID: On the street . . . ?

David grows sad.

NIGHTINGALE: It's not what you think. There's a certain freedom there that you don't have at other jobs. I kind of enjoy it.

DAVID: Stranger . . . ?

NIGHTINGALE: She's grown up.

DAVID: I miss her so much.

NIGHTINGALE: She was just here. She . . . she's good. She's talented. She's going to be a film director.

DAVID: She got that from you.

Nightingale turns to the food on the table.

NIGHTINGALE: I prepared some things you like. The food is getting cold. I haven't cooked in so long.

They sit down to dinner. David savors a bite.

DAVID: Delicious.

NIGHTINGALE: I can cook for you every day now if you like.

Pause.

DAVID: Night . . . I can't stay.

NIGHTINGALE: What?

DAVID: They treat me well up there, and they've always felt sorry for what they did to you. But, Night . . .

NIGHTINGALE: David, you're home.

DAVID: My work isn't finished. I can only stay a moment.

NIGHTINGALE: Only a moment. Only a moment. I guess that's how this universe works. You're away 20 years, and then we meet, for only a moment, and you're gone again. All of our dreams come true. Then, as if we're in another dream, we have to stumble on till we wake again.

Pause.

DAVID: If you saw them, you would understand what I need to do. They live under the most terrible conditions. They can't breathe. Nothing grows. Everything is slowly disassembling, becoming fragments, becoming sand. There's no reversing the process. It's happening to all the scientists that work on me. They're all . . . fragments of themselves. If one person's sacrifice can help them, it's worth it.

Pause.

Every day they hook me up to countless electrodes. They download things from me with the greatest urgency. I can only move the thumb and ring finger of my left hand. Sand is everywhere. I play with the grains of sand that blow into my hand, and let them sift through my fingers to the floor. With every grain that falls from my hand, I call your name.

NIGHTINGALE: I hear you.

DAVID: Every grain?

NIGHTINGALE: Every grain.

DAVID: The heart is faster than anything in the universe.

David brushes a grain of sand from his hand onto Nightingale's.

> Let this grain of sand from a distant star remind you, Night: as long as we truly live, time doesn't exist.

Nightingale takes the grain of sand.
> *Dim yellow-green light on the window. David turns to look.*

> I'm sorry, Night. It's time.

They embrace. As long as they can. Bright light pours into the window.

NIGHTINGALE: David . . . take me with you! Take me!

DAVID: I can't. You wouldn't survive the journey.

NIGHTINGALE: There must be a way! They can surely find a way . . . !

DAVID: It's not possible, Night . . .

NIGHTINGALE: Nothing is impossible! David . . . take me with you! Now!

The light is blinding.
> *Lights fade out.*

Scene 14

Lights up. The street. Only one stall. It is Nightingale's, but Hawker is tending to it.

HAWKER: *(peddling his goods)* "Time comes in two forms!" Don't be shy! Have a look!

Stranger enters with a camera in her hand. She is filming Hawker.

> Hey, Stranger.

STRANGER: Hawker.

HAWKER: Still shooting?

STRANGER: Tying up loose ends. Oh right, Hawker, I have a friend who's going to shoot a short feature. Interested?

HAWKER: You should know better than to ask.

STRANGER: I thought your dream was to be an actor.

HAWKER: Dreams are for dreaming about. Your mom left her stall to me. That's enough for me. There's no miracle to life. What's yours is yours. What ain't just ain't.

STRANGER: *(fumbling in her pockets)* Oh, I almost forgot. I finally deciphered the writing on this slip of paper my mom left. It's the number of a customer who inquired about a special watch. So I called her, and she's going to come and pick it up.

Stranger hands a watch to Hawker. Hawker examines it.

HAWKER: Time comes in three forms?

STRANGER: Right.

HAWKER: Never sold one of these. How much is it?

STRANGER: She didn't say.

A Customer approaches Hawker.

CUSTOMER 7: Any chance this one comes with a gold band?

HAWKER: You want this in gold? I think I have one. Hold on, it's in my car. *(to Stranger)* Take over for me.

Hawker exits.
The Mystery Lady enters, and sees Stranger.

MYSTERY LADY: Miss . . .

STRANGER: Yeah?

MYSTERY LADY: Did I talk to you on the phone?

STRANGER: Oh right, I got it for you.

Stranger gives the Mystery Lady the watch.

MYSTERY LADY: *(grateful)* Thank you! I thought you had forgotten.

STRANGER: Sorry for the delay. My mom gave instructions, but it's my fault for the delay, I didn't know whether you still wanted it or not.

MYSTERY LADY: That's okay, as long as I've got it now. *(examining the watch)* Wow, it's really got three hands! How much is it?

STRANGER: You have to ask the boss. He'll be right back.

Hawker enters with the gold watch.

HAWKER: *(to the Customer)* Look, sparkling gold!

CUSTOMER 7: Great!

HAWKER: *(handing off the watch)* Have a look.

Stranger points to Hawker.

STRANGER: *(to the Mystery Lady)* He's here.

Mystery Lady approaches Hawker.

MYSTERY LADY: *(to Hawker)* How much is this one?

HAWKER: That one? It's a special order. But I'll give you a good discount . . .

Hawker looks at the Mystery Lady. He is stunned. The Mystery Lady is stunned to see Hawker, too. They look at each other. Their bodies freeze in a pose of amazement, and stay frozen.
All other pedestrians, as well as the Customer, are also frozen.
Stranger sets her camera on the ground downstage, stands in front of it, and talks to it.

STRANGER: After that night, I never saw my mom again. In her room, I found a note that read:

"Stranger—Penefere isn't as far away as you think. Be well. Mom"

Hawker and I went looking all over for her. We searched like madmen. We visited every police station, and every hospital morgue . . .

I was at the end of my rope when, one day, I received a postcard. It had a tropical theme. There was no date or message on it. The beach and palm trees made me think of some island in the South Pacific. I took a closer look at the postmark. It read "Penefere." I searched for that place on the map, but couldn't find it. I went to the post office and asked them. They didn't know, either. They said that their job is to deliver the mail. Where it comes from is none of their business.

On closer look, I discovered two small figures in the distance. I recognized my mom, and a guy that looked a lot like my dad when he was younger. They were smiling, their radiance glowed from the postcard.

On closer examination, I saw that the "beach" was just a big poster board, behind which was a dark, menacing sky and swirling sand.

Then I looked again. The figures weren't there anymore, nor was the dark sky, or sand. Was it my imagination? Or had the Third Window of something or whatever opened in my mind, offering me a moment's glimpse?

Who knows? Maybe there really is a place called Penefere. And maybe it does have three moons. And maybe, on that distant star, within the swirling sands, you really can find something called happiness.

Lights fade out.

The End

Like Shadows

CHARACTERS

BRUCE, a middle-aged businessman from the San Francisco Bay Area, also seen in his 20s, second-generation Chinese American
PENELOPE, wife of Bruce, middle-aged, also seen in her 20s, Asian American
AI, daughter of Bruce and Penelope, a melancholy teenager
ALEJANDRO, a middle-aged Silicon Valley high-tech employee, neighbor of Bruce, also seen in his 20s, Latino
JOHANNA, Alejandro's wife, an award-winning real estate agent
EDIE, daughter of Alejandro and Johanna, an eccentric teenager
BOSS of a motorcycle shop, an old hippie, who could either be totally deluded or a true spiritual guru
V, abandoned imaginary friend of Edie's, a punk teenager
AH-FOK, middle-aged waiter at the Crystal Dragon Restaurant, also seen in his 20s, Chinese American
MUSICIAN'S SOUL, the soul of a jazz musician who sold out to Hollywood
POLICEWOMAN
POLICEMAN
RIDERS of motorcycles
WAITRESS at the Crystal Dragon Restaurant

Pedestrians, Photographer, Delivery Man, Patient, Funeral Home Representative

SETTING

Silicon Valley and other places in California, both now and 20 years ago

Like Shadows was first performed on December 21, 2007, at the National The-atre, Taipei, Taiwan, in Mandarin Chinese, directed by Stan Lai, produced by Performance Workshop, based on an earlier English version *Stories for the Dead* created and performed at Stanford University in 2006, with the kind support of the Institute for Diversity in the Arts, and the Drama Department of Stanford University:

Cast:
Yin Jao-der as Bruce
Ismene Ting as Penelope
Zhu Zhi-Ying as Ai
Chu Chung-heng as Alejandro
Hsu Yen-ling as Johanna
Stephanie Lai as Edie
Li Chien-chang as Boss
Bowie Tsang as V, movie audience, voice of young Ai
Hugh Shih as Rider, Policeman, movie audience, art therapy case
Ethan Wei as Rider, A-Fok, movie audience, Delivery Man
Vanessa Liu as Policewoman, Rider, Waitress, movie audience
Hank Pan as Musician's Soul

Scenic and Multimedia Design by Mathias Woo
Lighting Design by Michael Lee-Zen Chien
Costume and Style Design by Suzan Ting
Video Imagery by John Wong
Original and Impromptu Music by Hank Pan and Stan Lai

Produced by Nai-Chu Ding
Executive Produced by Hsieh Ming-Chang

Photo: *Like Shadows*, National Theatre, Taipei, Taiwan, 2007, Scene 22. Photo by Franco Wang.

Prologue

Musician's Soul is playing a mournful saxophone riff—"Song for Penelope." He (or she) wears a tuxedo and is barefoot.

The characters cross the stage in a silent parade, as if they have just come out of a funeral.

V appears in a spotlight. She addresses the audience.

V: Hi. My name is V. As in the alphabet. Actually I don't know if I'm the right one to be telling this story, because I . . . well, let's just say that I'm invisible. Which isn't saying much, because a lot of us are invisible. That's not my claim to fame, or even to existence. It's just that this story is interesting to me from my invisible little platform where I sit and watch the world, seeing how things unfold, you know, the cycle of cause, condition, and circumstance.

V looks at the characters walking across the stage and points at individuals as she continues.

Anyway, this is the story of a guy named Bruce Lee. Not that one. Though this one was pushed to excel by the pressure that came with his name. So, Bruce Lee Wang, which was his full name . . . Hold on. Maybe this is not his story. This story is really about his wife Penelope, and, *(thinking)* well, maybe not. Anyway, Bruce and Penelope had a daughter named Ai, which is Chinese for "Love," who was friends with their neighbor's daughter Edie, who was my friend, and . . . Hey, I'm totally messing this up. And since I'm invisible, you didn't hear this.

Pedestrians leave the stage.

Scene 1

Alejandro and Johanna's living room. Dusk. Bruce, a middle-aged Chinese American man, sits on an armchair.

Alejandro and Johanna, middle-aged neighbors of Bruce, enter silently, downtrodden. They are dressed in black. Their daughter Edie, a teenager, follows. Alejandro sits down on the sofa, as does Edie.

BRUCE: How's it going, guys? Any suggestions for dinner?

JOHANNA: There's some leftover pad thai in the fridge, but . . .

BRUCE: I'm sorry, but that pad thai doesn't look so good. And by the way, you don't have anything to drink in there.

JOHANNA: You know, we don't have anything to drink in there.

BRUCE: That's what I was saying.

JOHANNA: Is water OK?

ALEJANDRO: Water's okay.

BRUCE: I'll pass.

Edie gets up to leave.

JOHANNA: Edie, don't go. Stay for dinner.

EDIE: I have to talk to Ai.

JOHANNA: *(sudden explosion)* NO! YOU ARE NOT GOING OUT NOW.

Edie exits. Johanna takes a look at Alejandro.

BRUCE: *(laughing)* You don't have anything to eat. How can you expect her to stay?

JOHANNA: I'll go heat up the pad thai.

Bruce shakes his head in disdain. Johanna exits to the kitchen. Alejandro stands and goes to the window, gazing pensively out.

BRUCE: *(at Johanna in the kitchen)* There's a ton of lobsters in my fridge. Wild Tasmanian. They'd be 50 bucks each wholesale! It's easy. I can just go get them. Or we can all go over to our place and Penelope can boil them up when she gets home. I mean . . . Are you guys OK?

ALEJANDRO: *(softly)* Oh Bruce . . . Bruce, what the fuck is going on with you?

BRUCE: Hey Alejandro, um I don't know how to say this. Have you seen Penelope? I'm afraid something's happened to her.

Johanna returns from the kitchen.

JOHANNA: *(forcing a smile)* It'll just be a minute.

BRUCE: *(smiling back)* Sure you don't want those lobsters? I can go get them. Or we can go for dim sum.

Johanna breaks down and cries on the sofa. Alejandro goes to comfort her.

Johanna, what happened? Are you all right?

JOHANNA: I just can't believe that Penelope's . . .

Pause. Johanna composes herself. Sound of microwave oven ring.

The pad thai.

Johanna exits to the kitchen.

BRUCE: Wait, what about Penelope? What happened? Johanna, why aren't you talking to me? Why are you ignoring me? Alejandro! Listen to me!

Alejandro sits on the armchair. He shakes his head. Bruce sits next to him, troubled.

Alejandro, I need to level with you. I'm losing it. My head . . . Everything's a blur. Sometimes I don't know where I am. It's like a dark tunnel. Behind me is a glowing light, shining on me, but I turn and it's gone, like a memory, and it's dark again. I guess I just need some rest. I'll be okay if I get a good night's sleep. Problem is, I can't. I have these horrible nightmares.

ALEJANDRO: *(slowly and intensely)* Bruce, you motherfuckin' son of a bitch!

Alejandro stands and exits. Bruce does not know how to react.

Scene 2

Sound of a motorcycle occasionally being revved up. A motorcycle shop, with a workspace, a counter, and a waiting area. A sign says "We Fix Angels."
Ai sits on a workbench, in work clothes, working on an old motorcycle. She is a teenager with a melancholy demeanor.
A customer, Rider 1, enters. Ai stands at the counter.

AI: Welcome to Fallen Angels' Bike Shop. What can I do for you?

Rider 1 stands there fumbling with his keys. Edie enters the shop.

EDIE: Hey Ai!

AI: Hey Edie. You made it.

EDIE: Still working on that beat-up old bike?

AI: Yeah. Boss wants me to figure out how to put it back together.

EDIE: A lot of people came.

AI: Great.

EDIE: I think it's really okay that you didn't go. A lot of people said a lot of things. But it was so awkward, because people didn't know what to say, and they had to avoid saying this and that.

Rider 1 rings the bell on the counter.

AI: *(to Rider 1)* I'm here to help if you want. Otherwise . . .

EDIE: There were these beautiful slides that they showed to music, and there was this one really cute picture of you when you were small, in costumes, with wings, and your mom had this parasol . . .

Boss enters from the back room. He is dressed like an old hippie, and speaks with almost hypnotic persuasion.

BOSS: Can't put it together, right? Well, my child, that's because you're not together.

EDIE: Hey, take it easy, you don't know what she's going through.

BOSS: *(to Rider 1)* Have you been helped?

RIDER 1: Oh, my bike just needs some air.

BOSS: *(deliberately)* Is that—all?

RIDER 1: Yeah. Just air.

Pause.

BOSS: In that case, let's pump it up.

Boss and Rider 1 exit. Another customer, Rider 2, enters from outside. Ai goes to the counter.

AI: Welcome to Fallen Angels' Bike Shop. What can I do for you?

RIDER 2: *(secretly)* Am I in the right place?

AI: Depends on the problem.

RIDER 2: *(sighing)* I've lost it.

AI: You've lost . . . ?

RIDER 2: My drive.

AI: For biking?

RIDER 2: If you don't know what I'm talking about, I'm out of here.

AI: No, no. Please stay. If it's just your drive, I'm sure that my boss can help you. Look at me, I've lost my wings.

RIDER 2: You what? No way! How did that happen?

AI: It's a long story. Now I've lost my mom.

RIDER 2: What? I'm . . . so sorry.

Edie stands to console Ai. Sound of a motorcycle leaving. Boss enters from outside.

BOSS: So tell me what's the problem? Have you physically injured your wings?

Rider 2 looks around, and at Edie.

RIDER 2: No. It's just stress from my job. A general weariness with humanity, and disillusionment with the human condition.

Pause.

Are you sure we can talk here?

BOSS: Your mind needs further expansion. Let's go to the back. I've got something for you.

Boss and Rider 2 exit within.

EDIE: Look. You shouldn't be working today. Come home and stay with me. Mom and Dad won't mind.

Boss and Rider 2 enter from within.

RIDER 2: Thanks. I feel better already.

BOSS: My pleasure. Ai, could you sign her out?

AI: Yeah, sure.

Ai goes to the counter and takes out some paperwork.

Please fill this out so we have you in our database. And that's the number to call in case of emergency.

RIDER 2: *(signing)* Thanks.

Rider 2 finishes the paperwork and exits.

EDIE: That was fast.

BOSS: It was just a quick reboot to the status of non-ego.

EDIE: What?

Scene 3

Penelope's art studio in Bruce and Penelope's house, next door to Alejandro and Johanna's. A desk, an easel, art supplies, frames, paintings, and an armchair.
A Policeman is looking through some files on the desk. A Policewoman enters with Johanna.

POLICEMAN: We want to thank you for taking the time to help us. Have you ever been in this room?

JOHANNA: *(emotional)* Of course! It's her studio!

POLICEWOMAN: The studio of the deceased?

JOHANNA: We were always in here, when the men were downstairs, watching the game and . . . *(breaking down)* So much was said in here. So much life was lived here.

POLICEMAN: We have some questions to ask you about the deceased.

JOHANNA: I don't get it. Why are you searching her studio? She's the victim! The victim!

POLICEMAN: We noticed there are a lot of receipts in her drawers—plane tickets, lodging, rental cars . . .

JOHANNA: Yes. She was an art therapist. She traveled a lot. For inspiration.

POLICEWOMAN: We're wondering if you know anything about a person named Chaz.

JOHANNA: *(surprised)* Who told you? I'm the only one who knew about him.

POLICEWOMAN: Well, apparently not.

JOHANNA: He was . . . an old boyfriend of Penelope's. Before Penelope met Bruce. He's an adventurer.

POLICEMAN: Can you give us his last name?

JOHANNA: Sure. It's . . . Strange, we all simply called him "Chaz." I . . . how could I not know? It's so weird, I've known him all these years.

POLICEWOMAN: How many years?

JOHANNA: All these years. Wow, I'm thinking, did I forget, or did I never know it?

POLICEMAN: Where did you meet this Chaz?

JOHANNA: At the . . . well, no, I didn't meet him that time. It must have been at the office party when . . . Wait a minute. He didn't show up that time.

Pause.

POLICEMAN: So you've never met him.

JOHANNA: That's not possible! I . . . I can't believe it!

POLICEWOMAN: But you knew him.

JOHANNA: Intimately.

POLICEMAN: What?

JOHANNA: No, I mean, you know, I . . .

POLICEWOMAN: So after the deceased married Bruce, she continued to see Chaz?

JOHANNA: No. She, well, yes, once in a while they'd catch up.

POLICEWOMAN: So you would describe it as a sexual relationship?

JOHANNA: How could you say that?! She loved Bruce! She loved Ai! No one knew! I was the only person she told about this! Yes, they were having an affair.

POLICEWOMAN: For how long?

JOHANNA: Um, she broke up with him before she married Bruce. And she um, after a few years, started seeing him again.

POLICEWOMAN: So you would say they were on and off for about . . . 20 years?

JOHANNA: Yeah . . . most of the time on. I mean . . .

POLICEWOMAN: Would you happen to know if there were any gifts from Chaz she was hiding from Bruce?

Johanna gets a key from under the chair, and opens a box on the desk, revealing various mementos inside. The officers examine the memorabilia.

You're the only one who knows where that key is hidden?

JOHANNA: Just me and her. It has mementos, hotel tickets, songs he wrote for her . . .

POLICEMAN: So he's a composer as well as an adventurer.

JOHANNA: Yes, there's a cassette of a song that he wrote for her . . . jewelry he gave her . . .

POLICEMAN: Do you know the make of car he drives?

JOHANNA: A blue '64 Corvette. He also has a plane. He's very wealthy.

POLICEMAN: Can you give us a physical description?

JOHANNA: Tall, sandy hair, very athletic build. She described him to me in detail. He was gorgeous. Chiseled.

POLICEMAN: His ethnicity?

JOHANNA: Quite interesting. His mother was a Swedish princess. His father was a descendant of British royalty.

POLICEWOMAN: Which house?

JOHANNA: I don't know. Tudor? I'm not into British history—I think the parents knew Princess Diana.

POLICEMAN: Do you know where he lives?

JOHANNA: Look, I promised Penelope I wouldn't tell anyone about this. I hope you appreciate that this is a little difficult for me.

POLICEWOMAN: *(gathering her things)* Well, thank you for sharing all this with us.

JOHANNA: *(suddenly emotional)* Why go after Chaz? There's nothing there for you! Leave Chaz in peace! It was Bruce who did this! Chaz has nothing to do with this! Can't you be more considerate of MY feelings?

Pause.

POLICEMAN: We're just trying to figure out a possible motive.

JOHANNA: *(exasperated)* But you know the motive! It's obvious! Bruce must have found out about Chaz, she was at the Mystic Cove Inn and . . .

POLICEWOMAN: In that case we also have reason to protect Mr. Chaz, wherever he may be.

JOHANNA: Right! Search for him! Find him! Find Chaz!

Scene 4

Alejandro and Johanna's living room. Alejandro sits on the sofa, holding a book of poetry, lost in thought. Bruce stands nearby.

ALEJANDRO: *(reading to himself)* "Down another cup of wine, my friend.

West of the mountain pass, there are no familiar faces."

BRUCE: Isn't that beautiful?

ALEJANDRO: So beautiful.

BRUCE: I'm glad you're reading Wang Wei, Alejandro. I thought that one of these days you'd catch on to Chinese poetry. You can keep that book if you want.

ALEJANDRO: And so sad.

BRUCE: Yeah. You know, I haven't been able to sleep.

Alejandro closes the book and sighs.

> You don't look so good, man. What's wrong? You can tell me.

Johanna enters, with the keys to Bruce's house in her hand, and the box of Penelope's mementos.

BRUCE: Hi Johanna, what's in the box?

ALEJANDRO: What's in the box, honey?

JOHANNA: *(tucking the box under her arm)* Nothing. Some stuff that Penelope left me. Sort of. I guess.

Johanna and Alejandro embrace to console each other. Johanna exits toward the bedroom.

BRUCE: Wait, Johanna, what stuff are you talking about? Where's Penelope? Wait a minute, I've seen that box before. Does that box look familiar to you, man?

Bruce exits, following Johanna.
Edie and Ai enter from outside.

EDIE: Dad, I'm home.

ALEJANDRO: Hey, honey.

EDIE: Is it okay if Ai stays with us? She's been going through a lot, and I just feel like I need to have her around.

Johanna enters.

AI: It's really too much trouble.

JOHANNA: Oh honey, so you're saying that . . . ?

Edie sits on the sofa, pats the seat, inviting Ai to sit next to her.

ALEJANDRO: So you're saying that you'd like Ai to stay here?

EDIE: Is that OK?

AI: I really think it's . . .

ALEJANDRO AND JOHANNA: *(in unison)* Sure!

JOHANNA: We'd love to have her!

EDIE: *(to Ai)* Don't worry!

ALEJANDRO: It's true. Edie, you should have thought of that long ago.

JOHANNA: Right. Ai shouldn't be staying all alone in that big house.

AI: Are you sure?

JOHANNA: It's no problem at all. There's that extra mattress we can bring into your room, and I can get you all the stuff Ai needs. Toothbrush, toothpaste . . .

EDIE: Mom, she has her own toothbrush.

JOHANNA: Oh, that's right.

ALEJANDRO: We just want to make sure she has everything.

AI: Thanks.

A slight pause. Edie glares at her parents.

ALEJANDRO: You're welcome, Ai!

JOHANNA: Any time!

Edie stands to go. Alejandro and Johanna follow her.

EDIE: Let's fix the bed.

AI: Can I help?

EDIE: No it's fine.

ALEJANDRO: Ai, I just want to say, really, please make yourself at home!

The three exit, leaving Ai alone.
Bruce enters again.

AI: Dad?

Bruce looks around.

Dad, you shouldn't be here.

BRUCE: Are you talking to me?

AI: Yes, I am. Do Alejandro and Johanna know you're here?

BRUCE: Of course. They're my neighbors.

AI: Dad, come on. You have to call the police.

BRUCE: Look, whoever you are, I'm going through a very tough time here. I can't sleep. I think I'm losing my grip. Should I know who you are?

AI: Dad . . . Come on. I'm Ai. Your daughter.

BRUCE: That's unfair.

AI: No, you're being unfair. Look, I don't want to be the one who has to call the police.

BRUCE: Whoever you are, I'm just trying to find Penelope.

AI: That's not funny at all.

Ai hears footsteps.

Dad, someone's coming, do you want to hide?

BRUCE: What for, why should I hide?

Edie enters.

EDIE: Hey Ai, your room's ready. Are you OK? I heard you talking to someone. Who were you talking to?

Ai looks at Bruce.

AI: Uh . . . you don't see anybody?

JOHANNA: *(offstage)* Excuse me! Edie! Can I get some help here? . . .

EDIE: Okay, I'll be right there . . .

Edie and Ai exit, leaving Bruce alone. Ai glances at Bruce as she leaves.

Scene 5

The Crystal Dragon Restaurant, a Hong Kong–style tea restaurant.
Musician's Soul sits by himself at one table, working on a song, his saxophone by his side.
A Waitress and middle-aged waiter Ah-Fok [pronounced FOOK] are cleaning up. Ah-Fok notices something wrong with the way the Waitress is setting a table.

AH-FOK: You got it wrong! Soy sauce left, vinegar right. That's the way we Chinese do it—man left, woman right!

Ah-Fok changes the setting.

WAITRESS: So soy sauce is man?

AH-FOK: You gotta get it right! All our customers are regulars. They like everything the same.

WAITRESS: Whatever.

AH-FOK: Not whatever! I've been working here since before you were born.

Ai and Edie enter, and sit at a table.

This is a regular customer. You watch.

EDIE: *(to Ai)* No way in hell! You can't be serious!

AI: It's true!

Ah-Fok goes to Edie and Ai's table, giving them menus. The Waitress watches, like an apprentice.

AH-FOK: Good evening, ladies. Here for breakfast?

EDIE: Hi Ah-Fok.

AH-FOK: Hi Edie, hi Ai.

AI: Hi Ah-Fok.

AH-FOK: Edie, let me make you a strong cup of *yuenyeung,* how's that?

EDIE: Thanks, Ah-Fok. You're the best.

AH-FOK: Same for you, Ai?

AI: No thanks. I'll just have some iced milk tea.

EDIE: Iced milk tea is a good choice.

AH-FOK: No problem. *Yuenyeung* is too strong for Ai.

Ah-Fok exits, gesturing for the Waitress to follow. The Waitress looks puzzled.

AI: I tell you, it was him. I saw him.

EDIE: No way, isn't your dad on the run?

AI: That's what I thought. I told him to turn himself in. It was so weird. He was sort of spaced out, wandering around, and he didn't recognize me.

EDIE: Are you sure? I didn't see anybody.

AI: That's why it was so weird.

Edie is in thought. Ah-Fok approaches the table.

AH-FOK: So what will it be, Edie?

EDIE: I'll try cuttlefish balls with wontons.

AH-FOK: One cuttlefish balls with wontons . . . and?

AI: I'll just have salted fish steamed with pork.

EDIE: Salted fish steamed with pork?

AH-FOK: Over rice?

AI: Yes, please.

Edie nods to Ah-Fok.

AH-FOK: No problem.

AI: Thank you.

AH-FOK: You're welcome, Ai.

EDIE: Wait a minute. Let's also get some dim sum. Some shrimp roe siu mai, turnip cakes, steamed spareribs, and . . . *(looking at the menu)*

AI: Can I get some taro dumplings?

EDIE: You want taro dumplings?

AH-FOK: No problem. Wow, you guys are hungry tonight!

EDIE: It's Ai.

AI: No, come on, we just need to eat.

AH-FOK: Well, Ai, it's good that you have an appetite, after all that's happened to your family. I'm so sorry about your mother. She used to come here all the time, even before she was married to your dad. Well, what can I say? . . . I'm so . . .

Ah-Fok sighs and tears up.

Sorry. Let me get your order.

EDIE: Thank you. You're so considerate.

AH-FOK: No problem, Edie.

Ah-Fok exits.

AI: Are you sure your parents are okay with me staying over at your house?

EDIE: I don't think they care. You know, I don't think my parents are there any more than yours are.

Waitress confers with Ah-Fok in the background, pointing at Edie and Ai.

AI: How so?

EDIE: They never understood. Some of the things I wanted were really, really important. Like my friend V.

AI: Tell me about V.

EDIE: V was my best friend, I told her everything. We talked on the phone all the time. And she understood. But all they would say was "stop talking on the phone all the time." So what's more important? My mental health or you paying a bigger phone bill? One day V needed me to come over. It was a real crisis. So I asked my dad to take me to V's house. I remember I snatched his newspaper. And he was like, who's V? And you shouldn't snatch newspapers. Who's V?! Like only my best friend in the whole wide world aside from you! Who's V!

Ah-Fok and the Waitress enter, each with a mug. The Waitress looks at Ah-Fok, who motions for her to serve Ai.

WAITRESS: *(to Ah-Fok)* Here?

Ah-Fok nods. Waitress and Ah-Fok serve the drinks. Ah-Fok gestures to the Waitress.

Ai, I'm so sorry for what happened to your mother. Please accept my deepest condolences.

AI: Thank you.

Waitress and Ah-Fok exit. Waitress suppresses a laugh. Ah-Fok scolds her.

What happened to V?

EDIE: My parents were getting ready to go to some stupid dinner. My mom was going to accept this award—"the Zimmerman Award for Excellence in Real Estate Services."

AI: Sounds important.

EDIE: They all sound important. They made it up. It was fake.

AI: How do you know?

EDIE: Because my mom wanted to get this other prize so bad, the Musselman Award for top sales in the Peninsula, but this other realtor got it, so Mom and her firm invented this Zimmerman Award and gave it to themselves.

AI: Zimmerman?

EDIE: My mom's a Dylan fan. *(pointing at herself)* Haven't you noticed her taste in names?

Pause.

So they were going out to this big awards function, and I remember going up to them saying I need to go to V, and they were like, V can wait. Man, it was so late, and so dark, how could V wait? They were totally clueless! And they just drove off . . . and . . . after that night, I never saw V again. *(breaking down)* I should've been there for her. Right? It was my fault!

AI: No, it was not your fault.

EDIE: No, it was my fault. I could've run, run two hours to her house! I could've called an ambulance! And you know, years later, the word went out that I abandoned her on a mountaintop. How ridiculous is that? I was just a little girl! How could I abandon her on a mountaintop?

Edie is in despair. Ai consoles her.
V enters and addresses the audience.

V: Hey again. Can you guys see me? Well you're not supposed to . . . so don't lie to yourselves. *(pointing at Edie)* She used to see me . . . Edie. It was only because of Edie that I exist. I was imagined by her. One day we had an argument about her parents, and she exiled me to this barren mountaintop. In the dense fog. And since . . . she's never seen me again.

I miss her. How I wish someone could listen to me, to hear me tell her, I've always been here. For her, waiting, for her to remember me.

I know what you're all thinking: if an entity was only seen by one other entity throughout its existence, does that entity exist? Of course that is a syllogistic paradox on an ontological query. When a tree falls in a forest, yeah yeah . . . So did I ever happen? Was I ever me? Am I on the list of "sentient beings"? A species sitting somewhere undiscovered, unheard of, un . . . known. "I think, therefore . . ." hmm . . . But do I really? . . . This is not helping me. I'm stuck and confused, in a place I can only describe as "between." I'm in the "between" state. But I guess so is everyone. Between what? I don't know. Between sleeping and waking, between imagining and being imagined, between abandoning and being abandoned, between the constant oscillations of day and night, springs summers autumns winters, life and death, death and rebirth, rebirth and more life, between a breath and another breath, and more betweens, and more birth and death of breaths, and more lives, and more deaths. Again and again. Forever.

Edie and Ai finish their meal and leave the restaurant. They try to flag a taxi in the rain. V hovers around them, continuing to talk to the audience.

Ever since Edie abandoned me, I've been floating around aimlessly . . . like a wave in space, a cloud in the sky. It's actually kind of cool. I can meet all these other abandoned entities, *(pointing to Musician's Soul)* like Christina. She's the soul of a musician who went to Hollywood and lost that "thing you lose in Hollywood." She's that lost thing. I love what she plays. I'm almost certain that sometimes Edie can hear her.

Musician's Soul picks up his saxophone and plays "Song for Penelope."
Edie looks around, as if she is hearing something.
Edie and Ai exit, V watching.

Scene 6

Edie's bedroom. Early morning. Ai sleeps on the floor, Edie on the bed. Bruce squats in the corner.
Ai sits up, unable to sleep. She sees Bruce.

Ai gets up, puts on a jacket, and leaves, Bruce following.

They cross the street. Musician's Soul continues to play, as Pedestrians float by. Ai and Bruce thread through the people.

Ai arrives at a cemetery. She goes to Penelope's grave, eyeing Bruce, who is following at a distance.

Ai addresses the grave.

AI: *(to the grave)* Mom . . . I'm sorry. I didn't come yesterday. There's so much I want to say to you, but I just don't know how. I never knew how. Why is it that all these years we've been so cold to each other, when deep inside all I feel is warmth? Mom . . . I'm sorry I never learned how to talk to you. I hope you are well, wherever you are.

Ai kisses her hand, and touches the tombstone. She stands aside. Bruce approaches the grave. He inspects the tombstone.

BRUCE: *(to himself, surprised)* Penelope? What . . . ?

Bruce turns. Ai is gone.

What kind of a dream is this?

Scene 7

Alejandro and Johanna's house. Alejandro and Johanna are each on the phone, tending to their respective business.

JOHANNA: *(on the phone)* Do you know who you're talking to?

ALEJANDRO: *(on the phone)* No, no . . .

JOHANNA: *(on the phone)* You're talking to the recipient of the Zimmerman Award! The Zimmerman Award! I've nurtured you since you were wet behind the ears, but you screwed me over! . . .

The two police officers enter from within, with Edie.

POLICEWOMAN: We want to thank you for your time, Edie . . .

ALEJANDRO: *(on the phone)* No, no, just because Samsung did something doesn't mean we have to follow their ass. Look, THEY follow us, we don't follow anybody . . .

JOHANNA: *(on the phone)* Today you made a Zimmerman Award recipient look like a piece of worthless crap! . . .

POLICEWOMAN: Uh, we had one more question. We wanted to know, with all the time you spent at the deceased's house, did you ever notice any other men besides Bruce there?

EDIE: No.

ALEJANDRO: *(on the phone)* Look, I'm under enormous stress . . .

JOHANNA: *(on the phone)* Look, I'm under enormous stress . . .

ALEJANDRO: *(on the phone)* You have no idea what I'm going through! . . .

JOHANNA: *(on the phone)* You have no idea what I'm going through! Yeah, well you can . . .

ALEJANDRO: *(on the phone)* Fuck off! *(hangs up)*

JOHANNA: *(on the phone)* Fuck off, too! *(hangs up too)*

EDIE: Maybe Ai did.

POLICEWOMAN: Ai?

EDIE: Officer, can I request that you not interrogate Ai, because I really don't think she can handle it.

Policeman looks at Alejandro. Alejandro gestures "Don't."

POLICEMAN: We're done here. Ai has been through enough.

EDIE: Thank you, officer.

POLICEWOMAN: Thank you Edie, you may go now.

Edie exits within.

POLICEMAN: I guess we didn't come at a good time.

POLICEWOMAN: Looks like you guys are pretty busy.

ALEJANDRO: No . . .

JOHANNA: NO!

ALEJANDRO: No . . .

JOHANNA: NO! Just . . . Please have a seat.

Edie enters, with a sporting bag.

JOHANNA: Going to soccer practice, honey?

EDIE: Mom, that was last year.

JOHANNA: Right, right, of course . . . that was . . .

ALEJANDRO: Yeah, yeah, so now you're going to . . . ?

Edie exits.

Kids.

POLICEWOMAN: Um, I was talking with Edie . . . and she mentioned a girl named "V."

ALEJANDRO: "V"?

Pause. They think.

JOHANNA: Ha, V was Edie's imaginary friend, when she was a kid. She would talk to her every single day.

ALEJANDRO: Right. *(as if awakening)* Look, we're talking about Penelope's murder, here, what the fuck does V have to do with anything? Pardon my Chinese . . .

POLICEWOMAN: You never know.

ALEJANDRO: What do you mean "You never know"? V was a product of Edie's imagination! When they were kids, Edie and Ai would run around with these wings on their backs, saying they were angels, and Edie was always talking to V, who didn't exist.

Pause.

POLICEWOMAN: So when did Edie stop talking to V?

JOHANNA: Honestly, officer, does this really have anything to do with Penelope's murder?

POLICEWOMAN: I don't know.

Pause.

JOHANNA: I don't know, all of a sudden she just didn't talk to her again.

ALEJANDRO: We mentioned it to the doctor, and he said it's normal for children to have imaginary friends, or to think they were angels or whatever.

JOHANNA: They weren't doing drugs; they weren't getting pregnant.

ALEJANDRO: So what is the problem with that?

POLICEWOMAN: Um . . . Just off the record . . . I'm just wondering . . . I mean . . . What if I'm imaginary, and you're imaginary?

Pause.

JOHANNA: What?

POLICEWOMAN: Like we don't exist?

JOHANNA: But we do! We certainly do!

ALEJANDRO: *(laughing)* Check my PG&E bill for proof!

POLICEMAN: We should be getting back.

JOHANNA: *(laughing)* Right, in your imaginary police car, to your imaginary police station!

They all laugh.

POLICEMAN: Right. Well, we really appreciate your time, Mr. Chavez, particularly for coming down to the precinct earlier today.

The Policeman shakes Alejandro's hand sincerely. The officers exit.

JOHANNA: What was that about, honey? When did you go down to the precinct?

Alejandro's mood changes. He pours himself a drink.

ALEJANDRO: I haven't had a chance to tell you, honey. I went to see him this afternoon.

JOHANNA: See who?

Edie enters, with Ai.

EDIE: *(to Ai)* Looks like the cops just left.

ALEJANDRO: Edie, Ai, come here, please. It'd be best to hear this together.

Alejandro points to the sofa. Edie and Ai sit.

I have to tell you guys something. I want you all to be brave. I got a call from Bruce a few nights ago. He told me he had decided to give himself . . . a good night's sleep. Then he hung up. This morning, I got a call from the police. They told me they found Bruce's body on a beach in Big Sur—with a gunshot wound to his head.

Pause.

JOHANNA: What? Bruce is . . . ?

Johanna breaks down. Ai stands up to go to her room. Edie follows.

ALEJANDRO: Edie, are you . . . ? Are you guys OK?

AI: Thanks, I'll be fine.

EDIE: I think she needs some time by herself.

AI: Yeah.

ALEJANDRO: Of course. Ai, I'm so sorry. I hope you can forgive me for breaking the news to you in this way.

AI: No. It's actually helping me start to make sense of it all, in a weird way.

EDIE: Because you saw him in this house, AFTER he . . .

ALEJANDRO: What?

EDIE: Nothing, Dad. It's complicated.

AI: *(as she goes)* But thank you, Mr. Chavez.

Edie and Ai exit.
Johanna composes herself.

JOHANNA: Where did they find him?

ALEJANDRO: Near the Mystic Cove Inn.

JOHANNA: So he was hiding there all this time.

ALEJANDRO: No, dear. They actually checked the gas receipts in his car. He'd been all over. He'd even purchased a plane ticket to China and was going to leave from Seattle. But for some reason he gravitated back to . . .

JOHANNA: Where they fell in love. Where they had their honeymoon. Where they . . .

Alejandro breaks down.

Honey, I'm sorry. Is there anything you want to share?

ALEJANDRO: You wouldn't want to have seen him.

Bruce enters, and wanders about.

JOHANNA: Tell me how bad it was . . .

ALEJANDRO: *(in anguish)* Johanna . . . his whole face was gone.

Johanna comforts Alejandro.

JOHANNA: I'm going to make dinner. Is steak OK?

No answer. Johanna exits.

BRUCE: What was that all about?

ALEJANDRO: Why, Bruce? Why'd you do that? I couldn't even recognize you today.

BRUCE: I don't understand.

ALEJANDRO: You didn't think about your friends, did you? You didn't think about who'd have to go down and identify your fucking body, did you?

BRUCE: If you want to tell me something, don't talk in riddles.

ALEJANDRO: That's so cruel, Bruce, *(angry)* and stupid! What a fucking asshole! Pardon my Chinese.

Alejandro exits.

Scene 8

Fallen Angels' Bike Shop. Ai is filling out forms for a customer, Rider 3. Rider 4 stands on the side watching.

AI: So we're talking about a fear of heights.

RIDER 3: More. It's a greater fear. Of my inadequacy. My insignificance in the grand scheme of things.

AI: Could be the current planetary magnetic fields. They play on us all. It's temporary. Not like me. I've lost my wings.

RIDER 3: No shit. You what?

RIDER 4: Man, if you need to fix your bike, you need to line up behind me. Otherwise I can refer you to a nice shrink across the street.

AI: *(to Rider 4)* I'll be with you in a minute. *(to Rider 3)* Is there anything else?

RIDER 3: I need Boss.

AI: Let me check his availability for you.

Ai goes into the back room.

RIDER 4: Look, if you need confidence to bike, you shouldn't even be on the road.

RIDER 3: I would say we're talking different levels of biking, and a different kind of road.

RIDER 4: What?

Boss emerges from the back, with Ai. Edie enters to hang out in the shop.

EDIE: Hi Ai!

BOSS: *(to Rider 3)* I heard you're having some problems with heights.

RIDER 3: Related to fear.

BOSS: You're feeling crushed by the immensity of the human quandary, you feel like no matter how much you fix, you're not even making a dent.

RIDER 3: *(emotionally)* Boss . . .

BOSS: Well, come on to the back. Let's "fix" *you* first.

Boss takes Rider 3 into the back room.

RIDER 4: What's in the back room?

Edie shrugs her shoulders.

AI: It doesn't concern you.

RIDER 4: Look, I don't understand, I came first, and no one comes to help me, and . . . What happens back there?

Johanna and Alejandro enter from outside and stand in the doorway, tentatively. Johanna holds an address in her hand.

AI: Look, with some people the problem is the bike, with others there are other issues that take precedence. I'm happy to help you now. What's the problem?

Boss reemerges from the back room.

RIDER 4: So you're the boss here?

BOSS: Yeah.

RIDER 4: Your name?

BOSS: Boss.

RIDER 4: Well, boss, I need to get back on the road right now.

BOSS: Fallen Angels' Bike Shop isn't about getting back on the road. It's about the air.

RIDER 4: So get me in the air. Now!

BOSS: Thank you for your time, but we reserve the right to refuse service to anyone.

RIDER 4: This is outrageous! I want to know what happens in the back!

AI: Listen, do you want your bike fixed or not? There's another shop across the street.

BOSS: This is a place for REAL angels, OK? Would you please leave the premises?

RIDER 4: What the . . . ? I'm a real angel! We're the real angels! Who needs YOUR back room? We got our own back room!

Rider 4 storms out. Boss exits within. Johanna and Alejandro enter meekly.

JOHANNA: So this is where Ai works.

EDIE: You followed me?

JOHANNA: Let's just say, we were worried.

ALEJANDRO: About Ai.

EDIE: Well, showing up here is surely a weird way to show it. Right, Ai?

AI: Look, I'm really busy today. I'd appreciate if you all got out of here.

JOHANNA: We're caring for you now, Ai. That's why we want to know where you—and Edie—are all the time.

Boss reenters from the back with Rider 3, who seems totally relieved.

RIDER 3: Wow! That was amazing!

BOSS: Just happy to be of service.

RIDER 3: It seems as if in an instant my mind is expanded, and I'm seeing things like through a top-shot wide-angle lens.

BOSS: Good. Consider yourself fixed. Please sign her out, Ai.

AI: *(to Rider 3)* Do we have you in our system?

RIDER 3: No. It's been ages. I need updates on everything.

AI: *(to Rider 3)* Sure, no problem. I'll make certain you can access all the information.

Ai signs Rider 3 out. Johanna and Alejandro look at each other.

JOHANNA: *(to Boss)* Hi, I'm Johanna Chavez of Green Lawns Realty, I'm taking care of Ai.

BOSS: Oh really? Well, I'M taking care of Ai.

JOHANNA: *(befuddled)* Um . . .

ALEJANDRO: And you are . . . ?

BOSS: You can call me Boss.

ALEJANDRO: Okay. Whatever. I guess we should thank you. I'm a strong believer that teenagers should have experience in the workforce and . . . *(suddenly losing it)* This is ridiculous!!

Pause. Rider 3 embraces Boss.

RIDER 3: Thank you, Boss. You've got the stuff that really makes me fly. I feel energized to be back workin' the streets again!

BOSS: Go in peace.

Rider 3 exits. Alejandro and Johanna are flabbergasted.

JOHANNA: Edie, what's really going on here?

ALEJANDRO: Are there drugs back there, Edie? Listen, I hung around bikers when we were younger, and they did some crazy things.

AI: Lay off her. She's here to pick me up.

ALEJANDRO: Have you been doing drugs with Ai?

JOHANNA: Are they shooting marijuana back there?

ALEJANDRO: How much is Ai making an hour? We'll give her double.

AI: No, I'm learning so much here. How to put together things that have been taken apart. I've never done this in my life!

BOSS: Ai, please be more polite. These people mean well.

ALEJANDRO: Look, I don't like the way you're playing along here. That makes you an accomplice, you know.

BOSS: Ai, tell them about Fallen Angels' Bike Shop. It will help.

AI: Is that an order?

BOSS: Let's just say that's part of your . . . rehabilitation.

EDIE: *(to her parents)* Just listen!

Edie points to a bench. Johanna and Alejandro sit on the bench. Ai collects herself, and addresses them.

AI: Fallen Angels' Bike Shop is not a shop for bikes, but for fallen angels. I'm a fallen angel. I'm trapped here because I lost my wings.

ALEJANDRO: This is absolutely crazy.

EDIE: Shhh . . .

AI: Actually, my wings were stolen. By my father, when I was seven. So I'm stuck here. I can't go home.

Johanna is restless.

EDIE: *(to her parents)* Mom, please be patient.

BOSS: Sit down, my child.

Ai and Edie sit on the workbench.

The time has come for you to gain a deeper understanding and appreciation of yourself, your current situation, THE current situation of your reality.

Both of your parents are now dead. That is quite unfortunate. For reasons we can only guess at, your father, whom you have observed, seems to be lingering, though your mother seems to have moved on, on toward the place she aspires to go to.

Why is your father lingering? Why does he not go? For one, he does not understand that he has died. That in itself is not remarkable. We all do not understand that we are fundamentally dead.

Boss glances at Alejandro and Johanna.

The lack of recognition of our true status keeps us stuck, unable to progress. It is your sacred mission, Ai, to awaken your father to the reality of his death, and this, in turn, will liberate you.

AI: Awaken him? How?

BOSS: By telling him his story. By reminding him who he is, how he got to be who he is, all of the causes that have simmered into their effects. He has forgotten who he is. That's why he is stuck where he is. In the Bardo. Between. That's why we're all stuck where we are, between, in the Bardo. *(pointing to Alejandro and Johanna)* I'm talking about you two as well!

Pause.

ALEJANDRO: What kind of shit is this? Who's "lingering"? YOU'RE LINGERING! *(pointing at Ai)* She's lingering! *(pointing everywhere in the air)* Everyone's lingering! That's an easy one! What the hell are you doing to these kids?!!

EDIE: Dad, please, we're just coming to the point.

JOHANNA: Edie, enough is enough! You are leaving this instant, with or without Ai!

ALEJANDRO: You watch it! I'm going to report you, Boss!

Alejandro and Johanna grab Edie and storm off.
Silence.

AI: Tell my dad his story? But I don't really know it.

BOSS: Your viewpoint and concern are crucial. Tell him what you know. His memory may then be filled in by others.

AI: Others?

BOSS: In the wind, the rain, a stranger's face, a voice, a sound . . .

Pause.

> Go, Child.

Scene 9

Edie's bedroom. It is past midnight. Bruce squats in the darkness, watching Edie and Ai, who are asleep.
> *Ai wakes. They see each other.*

AI: Dad.

BRUCE: Don't keep calling me "Dad," I'm finally figuring things out. THIS is a dream. All I have to do is wake up, and everything will be fine.

AI: This isn't a dream, Dad, unless death is a dream.

BRUCE: You see? Everything you say, it's all part of this crazy logic . . .

AI: Dad, do you know what happened?

BRUCE: It doesn't matter. Once I wake up, I'll find my wife Penelope lying beside me, and I'll tell her I had this crazy, crazy dream, where . . .

AI: Where you killed her.

Pause.

BRUCE: How did you know?

AI: They all went to her funeral. They had a closed casket ceremony because the body wasn't presentable.

BRUCE: No, no, it's not possible!

AI: Then you went to Big Sur and shot yourself in the head.

BRUCE: No . . . no . . . that's ridiculous! If that were true, how could I be sitting here talking to you?

AI: You tell me! I'm waiting for YOU to disappear, because if you're a figment of my imagination you'll go away. If this is MY dream, I'll wake up, and Mom will still be alive, and . . . Daddy! . . .

Ai breaks down and cries in Bruce's arms.

BRUCE: I'm sorry . . . I'm sorry if I did anything to . . . but I'm here . . . Help me figure it all out.

Pause.

AI: Dad, I need to tell you a story.

BRUCE: A story?

AI: Once upon a time, there was a man named Bruce, his wife Penelope, and their daughter Ai. They lived happily in a faraway place called California. Bruce's parents had come there in the illusion that they would have a better life for themselves. But they wound up running a laundromat for the rest of their days. They consoled themselves with another illusion: that their son Bruce would fare better, thus validating all their previous illusions, and, empowered by the name they had given him, he seemed to do so. Bruce was driven to excel by this image, to transcend, but no matter how well he did, he was forever driven by this sense of inadequacy.

Do you remember? How it all started? Once upon a time, there was this place called the Crystal Dragon Restaurant . . .

Scene 10

The Crystal Dragon Restaurant, late 1990s. Alejandro sits at a table. Ah-Fok, the waiter, brings a cup of milk tea. They are both younger.

ALEJANDRO: Hey, waiter. Is this milk tea any good?

AH-FOK: Come on, Sir, our kitchen all comes from Hong Kong. You drink, you find out.

ALEJANDRO: Okay. I have a friend who'll be in a hurry. Why don't you bring her a cup of coffee, now?

AH-FOK: Sure, no problem.

Ah-Fok exits. Bruce enters.

BRUCE: What's going on?

ALEJANDRO: Sit down, Bruce.

Bruce sits impatiently.

> Look. Just meet her. If you don't like her, go. By the way, I said the same thing to her.

BRUCE: Why here?

ALEJANDRO: She's opening an exhibition a few blocks away. She chose the place.

BRUCE: An exhibition? I thought she was a coworker of yours.

ALEJANDRO: She's an artist. Our boss bought some of her paintings, and then he asked her to do some decorating for us. She's very talented.

BRUCE: Look, I'm just not in the mood for this. We're predicting a rise in sushi restaurants despite what the market seems to be saying, so I'm concentrating all my energy on work. I have no time, no desire, no interest, I don't even look at women. I won't be very talkative . . .

ALEJANDRO: You're talkative right now when the topic is sushi.

Penelope enters. She is in a hurry. Ah-Fok enters with her, bringing coffee.

AH-FOK: *(to Penelope)* Welcome, Miss Chen! Just seat yourself.

PENELOPE: Thanks, Ah-Fok, I'm actually . . . *(seeing Alejandro)* Hi Alejandro, sorry I'm late.

ALEJANDRO: Hi Penelope!

Penelope hugs Alejandro. Bruce is taken by her.

PENELOPE: What's up? I have to be back in 10 minutes.

ALEJANDRO: Penelope, I'd like you to meet my friend, Bruce.

PENELOPE: Nice to meet you.

Penelope holds out her hand. Bruce accidentally knocks over the tea; Alejandro knocks over a chair.

AH-FOK: Whoa!

BRUCE: Sorry.

They shake hands.

ALEJANDRO: I, well, got you some coffee.

Ah-Fok comes to clean up.

AH-FOK: So you're the one they waiting for! *(to Alejandro)* She doesn't drink coffee. She needs a strong cup of *yuenyeung*.

ALEJANDRO: What's that?

AH-FOK: Tea mixed with coffee together. Very potent. Like mating quails.

PENELOPE: Thank you, Ah-Fok.

BRUCE: Ah-Fok? Get me one of those, too.

AH-FOK: No problem.

Bruce and Penelope sit down. Ah-Fok exits.

ALEJANDRO: Relax, Penelope. Get something to eat before your opening. I hear the dim sum here is pretty decent. *(to Bruce)* Penelope's opening this solo show called *Bound Feet*. It's incredible. *(to Penelope)* I wanted you to meet Bruce because he's very interested in the psychological value of abstract art.

BRUCE: It's actually something I know nothing about. Seriously. *Bound Feet*? So you feel . . . bound?

PENELOPE: Aren't we all? By our collective past. Our bodies. Our minds. Our concepts. There's so much beyond what we live, what we imagine life to be.

Pause. Penelope checks her watch.

I actually have to leave in about eight minutes, sorry.

BRUCE: I'm fascinated.

ALEJANDRO: Yeah. Bruce's um . . . fascinated.

PENELOPE: So what do you do, Bruce?

BRUCE: Something totally unfascinating. I import seafood for wholesale.

ALEJANDRO: Kind of, you know, fishy business. He binds crab feet. Ha ha. Oh. That's terrible.

Ah-Fok enters.

AH-FOK: Excuse me, Miss Chen. There's a phone call for you at the front desk.

PENELOPE: Thank you. *(standing)* Sorry.

Penelope exits.

ALEJANDRO: What do you think?

BRUCE: Um . . . I mean, I'm speechless, I guess.

Penelope returns.

PENELOPE: Sorry, sorry.

ALEJANDRO: It's okay.

PENELOPE: *(to Alejandro)* It was Chaz.

ALEJANDRO: Ah. I didn't realize that the two of you were . . . ?

PENELOPE: Well, let's just say we've got some things to work out.

ALEJANDRO: Is he waiting for you at the gallery?

PENELOPE: *(rather pissed)* No, he's not. He suddenly decided to go abroad, so he's going to miss the opening.

ALEJANDRO: Some urgent business?

PENELOPE: He's writing music for a film. He needed inspiration, so he flew to Spain. He's so impulsive!

ALEJANDRO: *(to Bruce)* Chaz is a . . . um, composer, and an aviator . . . *(to Penelope)* He took his own aircraft, correct? I guess if you fly your own aircraft, you have the right to be impulsive! Ha ha . . .

Pause. Bruce gazes at Penelope.

BRUCE: Penelope, may I have the honor of escorting you back to the gallery and attending the opening of your exhibition?

Pause. They gaze at each other for a moment. Penelope's beeper buzzes. She checks it.

PENELOPE: Oh shit, I . . .

Penelope exits, tipping Ah-Fok as she goes out.

BRUCE: Did I say something wrong?

ALEJANDRO: No, no.

BRUCE: Is it this Chaz guy?

ALEJANDRO: Don't worry about it. She's a busy girl, gets all sorts of calls.

Bruce stands and follows Penelope out.

Scene 11

Sound of waves. The Mystic Cove Inn. Bruce and Penelope lie on the bed, after sex.

BRUCE: *(looking out)* How amazingly silent. The silence grows with the waves.

PENELOPE: This room is special. The tide rises overnight, so in the morning, we will be enveloped.

BRUCE: So you know this room well.

PENELOPE: No, I . . . Well I've . . .

BRUCE: Shhh. Don't say anything. At this moment, I don't have a care in the world.

They embrace.

PENELOPE: I come to this place to be alone.

BRUCE: Alone?

PENELOPE: To be.

BRUCE: To be.

PENELOPE: One with the waves. To be . . . with myself.

BRUCE: To be unbound.

Bruce picks up Penelope's exhibition catalogue and reads poetry of Wang Wei from it.

"Go now, and ask me nothing more,

The white clouds will drift on for all time."

I love this. And your painting that was inspired by it. Which I now own. What genius, to pair Chinese poetry with abstract art.

PENELOPE: Why did you choose that one?

BRUCE: It blew me away . . . the fragility, the hidden emotions, the wanting to be seen, be heard, the yearning to unbind yourself, to unwrap into something totally new. It was almost as if the poem about parting was referring to parting with yourself . . .

PENELOPE: I can't believe you saw all that.

BRUCE: How could I see it if I didn't know it myself?

PENELOPE: I'm sorry.

BRUCE: Why sorry?

PENELOPE: To infringe on your emotions. To push you toward vulnerability. To remind you of the pain.

BRUCE: Isn't that what art is all about?

PENELOPE: No. Painting has more and more become a kind of therapy for me. I feel uncomfortable parading it. Who goes around showing their therapy sessions in public?

BRUCE: I dunno. Rothko? De Kooning? Most everybody.

PENELOPE: But it's so private. To exhibit it feels almost . . . obscene.

BRUCE: Which means you have a better sense of decency then they.

Pause.

Sound of a beeper. Penelope checks her beeper.

PENELOPE: Oh shit. It's Chaz . . . I have to call him. Sorry.

BRUCE: No problem.

Penelope calls from the bedside phone.

PENELOPE: Hi, look, you can NOT just page me anytime you want anymore. We're over, over, you got that? . . . What are you trying to do? Monitor my every move? Shit, you're the one who flew away! ... Who's crazy? Well, you're right! I'm crazy! OK? Goodbye, Chaz! Is that crazy enough for you?

Penelope hangs up and weeps softly. Bruce watches.
  Ai enters. At the same time, V and Musician's Soul enter. Penelope exits.

AI: Dad, are you remembering things?

Musician's Soul plays a mournful saxophone solo.

  'Cause I can't remember things that happened before I was. You have to try! You have to tell me this story.

Bruce seems to start hearing the music. At this point, V takes over the narrative, which Bruce hears.

V: They fell in love that night at the Mystic Cove Inn in Big Sur. A strong bond was forged between them, built on the basis of fragility, and thus the bond was by nature fragile. They got married. They honeymooned there, and vacationed in nearby Santa Cruz. There was this photo studio on the boardwalk where they could take photos in ridiculous poses. They had a great time, a silly time, on that boardwalk. They had a baby girl.

BRUCE: A beautiful baby girl.

V: A joyful girl, radiant. They named her "Ai"—Chinese for "Love." For a time, she did embody her namesake. She was—Love.

BRUCE: Ai.

V: Bruce's fortunes were on the rise. Many new, high-end sushi restaurants in the region were supplied by his company. *Hotate, uni*, the best bluefin *otoro*. They bought a house, in a gated community in Redwood City, next to his buddy Alejandro, who worked in the budding tech industry on the Peninsula, and who had a daughter too, with his wife Johanna, whom they named Edie. Penelope turned from pure art to art therapy, and she worked out of her studio at home, developing a respectable clientele whom she guided through their lives. The two families spent a lot of time together. They even went back to that boardwalk together.

Scene 12

*A photo studio on the Santa Cruz Beach Boardwalk, with a rack of odd clothes
for customers to try on, plus cheesy backgrounds with cutouts where they can
insert their heads.*

    *Bruce and Penelope are posing with their heads in a cutout of a body
builder and a beach bunny for the Photographer.*

BRUCE: *(looking at the cutout)* The classic boardwalk pose.

PENELOPE: Sure, he's got to have muscles, and she's got to be blonde.

BRUCE: It is what it is. Come on.

PHOTOGRAPHER: Ready . . .

*The Photographer snaps a photo. Penelope and Bruce laugh.
Penelope picks out a Victorian dress for the next shoot.*

PENELOPE: Hey let's try this one next. Every time we come here, I want to
    try this one, but we always forget.

BRUCE: Are you sure? Then what do I wear?

PENELOPE: Whatever. We have to get Ai in here, too. Where'd she go?

BRUCE: She was just here . . .

PENELOPE: Did she run off with Edie again?

They start looking for Ai.

    Ai!

BRUCE: Ai! . . .

Penelope exits. V continues.

V: Ai's best friend was Edie. Edie's best friend was me.

Pause.

    But I digress. Ai was a bit strange, as are we all, in that she believed
    that she was an angel disguised as a little girl. And so she lived
    her life in such a delightful spirit of giving and compassion—of
    "Ai"—Love.

BRUCE: Ai . . .

V: But something happened along the way.

BRUCE: A lot happened along the way.

V: Tell me about it, Mr. Wang.

BRUCE: Business picked up. The demand was insane. I soon had a branch office in LA. Cash was flowing in. I flew my Japanese suppliers in from Tokyo, and took them everywhere, to Vegas, where I showed them a good time. Knocked their socks off! And their pants.

V: Is that where you met Annette?

BRUCE: What? How did you know about Annette?

V: I see things. From my little platform. Tell me about her?

BRUCE: No, she's of no consequence.

V: On the contrary, Sir, I believe she is.

BRUCE: I met her at the club where I took my clients. We had a great time. She was . . .

V: Blonde with big boobs.

BRUCE: No, no, she was nothing like that. She was very down to earth. Unlike all the others who were climbing on my clients' laps. She was . . . homey.

V: Like a homecoming queen.

BRUCE: Yes. No . . . no.

V: So you hired her.

BRUCE: Just happened to be an opening.

V: For mistress. Are you sure your wife was unaware of this affair?

BRUCE: Of course! It was so discreet.

V: So everything was coming up roses.

Pause.

BRUCE: Yeah, roses . . .

Scene 13

Bruce's house. A Delivery Man brings flowers to Bruce's door. Bruce opens the door.

DELIVERY MAN: Delivery for Penelope Chen.

BRUCE: You mean Penelope Wang?

DELIVERY MAN: Sign here, please.

Bruce signs and brings the flowers into the house, where Alejandro sits in the living room. Delivery Man exits.

ALEJANDRO: For Penelope?

BRUCE: *(reading the card)* "Happy Birthday." Shit. I forgot.

ALEJANDRO: From?

BRUCE: *(looking at the card)* What the . . . ?

ALEJANDRO: What the "what the"?

BRUCE: Remember this guy named Chaz?

ALEJANDRO: Chaz Pendleton?

BRUCE: Is that his name?

ALEJANDRO: Wrong. Pemberton. Chaz Pemberton.

BRUCE: Whatever. Have you heard from him lately? What the hell is going on with this guy? Is it money he's after? Is that it?

ALEJANDRO: Don't be childish. Chaz wouldn't be after your money. You play with fish in the marketplace. This guy plays with antique planes and châteaux in France, man. Take it easy.

Bruce pulls an Oxford Dictionary from the bookshelf, in which is stashed a handgun, in the cut-out pages, which he takes out.

BRUCE: Take what easy? My wife's ex-boyfriend sends flowers to my home on the occasion of her birthday. The proper thing to do now would be to thank him, in person.

ALEJANDRO: What the . . . ? Shit, where the fuck did you get that? Put it away. I thought you weren't into weapons.

BRUCE: No, I'm not. This thing's been lying here in the safest place in the house—this Oxford Dictionary—for years.

ALEJANDRO: Since when?

BRUCE: Remember that night when we took the kids out for green tea ice cream?

ALEJANDRO: You're talking years ago, man.

BRUCE: Whatever. We were sitting in the Crystal Dragon, and Ah-Fok brought them green tea ice cream, and he didn't even charge us, and the two of us were talking about gun control, remember?

ALEJANDRO: Yeah, you said how ridiculous it is that the two of us, after taking our kids out for ice cream, could tuck them into bed, and then go out and each buy a gun. I remember that.

BRUCE: And so I did.

ALEJANDRO: You what?

BRUCE: That night, in a fit of cynicism, I went out and bought this Chinese-made piece at Walmart.

ALEJANDRO: You fucking what?

BRUCE: And it's been sitting here soaking in the Queen's English ever since. In its own, insulated Chinatown. Time to unbind it. Time for it to lose its virginity.

Bruce takes out the gun again.

ALEJANDRO: C'mon, Bruce, cool it. Hey! You're Bruce Lee! Would Bruce Lee ever hold a gun in his hand and shoot the bad guys? No way! He would *(making a kung fu pose)* "Ai-eeeee!"

Bruce plays with the gun.

BRUCE: I'm Bruce Lee Wang. I do things differently. Tell me about this guy. Chaz.

ALEJANDRO: Chaz? What can I say? Talented guy. Tall, attractive, and independently wealthy.

BRUCE: Keep going. Tomorrow he cures cancer. What I want to know is, why did they break up? Why drag me into this long protracted mutual whatever?

ALEJANDRO: He couldn't commit. I don't know, that's what Johanna tells me. There was some deep dark secret about him, so he couldn't commit.

BRUCE: To Penelope?

ALEJANDRO: To anyone. To love. Something about a fiancée who died because of him. Some tragic accident.

BRUCE: Have you ever met him?

ALEJANDRO: Of course.

BRUCE: Where?

ALEJANDRO: At a couple of Christmas parties.

BRUCE: What was he like?

ALEJANDRO: I don't really remember. I was pretty drunk. I mean . . . the first time, he didn't show. The second time, *(thinking)* he didn't show up either. Yeah.

Bruce plays with the gun.

Just put it away, OK? Let's just monitor the situation. It can't be anything serious.

BRUCE: No? Remember last weekend? Penelope went on this three-day retreat with her group of art therapists?

ALEJANDRO: Yeah? So?

BRUCE: She wouldn't tell me where she went. Said it was a secret! So who knows where she went! Where do art therapists go for retreats?

ALEJANDRO: Listen to yourself. Are you serious, man? Look, if you're really concerned, check her credit card, man.

BRUCE: I did. Nothing.

Pause.

ALEJANDRO: So don't worry.

Scene 14

In Penelope's studio, the flowers are in a vase. Penelope concludes a session with a Patient, who has just finished a painting. Penelope studies the painting.

> PENELOPE: That's beautiful. There's so much you have started to reveal. But look at all the things that remain hidden, bound in the darkness.

The Patient starts weeping.

> PATIENT: How can you see that?

> PENELOPE: How could I see it if I didn't know it myself?

Pause. The Patient embraces Penelope.

> PATIENT: Thank you, Penelope.

> PENELOPE: You're welcome. You've come a long way.

> PATIENT: But so far to go.

> PENELOPE: See you next time.

The Patient collects her things and leaves. Penelope starts cleaning up. Johanna enters.

> JOHANNA: Penelope, you are just amazing. Every time I see one of your clients walk out of here, I see how you've transformed them.

> PENELOPE: Thank you, Johanna.

> JOHANNA: It's as if you show them what's really going on inside them.

> PENELOPE: What's really going on inside all humanity is that everybody is unsatisfied with some deep, fundamental desire that has not been fulfilled.

Pause. Johanna sees the flowers.

> JOHANNA: What a beautiful bouquet! How romantic of Bruce! Well, my man should see this and learn from it.

Johanna takes the card. Penelope tries to grab it.

> C'mon, let me see what's written here . . .

Johanna reads the card. She is astonished.

Penelope, how could you leave this lying on the table? What if Bruce saw it?

PENELOPE: He signed for the delivery.

JOHANNA: What? And?

PENELOPE: Nothing.

JOHANNA: So . . . *(astonished)* What's going on? You're seeing Chaz again?

PENELOPE: We hadn't been in contact for over three years. I can't believe he remembered my birthday!

JOHANNA: How romantic! . . . But did you tell him you're now happily married and have a lovely daughter, and that he shouldn't be . . . ?

PENELOPE: He just ended a mutually abusive relationship. He's not in good shape.

JOHANNA: No?

PENELOPE: He says he misses the time we spent together in Provence, and that he wants me to join him there again. Oh, I shouldn't be telling you any of this! The bottom line is, I would never say yes to him!

JOHANNA: Right! Penelope, I'm so proud of you.

Pause.

But are you sure?

PENELOPE: How could I?

JOHANNA: Maybe you could consider . . . just one trip. Look, you counsel so many people, why not Chaz?

PENELOPE: No! I couldn't!

JOHANNA: Why not?

PENELOPE: You really think so?

JOHANNA: No. *(pause)* Absolutely no!

Scene 15

Bruce enters the studio with Ai and V following.

V: The next year, Chaz did not send flowers.

BRUCE: *(to Ai)* Maybe it was because I kept so close an eye on her. I was like a one-man full-court press. For a time everything was . . . clean. But something had changed. I continued to have my suspicions. I knew they were somehow corresponding, or even meeting, but there was no evidence whatsoever. I felt so inadequate. In my despair, I found a way to get back at her.

AI: How?

Pause. Bruce is in thought.

BRUCE: That day. Ai was seven. It was a cold, rainy night. There was a Christmas play at school. Her mommy was giving her a bath.

AI: My wings . . .

Penelope's studio. Offstage is a bathroom. Sound of running water. Ai, age seven, is taking a bath, singing and playing. Bruce stands in the doorway. Penelope comes out of the bathroom, with wings in hand. She hangs the wings on the coat tree.

PENELOPE: *(toward the bathroom)* Yeah, bubbles! Right, honey, tonight you get a bubble bath, just as you asked for! . . .

Penelope turns to face Bruce.

Bruce, I'm going to ask you one question, which I've avoided for some time. And I only want the most honest of answers. *(very angry)* What the fuck is the deal with Annette?

The singing stops from Ai's bathtub.

BRUCE: I don't know what you're talking about.

PENELOPE: Don't make me a fool. I've suspected you were having an affair for a while. And this afternoon she called and asked for Brucey. She said I was of no use to you anymore. I hung up on that bitch, and she called me back.

BRUCE: Crazy.

AI: *(offstage)* Mommy, Mommy . . .

PENELOPE: I want answers.

Penelope goes to the bathroom to take care of Ai. Bruce sits by the desk.

PENELOPE: *(offstage)* Wow, Ai, that's so cute! You're covered in bubbles! Yeah!

AI: *(offstage)* Thank you, Mommy.

Penelope comes back out.

BRUCE: You want answers? Then you go first.

PENELOPE: What?

Bruce feels for a key under the chair, and uses it to open the box on the desk. Bruce takes out mementos.

BRUCE: This box. I didn't say anything. For years. Just quietly observed your memorabilia slowly stacking up. All these B&Bs. Restaurants. Even places abroad! France! Spain!

PENELOPE: All the places you've never had the time to take me.

BRUCE: All the places Chaz has had the time to take you. I think it's time you explained this all.

PENELOPE: So you really don't get it. No wonder we're so far apart.

BRUCE: Don't stall.

Penelope looks at Bruce, shaking her head in disbelief.

PENELOPE: Okay. Well now I'm going to reveal to you the greatest and stupidest secret in the world, which I thought you knew all along: I made it all up!

BRUCE: Right. You made this guy Chaz up.

PENELOPE: I did. I made up all this stuff. Isn't it so obvious? Do you know anyone who's actually ever met him?

BRUCE: You wrote this letter, you sent this postcard abroad to be sent back so it would have a foreign postal stamp, you took this picture of yourself by the Riviera . . .

PENELOPE: Have you ever heard of Photoshop?

BRUCE: Right. And you ordered flowers for yourself on your birthday last year.

PENELOPE: That was easy.

BRUCE: Right, that was easy. You wrote the card, and signed it yourself.

PENELOPE: Don't you recognize my handwriting?

Bruce takes out a sheet of music notation.

BRUCE: And what's this? "Song for Penelope"? Which film did he write this for? Since when did you learn how to write music?

PENELOPE: Read it. Read the lyrics.

BRUCE: *(reading)* "Down another cup of wine, dear.

West of the mountain pass, there are no familiar faces . . ."

God is that cheesy or what!!

PENELOPE: Cheesy, sure! Don't you recognize it? It's plagiarized from Wang Wei, your favorite poet that I introduced you to.

BRUCE: What? So this guy Chaz is using Wang Wei to write a love song to my wife? What the . . . ?

PENELOPE: Right! What the . . . ! I made it all up. Impossible? Abnormal? Since when was I normal? Chaz gave me a sense of self, a sense of existing, of being worthy, a chance to unbind myself! That first time we met at the dim sum place, didn't his call to me make you feel that I was more worthy of your attention? Am I the only girl you've gone out with who's ever used that old trick? Are you sure that those high school cheerleaders you were trying to date really had so many guys lined up? Bruce, can't you feel that I've been shouting out to you? Last year, those flowers on my birthday, couldn't you feel that I was shouting out a warning: "Danger! Deep water!" Wait a minute. What am I saying? You're the one who's having an affair with a 23-year-old stripper with fake tits, who is now your secretary.

BRUCE: Annette is not the issue. And they are not fake.

PENELOPE: Oh my God . . .

AI: *(offstage)* Mommy, can you come here?

Penelope sits down, emotional. Bruce goes to the bathroom.

BRUCE: What do you want, baby?

AI: *(offstage)* I want mommy.

BRUCE: She's busy right now. You play with Duckie, OK? Duckie keeps you company, OK?

Bruce comes back from the bathroom.

So tell me about Chaz, huh?

PENELOPE: What about Chaz?

BRUCE: Perfect boy. I want to hear about him. Talented, rich, writes songs, great cook. Great fuck.

PENELOPE: The greatest!

BRUCE: Tell me what it's like to fuck in a château, surrounded by lavender fields.

PENELOPE: The scent of lavender permeates my senses as I let myself go in wild abandon!

Silence.

He doesn't exist, Bruce. The château doesn't exist. The greatest fuck doesn't exist and never will. Bruce, do you really want to believe that Chaz is a better cook than you are, a better fuck than you are? And now you use him as an alibi to go out to prove that you're better than him? Shit! He doesn't exist! But this fake person has pushed you into doing something that is real, deadly real.

BRUCE: You started this, Penelope. You're the one having an affair with Chaz.

PENELOPE: Who started what? He only exists when I NEED him to exist! If it were real, would I ever let you find the key? Under the chair? The stupidest place to hide anything? That's not the point. Your girlfriend called me. She actually told me to seriously consider divorcing you now, because you told her you would give me a great deal once we divorced. You'd cover college for Ai, and be very generous with me. Is that what you told her? Did you really say that kind of shit?

BRUCE: That kind of shit is said by many men every night in the throes of carnal passion.

AI: *(offstage, crying)* Mommy, Mommy . . .

PENELOPE: How long have you known her?

BRUCE: Three months. How long have you known Chaz?

PENELOPE: All my life.

BRUCE: That's what I thought!

PENELOPE: *(pointing)* In my head! Dammit, Bruce!

AI: *(offstage)* Mommy, Mommy . . .

Penelope grabs her coat, puts it on, and enters the bathroom door. Sound of thunder.

AI: *(offstage)* Mommy, why are you crying?

Sound of Penelope bundling up Ai after her bath.

BRUCE: Where are you going? Where do you think you're taking her?!!

Penelope brings the child Ai out of the bathroom, covered in towels, and rushes out. Sound of thunder.

PENELOPE: Did you forget?! She's in the school play! She needs to be onstage! And you need to be in the audience! She's an angel! An angel!

BRUCE: NO! You're not going out in this rain!

PENELOPE: Go fuck yourself, Bruce!!

AI: Mommy, my wings . . . I need my wings . . .

Penelope exits with Ai in her arms.

BRUCE: No! No!

Bruce stares in front of him, blankly. On the coat tree, the wings start to glow. Bruce is attracted by the glowing wings. He goes to them. He picks them up.

NO! NO!

Scene 16

The Crystal Dragon Restaurant. Bruce and Ai sit at a table. Ah-Fok cleans up around them. Musician's Soul sits at a table playing the saxophone softly.
Ai continues her story.

AI: And after that day, Bruce never acknowledged his daughter again. It was like she was invisible. Ai went to school, by herself. Her dad never sent her or picked her up; her dad never did anything with her, never played with her, never did homework with her, never took her to Disneyland, never even took her out for dinner. And after she dropped out of school, her dad never even noticed, never even asked. She was grounded, on this chemical-filled earth, left to rot in the slime, without her wings to lift her out of the muck.

BRUCE: They weren't real. They were a toy.

AI: I need them back. Please. Figure out everything, figure out who you are, and give me back my wings. Please.

Edie enters, and sees Ai.

EDIE: So there you are! I've been looking all over for you!

Edie sits, and Ah-Fok approaches her with two menus.

AH-FOK: Good morning, Edie. The usual?

BRUCE: We should have some breakfast.

EDIE: Can I have some siu mai, shrimp dumplings, and turnip cakes?

AH-FOK: Sure thing.

AI: Can I just have some plain congee?

EDIE: Ai just wants some plain congee.

AH-FOK: No problem. How about some salted duck eggs?

AI: No.

EDIE: Too rich.

Ah-Fok starts collecting the menus.

AH-FOK: As you wish!

BRUCE: Can I get some Canton fried noodles with an egg? I know you don't serve fried noodles in the morning, but you know the kitchen'll do it for me.

AI: Can I also get some Canton fried noodles with an egg?

EDIE: What? You want Canton fried noodles with an egg?

AI: It's for my dad.

AH-FOK: That comes with a side of wontons or milk tea.

BRUCE: Wontons.

AI: Wontons.

EDIE: Wontons.

AH-FOK: Wontons it is. Hungry today, huh, Ai?

AI: It's for . . .

BRUCE: You bet. Crazy hungry.

Ah-Fok leaves.

EDIE: Who are you talking to?

AI: My dad.

EDIE: Where is he?

AI: Right here.

BRUCE: Hi, Edie.

EDIE: Am I supposed to see him?

BRUCE: I'm right here, Edie.

AI: He's right here. If you want to have a conversation with him, I can mediate.

EDIE: But he's dead. What's he doing here?

AI: Good question. You see, Dad?

BRUCE: What's wrong with Edie?

AI: There's nothing wrong with Edie. You're dead.

EDIE: So your dad's sitting *(pointing)* HERE in this chair?

AI: Yeah.

BRUCE: Yup, how are you doing, Edie?

EDIE: Hiii Bruce. And you know what? V's here, too. Hi, V.

Ah-Fok comes back with food.

AH-FOK: Hi ladies. Let's get started. Where do you want this extra bowl of wontons?

BRUCE: That's for me.

EDIE: *(pointing)* There is fine.

BRUCE: This guy's been working here for ages.

Musician's Soul starts playing. V appears.

V: *(to Bruce)* Look closely at him.

V sees Edie, and stands in front of her. But Edie doesn't see V.

AH-FOK: Look, I'll hold the order of fried noodles for now, and when you need it, just let me know. Just so it doesn't go on your bill until you actually eat it.

EDIE: Thanks Ah-Fok. You are so considerate.

BRUCE: Wait. You're talking about my fried noodles! Fire them up! Now! And bring me some sriracha sauce!

Ah-Fok exits.

Hey! Why is everyone ignoring me? I'm sick and tired of this! You can pay for this yourselves!

Bruce stands to go.

AI: Dad! Wait! I have to finish my story!

V: Yes, Mr. Wang, please listen.

BRUCE: No! Get away from me, whoever you are! Whoever all of you are!

Bruce exits in a rush.

EDIE: *(ironically)* Hi V, nice seeing you today. How are things on the mountaintop? Has the fog cleared?

AI: I am not making this up.

EDIE: *(laughing heartily)* Of course not. Right, V?

AI: This is not funny, Edie.

V: *(gesturing to herself)* I'm here, Edie! Here!

Ai exits. Ah-Fok watches.

Scene 17

Penelope's studio. Bruce squats in a corner.
Penelope enters and starts setting up a canvas for a counseling session.
Penelope sees Bruce and is startled for a moment.

PENELOPE: Bruce? What are you doing there?

BRUCE: I'm . . . what am I doing?

PENELOPE: Not at work today?

BRUCE: I thought you didn't schedule any sessions for Wednesday afternoons. Wait a minute. I said this before.

PENELOPE: There's a special case today.

BRUCE: And that's what you replied.

PENELOPE: What? Are you okay, Bruce?

Bruce stands in the doorway.

BRUCE: I stood in the doorway, and said: *(to Penelope)* I was thinking, let's go to a movie. Cancel your appointment. Right, that's what I said.

PENELOPE: I can't.

BRUCE: And that's exactly what you replied. Who is it?

Edie enters.

PENELOPE: Hey. Come on in. Have a seat.

BRUCE: Edie?

EDIE: My mom told me to come. So I'm here for therapy?

PENELOPE: *(to Bruce, waving)* Bye.

Bruce stays on, watching as Bruce in the present.

BRUCE: Wait a minute. Why is this important?

They do not see or hear him.
Edie looks at the paintings around her on the ground.

EDIE: Wow! So this is where all the psychos come! You know, Ai and I never used to dare to come here and play. We always felt this place was . . . weird.

PENELOPE: Those who come for art therapy aren't necessarily psychos.

EDIE: But I am, right?

PENELOPE: Of course not!

EDIE: That's okay. Whatever. I don't mind. So I have to paint something, is that it? Shall we start?

PENELOPE: Sure. There are lots of different things you can use. How about crayons?

EDIE: You think I'm a kid, so you give me crayons?

PENELOPE: No, lots of grown-ups use crayons. They're good for expressing colors.

EDIE: So what do you want me to draw?

PENELOPE: Anything. This isn't a drawing contest. Just draw whatever you feel like. Something simple.

EDIE: And then you're going to use what I draw to analyze my quirky personality. Is that it?

PENELOPE: Right. No! I meant . . .

Johanna enters with a bubble tea drink.

JOHANNA: *(awkwardly)* Hi. *(to Edie)* I got some bubble tea, the kind you like.

Johanna gives Edie the tea, then brings Penelope to the side.

Edie starts drawing with her crayons.

(softly, to Penelope) Thanks for doing this.

PENELOPE: In our line we usually don't counsel people we know.

JOHANNA: I understand. Thanks so much. Any clues about what's really going on with her will be so helpful to me.

Johanna turns to Edie.

How's it going?

EDIE: Mom, you should try this sometime too.

PENELOPE: I'll call you when we're done.

JOHANNA: Right. *(to Edie)* Okay, Honey, I'll see you later! *(cheering)* Yay!

Johanna exits awkwardly.

PENELOPE: So how are we doing?

EDIE: Done.

Edie has drawn two matchstick girls.

PENELOPE: Two girls. Do I know them?

EDIE: One is me. The other is my best friend.

PENELOPE: Who?

EDIE: Ai.

Pause.

PENELOPE: Very good. So . . . this is Ai playing with you?

EDIE: Yea. Just now.

PENELOPE: *(surprised)* What?

EDIE: This afternoon.

Pause.

PENELOPE: Did you have a good time?

EDIE: I guess we did. I did. I don't know if she did or not. I'm not sure she's happy where she is. But she's my best friend in the whole wide world. Look, I drew us having green tea ice cream, and cutting her birthday cake. It's her birthday today!

PENELOPE: Today?

EDIE: Right. The 24th. Ai's birthday.

Pause. Penelope suddenly grows sad.

PENELOPE: Edie, can you please tell me—was she happy today?

EDIE: It was okay. That's just how she is, you know, not very expressive, can't quite tell. But one thing you may not know, because she never says it, but I know, is she really loves you two. She's always thinking of you, moment to moment, always wishing you the best.

Penelope is speechless. In her sorrow she embraces Edie.
A long moment. She lets go, and goes into the bathroom.

Are you OK? Can I go now? I finished my drawing. I'm going now. Goodbye.

Edie exits, followed by Bruce.

Scene 18

The studio takes on a surreal quality. Johanna sits with her feet up on the desk, the key to the house in her hand. She peruses Chaz's memorabilia. A bottle of whiskey is on the desk.
The Policeman and Policewoman enter. The Policeman carries a large sandwich.

POLICEWOMAN: Well Johanna, we're wondering if you know anything about a person named Chaz.

JOHANNA: *(surprised)* Who told you? I thought I was the only one who knew about Chaz.

POLICEMAN: Apparently that's not the case.

POLICEWOMAN: But we know you know the most.

JOHANNA: What do you want to know?

POLICEMAN: How about starting with a full name?

JOHANNA: Charles Fabio Landis III.

POLICEMAN: Address?

JOHANNA: One sixty-eight Spindrift Road, Carmel-by-the-Sea. It's a gated estate with 270-degree panoramas of the sea.

The Policewoman goes to make a call.

POLICEMAN: So you've been there to his house?

JOHANNA: Yeah. *(to Policewoman)* No need to check, he won't be there.

POLICEMAN: Where is he?

JOHANNA: He flew to his summer home in the South of France. He's smart. He wouldn't stay here with everything that's going on. He'd be very sad about Penelope and wouldn't want to be here.

POLICEMAN: A house in France?

JOHANNA: A château in Aix-en-Provence. It overlooks lavender and sunflower fields. The fresh scent of lavender in blossom teases your sense of smell as you take breakfast on the patio.

POLICEMAN: So you've been there?

JOHANNA: I, uh . . .

POLICEWOMAN: *(back from phone call)* So Chaz was pretty convenient for Penelope. Like her own delivery service. Could order takeout whenever she wanted.

JOHANNA: Yeah, he would drop everything for her. He'd come in his blue '64 Corvette or his airplane.

POLICEMAN: Did you detect any seasonal pattern to these outings?

JOHANNA: Seasonal? Actually, whenever she had a fight with Bruce. Yeah, she would need some time away and would go away with Chaz. Also when she found out that Bruce was seeing someone else, this 23-year-old stripper, whom he brought into the company and made his personal assistant, she would just take a vacation.

POLICEWOMAN: So Johanna, when was the last time you took a vacation?

JOHANNA: I haven't taken a vacation in, gawd, 20 years, since my honeymoon. *(laughing)* Real estate doesn't give you a lot of time to leave the country if a sale is pending.

POLICEWOMAN: You didn't have it like Penelope did. Whenever she wanted, Chaz would take her somewhere exotic, pamper her. Cook for her. Write songs for her. Love her the way she wanted it. No questions asked. It was perfect.

JOHANNA: Perfect. Yeah. Yeah. It was perfect for her. Penelope had it all.

POLICEWOMAN: Yeah, but what did she do for him?

JOHANNA: What did she do for him?

POLICEWOMAN: What did she do for him?

JOHANNA: Nothing. Penelope never did anything for him. He was waiting on her hand and foot.

POLICEWOMAN: Poor Chaz. No one was ever there for him.

JOHANNA: Wrong. I was there for him.

POLICEMAN: You?

JOHANNA: Whenever he needed something he would come to me. What did Penelope know about weekends with Chaz? He would take me to France and Spain and Europe and take me away from Alejandro, from real estate, from Edie. He was my vacation.

POLICEWOMAN: *(writing)* So you're telling me that YOU'RE the one who was having an affair with Chaz?

The officers wander away, leaving half a sandwich on the desk.

JOHANNA: You bet. Damn right. Oh, don't tell Alejandro.

Johanna's cell phone rings. She comes out of her daydream and picks up the phone. The room returns to normal.

Hi honey . . . Nothing, I'm just helping clean up some of Penelope's stuff. Yeah, I'm next door. I'll be right back. Oh, I left half of my sandwich for you. I'll bring it to you. Bye.

Johanna hides the whiskey, checks her breath, and exits with the sandwich and keys.

Scene 19

Crystal Dragon Restaurant. Late night. Bruce sits at a table. Ah-Fok is cleaning up. A homeless-looking man with a ragged coat sits at another table, eating, his back to us. Musician's Soul continues to sit at his own table, working on a song.

BRUCE: Can I get a menu?

Ah-Fok sits at the table.

　　　　Rough day, huh? Me, too.

Ah-Fok starts shaking his head.

　　　　What's the matter with you?

Ah-Fok stands, clears a tray of dishes, and leaves. V enters and sits at Bruce's table.

V: What's up?

BRUCE: Go away.

V: Hey, you look dead. Tired. People giving you a hard time?

BRUCE: There are plenty of tables. We don't have to share.

V: Are you feeling lonely?

Ah-Fok comes back and sits at the same table as them. He takes out a calculator and starts to tabulate the day's checks.

BRUCE: Hey, Ah-Fok. Your restaurant has gone to the dogs. It used to be clean and respectable. Look at what kind of underage girls prowl around here now!

V: You still don't know why everyone ignores you? It's not because you're lonely. It's because you're dead.

BRUCE: If I am, then so are you.

V: Wrong.

BRUCE: So we're not.

V: Your logic is a bit thin. *(holding out her hand)* I never had a chance to introduce myself. I'm V, Edie's friend.

BRUCE: Should I know you?

V: "Should I know you?" That's the story of my existence.

Ah-Fok is still sitting, doing his accounting.

BRUCE: Hey, can I get a menu?

V: Don't you get it, Bruce? He just can't see you. Actually this guy's been working here for a while. Check out his name tag. Have you ever? Probably not. No one usually does, with anyone they're not interested in. And so all those name tags are made for nobody.

Bruce examines the waiter's name tag.

BRUCE: Why does Ah-Fok's name tag say "Chaz"?

V: All these years you've been coming here, but you never noticed his English name, huh?

BRUCE: *(angrily)* He's Ah-Fok!

V: Your wife, on the other hand, has been quite inspired by this dashing man.

BRUCE: What do you mean?

V: You can't put the pieces together.

BRUCE: *(puzzled)* So this . . . is Chaz?

V: I don't know, you tell me. Your wife's lover.

BRUCE: But this is Ah-Fok! What's going on?

V: Penelope's been coming here longer than you have. When Penelope needed to dream up a name for an "excuse" of hers, before she even met you, he was her inspiration.

BRUCE: *(starting to see clearly what has happened)* No way! This is . . .

The homeless-looking man, who has been sitting at another table, sheds his coat and is revealed as Boss. Boss addresses Bruce.

BOSS: This is not making sense, because it's starting to make sense, right?

Ah-Fok, who is sitting next to Bruce, is a bit taken aback.

BRUCE: What? Who . . . ?

BOSS: You think, therefore you are. But whatever you think is not necessarily what IS.

Ah-Fok suddenly feels a little unsettled. He steps aside. Boss comes and sits at Ah-Fok's seat, opposite Bruce.

BRUCE: Say whatever you like. You're all part of this dream of mine, and when I wake up, you'll all disappear.

BOSS: Wishful thinking, Bruce. You're in the Bardo.

BRUCE: What?

BOSS: You're "between," in the gap, stuck, in the state after death. I'm here to read to you. This is one of my favorites, works every time in crucial moments. *The Tibetan Book of the Dead.* Listen and tell me that none of this is happening:

Boss takes out a large book and begins to read loudly, in almost a chanting rhythm. Musician's Soul plays in accompaniment.

"O son of noble family, the moment of your death has arrived. In this period between death and rebirth, with such an intangible body, you will experience many things, like in a dream. You must strive to awaken, and understand everything that you have done, and then let it go . . ."

Ah-Fok comes over to stop Boss.

AH-FOK: Sir, please, you can't do that here.

BOSS: I can't do WHAT here? You have no idea what I'm doing, man.

AH-FOK: But . . .

BOSS: But there's nobody here, so no harm, no foul, OK?

BRUCE: What do you mean, "there's nobody here"?

BOSS: Be quiet. Your job is to listen. Carefully!

Ah-Fok, slightly ruffled, exits.

"With such an intangible body, in the 'between' state, you will see your home and family as though you were meeting them in a dream, but although you speak to them, they will not reply; and you will see them weeping, and realize, 'I am dead, what shall I do?' and you will feel intense pain like the pain of a fish rolling in hot sand . . ."

BRUCE: But no one is weeping, and I don't feel any pain. And I can talk to my daughter. At least, she claims to be my daughter.

BOSS: Well I hope that continues to be true, but I doubt it. You're on your way, Bruce, to wherever you should be going. And I doubt if that's a very nice place.

Pause.

You killed yourself, Bruce. Shot yourself in the face, in a moment of lucidity after a savage spree of anger, jealousy, and confusion.

BRUCE: No way.

BOSS: Look, Bruce, you don't make a shadow. Stand up, look at the lights.

Bruce points at V.

BRUCE: She doesn't have one either.

V: Never did. Never will. That's the point.

Ah-Fok reenters, with the Policewoman.

BOSS: Whoever you're talking to is another figment of the Bardo.

POLICEWOMAN: Well, whoever YOU'RE talking to, Sir, is certainly another figment of YOUR imagination. I have to ask you to leave.

BOSS: *(to Bruce)* Don't mind her! You must focus! You must remember the end of your story!

BRUCE: The END of my story?

BOSS: It was only a week ago.

BRUCE: A week ago?

BOSS: FOCUS!

POLICEWOMAN: Please, Sir, I'm warning you for the last time . . .

Boss gestures to the Policewoman to cool it for the moment.

BRUCE: I drove to work. There was some meeting that I left from feeling very angry.

BOSS: Right.

BRUCE: Who then? Who was I angry at? Annette? But she can't live without me.

BOSS: You got her a place on your company's board. And in return for your great benevolence, she totally screwed you over. She siphoned funds from the company and made it look like you did it, and the board fired you, Bruce!

AH-FOK: *(frightened)* Bruce?

Ah-Fok looks around the air.

BRUCE: That's impossible. They can't fire me. It's my company! I built it from the ground up!

BOSS: It's called denial. It's coming back to you, eh?

BRUCE: *(remembering)* She was playing me. Shit!

BOSS: She fired you, Bruce.

BRUCE: Fuck!

BOSS: It was a good one, wasn't it? Now focus! In all the varying shades of reality, now you must come to terms with the one that is YOURS!

BRUCE: No! It's not possible!

BOSS: Visions of Johanna . . .

BRUCE: What?

POLICEWOMAN: *(forcibly grabbing Boss)* Sir, I'm sorry, but . . .

BOSS: *(to the Policewoman)* Don't do this. Not now. This is a crucial moment in the recognition of a being trapped in the Bardo. The moment of release!

POLICEWOMAN: Sorry, Sir, but you'll have to release beings trapped in the whatever outside the premises.

The Policewoman grabs Boss and escorts him out.

BOSS: No! No! *(to Bruce)* Take it back a week! What happened that day? You have to remember, in order to release yourself!

The Policewoman escorts Boss out.

AH-FOK: Wait! He didn't pay!

BOSS: *(screaming to Bruce as he exits)* Johanna's aunt! . . .

Bruce stands and wanders off, with purpose.

Scene 20

Alejandro's living room. Johanna is drinking. Edie enters and moves stealthily to exit.

JOHANNA: *(very high strung)* Edie! Where are you going?!

EDIE: To . . .

JOHANNA: Don't say "To see Ai."

EDIE: Mom, actually, I'm going to see Ai.

JOHANNA: One more word and I'm going to—

EDIE: Mom, what the hell is going on with you?

JOHANNA: *(hysterical)* What the hell is going on with me? What the hell is going on with you? How the hell do you expect me to go on like this? Huh? You tell me! HOW ARE WE TO GO ON LIKE THIS?!!

Edie shakes her head and heads for the front door.

You dare take one step out that door and . . . !

Edie exits.

Okay. If that's what you want, then Okay! Okay!! Okay!!!

Johanna hysterically tears the cushions out of the sofa and throws them around the room.

Okay!!! Okay!!! Okay!!! . . .

Johanna sits back on the cushionless sofa, blank eyed.
Enter Bruce, with a wild glow in his eye.

BRUCE: Johanna, where the hell is Alejandro? He isn't picking up.

JOHANNA: *(unnaturally calm)* He's on a managers retreat, no phones allowed.

BRUCE: How come I didn't know?

JOHANNA: Ask yourself, jerk.

BRUCE: I beg your pardon?

JOHANNA: You don't seem to be available much yourself these days.

BRUCE: Wait a minute. Aren't you supposed to be visiting your aunt in Seattle with Penelope?

Pause.

JOHANNA: Some last-minute business came up. A pending sale. I couldn't leave.

BRUCE: So Penelope went by herself to Seattle, to see your aunt, whom she does not know.

JOHANNA: She actually, well . . .

BRUCE: So you guys are in this together? I thought this Chaz business was over. Tell me where she's gone with Chaz.

JOHANNA: Chaz? You think this is about Chaz?! This isn't about Chaz, it's about Annette.

BRUCE: Don't talk to me about that bitch.

JOHANNA: So Annette's a bitch now. That's great! Now we know even more about why Penelope needs time to herself right now.

BRUCE: Just tell me when Chaz came back from abroad.

JOHANNA: Man, are you clueless. Chaz has been back for a year!

Pause. Bruce looks blank.

Look, Penelope needs time away from you and your constant hammering. Where she can find herself. She needs space. She needs to be away from you, in her own place at the Mystic Cove Inn, where she always goes.

Bruce exits.

Let her be by herself this weekend. Let her find herself and unbind . . . Bruce, I'm talking to you, you can't just walk away like that! *(to herself)* Holy shit! What did I just say?! Did I say . . . ?

Scene 21

Sound of waves. Penelope sits by the window of her room at the Mystic Cove Inn. Loud knocking.

BRUCE: Open the door, Penelope! Tell Chaz I'm here! I've caught you!

PENELOPE: Sorry, he's not here. I'm just looking out the window, by myself, Bruce. And will you keep it down? People are trying to relax here.

BRUCE: Open the door NOW! Don't give the coward time to run off.

PENELOPE: I'm not sure he would if he could, Bruce.

BRUCE: Open NOW! . . .

Penelope opens the door. Bruce rushes in and searches frantically everywhere.

Tell him to come out! Be a man! Now!

PENELOPE: You really don't get it, do you? I'm always alone here. Didn't I tell you, Chaz doesn't exist?

BRUCE: How could you, Penelope? This is our room! OUR ROOM! We made love on THAT BED for the very first time!

PENELOPE: Precisely. That's why.

BRUCE: So this is where you've been coming all the time, with him, to desecrate the memory of our love.

PENELOPE: I come here, to eulogize the memory of our love. To figure out how I can stand up and navigate through the ruins of my life. To be one with the waves, close to the silence. Remember? "Go now, and ask me nothing more, the white clouds will drift on for all time."

BRUCE: Stop the fancy stalling. Tell him to come out, now!

PENELOPE: Give me a break, Bruce. The way you've been screwing around, you have to cut me some slack. I need my time alone here.

BRUCE: With Chaz.

PENELOPE: With Chaz? You just don't get it! Yes! With Chaz! We come here all the time to fuck like animals.

BRUCE: So you admit it!

PENELOPE: *(laughing)* Actually, you and Annette should come here to fuck sometime. On this bed.

Bruce pulls out a gun and holds it in front of her. Penelope is not affected.

BRUCE: Annette can screw herself. She's running the company now.

PENELOPE: What?

BRUCE: She screwed me over. They voted me out. I'm no longer in control of . . . anything. Everything I ever . . . ever . . .

Bruce is trembling.

PENELOPE: What a surprise. How astonishing. Certainly no one ever saw anything like this coming.

BRUCE: Shut up!

PENELOPE: So you poor boy, Bruce, boo-hoo. You're coming here to cry in my lap? I'm sorry. I'm quite busy today!

BRUCE: With Chaz! Tell him to come out!

Bruce runs around searching.

PENELOPE: So what do you want to do, Brucey? You've lost everything. You lost your wife long ago. Now you lost your company to the bitch who suckered you into hand-feeding her the business. You pack a big piece, come to take it out on a guy named Chaz, who is certainly the root of all your problems, right?

BRUCE: Shut up and get him out here!

PENELOPE: Right! Take Chaz out with that big gun of yours, prove that your dick is every inch as big as his, right?

BRUCE: Where the hell is he? In the bathroom? In the closet?

PENELOPE: Try under the bed! Oh, I think he sneaked out through the patio! Go! Chase him!

BRUCE: *(searching)* You bastard! Come out and show yourself!

PENELOPE: He's here. Don't you see him?

BRUCE: Where?

Bruce points the gun at Penelope.

TELL ME!!

PENELOPE: *(pointing to her head)* HERE! HERE!

BRUCE: I'M GONNA SHOOT THE BASTARD!

PENELOPE: SHOOT THEN! BECAUSE CHAZ IS RIGHT HERE.

BRUCE: WHERE?!

PENELOPE: I told you long ago. He's here! *(pointing to her forehead)* IN MY HEAD!

Penelope grabs Bruce's hand and points the gun at her forehead.

And you can never beat him. He'll always be greater than you! He'll always love me more than you do! He's in every way better than you! There's only one way to beat him! SHOOT! SHOOT! Kill him right now! C'mon! NOW!!

BRUCE: NO!

PENELOPE: YOU LITTLE PIECE OF SHIT! DO IT!

Bruce shouts.

BRUCE: NOOOOO!!!! . . .

Blackout. A gunshot.

Scene 22

Lights up. A funeral home. Bruce's funeral. Musician's Soul plays a dirge. Alejandro is addressing the guests from the podium. Bruce's casket lies behind the podium.

Johanna, Edie, and Ai sit in the first row. Others, including Boss, Ah-Fok, the Policewoman, and V, are all present.

ALEJANDRO: I remember when I first met Bruce in our freshman year at college. It was in the dining hall. I went over, said a couple of the guys are going out partying if you want to come. And he said no, I still haven't finished my planning. I thought it was for some school project. But no, it was for life. He was planning when he would start his own company, when he would make his first million, what kind of house he would buy for his parents, what year he would marry, have children . . .

Alejandro finds it hard to continue.

He was my brother. Anytime I needed him, for anything, he was there for me. And when he needed me the most . . .

Alejandro grows emotional.
Pause. He calms down.

Rest in peace, as best you can, brother.

Alejandro sits. Johanna goes to the podium.
Bruce enters and sits in the back.

JOHANNA: Today we gather together here to commemorate the life of a dear friend of ours, who . . . who . . . *(pause)* I can't do this! No, this is not a commemoration. It's a confession. I'd like to confess to all of you here, I'm the one who really killed Bruce!

Alejandro stands and escorts Johanna off the podium, back to her seat.

ALEJANDRO: It's okay, dear. Come on . . .

JOHANNA: *(shouting)* And I'm the one who killed Penelope, too! Me! It was me!

Johanna breaks down. Alejandro leads her back to her seat.
The Policewoman comes up to the podium. She is dressed in civilian clothing.

POLICEWOMAN: Hello. These past weeks, working on Mr. and Mrs. Wang's case, I have come to realize that the officer me was not the real me. And so this morning, I resigned from the police force. Effective starting now, I am full-time hard at work on completing my first novel, *The Fundamental Illusion of Penelope.* I want to thank you, Bruce Lee Wang, wherever you are, for doing something that has made a difference, for me.

The Policewoman exits the room.
Silence.
Ai steps up to the podium. During the following, the mourners all go to the casket and throw flowers onto it.

AI: Dad, I can see you. Following me around. Visiting places in your past. Tracing the steps that have brought you here today, to this moment. What's going through your head? Are you thinking about all those times you didn't take me to school? Or pick me up? Or visit me at work? You weren't there. And you're not there now. But it's okay now. You need to move on. Please. You need to go, and to let me go. I've finished telling your story. You need to give me back my wings.

Pause.

BRUCE: I'm starting to feel it now. The cold, the pain that he *(pointing to Boss)* told me about. I think I'm on my way. And I'm seeing that you ARE my daughter, yes, you are Ai. It's clear to me now.

AI: Of course I'm Ai. Dad, that's the easy part.

BRUCE: No, baby, you don't get it.

AI: I don't get what?

BRUCE: Ai, you died that night.

AI: What?

BRUCE: That night when your mom rushed you out of the bathtub.

AI: What?

BRUCE: It was a flash storm. I screamed and pleaded with your mom not to take you, because of the state she was in. She was completely beside herself...

AI: Because of you.

BRUCE: Because of me. The car skidded and smashed into a tree, totaling the whole right side of it. That's where you were sitting, Ai, my baby...

AI: What? Dad, this is no time for jokes.

BRUCE: I'm realizing that this is no joke, baby. I'm so sorry, I never forgave your mom for driving out that night. Never. That night created an unbridgeable chasm between us. But it was my fault to begin with. You were a helpless victim in an unstoppable storm.

AI: That's not possible, Dad. I'm here! I'm...

BRUCE: Ai, my little baby girl, never thought I'd see the day when you grew up. The last time I saw you, you were still a cute little seven-year-old kid . . .

AI: No! Edie! Tell me it's not true.

Edie is silent.

Boss! Tell me! Tell me it's not true!

BOSS: It's true, Ai.

AI: That's impossible! I helped you in your shop! How could I help your customers if I wasn't there!

BOSS: The customers that were able to see you were real angels. All of the other customers couldn't see you. Think about it.

Ai turns to Edie.

EDIE: Boss is right.

BOSS: One can only see what one's mind is capable of accepting. Some of us can see things that others cannot. Edie is one of those, too.

Edie consoles Ai.

EDIE: It's true, Ai.

BOSS: The accident that night was so traumatic for you that you stayed on the site for months. I saw you, just as I see many others in similar situations: a little girl, wandering around the roadside, lost, and I decided to take you in, even though you are not an angel.

AI: I'm not . . . ?

BOSS: Those wings you failed to bring to the school play don't make you an angel. Maybe understanding you are an ordinary girl will help release you.

EDIE: We all felt so much grief after you died, Ai. For me, I thought the world would forever be a dark place. Then for some reason I started seeing you, and light came back into my life. You were still around. It hadn't sunk in for you, I guess. I told my parents, but they wouldn't believe me, and they didn't dare tell your parents. But I kept seeing you, and talking to you. After a few years, they accepted you just to humor me.

AI: They can't see me?

Johanna and Alejandro stand nearby, without seeing Ai.

EDIE: Mom, tell her.

JOHANNA: Tell who?

EDIE: Tell Ai that after she died, you never could see her. You were only playing along.

Johanna gestures as in "What the . . . ?" Alejandro motions to Edie as if asking "Where?" Edie points in another direction.

ALEJANDRO: *(at the direction Edie pointed)* No, no, we'd never do that, right, Ai?

Alejandro is speaking in the wrong direction. Horror grips Ai.

AI: No. Alejandro! Johanna! I'm here! Here!

EDIE: They don't have a clue where you are. *(pointing elsewhere)* She's over there, Dad.

ALEJANDRO: Of course!

Alejandro bumps Johanna with his elbow.

JOHANNA: Anything you say, honey . . .

EDIE: *(pointing at Ah-Fok, who is weeping quietly)* And look how accommodating Ah-Fok always was. Whenever I went to eat, and was talking to you, he would know that you were there, and he played along so skillfully. Unlike my parents.

Ai is in shock.
Boss takes out his big book again.

BOSS: Now it is time to tend to you both. Bruce and Ai, it's time. *(reading in a chanting tone again)* "O son of noble family, your mind no longer enjoys the support of a physical body, and rides the horses of the wind like a helpless swaying feather. You say to mourners at your funeral, 'I am here, stop your mourning,' but they will not perceive you, and so finally you will realize, 'I have died,' and you will start to feel great pain . . ."

BRUCE: No!

AI: No! No!

The Policeman enters. He suddenly handcuffs Boss, apprehending him.

BOSS: What is this . . . ?? You can't . . .

POLICEMAN: *(reading the name)* Rufus Buster Hicks, you are under arrest for trafficking in illegal substances, kidnapping minors, and soliciting hallucinogenic drugs.

BOSS: What the f . . . ? This is totally untrue! Totally unfounded! You can't do this to me!

POLICEMAN: You have the right to remain silent . . .

The Policeman leads Boss away. Alejandro pumps his fist at the Policeman in a gesture of unity.

BOSS: Silence my ass! I AM BOSS! BOSS! ARRESTING ME WILL SERIOUSLY UPSET THE EQUILIBRIUM OF THE CELESTIAL SPHERES, AND YOU WILL BE HELD RESPONSIBLE BY THE HIGHER AUTHORITIES! Oh shit! . . .

The Policeman exits with Boss.
Musician's Soul plays "Song for Penelope" as all the mourners stand to leave. Penelope appears, in Victorian dress, with parasol, upstage, in the distance, before a bright light.

BRUCE: It's time.

ALEJANDRO: *(to Edie)* Honey, we have to be on our way now. On our way . . .

Ai embraces Edie.

EDIE: I'll miss you, Ai.

Johanna and Alejandro try to take Edie's hand to leave, but she is in the midst of parting with Ai.

JOHANNA: *(to Alejandro)* She's saying her goodbyes.

ALEJANDRO: *(to Edie)* Take your time. We'll wait for you.

EDIE: No, Dad, please. I need to be by myself. I'll walk home. Really. I'll be fine. Thanks.

ALEJANDRO: Sure, honey. *(to Johanna)* Then let's go. She needs to be . . . by herself.

JOHANNA: So where are we going?

ALEJANDRO: *(checking his watch)* I don't know. It's too early for my meeting.

JOHANNA: *(checking her watch)* Yeah, me too. Didn't think the service would be so fast.

ALEJANDRO: I guess we're . . . kind of between.

JOHANNA: Yeah. Between . . .

Johanna and Alejandro exit.
    As Edie watches, Bruce comes to Ai.
    Bruce embraces Ai.
    Bruce slowly crosses toward Penelope. Ai follows.
    Edie stands next to V, whom she can now see.

EDIE: *(to V)* Do I know you?

V sings to the music.

V: *(singing) Morning rain has settled the dust,*
    The willows by the inn are fresh and green.
    Down another cup of wine, my friend.
    West of the mountain pass, there are no familiar faces.

In the distance, Penelope, Bruce, and Ai are reunited for a brief moment, then they all go their separate ways.
    Lights fade out.

    The End

The Village

CHARACTERS

Main characters, first generation

HANBIN, surname Chao, age 20s–60s, from a humble Beijing family, a Chinese soldier who fought in the Second World War and the Chinese Civil War, retreated with Chiang Kai-shek's Nationalist Chinese Army to Taiwan in 1949, and works on an Air Force base as a transport driver
YEN, surname Chien, age 20s–70s, Hanbin's wife, from a wealthy Beijing restaurateur family
GRANNY CHIEN, Yen's mother, former restaurant owner from Beijing, originally from Tianjin City in northern China
CHU, full name Chu Chuan, age 20s–70s, a simple man from Qingdao, Shandong Province, who has a similar background to Hanbin, and is now also a transport driver on the Air Force base
MRS. CHU, née Chen Hsiu-er, age 18–70s, Chu's wife, an uneducated local woman from Chiayi, Taiwan, who at the start speaks only Taiwanese dialect and no Mandarin. In later acts she speaks decent Mandarin with a Taiwanese accent and sell dumplings
NING, full name Chou Ning, age 20s–70s, former fighter pilot in the Nationalist Chinese Air Force, a jovial spirit from Shanghai
RUYUN, surname Leng, age 20s–70s, elegant woman from Hunan Province in China, former wife of the fighter pilot Li Tzu-kang, later married to Ning
LI, full name Li Tzu-kang, age 20s–70s, a fighter pilot in the Air Force, and a war hero during the Sino-Japanese War and the Chinese Civil War

Other characters, first generation

WEI CHUNG, middle-aged man whose true identity is unknown
WEIRD, surname Chi, age 20s–70s, a neighbor in the Village who speaks in a dialect that nobody understands, not even a word
WU, age 20s–70s, a former fighter pilot who rises in the ranks after coming to Taiwan to become a General, originally from Sichuan Province in China, living in the much more spacious officers' housing nearby
MRS. WU, age 20s–70s, Wu's very proper wife
MRS. TSUI, age 20s–70s, manager of a neighborhood money fund in the Village, and mother to Big and Li'l Spice
GRANNY LU, a mysterious and elegant old woman, with white hair and a cane, impeccably dressed in traditional Chinese cheongsam. Little is known of her origins or what she does

ATTENDANT of Granny Lu, age 20s–40s
HUANG, a local Taiwanese man, owner of a carpenter's shop in the town of Chiayi, outside of the Village
MUTT, Huang's assistant

Second generation

BIGS, nickname of Chao Li-wen, 18 to middle age, eldest daughter of the Chao family
DEUCE, nickname of Chao Li-ming, 17 to middle age, second daughter of the Chao family
SMALLS, nickname of Chao Tai-sheng, 16 to middle age, son of the Chao family
OX, nickname of Chu Chien-kuo, 18 to middle age, eldest son of the Chu family
CART, nickname of Chu Chien-tai, 17 to middle age, second son of the Chu family
FATS, nickname of Chou Nian-k'ang, high school student, only son of the Chou family
BIG SPICE, 18 to middle age, eldest daughter of Mrs. Tsui
LI'L SPICE, 17 to middle age, second daughter of Mrs. Tsui
WU CHIA-KUANG, high school student, son of General Wu and Mrs. Wu

Others

Act One: Officers (2), Tang Songren, Tang's Wife, People Waiting in Line, Flagmen, Workers, Other Villagers
Act Two: Mr. Chang, Teachers (2), Tough Outsiders, Clerk, TV Host (voice), Military Police (2)
Act Three: Pedestrians in Taichung, US GIs, Bouncer at the Bar, Ladies Playing Mahjong (3), Wu's Attendant, Other Villagers, Templegoers, Woman in Red
Act Four: Pedestrians in Taipei, Tour Guide, Granny Yang, Hanbin's Relatives, Chu's First Wife, Chu's Elder Son, Chu's Daughter-in-Law, Ning's Sister, Ning's Nephew, Restaurant Waitress, Gamblers (2), Pit Boss, Casino Waitress, Andy, Cart's Vietnamese Wife, Smalls's Wife, Smalls's Daughter, Deuce's Husband, Bigs's Husband, Other Villagers, Other Children of Second Generation

SETTING

The main location is Formosa Village #1, a fictional military dependents' village (*juancun*) in the town of Chiayi, southern Taiwan, from 1949 to 2006. Such villages provided basic housing for the over one million military personnel and their dependents who retreated to Taiwan from China in the aftermath of the Chinese Civil War in 1949. People from all provinces of China were packed into these crowded refugee centers, speaking different dialects, cooking different foods. Within this diversity, they shared one common sentiment: the desire to go home. That wish would be denied them for almost four decades.

The Village was first performed on December 5, 2008, at the National Theatre, Taipei, Taiwan, written by Stan Lai, based primarily on childhood stories of Wang Wei-chung, in collaboration with Wang and the original cast, directed by Stan Lai and Wang Wei-chung, produced by Performance Workshop:

Cast:
Chu Chung-heng as Hanbin
Ann Lang as Yen
Feng Yi-gang as Chu
Wan Fang as Mrs. Chu
Sung Shao-ching as Ning
Hsu Yen-ling as Ruyun
Yen Yi-wen as Granny Chien, Mrs. Tsui and others
Chou Heng-yin as Granny Lu, Big Spice, and others
Michael Huang as Li Tzu-kang
Renzo Liu as General Wu and others
Ting Ting Hu as Bigs and others
Vanessa Liu as Deuce and others
Ethan Wei as Smalls and others
Jack Na as Ox and others
Hsiao Cheng-wei as Cart and others
Hugh Shi as Wei Chung, Fats, and others
Ashley Huang as Lil' Spice, Granny Yang, and others
Tseng Hsin-yu as Huang, MP, Bouncer, and others
Seng Soo-ming as Weird Chi and others

Charles Hwong as Attendant, Mutt, MP, Chia-Kuang, Andy, and others
Lin Chia-hsuan as Teacher, Waitress, and others
Igor Cvetkovic, as G.I. and Bigs' Husband
Wang Wei-chung as Narrator

Scenic Design by Austin Wang
Lighting Design by Michael Leezen Chien
Costume Design by Lei and Christine Suzuka

Produced by Nai-chu Ding
Executive Produced by Mingchang Hsieh

Photo: *The Village*, National Theatre, Taipei, Taiwan, 2008, Act 1, Scene 4. *Standing, from left*: Wei Chung (Hugh Shi), Hanbin (Chu Chong-heng), Granny Chien (Yen Yi-wen), Yen (Ann Lang), and Chu (Feng Yi-gang). *Sitting, from left*: Li Tzu-kang (Michael Huang), Ruyun (Hsu Yen-ling), Mrs. Chu (Wan Fang), and Ning (Sung Shao-ching). Photo by Franco Wang.

Part One

Prologue

A bulldozer razes a group of rundown shacks.

Granny Lu, an elegant elderly woman with white hair and walking stick, formally dressed in a dark cheongsam, walks slowly and gracefully through the rubble.

Smalls enters and speaks directly to the audience. He is middle aged, dressed in a smart business suit.

> SMALLS: It was 1949. The Chinese Civil War had just ended. The Communists had won and taken over China. My parents were on the losing side—the Nationalists, who, led by Chiang Kai-shek, organized a chaotic mass evacuation to the island of Taiwan, off the southeast coast of China. Over a million soldiers and civilians were displaced in this exodus. The plan was to quickly organize a counterattack, defeat the Communists, and recover all of China. Then they could all go home.
>
> That never happened.
>
> In the chaos, my parents were shipped to a town in southern Taiwan called Chiayi, where they were assigned to live in hastily built, temporary housing, named "Formosa Village #1." Those temporary quarters became our permanent homes. A few years ago, after over 50 years, after being condemned as uninhabitable, our village was finally scheduled for demolition. In fact, it was pretty much uninhabitable from day one. I called everyone and proposed we all gather on New Year's Eve for one last dinner there before our village was torn down. I brought my daughters to the gathering, to show them where I grew up, this village we all came from . . .

ACT ONE, 1949–1950

Scene 1: Address Plaques

A loudspeaker announcement.

> ANNOUNCEMENT: Attention, all noncommissioned officers and dependents. Please gather at the big tree with your identification papers . . .

A big tree, under which are two Officers in uniform, looking through documents at a makeshift desk. A lineup of refugees, looking mostly ragged.

In line are Hanbin, a young man in plain military khakis; his wife, Yen, her hair permed, dressed in a proper Chinese cheongsam, and her mother, Granny Chien, also dressed in a cheongsam.

> YEN: *(Beijing dialect, to Hanbin)* Hey, Yang, can they hurry it up? I'm sweating. I need a shower.

> GRANNY CHIEN: *(Tianjin dialect)* Are you sure we'll get a unit, Yang?

> HANBIN: *(Beijing dialect)* Don't worry. There won't be a problem.

> OFFICER 1: Listen up, everyone! Once you are assigned your unit number, go directly to the office to complete the paperwork. Next is *(shouting a name)* Tang Songren.

Pause.

> YEN: Hurry it, whoever you are! Pick it up!

> OFFICER 1: *(shouting)* Tang Songren?

Wei Chung, a casually dressed, middle-aged civilian, steps out of the line, and goes to the front.

> WEI CHUNG: *(Sichuan accent)* Here!

> OFFICER 2: Your papers?

> WEI CHUNG: I lost them on the ship.

> OFFICER 2: *(eyeing him suspiciously)* Your dependents?

> WEI CHUNG: They're . . . *(pointing)* over there by that tree.

> OFFICER 2: Are you really Tang Songren?

> WEI CHUNG: Yes, I am.

> OFFICER 2: So tell me how to write it. Which character for "Song" and which for "ren"?

> WEI CHUNG: "Song" as in "Song dynasty"; "ren" as in "benevolence."

> OFFICER 1: *(looking at his list)* Dammit, got 'em both wrong!

> OFFICER 2: Get out of here!

Wei Chung gets back in line, unruffled.

YEN: Did you see that? Someone just tried to bum a unit!

OFFICER 1: Tang Songren! Last call!

The real Tang Songren fights through the line from the back, with his family.

TANG SONGREN: HERE! *(to his wife)* Hurry up! . . .

The Officer checks his ID papers, stamps a document, and hands him a plain door plaque with the address number.

OFFICER 1: *(proclaiming officially for all to hear)* Tang Songren, Unit 97!

OFFICER 2: *(pointing for Tang)* Report over there.

Tang and family exit.

OFFICER 1: Now listen carefully! Don't waste time. Answer as soon as your name is called! *(reading from the list)* Chou Ning.

NING: *(Shanghai accent)* I'm Chou Ning.

Ning steps out of the line and takes out his ID papers. He is dressed in neat officer's khakis. The two Officers stand at attention and salute him.

OFFICERS: *(saluting)* Greetings, Officer!

YEN: What's going on?

OFFICER 1: Sir, this isn't housing for fighter pilots like you. This is soldiers' quarters. You should report to the section for officers.

NING: They're filling up over there. I'm quite happy here.

The two Officers discuss among themselves.

GRANNY CHIEN: Oh no, there's even an officer ahead of us.

YEN: Hey! You cut the queue!

HANBIN: Shh! Officers have priority. What's more, he's a pilot!

OFFICER 1: *(to Ning)* Where are your dependents, Sir?

NING: My mother's arriving on the first ship.

Pause. Officer 1 stamps a document and gives an address plaque to Ning.

OFFICER 1: *(proclaiming)* Chou Ning, Unit 98!

OFFICER 2: Report over there.

NING: Thank you.

OFFICER 1: Next: *(looking at his list)* Chao Hanbin.

Pause. No one answers.

CHAO HANBIN!

YEN: Hurry it up, whoever you are!

Nobody responds. Wei Chung steps out, tempted to give it another try. Suddenly, as if waking from a dream, Hanbin raises his hand.

HANBIN: HERE!

Hanbin moves toward the head of the line with his baggage. Both Yen and Granny Chien are stunned.

Excuse me, excuse me . . .

OFFICER 2: What took you so long?

Hanbin comes forward to the table and takes out his ID. Yen and Granny Chien follow, but are confused.

YEN: *(to Hanbin)* Tell me what's going on?

HANBIN: Shh . . . Don't say anything.

Officer 1 stamps a document and gives an address plaque to Hanbin.

OFFICER 1: *(proclaiming)* Chao Hanbin, Unit 99!

HANBIN: Thank you.

OFFICER 2: Report over there.

Hanbin takes Yen and Granny Chien to the side to gather their things.

YEN: *(in disbelief)* Wait a minute, Yang. You're telling me your name isn't "Yang"?

HANBIN: *(softly)* I'll explain later.

YEN: Who the hell are you?

HANBIN: Are you lucky to be alive or not? Didn't I manage to bring you and your mom over here?

YEN: Who is Chao Hanbin?

HANBIN: Me.

YEN: But aren't you Yang?

HANBIN: Later. Let's go.

YEN: So who in the hell did I marry?

GRANNY CHIEN: Later . . .

Hanbin, Yen, and Granny Chien exit.

OFFICER 1: *(looking at the list)* Wei Chung!

Pauses. Nobody responds.
Wei Chung looks around, sees no one answering, and raises his hand.

WEI CHUNG: *(standard Mandarin)* Here! Here!

Wei Chung steps to the front of the line again. The two Officers look at him in disbelief.

OFFICER 1: I called for Wei Chung. How come it's you again?

WEI CHUNG: Oh, I was confused. I am Wei Chung.

OFFICER 2: So your accent changed with your name? Papers?

WEI CHUNG: I told you they were lost on the boat.

OFFICER 2: Which "Chung"?

WEI CHUNG: Of course it's "Chung," as in "Chunghua," the Republic of China!

OFFICER 1: Date of birth?

Ning, who has not yet left the area, interjects.

NING: He's Wei Chung.

OFFICER 1: *(not believing him)* Sir, please . . .

NING: It's true. Really. I met him in Chungking.

OFFICER 1: Sir, we can handle this . . .

NING: Look. We're all far from home. No need to stand on such
formalities.

Ning exits.
Reluctantly, the Officer stamps a document and hands Wei an address
plaque.

OFFICER 1: *(proclaiming)* Wei Chung, Unit 101!

OFFICER 2: *(threateningly)* I'm letting you stay in this unit until the real
Wei Chung arrives, do you hear me?

WEI CHUNG: I am the real Wei Chung.

Wei exits.

OFFICER 2: Damn smart, aren't you?

Scene 2: Moving In

Two simple one-room shacks, with empty ground in between on which stands a
telephone pole.
Only structural pillars and frames of the houses are seen on the stage, so
the audience can see through the walls. Hanbin's house is stage right, Ning's
house is stage left. They are all unpacking. Hanbin is working cheerfully, while
Yen and Granny Chien are still trying to figure out what happened.

YEN: So who on earth did I marry? Mr. Chao or Mr. Yang?

GRANNY CHIEN: Hey, Yang, is there a stove?

HANBIN: Give me a moment and I'll set one up.

YEN: I thought we would fly to Taiwan. *(sarcastically)* Didn't you say you
were a fighter pilot?

HANBIN: I said I drove transport for fighter pilots.

YEN: Ha! Now you say it clearly! Shame on you! When we first met,
you wore one of those leather bomber jackets with a scarf made of
parachute silk, and you said you were *(slurring)* "transpurred fighter
pilot"! Of course I took you for a pilot! Turns out you're only a regular
soldier! You conned me into coming here. I need you to fly me back
home! I'm going back to Beijing to find me a real pilot who'll fly me

over to Manchuria for a barbeque, just like my classmate Pei-lan, who married a real fighter pilot!

GRANNY CHIEN: Who died in battle. You envy that, too?

Stage left, Ning is putting things in order in his spartan room, which has a temporary cot for a bed, and a chair. Wei Chung approaches Ning's front door holding a bottle of liquor and knocks.

WEI CHUNG: Officer Ning!

NING: Who's there?

WEI CHUNG: I wanted to thank you, Sir! I brought a little something for you.

Ning opens the door.

NING: Please come in. Have a seat.

At Hanbin's.

YEN: I'm thirsty! I want some iced Beijing plum juice!

At Ning's. The two open the bottle of liquor.

WEI CHUNG: I didn't come here to Taiwan by choice.

NING: Everyone has their story.

WEI CHUNG: I was a merchant, with business in Shanghai, Amoy, Hong Kong, Japan . . . I was about to return home that day. I had a boat ticket, but they shut down all the damn ports!

NING: And your real name is . . . ?

Pause.

WEI CHUNG: In times like these, many things are best forgotten. Just call me Wei Chung. *(raising his glass)* Bottoms up!

The two drink.
At Hanbin's.

YEN: So where's the rest of this house? How can we live in such a small space?

HANBIN: Don't worry, it's only temporary.

Granny Chien takes out a rolling pin.

YEN: Mom, why did you bring a rolling pin all the way from Beijing?

GRANNY CHIEN: Silly girl. This is your grandmother's rolling pin. She founded the Fortune using this! With this in hand, you can make a living anywhere.

YEN: *(depressed)* I was scheduled to enroll in Beijing University in the fall.

GRANNY CHIEN: Hey, Yang, do you think we can go home before the Tomb Sweeping Festival next spring?

HANBIN: No problem. We're going to mount an offensive, defeat the Commies and be back home before Chinese New Year.

YEN: I need a shower. I demand a shower!

Hanbin suddenly slaps her.

(surprised) What?! You dare hit me?!

GRANNY CHIEN: What are you doing!

Hanbin looks at his palm—he has killed a mosquito.

HANBIN: I guess Formosa really is a "precious island." Look at how huge this mosquito is!

Chu, a tall man from Shandong wearing the same plain khakis as Hanbin, enters with a shy, pretty young woman, Mrs. Chu. He motions at Mrs. Chu to stand aside, then knocks on Hanbin's side window.

CHU: Hey, Yang!

YEN: Someone is calling you, charlatan!

Hanbin opens the little window and sees Chu.

HANBIN: Oh, hi, Chu! Let's talk outside.

Hanbin steps outside and meets Chu at the door.

YEN: Where are you going? I need to listen to some music!

Yen takes out a portable gramophone from her luggage and starts to set it up.

CHU: *(Shandong accent)* Not bad!

HANBIN: Thanks. Uh, from now on, can you please call me "Chao"? Don't call me Yang.

CHU: Aren't you Yang?

HANBIN: Yeah, but . . . just call me Hanbin.

CHU: Okay, Hanbin, Yang, whatever, I have a situation.

HANBIN: Uh-oh. Been drinking again?

CHU: No, no. Look. *(to Mrs. Chu)* Come on over here!

Mrs. Chu joins them, bashfully. Hanbin recognizes her.

HANBIN: Wait. Isn't she the waitress from the roadside food stall?

CHU: That's her.

HANBIN: So you two are together?

CHU: We're actually further down the road than that . . . *(pointing at Mrs. Chu's abdomen)* She's . . .

HANBIN: No way!

CHU: Well, yes, there is a way.

HANBIN: Then . . . let's see . . . uh, we can figure out how to put you up . . .

CHU: No, no, Yang, I mean Hanbin, I'm not asking to intrude on you guys. I'm just looking at this empty space between your unit and the guy next door.

Chu points at the empty space between Hanbin's and Ning's.

This would work just fine for me.

HANBIN: *(in disbelief)* But there's nothing there!

CHU: Put a roof over it and it'll do.

HANBIN: But there's a telephone pole in the middle!

CHU: The better to tap electricity.

HANBIN: That pole was brought over from Nanjing. When we go back it will have to be moved back according to its serial number!

CHU: I'll personally see to that.

Mrs. Chu speaks, in pure Taiwanese dialect, which is not understandable by the men, who come from mainland China. She cannot understand their language either.

MRS. CHU: *(Taiwanese dialect)* What's going on?

CHU: Later.

MRS. CHU: Can't understand a word.

CHU: Yang, I mean Hanbin, please. I'm counting on you. You've had my back all the way here.

YEN: *(opening the window)* I need a shower!

HANBIN: But I can only speak for myself.

CHU: *(pointing at Ning's house)* Then can you put in a word for me?

HANBIN: Surely.

CHU: Much appreciated.

Hanbin and Chu walk over to Ning's, stage left, leaving Mrs. Chu where she is.

HANBIN: Sir!

CHU: Reporting, Sir!

NING: Who's there?

Ning comes to open the door.

HANBIN: May I have a word with you, Sir? I'm your neighbor. *(saluting)* Sergeant Chao Hanbin.

CHU: *(saluting)* Sir, Sergeant Chu Chuan reporting!

Ning steps outside to talk to them. Wei Chung listens from the doorway.

HANBIN: Sir, we have a situation: Your unit is number 98. I'm next door, in unit 99. In between, uh, we're, um, short a number.

NING: *(confused)* We're what? We're not short or anything here.

CHU: I mean . . . I'd like to shore up a number in between.

NING: What?

HANBIN: *(pointing at Mrs. Chu)* Sir, he has family now.

Ning sees Mrs. Chu. Pause.

CHU: Sir, my buddy Hanbin has no objection in this matter.

Wei Chung speaks up.

WEI CHUNG: *(rudely)* Are you kidding me? I live right behind. You're going to be blocking my way!

NING: *(calmly)* Who's kidding who? These are crazy times. I've seen troops and horses competing for the same shelter. I even heard someone claimed he was someone else and he actually succeeded in bumming a unit!

WEI CHUNG: *(switching his tone immediately)* Did you hear that? My big brother has spoken! Any objections?

CHU: Not me.

HANBIN: Nope.

WEI CHUNG: Then come by for a drink when you're free.

Wei Chung exits.

HANBIN: Thank you, Sir!

Ning surveys the empty space, puzzled.

NING: *(to Chu)* You were saying you want to put up—a roof here?

CHU: Easy.

HANBIN: But what about flooring?

CHU: Isn't there ground here?

HANBIN: What about windows?

CHU: Your windows are my windows.

Yen's gramophone is now set up, and she manages to play a record. An Italian tenor's voice is heard from the gramophone, singing the aria "Amor ti vieta." Everyone stops to listen to the music. Yen smiles for the first time. Everything seems to stop for a moment.

Scene 3: The Flag-Raising Ceremony

New Year's Day, 1950. It is a cold day. The villagers gather for the flag-raising ceremony, a patriotic event held every January 1. Most of the villagers look rough and ragged, except for a few, like Yen and Granny Lu, who always make a point to be well dressed. Two Flagmen prepare the flag of the Republic of China.

OFFICER 1: TEN-HUT!

The ragged men, women, and children stand at attention, facing the flag, with as much dignity as they can muster. Latecomers insert themselves into the formation. Just when the two Flagmen are about to raise the flag, Hanbin rushes in, carrying a torn and tattered flag.

HANBIN: Hold on, Sir! Can we use this one?

Officer 1 opens up Hanbin's battered flag, with a puzzled look.

OFFICER 1: But this is torn and tattered. Where did you get it?

HANBIN: A comrade of mine carried it on his back during the Battle of Xubang.

OFFICER 1: *(to Flagmen)* Replace it.

Flagmen switch to the torn flag. Hanbin gets into the formation and stands in front of Yen.

YEN: Which comrade was this?

HANBIN: Don't ask.

YEN: Come on, tell me. Who was it?

HANBIN: Don't ask.

YEN: Who?

HANBIN: Chao Hanbin.

YEN: What . . . ?

OFFICER: TEN-HUT! . . . All salute!

All salute. The torn flag rises to the Flag Song.

Scene 4: The First New Year's

Chinese New Year's Eve, February 16, 1950. The three families are busy preparing for the festive dinner, as best they can. As time has passed, more things appear in each household: a chair here, a cabinet there. Everyone is dressed for cold weather, in as festive a way as possible. Stage right, Granny Chien is making dumplings, while Hanbin kneads the dough and Yen watches.

The Chu's house, in between the other two, is now livable, with the roof and walls in place, connecting all three units in a line, but the telephone pole is still in the center of the house. Chu is writing a New Year's couplet in calligraphy, on red paper. Mrs. Chu stands outside the door and stares longingly into space, her pregnancy more obvious. Chu steps out and gestures for her to go inside. They can barely communicate. Neither speaks standard Mandarin. Chu's thick Shandong accent is barely understandable; Mrs. Chu's pure Taiwanese dialect cannot be understood by any villagers.

> CHU: What are you doing standing outside? Come in, it's cold outside. *(pointing at the calligraphy)* Look.

> MRS. CHU: That's really good calligraphy. But what does it mean?

> CHU: "Earth reawakens and spring blooms in Lu." "Lu" refers to Shandong, my ancestral home. Home, get it?

Chu pastes the banner on the telephone pole.

> MRS. CHU: I don't understand.

> CHU: You still can't understand?

Over at the Chao household, Yen is wearing a well-tailored winter vest.

> YEN: Didn't you say Taiwan was going to be warm? Who thought I would need my winter vest indoors?

> HANBIN: It's all good. The cold gives it a New Year's feel.

> YEN: Well, it doesn't. What kind of meat is this? It stinks! Is this dog meat?

> HANBIN: Come on, it's not that bad.

> GRANNY CHIEN: C'mon, Yen, it's New Year's, give Hanbin a break.

> YEN: Mom, we never had to do this ourselves. It breaks my heart to see you laboring so. You should have all your assistants doing these things!

HANBIN: What's there to be sad about? We're here together as a family.

Over at Chu's. Mrs. Chu gets ready to panfry a fish.

CHU: Are you sure you know how to cook the fish?

MRS. CHU: *(not sure what he's saying)* Hish?

CHU: Fish.

MRS. CHU: We've got one hish only.

CHU: Oh I get it!—Hish! *(Taiwanese, very distorted pronunciation)* "Wun hish." Taiwanese dialect isn't that hard after all! "Wun hish" . . .

Over at Ning's, Wei Chung enters with a bottle of whiskey.

WEI CHUNG: Happy New Year, Sir!

NING: Happy New Year!

Ning opens the door and lets Wei Chung in.
   Two good-looking young couples enter right—Air Force pilot Li Tzu-kang and his wife, Ruyun, followed by pilot Wu and Mrs. Wu. They are dressed elegantly, with long coats, clearly from a different social class. They check the door numbers. Ruyun carries a whole ham.

WU: Where does that bum Ning live?

LI: Number 98, up ahead.

WU: He lives *here*?

At Ning's.

WEI CHUNG: A toast to you, Sir! You're not flying during the New Year?

NING: I'm off duty.

WU: *(yelling)* ATTENTION, CHOU NING, you are hereby ordered to come to my house for New Year's dinner!

MRS. WU: You must come!

Wu and Mrs. Wu exit. Li and Ruyun knock on Ning's door.

LI: Happy New Year, Ning!

Ning opens the door.

NING: Happy New Year, Li! Was that Wu squawking?

LI: He's inviting you to his house for New Year's dinner, with all the trimmings!

RUYUN: *(handing the ham to Ning)* Ning, we brought you a little bonus for New Year's!

Ning takes the ham, and smells it.

NING: My God! A bona fide smoked Hunan ham!

LI: Right! I have no idea how a pampered damsel like Ruyun could have found something like this!

RUYUN: Hey, it's New Year's. I had to come up with something!

NING: Please come in. It's cold outside. *(to Li)* This is Wei Chung. *(to Wei Chung)* This is Li Tzu-kang, my Air Force Academy schoolmate, fighter pilot and national hero. His wife, Ruyun.

WEI CHUNG: Oh, a national hero! How are you, Sir? And you, Madam?

LI: We're having New Year's dinner at Wu's place. Come along.

NING: I'll pass. I'm fine by myself here.

RUYUN: Hey, Ning, I don't get why you are living here with the ground staff? You should have applied for the pilot's quarters.

NING: There was only one unit left and the other guy had a family, so I let him have it.

WEI CHUNG: He's such a kind man.

LI: *(seriously)* Listen to me. The ban they put on your flying can be lifted. Let me talk to our superiors.

NING: Thank you, Li, but I just don't have the heart to fly anymore. I'm fine here. Really.

LI: Stop being ridiculous, Ning, let's go over to Wu's! It'll be a lot of fun!

RUYUN: Madam Chen and her pretty sister will be there, too. Let me set you up with her!

NING: C'mon, Ruyun, the last thing I need is a girlfriend!

LI: Stop the fuss, let's go.

Li Tzu-kang and Ruyun drag Ning out. At the same time Hanbin carries a plate of steaming dumplings over to Ning's.

HANBIN: Sir!

NING: Don't call me Sir, my friend Hanbin! *(to Li and Ruyun)* This is my neighbor. *(to Hanbin)* This is Li Tzu-kang, my academy schoolmate and national hero. Ruyun, his wife.

HANBIN: *(saluting)* Another of our distinguished superiors! Sirs, we've made some dumplings, and it's New Year's, so I thought . . .

Chu and Mrs. Chu also come out of their small house to bring fried fish to Ning's.

CHU: Sirs, this fish we made . . .

MRS. CHU: *(Taiwanese)* "Wun hish."

CHU: This *(Taiwanese)* "hish" may be small, but fish symbolizes "abundance," so it's a custom for us to have fish for New Year's!

WEI CHUNG: Dumplings symbolize golden ingots. So now we've got ingots and abundance!

NING: Look. I'm by myself, why don't you all bring everything over to my place to eat?

HANBIN: I have a better idea. I fixed up a big table. Come to my place! Just bring chairs! *(enthusiastically)* Come on! Let's go!

Everyone goes to Hanbin's house, bringing chairs or stools.

NING: Will you join us, Li?

RUYUN: Aren't we intruding?

NING: Not at all! Hanbin's mother-in-law used to run the Fortune Peking Duck Restaurant in Beijing.

RUYUN: The Fortune? Wow. Their Peking duck was the tops!

Ning brings the ham and whiskey, and everyone brings their own chairs over to Hanbin's house, where the atmosphere turns festive. Granny Chien is cooking at a steaming stove set up in the corner.

CHU: *(entering Hanbin's house)* Hello, Auntie!

WEI CHUNG: *(to Li and Ruyun)* Come on, Sir! Everyone! Meet the great Air Force hero!

CHU: Come, Sirs!

YEN: Welcome, everyone!

HANBIN: The more the merrier!

NING: This is my schoolmate, Li Tzu-kang! He brought a Hunan ham!

Everyone sits around the makeshift table at Hanbin's. Wei Chung pours the whiskey.

HANBIN: *(to Yen)* Speed up the dumplings!

YEN: Yes, Sir!

WEI CHUNG: Let's all drink!

They drink. Yen brings a big plate of steaming dumplings to the table.

YEN: Listen up, everyone, my mom wrapped these dumplings herself! If we were in Beijing, you'd have to stand in line and pay a pretty penny to get an order!

LI: We pay! We pay! Ruyun, give me a red envelope for gift money!

HANBIN: Hey, she was just kidding!

GRANNY CHIEN: Don't listen to her nonsense. It's New Year's, so every one of you must have your share of gold ingot dumplings! Let's eat! Come, come!

Everyone eats the dumplings enthusiastically. The mood is festive. Ning suddenly yells out.

NING: *(shouting)* WHOA—!!

GRANNY CHIEN: What happened?

Silence. All look at Ning apprehensively.

NING: SOOO—GOOD!

All are merry, and get back to eating.

What's in the filling, Auntie?

CHU: Wow! I haven't had anything so delicious since I came to Taiwan!

MRS. CHU: *(Taiwanese)* So good! Delicious!

CHU: That's Taiwanese dialect for "delicious."

GRANNY CHIEN: What's in the filling? Sir, I wouldn't call this a proper jiaozi filling. I can't find any of the right ingredients here in Taiwan. The flour's not right, the vinegar's off. You'll just have to make do!

NING: *(in a bragging tone)* So tell me what kind of vinegar you need, Auntie?

GRANNY CHIEN: What kind of vinegar? We need Beijing vinegar! In old Beijing, we just call it—"vinegar"!

NING: One cask of old Beijing vinegar! Li will pick one up next time he flies over there!

GRANNY CHIEN: That's a tall tale if I ever heard one, kid! Who'd be able to fly back there?

LI: *(playing along)* Not so, Auntie! I normally fly missions right along the border. If I turn my nose slightly to the left, we have a landing in Beijing!

RUYUN: He's taking you for a ride!

GRANNY CHIEN: What a rascal!

CHU: *(playing along)* If that's the case, I want a big Shandong turnip!

YEN: I want a glass of Beijing iced plum tea.

HANBIN: Are you serious?

WEI CHUNG: I want some Sichuan red-hot chili pepper!

HANBIN: You talking about food or a girlfriend?

Everyone is merry.

LI: *(to Ruyun)* Write it all down, Ruyun. On my next mission, I'll stop over in Wangfujing, downtown Beijing, fetch everything, and have it all delivered by the Lantern Festival!

YEN: What a pipe dream!

RUYUN: Got it!

GRANNY CHIEN: What a bullshooter! Who's he kidding? Come on, everyone, eat up!

Hanbin stands to make a toast. Everyone's chopsticks pause for a moment.

HANBIN: *(clearing his throat)* My friends, this is our first New Year's dinner on the precious island of Taiwan. Though we're all far away from home, tonight we share our food together. *(raising his cup)* Let me wish you all health and happiness, and hope each and every one of us can return to our own homes for next year's New Year's.

CHU: Home for New Year's!

Everyone stands to drink.

ALL: Home for New Year's!

Everyone sits. It all feels a bit empty.

LI: *(sighing)* To tell the truth, troop morale is at a low. All the boys are thinking of home. I worry that some of them will snap and try to defect.

NING: We have to be strong, Li. We'll be fighting our way back soon!

WEI CHUNG: Soon, we'll be going back.

CHU: Well, you know, I'm a tough Shandong hombre, but when I boarded the ship headed here, I saw my hometown receding from view, getting smaller and smaller, and finally—it disappeared. I admit, my tears were flowing.

Silence.

Come, let's drink!

HANBIN: Let's not talk about unpleasant things.

All drink.

LI: Look on the bright side. This is our first New Year's dinner in Taiwan, and it will also be our last! Soon, we'll all be going back home!

Ruyun stands up, and addresses the table elegantly, small glass of wine in hand.

> RUYUN: It's so cold outside tonight, but we're all here inside together, so full of warmth. Mr. and Mrs. Chao, you are so lucky to have your mother by your side. None of our mothers are with us. Li hasn't seen his mother in two years.

She raises her glass to Granny Chien.

> Auntie, tonight you represent all of our mothers! Let us all drink to you!

Everyone stands and drinks.

> NING: Right!

> CHU: Let's all drink to Auntie!

> ALL: To mother!

> GRANNY CHIEN: Thank you! And Happy New Year, everyone! May you all enjoy good health!

> WEI CHUNG: May you live to a ripe old age!

> CHU: Happy New Year!

Everyone sits.

> *(explaining to Mrs. Chu)* Our mothers aren't here, and so . . .

> MRS. CHU: *(Taiwanese)* My parents are just nearby, but they've chased me out. It's all because of you!

She points at Chu and slaps him in the arm.

> ALL: What happened?

> CHU: Um . . . that sentence was too long. I didn't catch it.

Everyone laughs.

> HANBIN: She must be scolding you.

> MRS. CHU: *(Taiwanese)* Excuse me . . . I'm sorry . . .

Li is suddenly sad. He sings softly the patriotic song "On the Songhua River," from World War II.

LI: *(singing) My home lies on the Songhua River, in Manchuria . . .*

This breaks the silence. All listen, then softly join in singing.

ALL: *(singing) Forests and coal mines,*

   The soya and sorghum grow wild over the hills.

   My home lies on the Songhua River,

   In Manchuria . . .

While the singing continues, Ning stands, walks out of the house, and stares at the night sky. Hanbin and Chu follow him outside. The three stare into the starry night.

HANBIN: *(to Ning)* Sir, may I ask which direction is Beijing?

CHU: *(pointing at sky)* Is it that way?

NING: I haven't flown for a long time, I couldn't tell you.

Ning goes back inside and gets Li to come out. Meanwhile Yen has found an instrumental version of the song on a record, which she plays.

We have a question for you, Li. Me first: which direction is my hometown, Shanghai?

Li looks at the sky, then points.

LI: Find the North Star, then go west, then a little farther west. There. Shanghai.

Ning stares longingly in the direction Li has pointed.

   Silence.

HANBIN: Sir, what about Beijing?

Li looks at the sky, then points.

LI: Find the North Star, then go east, and then farther east. There.

Hanbin stares longingly in the direction Li has pointed. Silence.

CHU: And what about my hometown, Qingdao?

LI: A little farther, there's Shandong—Qingdao.

The men stand outside and gaze silently in the direction of their hometowns. Granny Chien steps outside, too, and stares into the starry night, as the music continues.

Scene 5: Under the Big Tree (1)

A young and fashionable girl, Bigs, the eldest daughter of Hanbin and Yen, enters and speaks directly to the audience. She is dressed in Go-Go Girl style from the sixties.

> BIGS: Time passed. This group of people from all over China started to learn how to get along. Some of them couldn't even understand one another. The big tree near the Village entrance became the place where everyone exchanged information.

Summer under the tree. Hanbin, Chu, Ning, Wei Chung, and Weird Chi ("Weird") sit on various stools and benches. Each is very opinionated, and seemingly authoritative.
> *Granny Lu moves slowly across the stage, followed by her attendant. The sound of an airplane. All look up at the sky and salute.*

> HANBIN: Did you hear? We're staging the major offensive soon.

> WEI CHUNG: The word is that our troops will be dispatched straight from Chiayi. General Dai Li has it all set up. and is waiting over there.

> HANBIN: That's possible. We've been here almost a year now. Enough time to set the table.

> CHU: *(curbing their enthusiasm)* There's just one small problem with your theory. General Dai Li is dead.

> NING: *(authoritatively)* That shows how much you know, Chu. The plane General Dai was on, which you with your intellect understand to have crashed on takeoff in Nanjing, actually wasn't able to land in Nanjing, so it flew to Shanghai, where it couldn't land either. How do I know? The pilot was a buddy of mine! And the real scoop is that all this speculation doesn't matter, because General Dai wasn't even on that plane. He got off long before!

Weird speaks. His dialect and accent are impossible for anyone to understand, not a single word. But out of courtesy or shyness, everyone acts as if they understand him. It doesn't help that his voice itself is gruff and his words are often slurred.

WEIRD: *(unintelligible)* Wertersduolap duddedoarsnine, deezbinquash-ioned beesmoney peeps. Eeterstrolley torsque.

Awkward pause. No one got it.

HANBIN: Well, that's not what I heard.

CHU: And what did you hear?

HANBIN: I heard that he didn't even board that plane in Nanjing.

WEI CHUNG: Wrong! He didn't even go to Nanjing!

WEIRD: *(heartfelt)* Zerrayshoos notting Namkin ang Namkin, duolap noogin choogin worz?

Awkward pause.
Mrs. Chu walks over to listen. She is very pregnant.

CHU: You guys are wrong. I've been to General Dai's grave in Xuzhou.

HANBIN: That's right. It's on a hill in Xuzhou.

NING: Hogwash! Which grave are you guys talking about? I'm the one who's been to what is alleged to be his real grave! It's in Nanjing!

WEIRD: Cheezukenamken eetdonmoddern, donmoddernerswine hobeebersinkeezdud?

Weird claps his hands to emphasize his point. Awkward pause.

NING: So you guys think you can fathom the mind of Chiang Kai Shek's top agent, the mastermind of all intelligence operations? Let me say that I cannot confirm where they supposedly buried him. The only thing I can confirm is: GENERAL DAI DID NOT DIE!

While they argue, two officers march by, and exit stage left.

CHU: He's dead as a doorknob!

NING: He's alive and kicking!

A scream, stage left.

WOMAN'S VOICE: *(screaming)* Ahhhh—!!!

All turn their heads toward stage left. Silence.

MRS. CHU: *(to Chu, Taiwanese)* Dinner's ready.

The gathering under the tree disbands as they all leave with heavy hearts.
Bigs speaks directly to the audience.

> BIGS: Formosa Village No. 1 was built near a military airstrip. Tensions
> were high across the Taiwan Strait, the stretch of water between the
> Nationalists on the island of Taiwan and the Communists on main-
> land China. Our brave pilots flew daily missions from Chiayi. The
> two sides often challenged each other in midair. For a villager, the
> greatest fear would be to hear the sound of a phone ringing in the
> late afternoon, or to see uniformed officers knocking on someone's
> door. What followed after would be the sound of a woman crying,
> and then we knew: another of our planes had gone down.

Scene 6: How to Make Tianjin Buns

In Chu's house, center, the pregnant Mrs. Chu is at her right-hand window,
which looks directly into Hanbin's house. She sees Granny Chien kneading
dough.
> *Granny Chien coughs.*
> *In the following scene, Mrs. Chu and Granny Chien cannot understand*
a word of what the other says. They converse through body language and
gestures.

> MRS. CHU: *(Taiwanese)* What are you cooking today, Auntie?

> GRANNY CHIEN: *(Tianjin dialect)* Mrs. Chu, you have quite a nose, to
> know that I'm making Tianjin buns.

Granny Chien waves at her and beckons her.

> Pork buns! Come, *(waving to Mrs. Chu)* let me teach you. TEACH
> YOU.

> MRS. CHU: Me come over? OK. I'm coming.

Mrs. Chu exits her house and goes next door to Hanbin's house.

> GRANNY CHIEN: I tell you, our Hanbin is really resourceful. He finally
> found me some decent flour, so I can make buns. *(pointing)* Tianjin
> buns.

> MRS. CHU: *(trying to imitate the sound)* Bunz?

GRANNY CHIEN: What did you say? I tell you, these aren't ordinary buns we're talking about. We're talking about *(with pride)* THE famous Tianjin buns!

Mrs. Chu nods, but doesn't really understand. Granny Chien explains patiently, with lots of hand gestures.

I hail from the city of Tianjin. Get it? Tianjin. Tian-jin.

Granny Chien takes the ingredients, Mrs. Chu watches intently.

Okay. Watch carefully. There's a secret to making Tianjin buns. Each bun contains a mixture of lean and fat pork. The ratio is adjusted in accordance with the seasons. Do you get it? Seasons? Do you understand "seasons"? Spring, summer, autumn, winter? The four seasons. FOUR SEASONS.

Mrs. Chu can't understand and chuckles.

You're laughing. Does that mean you understand or don't? *(thinking hard)* How can I explain? For instance, now, it's summer . . . *(using her hands expressively)* Hot . . . it's hot . . . you're sweating! . . . The ratio of fat to lean meat must be *(using her fingers)* three to seven.

MRS. CHU: Three? Seven?

GRANNY CHIEN: Then when it is winter, *(miming)* COLD, winter, got it? You've got to add a bit of fat, so the ratio becomes *(using her fingers)* FOUR TO SIX . . .

MRS. CHU: Four to . . . Oh! I get it! *(excited)* You mean the ratio changes with the weather!

GRANNY CHIEN: *(not understanding)* No, no, now don't rush to conclusions! Watch. Let me show you. Now it's summer, so the ratio is three to seven. Then when winter comes, it'll be your turn to make buns for me, ok?

MRS. CHU: My family runs an eatery, too . . .

GRANNY CHIEN: *(not getting it, but responding anyway)* Right . . . right . . .

Granny Chien demonstrates.

Okay. Now we're putting in the onion, ginger, and garlic, but careful, don't overdo it. My mother said that a true Tianjin bun must contain all kinds of flavors, and yet people can't describe how it tastes! That's what you call a real Tianjin bun! My mother taught me how to make them . . .

Pause. Granny Chien grows sad.

MRS. CHU: What's the matter, Auntie?

GRANNY CHIEN: Mrs. Chu, do you know Tianjin City? My home! My hometown! *(pushing to explain)* Home! My home! Tianjin! Tianjin City! MY HOME! HOME! . . .

Granny Chien shakes her head, and moves to the doorway, gazing out. Pause.

MRS. CHU: What's the matter, Auntie?

GRANNY CHIEN: *(in despair)* We're not going back. We're not going back. I'm never going to make it home.

Silence.
Mrs. Chu tries to comfort Granny Chien.

MRS. CHU: Don't be sad, Auntie. Come, let's make buns. Teach me how to make . . . uh . . . *(trying her best to imitate Mandarin)* TIANjeen ban—sai!

Mrs. Chu's pronunciation is so off it is entertaining to Granny Chien, who smiles.

GRANNY CHIEN: *(laughing)* Mrs. Chu, it's "Tianjin buns."

MRS. CHU: TIANjeen BAN—SAI!

GRANNY CHIEN: *(laughing)* Fine, let me teach you. Come . . .

The two continue to make buns.

Scene 7: New Lady of the Chou Household

Ning enters right, walking toward his house, followed by Ruyun. She is now dressed in a plain cheongsam, and is very quiet, in contrast to her elegance and vivacity at Chinese New Year. Two Workers follow, carrying Ruyun's luggage. They walk toward Ning's.
Yen enters left.

NING: *(to Ruyun, subdued)* It's right ahead. *(to Yen)* Hello, Mrs. Chao.

YEN: Hello, Ning . . .

Ning and Ruyun go inside Ning's. Ruyun remains completely silent and keeps her head down.

NING: *(to the Workers)* Just leave them here. Thanks.

The Workers put down the luggage and leave. Yen watches with surprise. She gestures for Mrs. Chu and Granny Chien to step outside and talk about it.

MRS. CHU: *(Taiwanese)* What happened? Isn't that Mrs. Li? Why so many things?

YEN: *(gesturing)* We just heard. Ruyun's husband, the pilot, Li Tzu-kang, the Air Force hero, he defected to the other side!

MRS. CHU: The other side?

GRANNY CHIEN: You're saying her husband defected to the Communists?!

YEN: SHH!

The Workers pass them as they exit.

MRS. CHU: What did you say?

YEN: His mission was behind enemy lines. *(gesturing)* His plane crashed, and now they say he's defected. Mrs. Li is all alone, and so Ning's taking care of her now.

MRS. CHU: What? Come to my house. We can listen to them.

The three go to Chu's together, eavesdropping through the shared window with Ning's house. Yen pushes Mrs. Chu away.

YEN: Allow me! You can't understand anyway.

At Ning's, Ning and Ruyun stand awkwardly.

NING: Ruyun, I must say first of all . . . Li was my classmate, and my sworn buddy. I absolutely believe in him. He couldn't possibly have defec—

Pause. Ning doesn't want to say the word. Ruyun remains silent.

Sorry, this place doesn't suit you. It's too small. You can sleep on the cot. I'll make you some tea. What kind do you like? I drink Longjing.

Silence.

> This can't be real! You can't even get a pension because they've branded Li a trait—But don't worry. The bond between Air Force comrades is like steel. I'm here for you, to take care of you. *(pause)* Even if I wasn't, someone else would be. Wu would be, surely, but he . . . he's married. So I'm sorry, you'll have to put up with this place . . .

Silence.

> These surroundings aren't what you're used to. To go to the bathroom, you'll need to use the public restroom outside. Let me show you . . .

Ning leads the silent Ruyun out the door.

> *(pointing)* See that tree? Go there, turn left, and your nose will pick up the trail.

Ruyun remains silent. The two go back into the house.

> Actually, I quite like this place. There's something about it. I feel at ease here on my own. I mean . . . *(realizing he has said the wrong thing)* I mean that we, I mean . . .

Hanbin and Chu come home from work. They stop outside their houses.

HANBIN: Listen, Chu, when you get home, not a word about Li.

CHU: Don't worry. *(sighs)* Never imagined he was a . . .

They enter their respective homes.

> *(shouting in Taiwanese)* I'm back!

The three ladies are startled.

YEN: You scared the hell out of me!

Yen keeps eavesdropping at the window.

MRS. CHU: Look! That Mrs. Li has moved in!

CHU: Listen, ladies: there is an unspoken code among fighter pilots. If anyone dies in a plane crash, the other pilots take care of the family. You women should keep quiet about such things.

MRS. CHU: But what happened? What's going on?

YEN: *(sighs)* At the New Year's dinner, nobody would have thought that he would defect to the Commies! Poor Mrs. Li . . .

Hanbin opens his shared window with Chu's house, and talks directly to the people at Chu's.

HANBIN: Yen, what are you doing over there?

ALL: Shh!

At Ning's. Ning steps toward his window.

NING: Oh Ruyun, there's one more thing you should know. If possible, don't open this window. If you do, you may find . . .

Ning opens the window and finds everyone eavesdropping. Everyone at Chu's ducks to hide, and even Hanbin, in the next house down, has to dodge. Everyone freezes.
Ning closes the window.
Pause. Ruyun finally speaks.

RUYUN: You know it's not true. Li is a hero! He would never defect!

NING: That's right. So they must be discussing, uh, the mooncakes for the upcoming festival!

YEN: That's right, mooncakes!

CHU: I wonder what filling they put here inside Taiwanese mooncakes?

YEN: Really! We are so curious!

CHU: *(to Yen)* Come home.

The party at Chu's breaks up. Yen and Granny Chien go back to their house.

Scene 8: Buying a Coffin (1)

Deuce, the second daughter of Hanbin and Yen, enters and speaks directly to the audience. She is a teenager, dressed in a high school uniform.

DEUCE: The Village was a self-contained world, where you could walk down the street and hear five different dialects at the same time. At dinnertime, you could open the back door and smell 10 different types of cooking from all over China. Once you got used to it, you wouldn't want to leave. But life can't always be sheltered. There were

times when we needed help from outside. My dad was the most
public-spirited person in the Village, always helping others. In times
of need, he was always the one who'd venture outside in search of
assistance . . .

A carpenter's workshop on a Chiayi city street outside the Village. The carpenter
Huang and his apprentice Mutt are in the shop. Hanbin enters. Huang speaks a
little bit of Mandarin, but mostly Taiwanese. Mutt only speaks Taiwanese.

HANBIN: Mr. Huang . . .

HUANG: *(Taiwanese)* Oh, it's that mainland guy. I helped repair his house.
May I help you? *(very rudimentary Mandarin)* HELP—YOU?

HANBIN: I need your help. I need you to make a wooden box for me.

HUANG: *(imitates Hanbin's Mandarin)* "Wooden box"? Oh, a box. What
size? *(Mandarin)* BIG? SMALL?

HANBIN: Let me draw it for you.

HUANG: Okay. Draw. Here . . .

Hanbin takes a pencil and draws on the table.

HANBIN: It's made of wood. Shaped roughly like this . . . length, five
feet . . .

MUTT: *(Taiwanese, joking)* Just right for a corpse!

Huang and Mutt share a laugh.

HUANG: *(Taiwanese, laughing)* Don't make jokes like that.

HANBIN: It's for a coffin.

Huang stops laughing.

We've had a passing in the Village, and I'm helping to organize the
funeral. I'm here to seek your help.

Pause.

HUANG: *(Mandarin and Taiwanese mixed, gesturing)* No . . . Look, we
make windows . . . we fix glass, we don't make that stuff. Come here,
look . . . *(pointing)* There's a coffin shop over there, round the corner
to your left.

HANBIN: I know there's a coffin shop over there. But I also know you can make a good one.

HUANG: No, you don't get it. We don't do coffins. They do. They have it all set up. You can order one for about . . . 100 Taiwan dollars. I can help you, put in a word for you, to bring the price down to 90. I think I can get it down to 90 for you.

HANBIN: But I don't have 90.

HUANG: How much do you have? I'll see what I can do.

HANBIN: I have 10 dollars.

Pause. Hanbin gestures.

Ten dollars.

HUANG: Hey, just the other day, I repaired a roof in your village, and that cost three dollars.

Huang gestures "three," Hanbin grabs his hand and shakes it.

HANBIN: Thank you, thank you . . .

HUANG: Wait, no . . .

MUTT: *(condescendingly)* If you can't afford it, just wrap the body in a straw mat, and . . .

HUANG: Shut your trap, Mutt!

HANBIN: Huang, we're all far away from home. We all thought we'd be going home soon. And now someone has passed . . .

Pause. Huang stares at his table.

HUANG: Well . . . maybe if we use this type of plywood, *(knocks his table)* we might save on the materials, and . . . *(thinking)* Seriously? Ten dollars?

Hanbin gives him the money and bows deeply to him.

HANBIN: Take it! Ten dollars. I bow to you! Thank you!

MUTT: Boss!

HUANG: Wait! But . . .

Scene 9: The Funeral (1)

A young man, Ox, the eldest son of Chu and Mrs. Chu, enters and speaks directly to the audience. He is good looking and athletic, dressed smartly in the style of the sixties.

> OX: The next day, the 10-dollar coffin was delivered to our village. That apprentice cursed all the way, thinking his boss had been cheated by the mainlanders. But then they found out who the coffin was for . . .

At Hanbin's house, the dining table has been removed, and a makeshift altar has been set up. Yen sits silently, dressed in black. Hanbin attends to those who have come to pay respects. Granny Lu walks slowly by, with her Attendant following. Huang emerges from the back, putting away his tools.

> HUANG: *(to his apprentice)* Will you be quiet? A promise is a promise! Stop harping on the price! . . .

The very pregnant Mrs. Chu, weeping openly, comes out of her house with a plate of hot buns, which she places on the Chao's altar. Chu is next to her. Mrs. Chu kneels in front of the altar.

> MRS. CHU: *(to the altar, mixing Taiwanese and Mandarin)* Auntie, the weather is growing cold. I followed your instructions and used the four-to-six ratio for the pork filling. I made these for you. Please see if they taste right. You taught me how to make them . . .

She cries, and speaks Mandarin.

> . . . TIANJIN BUNS!!

Chu tries to console her.

> MUTT: Let's get out of here, boss . . .

> HUANG: Shh. What's the matter with you? Are you blind? An elder has died. Where's your manners? Moron!

Hanbin steps out to talk to Huang. He has some cash with him.

> HANBIN: We are grateful to you, Huang. The neighbors have raised another 10 dollars to pay you so that you will not suffer such a loss.

Hanbin hands over the money to Huang.

> HUANG: No need! I mean it, Mr. Chao.

HANBIN: No, you must take it . . .

HUANG: No! Keep it!

Mrs. Chu suddenly screams.

MRS. CHU: AHHH . . . !!

Ruyun is just about to enter Hanbin's to pay her respects.

RUYUN: Hurry!

CHU: What now?!

HANBIN: Help! She's giving birth!

Chaos. Everyone is running around. They drag Mrs. Chu out. Yen sits silently in mourning.
Lights fade out.

ACT TWO, 1969–1970

Scene 1: Montage

A Mandarin pop song from the 60s.
Lights up. It is 1969. The three housing units have evolved over time. The furniture has improved. A youthful energy throbs through the Village. The first generation is now middle aged. Hanbin sits in a rattan chair outside his house. The telephone pole still stands in the center of Chu's, only with many extra wires on it. Chu sits at a tiny desk, doing paperwork. Ning relaxes, listening to Peking Opera on a small transistor radio in his house.
The second generation is already teenaged. Smalls, the son of Hanbin and Yen, is in high school uniform, which resembles military khakis. He speaks directly to the audience, and the scene unfolds like a montage, the characters entering and acting according to his narration.

SMALLS: So this group of travelers, who thought they would be going home soon, stayed on. From yearning of home, to realizing they weren't going home, they finally figured out that this was home. In the blink of an eye, almost 20 years have passed since the day of my grandmother's funeral. The baby boy who was born that day was named Chu Chien-kuo, nicknamed "Ox." Nicknames are important! Everyone from a village like ours has a nickname. The following year, my eldest sister, Chao Li-wen, was born. She got the nickname "Bigs." Ox and Bigs grew up separated only by a thin windowpane. They were definitely the most eye-catching couple in the Village.

Nineteen-year-old Ox is home, chatting with 18-year-old Bigs over at Hanbin's house through their shared window. They are young, fashionable, and good looking.
Cart and Deuce enter, both in student uniforms.

Ox's younger brother was nicknamed "Cart." Don't ask me why. I guess the Ox pulls the Cart. My second sister, Chao Li-ming, had the nickname "Deuce." Since our parents obviously nicknamed us in order, I got the nickname . . .

DEUCE: Hey Smalls.

SMALLS: *(to Deuce)* Hey Deuce, what's up? *(to the audience)* Cart and Deuce were also a hot item, but not many thought their relationship would last. Both my sisters were real lookers. Actually all us village kids were good looking, like some from other villages who were making a name in the entertainment business. Like the two hot sisters Big Spice and Li'l Spice, whose parents were Mr. and Mrs. Tsui. They were real showboats. Whenever they came home from school, we always tried to get their attention.

Big Spice and Li'l Spice enter. They are dressed rather revealingly. Fats, son of Ruyun and Ning, and Cart see them coming and do some kung fu moves to attract attention.

FATS AND CART: *(in unison, a kung fu shout)* HYAH—!!

Big and Li'l Spice stop and look at the two boys.

BIG SPICE: What losers!

Mrs. Tsui enters. She carries a book of accounts.

LI'L SPICE: *(trying to cover her short skirt)* Oh, hi Mom . . .

MRS. TSUI: Go home and put on some clothes!

Big and Li'l Spice exit.

SMALLS: Good day, Mrs. Tsui!

MRS. TSUI: Hi Smalls.

Mrs. Tsui tends to her own business.

> SMALLS: Mrs. Tsui was in charge of the savings club, a grassroots savings group she started. She's doing her monthly collection. The mothers all joined to help pay for their children's tuition.

Ruyun steps out of her house on the left. She is middle aged, wearing a plain cheongsam, but still elegant. She searches for her son, Fats. Smalls greets her.

> Good day, Auntie Ruyun.

> RUYUN: Hi Smalls.

Ruyun beckons to Fats, who goes back inside to do his homework.

> SMALLS: The year after she moved in, Ruyun gave birth to Fats. I don't know why, but everyone nicknamed "Fats" grows up to be pretty skinny. Anyway, everyone wondered if he really was Mr. Chou Ning's son. We thought he might be the son of Ruyun and her ex-husband, the defected Commie traitor Li. Ruyun worked as a housemaid, cooking and cleaning for a general's family in the officers' village opposite us.

Mrs. Chu pushes a cart with a sign that reads "Authentic Tianjin Buns" and chats with Yen. Weird passes by on his bike.

> My neighbor, Mrs. Chu, really was an enterprising lady. My grandmother not only taught her how to make pork buns, she even passed on her rolling pin to her. By the 1960s, Mrs. Chu's Tianjin buns were famous in Chiayi town. As for my mom . . . Well, she couldn't cook. So we grew up eating Tianjin buns. Mr. Chu decided also to go into business, capitalizing on his prime location to set up a small power company. He connected electricity to homes and collected very competitive monthly fees.

In front of Chu's. A villager passes by, and Chu steps out to collect fees from him.

> CHU: Please, Mr. Chang, don't put me in a difficult position. I'm not selling electricity; I'm providing a service. If you don't pay, I'm going to have to cut your service off.

Mr. Chang searches his pockets for some coins.

> CHANG: Take it.

> CHU: *(taking the money)* Thank you kindly.

Mrs. Chu has been stowing her vending cart for the night. She has seen everything.

MRS. CHU: *(to Mr. Chang as he passes by)* So sorry . . .

Mrs. Chu goes home. Her Mandarin is quite fluent, but she speaks it with a Taiwanese accent.

Cut, cut, cut; whose electricity are you using?

CHU: *(Taiwanese)* Don't meddle in my business!

MRS. CHU: You're siphoning public electricity, and you dare charge people for it?!

CHU: What do you mean by "public"!? "Public" happens to run through my "private" house! And don't think I don't work for it. Do you know how many times I have to climb up and down every day?

MRS. CHU: Right, wow, what hard labor! You even have account books and an office desk. If I didn't know better, I would think you were running a business! Big boss man! *(Taiwanese)* How much can you earn a month?

CHU: Just listen to you! You talk so loud now, just because you can sell a few lousy minced pork buns in the market?

MRS. CHU: Just listen to YOU! Would we have had this place to live in without the grace of Hanbin and Ning? And now people come to you for help, and you charge them! That's called *(Taiwanese proverb)* "A bolt without a nut!"

CHU: Hold on, what "bolt"? What "nut"? I don't get it!

MRS. CHU: Don't get it? *(Taiwanese)* Well, tough toodles!

CHU: Well, your selling buns is sure like *(retaliating with a Shandong proverb)* "A muckworm wandering in the garden."

MRS. CHU: Hold on, what are you saying? What "worm"? I don't get it!

CHU: You don't get it? Because you're not the right onion!

MRS. CHU: *(Taiwanese)* Foul-hearted man, die on an auspicious day!

CHU: So we're playing "Don't get it!" huh? Okay, don't get this: *(Shandong accent)* "The Land Goddess grasps for a grasshopper—totally off!"

MRS. CHU: Keep going, the more the merrier!

The two yell at each other in Taiwanese and Shandong as they exit into the back. Bigs continues the narrative.

BIGS: Just like Mr. Chu, my dad wasn't very good at making money. He was a truck driver who moonlighted by occasionally transporting other goods. But he didn't care. My dad loved helping others. People would come to seek his help for all sorts of matters, big or small . . .

Spotlight stage left. A school office. Two Teachers sit back to back. Hanbin, properly dressed, speaks earnestly with one of them.

HANBIN: Sir, this kid is really a good kid. He always bows whenever he sees an elder. It's totally beyond us how he would get in a fight.

Teacher 1 is not convinced. Hanbin continues. Deuce walks into the narrator's spotlight and narrates along with Bigs.

DEUCE: We were all dirt poor. We couldn't have afforded school if not for the state scholarship that subsidized the tuition of military children. The bar for the scholarship was unthinkably low—all you needed was to score a D for general conduct. And yet a hell of a lot of us still couldn't qualify.

Hanbin persists.

HANBIN: Sir, I'm begging you, please, Sir . . .

TEACHER 1: Okay, Mr. Chao, I'm raising his grade to a D. But just this once!

HANBIN: *(bowing)* Thank you, Sir!

Hanbin moves to the other Teacher. He speaks in almost the exact same tone.

Ma'am, this kid is really a good kid. He always bows whenever he sees an elder. It's totally beyond us why he would set your bicycle on fire . . .

Flyers float down everywhere from the sky. Smalls, Cart, and Fats run out to gather them. Deuce and Bigs continue the narrative.

BIGS: Sometimes we would get a shower of propaganda flyers from the other side, informing us how wonderful life was over there in Communist China, how great Communism was, and so on and so forth.

We weren't much into ideology, but if you could gather them, you could turn them in for a small cash reward.

Smalls and Cart examine a flyer.

SMALLS: "Chairman Mao is Taiwan's true hope." Yeah sure.

DEUCE: There was a time when there were no flyers, so my brother and Cart decided to forge fake ones and hand them to their teacher in the hope of cashing in . . .

In the classroom. Smalls and Cart stand in front of Teacher 1. Pause.

TEACHER 1: These look pretty genuine. There's just one problem. Of all the students in this school, why is it that only the two of you found these?

Pause. The two look at each other.

SMALLS: Scram!

Cart and Smalls run away.

DEUCE: After 20 years, that big tree near the entrance was still the main venue for discussing affairs of state. You know the guy who everyone called "Weird"? Well, still nobody could understand a word he said. I mean, China is vast, and there are so many dialects. In fact, we didn't even know where he came from.

Scene 2: Under the Big Tree (2)

The year 1970. Under the tree, the men are still talking politics. Same people, but without Wei Chung. An airplane flies over. Ning salutes the sky.
Granny Lu slowly crosses, with her Attendant behind her. The Attendant is middle aged, but Granny Lu seems timeless.

NING: Hey Hanbin, did you hear the news? We're purchasing new fighter jets!

HANBIN: Is that so?

CHU: One hundred brand new F-51s! It's a huge expenditure.

HANBIN: *(surprised)* One hundred F-51s? Do we need that many?

CHU: Do we need that many?

NING: I guess you think they're all for defense?

WEIRD: *(spirited)* Rooternootoo deponsoneeler, ocherosachersoon kayoonton!!

Awkward pause. His words are still absolutely unintelligible.

HANBIN: *(breaking the silence)* Okay, let's not go there. Did you see the article in the *Central Daily News*? It's a mess on the other side! It's this Cultural Revolution! People are eating tree bark!

NING: Therefore.

HANBIN: Therefore what?

CHU: Therefore the time is now! Time to fight our way back!

WEIRD: Atsabento owntertweens! Atsabootyton!

Pause.

HANBIN: Okay, so what's the strategy, Chu?

CHU: I have it all planned out: first we cross the Taiwan Strait and take Amoy. We'll only need one regiment.

HANBIN: Just one regiment? You must be joking. All Amoy went on vacation?

No one seems to agree. Weird shakes his head. Chu hurries to explain the rest of his plan.

CHU: So I AM joking. Amoy is there for the taking, but what would we need it for? The recovery of the mainland calls for a comprehensive plan. First we capture Amoy and leave one regiment there. Move south, take Guangzhou in a surprise attack. Go north, take on Shanghai straight on; like the autumn wind whipping the leaves around, we take it like a piece of cake!

NING: My God, Chu! It's a pity you're not a member of the Joint Chiefs of Staff! You don't get it. The problem is not about how we get over there, the problem is in handling all the logistics once we get there!

CHU: So who's going to handle all the logistics?

NING: *(firmly)* General Dai Li.

CHU: *(even more firmly)* He's dead.

NING: No way!

CHU: You've been harping on General Dai for a hundred years now!

NING: You're clueless when it comes to General Dai!

Weird shakes his head animatedly. Granny Lu walks in front of them. Her Attendant follows.

HANBIN: Hello, Granny Lu.

NING: Granny Lu . . .

GRANNY LU: Having a nice chat?

NING: Granny Lu, tell them, is General Dai Li dead or not?

CHU: Of course he's dead.

GRANNY LU: *(slowly)* Concerning this matter, you might want to ask Wei Chung.

Granny Lu walks slowly away. She and her Attendant exit.

CHU: Wait a minute. Have you seen Wei Chung recently?

HANBIN: *(surprised)* Are you kidding? You didn't know?

CHU: What?

NING: He's in.

CHU: Busted.

WEIRD: Goosserfronto booroofoo nabberstoo!

HANBIN: The secret police from Bureau 4 took him away.

WEIRD: Fooroo booroofoo!

CHU: Are you kidding?

NING: Wei Chung, Communist spy!

HANBIN: Over 20 years, and no one had a clue!

NING: You guys had no clue. But I knew everything.

HANBIN: The hell you did! Wasn't it you who stood up for him in the first place?

NING: The better to observe him in secret. He was always asking "When are we going to take action? When are we going to take action?" Right?

CHU: But I always ask that question, too!

NING: The way you ask is different. Wei Chung's eyebrows were always shifty when he asked! *(demonstrates shifty eyes)* Am I right? Am I right? *(conclusively)* You betcha!

HANBIN: *(sighing)* To think we had a Commie spy among us for 20 years! What has become of this world?

WEIRD: Yorksoos traroose!

Pause.

CHU: Wait a minute. So why ask Wei Chung about Dai Li?

Everyone looks at Hanbin, for no particular reason, but he feels obliged to answer.

HANBIN: Because . . .

Pause. They wait.

Well, General Dai and Wei Chung . . . they've both disappeared.

CHU: So what is that supposed to mean? Anyone who has disappeared knows the whereabouts of anyone else who has disappeared? If that's the case, all disappeared people would be together in one place! Sun Yat-sen and Yuan Shikai would be playing mahjong together, with Amelia Earhart doing tea service. Chang Tso-lin stands by, lighting a firecracker! Might as well throw in Mei Lanfang singing an aria!

Everyone enjoys the joke. Hanbin gets mad for once.

HANBIN: Enough already! Have you quite finished? I just made one comment and you ramble on and on!

CHU: You started it.

HANBIN: What do you mean? Granny Lu was the one.

Ning suddenly stands up and interrupts their argument.

NING: Enough! How childish! Donkey's eggs! We part in discord!

Ning exits.

Scene 3: The Bomb Shelter (1)

Bigs speaks directly to the audience.

> BIGS: The bomb shelter at the other side of the Village was where we, the second generation, wove our dreams. It was our secret headquarters, far from the harsh realities of life. This was where we talked about the mysterious, ageless Granny Lu. She lived at the entrance of the Village and had an attendant, but nobody knew what she did. Sometimes a big, black limo would come to pick her up, and she would disappear for months. To where? We imagined she had martial arts skills like "vaulting," and she could fly through the air, across the Taiwan Straits to carry out secret missions on the other side!

The bomb shelter, a dark, mysterious space. Cart, Deuce, Smalls, and Fats are here, with an unlit oil lamp.

> SMALLS: So I was gazing at the moon from our front yard one night when a shadow flew across the sky. *(gesturing)* Shoo!

> CART: Wow!

> SMALLS: I wasn't surprised in the least.

> FATS: Was it Granny Lu?

Cart and Smalls slap Fats on the back.

> SMALLS AND CART: *(in unison)* Don't interrupt!

> CART: Pay attention! *(to Smalls)* Then?

Fats is about to light up the oil lamp with a match but is stopped by Smalls.

> SMALLS: Damn it, Fats. Who said you could light that lamp?

> FATS: Why not?

> CART: How do you know what you'll see after lighting it?

> SMALLS: Right!

> FATS: *(growing scared)* I'm going home.

> SMALLS: Sit down! Give me the damn matchstick.

> DEUCE: Are you sure?

SMALLS: He doesn't believe it, sis, so here goes!

Smalls is about to light the lamp. Fats is scared.

FATS: No, don't . . .

SMALLS: Chicken!

Smalls lights the lamp. Fats is scared, but finds that nothing has happened.

Stop it. Back to the story. Do you know who practices martial arts here?

FATS: Granny Lu?

The two slap him on the back again.

SMALLS: Wrong! Do you have any idea who Granny Lu is? Does someone like her need to practice?

FATS: Then who?

SMALLS: Her attendant . . .

He randomly draws a name from the Chinese puppet theatre, sort of like saying "Howdy Doody."

Su Ya—wen.

FATS: Bullshit!

SMALLS: I swear I'm not bullshitting you! That day I came here in secret. Granny Lu was sitting here *(pointing)*, and that nerdy-looking attendant came out of there in martial arts attire!

The bomb shelter turns into an imaginary space. Granny Lu appears sitting sternly in a corner. The Attendant enters and somersaults spectacularly, practicing skillful martial arts moves.

He was training under her guidance, and man, did he show some fancy stuff! He used his "Dark Terminator Palm" to "Bang!" hit the ceiling! Man, the debris came showering down with a "whoosh." In an instant, he deflected all those pieces like a whirlwind scattering dust. Not a single piece of debris touched the floor! Damn, was he good!

Smalls starts emulating the Attendant's moves.

FATS: *(in awe)* Incredible!

SMALLS: You know how Granny Lu transferred her kung fu to her attendant? By just the slight movement of her fingertips.

CART: Damn!

Granny Lu moves her fingertips, and the attendant does another somersault.

SMALLS: Do you know what happened next? She saw me!

Granny Lu looks in Smalls's direction.

Her mouth didn't move, but she moved her fingertips again, and I heard her clearly say: "Come. Join in the training!" *(to Granny Lu)* No, Granny Lu! I can't . . .

FATS: What are you doing, Smalls?

Smalls acts as if he is practicing martial arts under Granny Lu's direction, but his moves are quite amateurish.

SMALLS: I realized then and there that Granny Lu wanted me to train along with her attendant and learn his moves. So I did, move by move. Man, though I didn't have a sword in hand, my whole body became infused with the sword spirit! *(posing)* The "Nine Swords of the Loner"! . . . *(posing)* the "Wave" posture . . . *(posing)* the "Turbulence" posture . . . Man, I was even turning frickin' somersaults!! . . .

The Attendant, who had been demonstrating all the moves as Smalls mentioned them, exits, at which moment Smalls falls to the ground.
  Silence.

CART: You suck, Smalls. You fell down.

FATS: Yeah.

SMALLS: You don't know shit. That's called the "Falling Down" posture.

DEUCE: I'm hungry. I'm going home.

Deuce exits.

SMALLS: Sis, wait for me.

Everyone exits except Fats, who is still soaking up what just happened.
  All of a sudden, Fats gets scared.

FATS: Wait . . . Wait for me.

Fats gets up and hurriedly exits.

Scene 4: Blackjack (1)

At Chu's, Ox is teaching Bigs how to play blackjack.

OX: Well?

BIGS: Hit me.

OX: Wrong. Look, I'm showing six, you already have 16. You should let me go bust.

BIGS: But I have a feeling.

OX: *(dealing a card)* Okay. You asked for it!

BIGS: Twenty-one.

OX: Sheer luck! By the laws of probability, you should have lost.

Ox deals again.

BIGS: What laws of probability? I had a feeling.

OX: Well?

BIGS: *(checking her cards)* Pass.

OX: *(astonished)* You can't refuse a card here! Look how great my hand is. You have to take one!

BIGS: But I don't want one.

OX: Nobody plays this way! Going by the laws of probability, you're sure to lose.

BIGS: None of your business. Are you playing or not?

OX: Okay, okay.

Ox deals a card.

BIGS: See? I win.

OX: Blind luck! Sometimes one's lucky, sometimes not. That's the way it is.

BIGS: It's not luck. It's a feeling.

Big Spice and Li'l Spice pass by, wearing even more revealing clothes than before. Ox stares at them.

OX: Wow! That's what I call a "feeling"!

Ox whistles at the girls.

BIGS: What are you ogling at?

OX: They're dressed so scantily because they want people to ogle them. I'm just obliging.

BIGS: I'm going home.

OX: What's the problem? Chicks like Big Spice and Li'l Spice are for fooling around with. It's not as if you're marrying them. How sad if they dressed like that and no one looked?

BIGS: Would you ogle at me if I dressed that way?

OX: You would never dress that way. I wouldn't allow it.

BIGS: Why not?

OX: You're not that type.

BIGS: What type?

OX: The fool-around type. They're chicks, you're my girl. There's a big difference!

BIGS: So you want to fool around with them?

OX: No, I don't.

BIGS: Yes, you do.

OX: Doesn't matter either way.

BIGS: Why not?

OX: Because it's just fooling around, like playing cards. After you're done, you just shuffle the deck and start afresh, understand?

BIGS: I'm playing a serious game with you now.

OX: What are we talking about?

BIGS: *(approaching Ox seductively)* Okay then, I'm going to fool around with you now.

OX: But I don't want to fool around . . .

BIGS: But I do.

OX: Okay. You said it! . . .

Ox pushes Bigs onto the bottom bunk bed in the crowded little one-room house. They start making out.

Chu enters right. He suddenly comes home and opens the front door. Bigs and Ox freeze, Ox on top of Bigs on the bed.

CHU: *(not paying much attention)* You're home, Ox?

Pause.

Taking a nap?

Pause. Bigs cautiously and quickly pulls away from Ox, slips through the back door, then enters her own house through the back door as Chu is facing away, as if she has done this many times.

Chu turns to look but sees only Ox in bed.

Wait. Did I hear Bigs's voice?

OX: Probably from next door.

Chu goes to the common window and opens it. Bigs is there. She acts like she has been there the whole time.

BIGS: Oh, hello, Uncle Chu!

CHU: You're home?

BIGS: Yes, I'm home.

Ox breathes a sigh of relief.

Scene 5: A Peeping Tom

Fats is doing his homework at home. There are two boxes of Christmas light parts in front of Hanbin's house. Bigs and Deuce stand at their door. Deuce is wearing a very short miniskirt.

DEUCE: *(impatiently)* What does Mom want us to do, sis?

BIGS: *(pointing to the boxes)* Assemble this stuff.

DEUCE: I have a date and I need to shower.

BIGS: I'm running late, too. Ox and I are going to catch a movie.

DEUCE: Then let's sneak off.

Yen comes out of the house.

YEN: Listen, both of you. Auntie Chu helped us get these from the cooperative. Let me teach you how to do it.

DEUCE: What a hassle. Why do we need these?

YEN: How could I keep you girls alive without this extra income? *(looking at Deuce's skirt)* Any shorter and you'll expose your panties!

They sit.

Okay, let me show you. There is a hole here, stick two pins inside and . . . *(breaking it)* Darn, it broke.

Mrs. Chu returns from the marketplace with her pork buns vending cart.

MRS. CHU: How's it going, Mrs. Chao?

YEN: Are these rejects? How come they broke?

Hanbin also comes home from work. He watches.

MRS. CHU: *(looking)* No, they're not rejects!

She takes up the pieces and shows Bigs and Deuce how to do it.

Look, there's an angle. You have to hook it up, and "pop," it's done.

YEN: "Pop"?

MRS. CHU: *(excitedly)* Mrs. Chao, let me show you something.

YEN: Okay. Both of you stay put.

Mrs. Chu brings Yen into her house to see their new TV. Bigs runs off, while Deuce goes to the back of her own house to take a shower.
Mrs. Chu shows off her new television to Yen. She turns it on.

MRS. CHU: Okay. Now watch.

YEN: *(coolly)* Oh my! It's a new television set. You're really something, Mrs. Chu.

MRS. CHU: Not bad, eh?

YEN: Not bad, not bad.

MRS. CHU: It's in color, makes for great viewing.

YEN: Hold on. Did you say this is a color TV?

MRS. CHU: Not really, it's black and white. But with this attached filter in front you get colors.

YEN: *(slightly condescending)* Wow, I get it. It's just like in the old days, when they took black-and-white photos and painted the lips red, and they became color photos! Why didn't you just buy a color TV?

Hanbin and Ruyun open their common windows and watch from either side.

MRS. CHU: I save money this way. *(to Hanbin and Ruyun)* In the future, you can come here to watch baseball!

Meanwhile, Fats sneaks away from his desk, and goes behind Hanbin's house to peep at Deuce bathing.

YEN: Well, I sure am getting a little dizzy watching all that movement. I'm going home to listen to my gramophone. Thank you kindly!

Yen returns home.

Hey Hanbin! Don't you see the neighbors have a TV?! I want one, too.

HANBIN: You can't just see something that the neighbors have and say you want it.

YEN: When did I ever ask you for a telephone pole? It's just a TV set!

She steps out and notices her daughters are gone.

Bigs, Deuce! Where did those two good-for-nothings go?

Big Spice and Li'l Spice pass by, dressed more revealingly than before.

My God, is it Big Spice and Li'l Spice? Haven't seen you in a while.

BIG SPICE AND LI'L SPICE: *(politely, in unison)* Hello, Auntie Chao.

Big Spice and Li'l Spice move on. Deuce runs from her house holding a towel. Fats rushes back to his house.

DEUCE: Dammit, Fats!

Deuce exits. Yen gets Mrs. Chu to come outside to see Big Spice and Li'l Spice as they walk away.

YEN: Mrs. Chu, come and look, now that's what I call color!

MRS. CHU: Oh my, Big and Li'l Spice.

BIG SPICE AND LI'L SPICE: *(politely, in unison)* Hello, Auntie Chu.

Big Spice and Li'l Spice exit. Yen and Mrs. Chu look puzzled. Hanbin and Ruyun also step out to have a look.

HANBIN: Something's different about them. Have they . . . ?

YEN: They took the plunge.

RUYUN: What?

YEN: They quit school to become bar girls in Taichung!

RUYUN: Where?

YEN: In the city. They work for the soldiers from the US Air Force base.

HANBIN: No wonder Mr. Tsui doesn't seem to be himself these days.

RUYUN: He didn't respond when I greeted him recently.

YEN: He hardly leaves his house.

MRS. CHU: You know what's been going around? People say that the money the Tsuis used to build their new second story was earned by their daughters, sitting on GI Joes' laps.

RUYUN: Enough.

YEN: My God, the deadline is day after tomorrow for the Christmas lights!

Mrs. Chu and Ruyun go back inside. Yen continues working on the Christmas lights. Hanbin goes home, too.

Deuce, Smalls, Ox, Cart, and Bigs enter and discuss their situation seriously in front of the houses.

SMALLS: Are you sure?

DEUCE: Positive, and it isn't the first time either!

CART: Damn.

They go to Ning's, passing by the other houses. Hanbin sees them.

HANBIN: What's going on?

CART: Hi, Mr. Chao.

SMALLS: Nothing, Dad. We're going to play with Fats.

Smalls, Ox, and Cart enter Ning's. Ruyun is cleaning. Fats is doing his home-work, but has a guilty look on his face.

Excuse us, Auntie Ruyun.

RUYUN: Come on in.

OX AND CART: *(politely, in unison)* Hello, Auntie Ruyun.

OX: Fats, so this is where you've been hiding?

CART: Fats, my God, you're home!

Ruyun is confused.

FATS: *(guiltily)* What's the matter?

OX: *(copying him)* What's the matter?

SMALLS: I don't get it. Why are you at home studying? I thought you were busy peeping at my sister in the shower?

Fats suddenly bolts out the back door. The three chase him. They run from one house to another, chasing Fats straight through each house.
General commotion. The three split up to block Fats, knocking over the boxes in front of Hanbin's house in the process. Fats slips away.

SMALLS: Block him!

OX: Fats, come out if you dare!

Ruyun comes out to look and stands right next to Smalls.

SMALLS: Fats, you motherfucker! *(discovering Ruyun right next to him, bowing and apologizing)* Excuse me, Auntie Ruyun.

RUYUN: Stop fighting. Let's find him so we can figure out what's going on . . .

OX: Dammit, Fats is over there!

The three look in one direction. Fats leads a group of tough-looking outsiders with clubs and knives on.

FATS: Goddam it, there they are!

SMALLS: Let's split!

The three run away.

FATS: Dammit! Get them!

The outsiders and Fats chase the three in and out of the houses. General commotion.

Scene 6: Discipline

The aftermath: Hanbin, Yen, Chu, and Mrs. Chu are in front of Hanbin's house, seeking to discipline their children, who are assembled before them, standing at attention. At Ning's, Fats holds a chair over his head, in punishment, supervised by Ruyun. Ning sits out front of his house, listening to the radio. They seem to be taking the task of disciplining their kids very seriously, but in fact they say random things, with a sense of authority.

YEN: *(to Smalls)* You should be doing your homework instead of always creating trouble!

MRS. CHU: *(to Ox)* She's talking to you two, too! Both of you have forgotten everything you learned in school.

DEUCE: I don't get it, Mom. Why punish us? Fats was the one peeping, he deserves to get beaten up!

OX AND CART: *(nodding)* Right!

YEN: *(to her children)* Be quiet, stand up straight! You snuck off and didn't do the work I gave you. Bigs, you should set an example for your sister, but you led the way.

Hanbin begins to sort out the facts in order to mete out punishment. Everyone looks to him for authority.

HANBIN: Are you sure it was Fats?

DEUCE: Double sure!

HANBIN: Fine . . . The Chao family will not be taken advantage of!

CHU: Neither will we Chus!

HANBIN: So whoever peeped at our daughter . . .

All wait in anticipation.

> We'll be damned if we don't peep back!

CHU: What?

BIGS: Uh, Dad, they don't have a daughter.

SMALLS: Dad, does that mean we can peep at Big Spice and Li'l Spice?

YEN: Hanbin, what are you saying!

HANBIN: That's not how you settle accounts! Every debt has its debtor.

CHU: Someone borrows from you but doesn't pay up. Can you go out into the street and randomly ask someone else to pay back?

DEUCE: Dad, what do you mean?

HANBIN: At any rate, the next time Fats showers . . .

YEN: Hanbin! What are you teaching your kids?

CHU: Hanbin, we await your instructions.

MRS. CHU: Right, Mr. Chao, lay down the law!

HANBIN: Okay. Everyone. The next time you shower . . .

All anticipate a just conclusion from the fair-minded Hanbin.

> Watch out.

Hanbin exits.

> DEUCE: What was that?

All exit.

Scene 7: The Movies

A small movie theatre in Chiayi town. Ox, Bigs, Cart, Deuce, Smalls, and Fats are here to see the latest Bruce Lee movie. Ox is buying tickets.

OX: Two student tickets, please.

CLERK: Fourteen dollars.

Ox gets two tickets.

OX: Thank you.

Ox hands out money to Cart, Deuce, Smalls, and Fats.

Okay. Here's 10 bucks each. Go take a stroll.

SMALLS: Thank you, Master Ox! Let's go.

Ox and Bigs go into the theatre.

FATS: But I want to watch the movie.

SMALLS: Watch your ass. They're on a date.

FATS: Then why can they go in?

SMALLS: Because they . . . *(slapping him on the back)* Fats, what happened to everything you ever learned at school?

DEUCE: Not another word from you.

SMALLS: Let's go for some shaved ice.

They exit.
    Inside the theatre, the film is playing. Ox has his arm around Bigs's shoulder. Sound of kung-fu fighting.

OX: My classmates tell me that Bruce Lee beats up 50 Japs in this scene.

BIGS: I've seen it already.

OX: What? With who?

BIGS: This guy from the Air Force Academy.

OX: When was this?

BIGS: Last week.

Fats comes back to the ticket office. He buys a ticket.

OX: So, I bet he took you to the cinema in uniform? Then?

BIGS: We had dinner, and he sent me home.

OX: Where?

BIGS: Some Western restaurant.

Fats comes in and sits in the seat right behind Ox and Bigs. He watches the screen in fascination.

OX: Fancy! Was it good?

BIGS: Just some ham or something, I don't really remember.

OX: Does your mom know about this?

BIGS: My mom likes him very much.

OX: So what do you think of me applying to the academy?

Pause. Smalls comes back to the theatre lobby, looking for Fats. He talks to the Clerk.

You don't think I can get accepted?

BIGS: Look, I'm telling you all this because I don't want any secrets between us. I actually don't like that guy.

OX: *(loudly)* If you actually don't like him, why would you go to a movie with him?

FATS: Keep it down, will you!

Bigs and Ox are surprised by the voice. Smalls enters the theatre.

OX: Fats! Get out of here!

SMALLS: Damn it, Fats! You really have the nerve!

FATS: Why can't I watch the movie?

Smalls chases Fats out, and they exit. The movie continues, with sounds of intense martial arts fighting.

BIGS: Sometimes in the dead of night, I imagine myself running and running, to a faraway place . . . so far . . .

OX: What about me?

BIGS: You're by my side.

Pause.

OX: We have to get out of here.

Silence. They continue watching the movie.

Scene 8: Three Flowers

A Western pop song of the era, such as "Smoke Gets in Your Eyes." At Hanbin's house. Cart and Deuce are listening to a record, singing along. Deuce pretends to hold a microphone.

DEUCE: Get ready.

CART: Here it comes . . .

They sing the climactic note together. Cart is way out of tune. Ning passes by outside and is visibly bothered by how bad it sounds. He goes straight into Hanbin's house without knocking or asking, as usual.

DEUCE: *(stopping the music)* Hello, Uncle Ning!

NING: Deuce, Cart! Singing?

DEUCE AND CART: Yes, sir.

NING: I thought you were slaughtering a cow.

He takes the flimsy, plastic bootleg record cover and examines it.

Western pop songs?

CART: Do you like them, too, Uncle Ning?

NING: *(flipping through their records)* Oh, you have Mandarin pop, too. *(looking at one in particular)* Chin Shan—excellent!

DEUCE: I saved up to buy it.

NING: Have you ever met Chin Shan?

DEUCE: No way!

CART: Right.

NING: Quite a handsome guy!

CART: Really? You know him?

NING: I saw him once at a recording session.

DEUCE: What! You've been to Taipei to watch a recording session?

NING: I have an old colleague who became a TV station exec. He invited me there.

DEUCE: Really? Who else did you see?

NING: All the stars! Hsieh Lei!

DEUCE: Hsieh Lei! Who else?

Long pause. Ning thinks.

NING: All of them!

DEUCE: Then can you help us get into the TV song competition?

NING: Of course.

CART: Really?

DEUCE: You're putting us on! That's not possible!

NING: Why would Uncle lie to you? All I have to do is write a letter!

CART: Can you ask him if there are any shows where I can show off my kung fu?

NING: Come on, Cart, you country bumpkin! For singing competitions, you have to sing! No one does kung fu!

DEUCE: I have an idea. Cart, we can surprise the judges by singing and doing kung fu at the same time.

NING: Deuce, do you have any nice clothes?

DEUCE: Nope.

NING: Cart, do you have a suit?

CART: No.

NING: Then too bad.

DEUCE: Uncle Ning, are you serious? You can really introduce us?

NING: Of course. I just have to write a letter, and if you guys don't go, I'll go!

Ning breaks into a Mandarin pop song, dramatically.

> *"Who'll love me?*
>
> *I wonder who will ever love me ..."*

Hey, Cart, didn't you say you wanted to do some kung fu?

CART: What?

NING: So go through with your plan: Deuce will sing, and you can be her bodyguard, and do your kung fu as accompaniment! Come on, let's use this song for practice!!

Ning plays a Mandarin pop song. Deuce sings along, while Cart does kung fu moves.

> DEUCE: *"You heartlessly threw me aside,*
>
> *Oblivious if I live or die,*
>
> *Who'll love me?*
>
> *Who'll love me ... ?"*

CART: *(swinging punches to the beat)* HYAH! HYAH! HYAH!

Deuce catches Yen coming home through the corner of her eye.

DEUCE: Look out, my mom's home!

CART: Her mom's home!

NING: Beat it!

Deuce hastily takes away the record and covers the gramophone. Ning and Cart rush out through the back door and arrive back at their respective houses in an instant. Deuce grabs her English dictionary and pretends to be studying hard. Yen enters.

DEUCE: L ... O ... V ... E ...

Yen taps her on the head.

YEN: Your dictionary is upside down.

Scene 9: Expectations

Bigs speaks directly to the audience.

> BIGS: So Uncle Ning really wrote a letter to his former colleague, and the TV station invited Cart and Deuce to the singing competition, *Three Flowers*. This was big news in our village! Unfortunately, my mom went to extreme lengths to keep my sister from going, so Cart became our village's sole representative.

Cart is preparing for his Taipei trip. He wears an ill-fitting suit. Chu sits in front of his house. Excitement is brewing.

> CHU: Tell me, Cart, what kind of a TV show is *Three Flowers*?

> OX: They give you the first line of a song, and you raise your hand if you can sing the next line.

> MRS. CHU: That calls for quick thinking. Can you handle it?

> CHU: Cart, competition is good experience. But don't worry too much about the outcome.

> MRS. CHU: Where did you get this suit?

> OX: This suit is the pits!

Fats comes over from his house with a notebook.

> FATS: Uncle Chu, I heard Cart is entering a competition in Taipei! We have a celebrity in our village! Autograph!

> OX: Starting now, you go through me, and pay for an autograph!

> FATS: Cart, why does my dad treat you so well? Better than he treats me. He's never very supportive of me.

> OX: You don't know how to sing. Why should he be supportive?

Bigs enters with a donation box, followed by Deuce and Smalls.

> BIGS: Uncle Chu, we've raised money for Cart to get a new suit!

> CHU: How can we accept this?

> BIGS: You must!

> DEUCE: *(looking at Cart)* Oh my god! What kind of a suit is this?

MRS. CHU: Weird lent it to him.

DEUCE: Uncle Weird owns a suit?

CHU: It's from the war era.

SMALLS: Man! Cart Chu, raise your hand and shout "here"!

CART: Here!

The suit is too tight. Cart can't raise his hand. Everyone laughs.

BIGS: This will not do! Cart needs a proper suit to go to Taipei. Our village is going to have a celebrity!

Bigs gives the donation box to Chu.

CHU: Well . . . Okay, thank you!

BIGS: Don't thank me; this is from the whole village.

CHU: *(bowing)* Thank you.

Ning enters in bubbly, flamboyant style, as if he is dancing onto a song competition stage.

NING: Hey, Chu, time for your boy to shine! Cart, come here.

CART: Uncle Ning.

NING: Listen carefully: Of the "three flowers," the first is the most important. You must get the first flower!

He suddenly breaks into song.

> *(singing) Diamond, diamond, sparkling bright*—and?

CART: *(singing) Like a star in the night . . .*

NING: That is correct!!

ALL: *(cheering)* Good going! He got it!!

DEUCE: *(singing to continue the quiz) The moon is like a lemon . . .*—and?

CART: *(singing) Hanging lightly in the sky . . .*

NING: That is correct! Got another one!

Everyone is merry.

ALL: Two flowers!

NING: Don't rejoice too soon. The third flower is always the most difficult. Listen carefully. I'm only going to sing this once:

(singing) I— and?

Cart pauses. Everyone is stumped.

You're done. Eliminated!

Pause. Everyone thinks hard.

CART: *(singing) I—my home . . .*

They all join in, singing the nostalgic song they sang at the first New Year's dinner.

ALL: *". . . is by the Songhua River, in Manchuria . . ."*

NING: Incorrect! This song has been banned. Take them all away!

All the villagers shake their heads, dissatisfied with Ning. Ox breaks into a nursery song.

OX: *(singing) I—have a small donkey, never do I ride . . .*

NING: Incorrect again! How juvenile! Bunch of donkey eggs.

Pause. Everyone thinks. Deuce breaks into a romantic song from the 1940s.

DEUCE: *(singing) I—walk down an endless path . . .*

Everyone joins in, singing and dancing to this romantic tango.

ALL EXCEPT NING: *(singing) I—gaze at distant clouds and trees . . .*

How many—

NING: *(interrupting them rudely)* INCORRECT!

SMALLS: Why?

NING: No need for any reason! YOU ARE INCORRECT!

HANBIN: Sir, there are a million songs starting with the word "I."

NING: Hanbin, did I sing "I"? Did I sing "I"? Listen carefully!

All listen.

(singing) Ahhh—ve Maria . . .

Ning swings and rocks as he dances away.

CHU: What the hell was that?

NING: Let's go for a drink.

Ning exits. Everyone is stupefied.

HANBIN: What bull!

Scene 10: The Competition

The Chu's television set has been moved out into the front yard for everyone to watch. Huang the carpenter is on a ladder, holding onto the antenna as he adjusts the reception.

SMALLS: Got it!

HUANG: Can you see?

OX: Got it! Don't move an inch!

SMALLS: It's starting! Hurry!

Everyone is excited. All take their place. Mrs. Chu brings out some steaming buns.

MRS. CHU: Everyone have some buns.

CHU: Pork buns!

The show's host is heard.

TV HOST: *(voice-over)* Good evening dear viewers, welcome to this week's competition . . .

RUYUN: *(pointing)* Hey, I see Cart! Over there!

ALL: *(cheering)* Hurray, Cart!

All the villagers point at the TV set and engage in small talk as they see Cart among the competitors.

TV HOST: Tonight we have 30 contestants from all over the island. The rules: If you raise your hand first and continue the song correctly, you get the first flower. Answer all three correctly and that's three flowers! Okay, let's start with the first song!

Music from a pop song.

> SINGER: *(voice-over, singing)* *In the rain, floating down . . .*

> DEUCE: *(raising her hand swiftly)* "Tears like Petals"!

> SMALLS: *(pointing)* Cart raised his hand!

> TV HOST: *(voice-over)* This young man, please continue.

> CART: *(voice-over, singing out of tune)* *Yellow petals, white petals . . .*

> CHU: Terrible.

The host pauses.

> TV HOST: Congratulations!

> ALL: *(cheering)* Way to go!

> TV HOST: Young man, where do you hail from?

> CART: Hello everybody, I'm from Formosa Village #1, in Chiayi.

The villagers jump up and down in ecstasy.

> ALL: Yea! Formosa Village #1!

> TV HOST: *(slightly condescending)* A dependents' village, huh? Very good, congratulations to this contestant from Formosa Village #1. You've got the first flower!

> HANBIN: He's going to get all three! I can feel it!

> TV HOST: How's your confidence level?

> ALL: *(drowning out Cart)* Great!

> TV HOST: Ready?

> ALL: *(drowning out Cart)* Ready!

> TV HOST: Now here comes the second song:

Music plays.

> SINGER: *(voice-over, singing)* *The night is deep . . .*

> DEUCE: Too easy, I prepped him on this one.

> YEN: "Country Path" from the Huangmei-style opera *Crimson Palm*.

> TV HOST: Please continue!

Silence. All watch intently, starting to grow uneasy.

CART: *(singing the musical accompaniment)* Ta ta ta ta . . . ta . . .

CHU: Sing the lyrics!

YEN: That's the bridge. He's okay . . .

Uneasy silence. All become perturbed.

CART: HYAH! HYAH!

TV HOST: Wait a minute, what are you doing? Boxing? Excuse me, young man from Formosa Village #1 in Chiayi, this is a singing competition. If you don't know the song you can't box your way out of a corner! Assistants, take him aside, please. *(gathering himself, with a chuckle)* To all our dear contestants, it is highly advisable that when you come to the competition, you be well prepared, or else . . . ahem . . .

Pause. Everyone stares at the screen. The TV Host chuckles and continues.

Now let's enjoy a professional rendition of "Lover's Tears."

Intro to the song, followed by sound of a songstress singing.
Long silence from the villagers. No one moves.
Ning quietly wipes away a tear. Chu stands up and bows to everyone.

CHU: *(to all)* I apologize to everyone.

Chu exits into his house. Fats cries out loud. Yen tries to comfort everyone.

YEN: Oh, it's just a TV show.

HANBIN: It's nothing, don't take it so seriously.

Ox shuts down the TV and moves it back home, with assistance from the sniveling Fats. Everyone takes their own stools and goes home.
Suddenly, Smalls breaks down and starts swearing.

SMALLS: Damn it, what the hell was he doing?! Cart! Damn it, Cart.

HANBIN: Smalls, what are you doing?

SMALLS: Damn you, Cart, you blew it! That means you aren't taking me to Taipei! WE'RE NOT GOING TO MAKE IT TO TAIPEI! GODDAM MOTHERFUCKER . . .

Ox grabs Smalls.

HANBIN: Stop it! It's just a TV show!

Smalls is escorted home, his shouting muffled. The TV and the chairs have been moved back inside. Only Granny Lu remains seated. Everyone else is gone. She raises her hand politely and sings out the correct answer, Chinese opera style.

GRANNY LU: *(singing)* Shadows swaying in the wind . . .

Birds shriek, a meteor streaks across the sky . . .

Not a single soul on the road . . .

Scene 11: The Gramophone Incident

Bigs appears in a spotlight as narrator.

BIGS: The greater the expectation, the greater the disappointment. After Cart came home from the big city, nobody ever mentioned the competition again. But Cart had embarrassed himself so badly that he never left the Village again.

Soon after, there was an incident involving my mom's gramophone: One day, Uncle Chu, who was a longtime Peking Opera aficionado, got hold of a classic record. He moved my mom's gramophone into the front yard . . .

Yen's gramophone has been moved to the front yard. Chu and Hanbin are listening to Peking Opera. Chu sings along in stylized falsetto as Hanbin claps along to the beat.

CHU: *(singing in falsetto)* Outside the Spring-Autumn Pavilion,

the storm rages.

What sad sound breaks the silence?

Two Military Police Officers enter left. They march toward the two. Chu, nervous, takes the needle off the record.

MILITARY POLICE A: What are you doing?

CHU: We're listening to Peking Opera.

MILITARY POLICE A: A man like you listening to Peking Opera?

HANBIN: Look, we're just listening to a record!

MILITARY POLICE A: *(looking at the record cover)* Peking Opera singer Cheng Yen-chiu? Isn't he . . . ?

MILITARY POLICE B: From the Commies' side.

CHU: What are you talking about? Cheng Yen-chiu is one of the four greatest actors of female roles, from the era predating the Commies!

MILITARY POLICE A: I don't care if he predates a scrambled egg. Where did you get this record?

CHU: A friend bought it in Hong Kong and brought it over.

MILITARY POLICE A: "Conveyance of smuggled goods!" Plus "Communication with the Enemy!" We are confiscating this evidence!

Military Police B takes away the record. Meanwhile, Smalls and Ox are smoking cigarettes behind the house.

CHU: What's the matter? Aren't we even allowed to listen to opera?

MILITARY POLICE A: Certainly you are! In the comfort of your jail cell. Arrest them!

Hanbin halts Military Police B and explains.

HANBIN: Sir, this is a misunderstanding. We're preparing a skit for the upcoming Mid-Autumn Festival talent show. We were rehearsing, we had no idea where this record came from . . .

Military Police B checks the gramophone.

MILITARY POLICE B: *(pointing at the gramophone)* This is also from the other side.

The two officers check the gramophone.

HANBIN: My wife brought this with us when we retreated from China.

CHU: Right. She brought it over from Beijing in 1949.

MILITARY POLICE A: You expect me to believe that? Refugees bringing a gramophone with them in their luggage? Who are you kidding?

HANBIN: It's true! I . . .

MILITARY POLICE A: Stand at attention! TEN-HUT! Don't move. We're confiscating this gramophone and record. Both of you stand properly and reflect on your wrongdoing! Smuggling and contact with the enemy!

HANBIN: Wait, that gramophone . . .

CHU: It . . .

Hanbin and Chu stand at attention. The two officers take the gramophone and exit left. They see Smalls and Ox smoking. Smalls and Ox attempt to run away.

MILITARY POLICE A: *(loudly)* Get over here!

Military Police B stops Ox and Smalls. Smalls tucks the lit cigarette inside his mouth with his tongue in one fluid move.

Stand at attention!

MILITARY POLICE B: Hand it over!

Pause.

MILITARY POLICE A: Your mouth!

MILITARY POLICE B: Open it!

Smalls opens his mouth. Smoke comes pouring out. Officer takes out the lit cigarette.

MILITARY POLICE A: Runaway from the circus? Stand properly! TEN-HUT! Head up, torso straight, belly flat, ass cheeks tight, hands flush!

Smalls and Ox stand at attention.

What is the matter with this village? We came here to nab mahjong gamblers and set the moral tone right. And we get people like you?

The two officers exit with the gramophone, the record, and the cigarette.
The four stand awkwardly at attention, not having been given orders to stand at ease.
Yen enters left and doesn't pay attention to how the four are standing. She passes by Hanbin and Chu.

YEN: This heat is killing me! Hanbin, I need to listen to some music. Play a record for me.

HANBIN: Uh . . . something happened to our gramophone . . .

Yen is about to go into the house.

YEN: What can happen to a gramophone? Wait. What are both of you doing standing at attention?

Yen suddenly sees Ox and Smalls standing, too.

What is Smalls doing there? What's going on?

SMALLS: Nothing, Mom. We . . .

The two Military Police Officers come marching back.

MILITARY POLICE A: ATTENTION!

Hanbin, Chu, Smalls, and Ox stand properly. Yen doesn't get it.

Engaging in small talk? Tell me: who does that gramophone belong to?

CHU: *(trying to cover)* It's mine.

YEN: *(angrily)* What are you saying, Chu? I hand-carried that gramophone all the way from Beijing in '49! It was a present from my Uncle De!

Hanbin and Chu try to hint to Yen to be quiet.

MILITARY POLICE A: So you're in this, too! Tell me: who is Uncle De?

YEN: I'm in what, too? How dare you take my gramophone? Who are you?

MILITARY POLICE A: Ma'am, you're dealing with two MPs of the Republic of China! *(to Police B)* Take this woman away!

YEN: *(still not getting it)* What?

Hanbin, Chu, Ox, and Smalls surround Yen. Chaos.

HANBIN: She's innocent. Don't arrest her. Arrest me instead!!

CHU: Please, it's all a misunderstanding.

MILITARY POLICE A: TEN-HUT!

Everyone, including Yen, stands at attention.
Pause.

Don't any of you dare move a muscle! Listen. I'm letting you all off today. But I want you to reflect! At this time of national crisis, what do we find you people doing? Listening to opera? Smoking?!

They march off and exit.

Silence. The five stand at attention, having not been given the order to be at ease.

Hanbin turns his head slightly to make sure the military police officers are gone.

HANBIN: *(at attention)* Smalls, when I'm done here, I'm stringing you up and giving you a good thrashing.

Ox laughs.

CHU: *(at attention, softly)* Ox, don't be too smug. You'll be hanging above Smalls.

Silence. The five stand at attention.

Weird passes by on his bike. He looks at them curiously.

WEIRD: Woowoo, wehorvil soomortic oosternuncie!

They all try to look natural as Weird exits.

Scene 12: The Bomb Shelter (2)

Ox and Bigs are in the bomb shelter, alone.

OX: Once you hear me whistle. That's the signal.

BIGS: Then we go.

OX: Out of here.

BIGS: Some night, way past midnight.

OX: Some night.

BIGS: We'll go to the coast . . .

OX: Where a ship will be waiting for us . . .

BIGS: We'll take the ship . . .

OX: A big ship.

BIGS: Our ship.

Silence.

To . . . ?

OX: Japan.

BIGS: No, America.

OX: We'll go to America and buy a big house, bigger than this bomb shelter, goddamit, bigger than the whole damn village!

BIGS: I'll never have to see my mom again, never have to share a bed with my sister.

OX: I'll never have to deal with a telephone pole in my house . . .

BIGS: No more neighbors eavesdropping!

OX: No need for secret meetings in the bomb shelter. We'll have our own bomb shelter!

Pause. Bigs and Ox look at each other.

You don't believe me, do you?

BIGS: You're the one who doesn't believe.

OX: Bigs, we must catch that ship together.

BIGS: If we don't make it, there's no other way out. If the ship leaves without us . . .

OX: I'll join the army, and then become a drifter.

BIGS: I'll go to Taichung and service the American GIs.

OX: I'll find you, drag you away, and beat you up.

BIGS: You said it.

OX: I said it. So we're agreed. Once you hear my whistle we set off.

BIGS: I can't wait.

Scene 13: The Argument

Inside their house, Yen and Hanbin are scolding Bigs. Next door, Mrs. Chu and Chu are scolding Ox.

Deuce is eating a big piece of watermelon by the window in her house, trying not to get involved.

Ning sits alone in front of his house, listening to the radio. Since they are so close to one another, everything can be heard by everyone.

YEN: Shame on you, Bigs!

BIGS: What about me?!

YEN: People say you were half-undressed!

BIGS: I was not.

YEN: I heard every time the two of you left the cinema, your clothes were in disarray, and it was the same at the bomb shelter.

BIGS: Who said that? Don't listen to rubbish.

YEN: I don't get it. If you want to talk to Ox, why must you talk inside the bomb shelter?

BIGS: Because we can't talk here.

YEN: Then just talk, why take off your clothes?

BIGS: Mom, I didn't!

HANBIN: Easy. Ox isn't a bad kid.

YEN: This has nothing to do with Ox.

BIGS: Then what does it have to do with?

YEN: Our village rules. Don't you understand? You can't be dating our own!

BIGS: Why not?

YEN: Our girls must leave if they want a future, even if it means marrying an officer from the village across from us! You can't date a guy from here! What future can he offer you? Nothing!

BIGS: So I should follow Big Spice and Li'l Spice? What a future they have out there, sitting on the laps of American GIs!

HANBIN: That's enough.

YEN: Bigs, how can you say that?

Silence. Deuce spits a watermelon seed into a bucket. The sound echoes.

BIGS: What a bright future, clinging to a half-drunk American soldier, whose hands are groping . . .

HANBIN: Bigs!

The Chus next door continue the scolding, directing it at Ox, who is standing at attention.

CHU: You heard it. Why give others the chance to say such things about us?

OX: Her mom is crazy. That's not my problem.

Yen answers from next door.

YEN: Who is crazy? How did you teach your kids? I was a preparatory student for Beijing University. Everyone in Beijing knows me—Chien Yen, the young miss of Fortune Restaurant!

MRS. CHU: *(to Ox)* You have to stop wasting her time.

OX: In what way am I wasting her time?

MRS. CHU: What do you have to offer her?

OX: You don't think I can provide a future for her?

YEN: *(next door, sarcastically)* Haha!

Ning is listening to his transistor radio.

NING: Bravo!

Though they are not in the same room, the dialogue weaves together as if it is one conversation.

YEN: Provide a future? Ox? Ox is the spitting image of his dad. Marry him and you'll end up steaming buns till you're old and your face is all wrinkled. *(begging her)* Bigs! I'm doing this for your own good! I don't want you to be like me! Marry the wrong man, and your life is over!

Hanbin is ruffled, but he decides not to intrude.

BIGS: Mom . . .

MRS. CHU: *(to Ox)* You couldn't even get into college, what are you going to provide?

OX: Nothing I say will convince you, so I'll show you what I can do.

MRS. CHU: Yes, show me how you can make a fool of yourself!

YEN: *(next door, hysterically)* All of you want to see us make fools of ourselves, right? When you marry Ox, I'll give you a big wedding present, I'LL HANG MYSELF FROM THEIR TELEPHONE POLE! I'LL DIE BEFORE YOUR EYES!

BIGS: Mom!

HANBIN: What are you saying, Yen?

MRS. CHU: *(to Ox)* It's your fault that they look down on us! She has a general's son courting her. Tell me, what do you have to offer?

OX: Oh, I get it. You mean he has more to offer so I should just give up? Dad, Mom, is this what you've taught me? Fine! I give up! I'm predestined to be useless! *(shouting)* EVERYONE FROM OUR VILLAGE IS PREDESTINED TO BE USELESS AND HOPELESS!

CHU: Stop it!

MRS. CHU: *(scolding Ox)* There are so many girls out there, why do you insist on chasing Bigs? You've seen her every day since you were a kid, aren't you tired of her yet?

YEN: That's right!

MRS. CHU: Just think. If Auntie Chao's mom hadn't taught me how to make Tianjin buns, you wouldn't even have had the chance to grow up and attend school. If her mother doesn't want you to be with her, then so be it! Break up!

BIGS: Mom, you're driving us into a corner.

YEN: For who? For who?

OX: Everything you say won't mean a thing. When the ship comes, I'm gone.

MRS. CHU: Where are you going?

OX: Don't say I didn't warn you.

Ox exits. Chu and Mrs. Chu chase him.

MRS. CHU: What crazy things are you saying? What ship?

Over at Hanbin's house.

YEN: What ship?

Bigs exits.

> Where do you think you're going? GO, THEN, AND WATCH ME
> HANG MYSELF! *(hysterically)* LET ME DIE!

*Yen breaks the window between her home and Chu's in a wild frenzy. Hanbin
and Smalls grab her and sit her down. She remains hysterical.*

HANBIN: Smalls, go and get your sister back.

Smalls hurries out. Yen cries and exits.
   *Silence. After the commotion, only Hanbin and Deuce, who's still working
on the watermelon, are left at home. Chu is the only one over at his home. Ning
is still sitting in front of his house, listening to the radio. Hanbin searches his
house for a drink.*

> There's nothing to drink. What has this home come to?

Hanbin stands in front of Deuce, watching her eat the watermelon.
   *Hanbin reaches out for a bite. Deuce holds the watermelon out of his reach.
She spits a watermelon seed into the bucket again, making a loud ping.*
   Silence.
   *Hanbin goes to the broken glass window, and directly addresses Chu
through the window.*

> Any beer in your fridge?

CHU: *(at the window)* Hang on.

Hanbin steps out. Chu gets the beer. They walk out together, passing Ning.

> Coming?

NING: All done over there?

Hanbin and Chu exit. Ning follows.

Scene 14: Breaking Vows

*Middle of the night. The three houses have now been turned 90 degrees, showing
a cross section of everyone asleep, on bunks, on the ground, everywhere.*
   *With his backpack in hand, Ox whistles a sound replicating the intonation
of "Bigs" at the back door of Hanbin's house. Bigs hears the signal, gets up, grabs
her jacket, and comes outside.*

BIGS: It's 3 a.m. What's up?

OX: It's 3 a.m.

BIGS: Why the backpack?

OX: The ship is here. Are you coming?

Bigs pauses. Ox grabs Bigs.

> I'm asking you again. If you hesitate, I'll know your answer. The ship is here, let's leave.

Slight pause.

BIGS: Okay!

OX: You hesitated.

BIGS: No, I didn't.

OX: What were you just thinking?

BIGS: Nothing.

OX: What was in your mind at that very moment?

BIGS: It's complicated! My dad, my mom. It's 3 a.m.! But if you want me to go, let's go.

OX: You don't believe in me.

BIGS: It's not that, I was just thinking . . .

OX: Don't think, Bigs.

BIGS: Ox, those things we said in the bomb shelter . . .

OX: Everything said in the bomb shelter was from the heart. I couldn't be more truthful.

BIGS: Fine. But . . . You're so rash? How can you not . . .

OX: NOT WHAT? YOU'RE RIGHT, JUST LIKE YOUR MOM SAID, I'M USELESS.

BIGS: No, that isn't what I mean . . .

OX: You don't believe in me, right?

BIGS: It isn't that. You know that, I . . .

OX: ALL OF YOU LOOK DOWN ON ME! THE WHOLE VILLAGE LOOKS DOWN ON ME. EVEN YOU DO!

BIGS: YOU'RE RIGHT! I LOOK DOWN ON YOU. SO DOES MY FAMILY! SO DOES THE WHOLE VILLAGE! WE ALL DESPISE YOU!! ARE YOU SATISFIED NOW? DOES THAT MAKE YOU HAPPY?

Silence. Bigs' words still seem to ring through the night air. Some people stir, but fall back asleep.
  Ox is surprisingly calm.

OX: One day . . . One day when we meet again, you'll see.

Bigs watches Ox leave.
  Lights fade out.

Part Two

ACT THREE, 1970–1975

Scene 1: The Blue Angel

Deuce address the audience.

> DEUCE: After leaving the Village, Ox drifted around. One night, my sister also left the Village. She went to Taichung City, to a bar called the Blue Angel on Wuchuan Road, to join Big Spice and Li'l Spice as a bar girl, providing "services" to US military personnel stationed nearby. That was a tremendous blow to my parents, and to us, too . . .

A street scene in Taichung, central Taiwan, home to a US Air Force base during this Vietnam War period. The entrance of the Blue Angel bar. Bigs and Big Spice stand at the doorway, dressed in revealing clothing and heavy makeup, enticing the mainly American soldiers who pass by. A tough-looking Bouncer sits at the entrance. Bigs and Big Spice wave to a passing GI.

> BIG SPICE: *(broken English)* Hey, there. Come in! Have some fun.

The GI goes into the bar with them, wrapping one arm around each.

> DEUCE: *(to the audience)* One day, Smalls took Cart and Fats on a train ride to Taichung to search for my sister. Smalls planned on beating up whatever US soldiers were in his path, and then bringing her back home. But when they got there, they didn't know where to look . . .

Smalls, Cart, and Fats enter. They look around, eyes wide, like deer in headlights. They stare at the bar, watch the pedestrians, and hesitate.

> SMALLS: Blue Angel. Damn it. Is this the one?

> CART: Is it this one?

Li'l Spice comes out of the bar on the arm of an American soldier.

> LI'L SPICE: *(to the soldier, English)* Hey you, be gentle!

They exit right.

> FATS: Wait. Isn't that Li'l Spice?

> SMALLS: Is it?

CART: Looks a lot like her.

SMALLS: Damn, did you see how that GI was fondling her?

Bigs comes out of the bar and waves to the American soldiers.

BIGS: *(English)* Hey, Joe. Come in, have some fun!

FATS: Hey Smalls, isn't that your sister at the door?

Smalls takes a look.

SMALLS: *(in denial)* No, that's not her!

CART: From the side it really looks like her.

SMALLS: My sister would never dress like that.

FATS: *(looking carefully)* It's her.

SMALLS: How do you know?

FATS: I've seen her with that little on before.

Fats realizes he has said more than he should.

SMALLS: *(slapping Fats's shoulder)* Goddam it, you peeped at both my sisters?!

CART: Fats, are you sure?

BIGS: *(English)* Hi there, come in, Joe . . .

Bigs brings a GI into the bar. The GI puts his arm around her. The boys watch in wonder.

SMALLS: Okay, here's the plan: we barge in, we rescue Bigs, then we smash up the place, burn it down, and go home.

CART AND FATS: *(meekly)* Roger that.

SMALLS: On "three."

CART AND FATS: *(meekly)* On "three."

Pause.

SMALLS: On "three."

CART AND FATS: *(meekly)* On "three". . .

They stare at the Bouncer.
　Cart runs away.

FATS: Cart? Where are you going? Wait for me!

Fats also ditches. Smalls is left alone, staring at the Bouncer, with clenched fists. The Bouncer is expressionless. He doesn't even look at Smalls.

SMALLS: Damn . . .

Smalls is resigned to give up, and exits.

Scene 2: The Help

Deuce addresses the audience. The sound of another patriotic song, "How Can I Forget Her?" is in the air.

DEUCE: Remember Ruyun? The one who lived in a big house with a big yard in the pilots' compound? Then her husband Li the fighter pilot, who was a national hero, defected to the Communists, and she came to live with her husband's classmate, our neighbor, the kindhearted Uncle Ning? Well, another of her husband's classmates, General Wu, also took good care of her. He employed Ruyun to clean and cook for his family. She'd been cleaning house for Wu since I was a child. Wu was later promoted all the way to general, and became the big shot of our village. Though Ruyun was the housemaid, she always insisted on wearing her pretty dresses to work. Many people mistook her for the lady of the house.

Afternoon inside General Wu's house. It is spacious and well appointed. Ruyun is in the kitchen, dressed in a plain but proper cheongsam. She smokes a cigarette, staring blankly into space. Mrs. Wu and three other properly dressed ladies are playing mahjong in the living room.
　Wu and Mrs. Wu are the couple who came to see Ning on the first New Year's Eve in the first act. They are now middle aged.
　Ruyun enters the living room from the kitchen and pours tea for them.

MRS. WU: You just can't stop winning!

MAHJONG LADY: It's my lucky day today.

MRS. WU: Ruyun, please prepare the special Sichuan dumplings we brought back the other day.

RUYUN: Yes, Madam.

Ruyun returns to the kitchen. General Wu enters the living room, buttoning his sleeves, with an air of authority.

WU: *(Sichuan accent)* Who's winning?

THREE LADIES: *(greeting Wu)* Good day, General . . .

WU: Carry on.

Wu enters the kitchen. His public face disappears. He talks to Ruyun extremely casually, as if she were his spouse.

What's for dinner, Ruyun?

RUYUN: Mrs. Chen brought us some Sichuan peppers. I'm making fish stew.

WU: Great! I have an official cocktail party to attend in the evening. But my uniform . . .

RUYUN: Is already mended.

Wu stands at the kitchen door, looking toward the living room.

WU: *(to his wife and ladies)* Spicy meat dumplings coming up!

Wu goes into the kitchen again.

RUYUN: Will you need your medals?

WU: Don't think so.

RUYUN: Your superior from Taipei is coming. Of course you'll need them.

WU: If you say so.

Ruyun helps put on Wu's jacket and medals.
She gets sad all of a sudden.

RUYUN: Were you aware that today is the 20th anniversary of Li's accident?

Silence. They share a moment of memory.

WU: *(reminiscing)* Li . . . We miss you, buddy . . .

RUYUN: *(emotionally)* I want to thank you, Wu. I don't know how I would have made it without you.

Ruyun is about to turn and leave, but Wu holds her still.

WU: Ruyun . . . I'm the one who wouldn't have made it without you.

They embrace.
 Wu's son, Chia-kuang, a quiet high school student in uniform, enters the kitchen from the back door. Wu and Ruyun quickly let go of each other.

Oh, you're home, Son?

MRS. WU: *(shouting from the living room)* Ruyun, are the dumplings ready?

Wu goes back to the living room, where his Attendant waits for him.

RUYUN: Right away.

Chia-kuang pokes around the kitchen and grabs something from the pot to eat.

That's not for you!

WU: *(to the ladies)* Have fun. I'm off to work.

In the kitchen, Chia-kuang sits down at the kitchen table. Ruyun takes out his report card.

RUYUN: *(to Chia-kuang)* I need you to have a look at this disgraceful report card! Your teacher made a special trip here to deliver it.

CHIA-KUANG: *(takes a look)* How dare he bring this shit here?

He throws the report card on the table.

RUYUN: Watch your mouth. You won't die if you don't cuss. Look at how many days you played hooky. What's going on with you?

CHIA-KUANG: You're not my mother. Don't give me any of your shit.

RUYUN: I warn you again, watch your attitude.

CHIA-KUANG: Don't think you can bully me just because my dad has your back.

MRS. WU: *(from the living room)* Ruyun . . .

CHIA-KUANG: You think I don't know you're a dirty spy's bitch!

Pause.

RUYUN: I dare you to say that again!

CHIA-KUANG: A dirty spy's bitch is also a dirty spy! You should be locked up! I'll get my dad to arrest you! ARREST THE DIRTY SPY!

Ruyun slaps Chia-kuang. At the exact moment, Mrs. Wu comes in the kitchen door. She is astonished.

MRS. WU: Chia-kuang, are you OK?

CHIA-KUANG: Leave me alone. *(to Ruyan)* Bitch!

Chia-kuang exits running.

MRS. WU: Who do you think you are? You're just the nanny, the housemaid!

The winning Mahjong Lady comes into the kitchen.

MAHJONG LADY: Calm down.

MRS. WU: Stay out of this.

Mahjong Lady goes back to the mahjong table. Pause.

Okay, Ruyun, I finally have had enough. All these years, you think I don't know what's been going on between you and my husband? Did I ever say anything? But if you think you can lay your hands on my baby, that's it! Go pack up your things, and don't bother coming in tomorrow.

Mrs. Wu goes back to the living room.

Carry on . . .

They continue playing mahjong. Ruyun is alone in the kitchen.

Scene 3: The Bomb Shelter (3)

Ruyun and Wu are meeting in the bomb shelter, a space that normally belongs to the teenagers. Wu tries to comfort Ruyun.

WU: Ruyun, my wife came from a wealthy family back home. You know that she's not very sensitive to the feelings of others. Please, come back. I guarantee she'll be fine.

RUYUN: Nothing changes. Why go back?

Pause.

WU: Fine. If you aren't going back, neither am I. I can apply for retirement in two years. Once I get my pension, we leave. You and I. We'll go to Taipei. We'll start up a restaurant!

RUYUN: You mean it?

WU: Of course I do. Really.

The two begin to imagine this.

RUYUN: If we really are leaving, we should go somewhere farther away.

WU: No problem. Let's go to America, to Los Angeles. I have many former subordinates there. I can hold court over there.

RUYUN: LA. We can start over there.

WU: We'll do some mean home cooking. We'll name the restaurant "Ruyun's Bistro."

RUYUN: No, no. It has to be called "General Wu's Palace." That sounds much more impressive.

WU: "Ruyun's Bistro" has a cozy feel to it. Those overseas Chinese are just dying to taste some real home cooking: Hunan ham, Sichuan dumplings, fish stew . . .

RUYUN: . . . Spicy chili chicken, fish-braised eggplant . . .

Deuce and Cart enter. They are surprised to see Wu and Ruyun in the bomb shelter.

DEUCE: Oh, uh, hi, Auntie Ruyun . . .

CART: General Wu . . .

DEUCE: Isn't this . . . ?

WU: *(seriously)* This is a bomb shelter. I'm carrying out an inspection.

He walks around as if inspecting the place.

    Very good, very safe . . . Okay, I'm leaving!

DEUCE: Okay.

CART: Okay.

Awkward pause. General Wu stays put. Deuce motions to Cart to go, and they exit.

General Wu continues his fantasizing.

WU: For dessert, your famous almond pudding will slay them! I can see the long line waiting for a table! . . .

Scene 4: Mind Your Business

Over at Ning's, Ruyun is home alone, writing a note. Fats comes home from school.

FATS: Mom, what are you doing home?

Ruyun doesn't respond. Fats sees the note.

What are you writing? Why don't you answer me?

RUYUN: Do your homework.

Fats takes out his textbooks.

FATS: Where's Dad?

RUYUN: I don't know.

FATS: Mom . . .

RUYUN: What?

FATS: I heard you were at the bomb shelter with General Wu just now.

RUYUN: What?

FATS: What were you doing there?

RUYUN: Mind your own business.

Fats suddenly throws down his pen.

FATS: You only help their son with his schoolwork.

RUYUN: You always have such good grades, there's no need for me to help you. But no matter how late, I come back and cook for you. So stay out of my business.

Mrs. Chu is back from the market with her vending cart. She hears the conversation and stops to listen.

FATS: Then thanks for your cooking! But you never tell me anything!

Fats breaks down crying.

RUYUN: What are you crying for?! Why are you asking so many questions?!

FATS: You never tell me anything! Why am I solving all these math problems? They're meaningless!

RUYUN: Stop crying! Is this how a boy should behave?

FATS: They say I'm not Dad's son!

RUYUN: You believe what others say? What about what I say? Do you care what I say?

FATS: I've always wanted to ask you, but you never say anything! I want to know where I came from. They say Dad can't have kids. They say he's a homo. So where did I come from?

Pause. Mrs. Chu continues to eavesdrop.

RUYUN: Look at me! Are you my son?

FATS: Mom, I've known this for a long time! I know that man is not my father. So why should I call him Dad?

Pause. Ruyun slumps down in her chair.

RUYUN: *(in deep despair)* I'm so tired! I'm tired to death!

Silence.
Mrs. Chu knocks and enters, bringing in some buns. She acts as if nothing has happened.

MRS. CHU: Hi, Ruyun, I'm experimenting on these buns, using dried radish as a filling. It's a new recipe! Try them and tell me if they will sell.

FATS: Thank you, Auntie Chu.

Ruyun stares ahead blankly.

Scene 5: Lugang Temple

Deuce speaks to the audience, as Ruyun comes out of her house and walks away from the Village.

DEUCE: That day, Ruyun finished the simple note she was writing, which Fats found on the table: "Don't look for me. I won't be back. I'm going where nobody can find me." The whole village began a frantic search for her . . .

To the aria "Amor ti vieta," the three houses start to revolve. All the villagers run back and forth, through the houses, looking for Ruyun.

CART: Auntie Ruyun!! . . .

ALL: RUYUN! RUYUN! . . .

MRS. TSUI: Ruyun! Don't overanalyze!!

Mrs. Tsui runs around, stopping every few steps to fold her hands to the heavens in prayer.

DEUCE: *(to the audience)* Ruyun went to the train station, where she bought a platform ticket. She stood on the platform, and watched as the northbound express approached at high speed, closer and closer . . .

Ruyun stands on the platform of the train station. A train approaches. The whistle grows louder and louder. Ruyun takes a deep breath, and prepares to jump onto the tracks. At the crucial moment, she holds back, almost falling to the ground as the train whizzes by.
The train has gone. Ruyun seems to come to her senses, but is still in a daze. She walks away.

She realized that she hadn't jumped.

She left the station, and randomly hopped on a bus that took her to Lugang, the ancient town with the famous temple to Matsu, goddess of the sea, protector of souls. There, she wandered into the Grand Temple, burned some incense, then stood before the goddess all afternoon, watching the pilgrims come and go.

Ruyun does all that, and stands watching as others beside her burn incense and bow devoutly.

And then, she went home.

Ruyun leaves the temple downstage and returns home.
It is evening. Ning and Fats sit quietly at home in despair. Ruyun opens the door and enters. The three face one another, in silence.

Scene 6: DIY Toilet

Daytime. In front of Hanbin's house, Hanbin and Huang are covering their noses, as is Weird. Cart addresses the audience.

CART: And so things returned to normal. One day, we detected a foul odor from our neighbor's house. It turned out to be Uncle Hanbin, trying to install a flush toilet after seeing the new one my dad had put in. But he couldn't afford it, so he asked Mr. Huang, the window fixer and coffin maker, for DIY help. It was a total disaster.

He exits.

YEN: There shouldn't be such an odor.

HUANG: Maybe we didn't use enough charcoal.

WEIRD: Zameesoodallit, rutchudeente dogsdoop.

Deuce walks by in a miniskirt, about to go inside.

DEUCE: Hi, everyone.

HANBIN: Where are you going?

DEUCE: *(with pride)* To use our new toilet!

HANBIN: *(stopping her)* You can't. It's still under construction.

DEUCE: Wasn't it finished yesterday? I told everyone we have a flush toilet! I saved it all for now. I knew you'd screw it up. Who puts in their own toilet?

Deuce exits in the direction of the public toilet.

HANBIN: I think we should consider starting over.

WEIRD: Woostoofoo? Dogsdoop joosoo!

Weird claps his hands to emphasize what he's saying. Chu comes out of his own house, having just used his own bathroom.

CHU: *(stretching)* What a great feeling to have a toilet in your own home! Hanbin, what are you all doing?

HANBIN: We're installing my toilet. My daughters have grown up, and it will be more convenient for them if they can . . . *(pause)* Forget it, let's drop the subject.

CHU: But you can't do this yourself. You need a professional! Oh, I see, Huang, you're here.

Awkward pause. Chu points at the window between his house and Hanbin's.

Then can you please have a look at this window? It's broken.

HUANG: No problem, I'll fix it for you.

CHU: Right. You're the only one who can fix it. The windows you made are crooked.

HUANG: Hey, don't blame me. Your house was built crooked.

Mrs. Chu comes out of the house.

CHU: Hanbin, say the word and Huang will replace the glass.

HANBIN: What do you need my approval for? The window's in your house. Do as you please.

CHU: What do you mean? It was YOUR wife who broke MY window.

Yen rushes out of her house.

YEN: What did I just hear? WHOSE wife broke WHOSE window? Who was the one who got my gramophone confiscated by MPs?

CHU: Wait a minute. How can you link these two matters together?

YEN: Because they are!

WEIRD: Oonuu! Doosdoont footoo!

CHU: Please keep your opinion to yourself, Weird, it's none of your business!

YEN: *(to Weird)* We'll let you know when we need your opinion, okay, Weird? Can't you see we're busy quarreling?

CHU: We are not quarreling! I never quarrel with anyone! I'm REASONING with you! Look: From my perspective, this is MY window; where you are is outside of MY house. If you insist it's YOUR window, that creates a new set of problems. It means that you've broken both YOURS AND MY windows, so you have to pay double!

YEN: You heard that, Huang! Please install two separate windowpanes so we can each open our own individual windows! And HE will pay for BOTH!

HANBIN: Enough!

YEN: How dare he say I broke his window! His "house" has no windows!

HANBIN: Enough. In the beginning . . .

YEN: In the beginning, did the Chu family live here?

CHU: In the beginning did the Chao family live here?

HANBIN: What the . . . ?

YEN: Ha! So that's how you want to play it? Fine! Let's talk about "in the beginning." Who brought our two families here in the beginning? We'll let THEM settle this window issue, okay? So Chiang Kai-shek and Mao Zedong are the responsible parties, we'll demand each of them to pay half, what do you say?

Pause.

CHU: Sounds good to me! Let Chairman Mao pay your half! I don't want his money!

Chu exits.

YEN: Who wants Mao's money? We're on the side of righteousness, so Generalissimo Chiang pays for us!

Pause. Yen points at Hanbin.

It's all because of you! You can't afford it, and yet you want your own bathroom! Your whole life has just been poor poor poor, that's why it stinks stinks stinks!

HANBIN: *(bursting out in anger)* ARE YOU DONE? AREN'T WE SHAME-FUL ENOUGH? IT'S JUST A WINDOWPANE! JUST BUY A NEW ONE AND INSTALL IT! BUT WHAT ABOUT OUR DAUGHTER? HOW CAN I GET HER BACK?

Silence.
Yen exits, in tears.
Mrs. Tsui enters.

MRS. TSUI: Hanbin, what happened?

HANBIN: Nothing. You?

MRS. TSUI: There's more graffiti at the public toilet.

HANBIN: But I just whitewashed it yesterday.

Hanbin exits in the direction of the public toilet.

Mrs. Tsui suddenly holds her nose.

MRS. TSUI: My, it stinks!

Scene 7: Forum at the Public Restroom

Outside the public restroom. The graffiti on the wall is Tang Dynasty poetry, but written childishly and with misspellings. The original line should read "Raising my head I gaze at the full moon, lowering it I think of home."
    Ning is studying the graffiti. Hanbin, Huang, Weird, Mrs. Tsui, and Mrs. Chu enter.

HANBIN: What gibberish! Look at all the misspellings!

NING: How juvenile. Donkey eggs. What illiterate would miswrite the characters in this famous poem? *(giving a wink)* Am I right? Am I right? You betcha!

MRS. TSUI: Watch out. He's got that shifty-eye look again.

Smalls and Cart enter.

SMALLS: Dad, we brought the paint.

MRS. TSUI: Whitewash it immediately.

Smalls and Cart begin to whitewash the wall. Hanbin suddenly stops them.

HANBIN: Hold it. Look carefully at how it's miswritten: "Gaze at the full moon" is written "Forget the full moon"; "hometown" has become "ancient fragrance." Either this guy is really off, or . . . could this possibly be some code?

NING: Something's fishy here.

Deuce emerges from the public restroom.

DEUCE: What's fishy? Someone just has bad spelling. Quick, paint over it!

An unknown pedestrian, the Woman in Red, passes by and takes a look.

NING: Deuce, pay attention! It's not that simple.

HANBIN: *(analyzing the text)* "Forget the full moon." When is the full moon?

NING: Every 15th of the lunar calendar.

HANBIN: So "forget the full moon" means . . .

NING: First day of the lunar month!

HANBIN: Everyone listen up! This is code language for a secret gathering!

WEIRD: Ohscreedoo gollyroot roocooshoonies!

NING: So the date is set. What about the place?

HANBIN: "Thinking of the ancient fragrance . . ."

NING: "Ancient fragrance" takes the place of "home."

DEUCE: Please, can you just stop it, everybody? Someone just happened to write the wrong characters! "Lower my head and think of ancient fragrance." "Ancient fragrance" refers to the smell in the public restroom. It means lower one's head and look at the shit, until one forgets about the moon! It's that simple, I do it every day!

Deuce exits.

HANBIN: Deuce, get out of here! Go home!

SMALLS: Wait a minute, Dad. Did you know there's an Ancient Fragrance Teahouse on Lanjing Street in town?

HANBIN: Really?

HUANG: Right. It's very dark inside. The women there offer special services.

SMALLS: That's right!

HANBIN: How do you know?

SMALLS: *(awkwardly)* Mr. Huang once, uh, described it to me.

Granny Lu enters with her Attendant following.

GRANNY LU: Having a nice chat?

SMALLS AND CART: *(in unison)* Hello, Granny Lu!

HANBIN: Granny Lu, does this look suspicious to you?

Granny Lu signals for the Attendant to leave. She looks at the wall.

NING: Today's the 29th of the lunar month. The day after tomorrow will be the first! Does it look to you as if Commie agents are plotting something?

GRANNY LU: *(very slowly)* I think . . .

All bend over to hear.

I think I need to use the restroom.

Granny Lu goes into the restroom. The Woman in Red exits. Ruyun passes by.

HANBIN: *(pulling Ning forward)* Granny Lu said she needs to use the restroom.

NING: Granny Lu has her own bathroom at home. Why does she need to come here?

HANBIN: Her house was the first in the Village to install a flush toilet!

WEIRD: Soustho oonta dallots!

HANBIN: Mrs. Tsui, can you please go in and see how she is?

Mrs. Tsui goes into the restroom. She comes out frightened.

MRS. TSUI: There's nobody inside.

HANBIN: No one there?

NING: *(authoritatively)* Granny Lu has given us the answer!

WEIRD: Soustho konetoo dallots!

SMALLS: What?

HANBIN: *(authoritatively)* Day after tomorrow, in the restroom of the Ancient Fragrance Teahouse, someone will disappear!

Pause.

WEIRD: Soustho moosantoo dallots!

HANBIN: Quick, paint over it!

Scene 8: Busted

Over at Hanbin's house, the atmosphere is solemn. Yen is beside herself with worry. Chu, Ruyun, Deuce, Smalls, Mrs. Tsui, and Mrs. Chu surround her and try to comfort her.

CHU: What happened? Why was Hanbin arrested?

YEN: What happened?

DEUCE: A few days ago, at the public toilet . . . there was a poem on the wall, and Dad whitewashed it. That's all!

SMALLS: I was there, too!

RUYUN: I saw it. Everyone was there.

MRS. CHU: That's right. Everyone was there! But there was a stranger.

YEN: Who?

MRS. CHU: A stranger. How would I know? That woman in red.

DEUCE: You mean the one beside me? Never saw her before.

RUYUN: Me neither.

CHU: Oh no!

Ning enters with a document. Everyone stands up.

NING: *(solemnly)* So we're all here.

YEN: What's going on? Tell me.

MRS. CHU: Have a seat.

NING: *(sitting)* I just came back from HQ. So the situation now is . . .

Ning pauses, then sighs.

MRS. CHU: Speak!

NING: The secret police are investigating Hanbin and Huang.

YEN: The secret police?

CHU: Oh, no!

NING: They say they were going to a secret gathering at Lanjing Street this afternoon, but were arrested before they could reach it.

YEN: What secret gathering? They were just going to the hardware shop to buy materials for the bathroom!

NING: Listen. A Commie spy was arrested in Chiayi town just yesterday. The secret police are everywhere! What were they thinking? I asked a colleague at HQ to get some more detailed information, and he told me:

Pause.

YEN: What did he say?

NING: He said, Ning, you need to stay out of this.

Everyone is shocked.

ALL: What?

NING: *(realizing he has said the wrong thing)* Don't get me wrong. He meant if I stay out of it, everything will be fine.

DEUCE: *(angrily)* Someone wrote some graffiti on the toilet wall, and my dad was arrested for cleaning it up! Well, I was there too! Why didn't they arrest me? Fuck all the secret police and military cops! Fuck all this!

NING: Lower your voice, Deuce!

MRS. CHU: What should we do now?

SMALLS: Auntie Ruyun, can you ask General Wu to help?

CHU: That's right! General Wu!

RUYUN: Of course. I'll speak to him.

SMALLS: Thank you, Auntie Ruyun.

Yen breaks down and kneels.

YEN: *(begging Ruyun)* Tell him Hanbin didn't do anything wrong!

RUYUN: I know. He's aware of that, and he'll help us.

Everyone tries to get Yen up.

YEN: *(wailing)* Hanbin, how will I get on without you?!

Mrs. Chu and Mrs. Tsui exit to their own homes to get some food.

NING: Hell, those secret police guys, they don't beat around the bush.

CHU: You're telling me! Wei Chung went in and never came out.

YEN: What?

Chu also realizes he has said the wrong thing.

NING: Nothing, don't get me wrong ...

SMALLS: Mom, Wei Chung was a real spy.

CHU: *(to Ning)* But you were buddy-buddy with Wei Chung, why weren't you arrested?

NING: I was detained! They interrogated me!

Mrs. Chu and Mrs. Tsui come back with some noodles.

CHU: What did they ask you?

NING: They asked me about my relationship with him. Hey, I had nothing to hide, so I didn't give a damn. *(heroically)* I thought, "What the hell! Let them confine me for life!"

YEN: What?

NING: *(realizing he has said the wrong thing, again)* Don't get me wrong! Those were only my thoughts. In my mind! It would never happen!

YEN: Not kidding?

NING: No. Don't worry, Yen, if he didn't do it, he didn't do it. If a person sits on ice long enough, the truth will come out.

Everyone is shocked.

YEN: Ice?

NING: I meant iced water. That's what I meant.

Everyone comforts Yen.

MRS. CHU: Come on, it's no use overthinking things. Let's have some noodles ...

Everyone eats.

Scene 9: Seeking Assistance

Granny Lu's house. A mysterious aura. Granny Lu sits on an antique Chinese chair. The Attendant brings in Smalls and Deuce, who look around in awe.

SMALLS: Hello, Granny Lu ...

GRANNY LU: *(in her stately way, as if talking to children)* Here to play?

SMALLS: We're not here for fun, Granny Lu. Did you hear that my dad has been arrested? We . . . Please help us!

DEUCE: Please, Granny Lu. We've had no news at all!

GRANNY LU: *(slowly)* How is your sister?

SMALLS: *(puzzled)* Granny Lu, we're talking about my dad. He's in trouble!

GRANNY LU: Excuse me.

She stands.

SMALLS: Granny Lu, what about my Dad?

GRANNY LU: I need to go out now.

She exits within.

SMALLS: Hey, what about my dad? Will you help him, please . . . ?! Granny Lu!

Smalls and Deuce are restrained by the Attendant, who points in the opposite direction and asks them to leave.

Scene 10: Homecoming

Smalls and Deuce leave Granny Lu's. They come home. Hanbin has come back, and is sitting quietly in the rattan chair in front of the house, but nobody notices.
The atmosphere is still tense over at Hanbin's house.

SMALLS: Mom, we're back. Damn it! It was useless to go to Granny Lu.

Smalls goes outside to think things through, walking past Hanbin.

HANBIN: Hey, Smalls.

Pause. Smalls sees his father.

SMALLS: Dad? MOM! DAD IS BACK!

They all rush out to greet Hanbin.

YEN: Hanbin, you're back!!

HANBIN: I'm fine . . . Just sitting outside for a bit, enjoying the sunshine.

CHU: Hanbin! You're back!

Yen is in tears.

HANBIN: Come on. Why are you crying, Yen? I'm fine! Fine!

MRS. TSUI: Hanbin, I'm sorry I asked you to go to the public restroom . . .

HANBIN: It's okay! It wasn't so bad. It was an experience.

Mrs. Chu goes back to her home. Ning hunches down in front of Hanbin.

NING: Hey Hanbin! Do you recognize me?

Hanbin looks at Ning carefully.

HANBIN: Wei Chung?

Yen and the others are worried.

NING: Hanbin! Don't frighten me . . .

HANBIN: *(laughing)* Just toying with you, Sir! What could possibly happen to me? If the sky falls down, Hanbin is here for you.

DEUCE: Dad, what did they do to you?

HANBIN: What could they do to me?

DEUCE: Did they make you sit on ice?

HANBIN: *(seriously)* Don't mention the word "ice" in front of me, OK?

SMALLS: Really?

Yen is about to cry.

HANBIN: Just joking!

YEN: Hanbin, don't frighten us!

Ruyun enters.

RUYUN: Hanbin, you're finally back!

Hanbin stands up and shakes Ruyun's hand sincerely.

HANBIN: *(seriously)* Ruyun, I must thank General Wu.

RUYUN: Think nothing of it. Good to see you back.

Mrs. Chu enters with special string noodles.

MRS. CHU: Have some string noodles!

HANBIN: This is . . . ?

CHU: It's a Taiwanese tradition.

MRS. CHU: It's a tradition, to get rid of bad luck.

Hanbin sits down, but gets up immediately.

HANBIN: Whoa . . .

ALL: What happened? What happened?

HANBIN: Just joking.

ALL: Oh!

YEN: It's not funny at all.

DEUCE: You have to finish the noodles to clear out the bad luck.

Scene 11: It Should Rain Now

The night of April 5, 1975. Deuce is alone under the tree, smoking. Bigs enters with some shopping bags. She is dressed fashionably. Deuce senses someone approaching and hides her cigarette. She sees it is Bigs.

DEUCE: *(surprised)* Sis!

BIGS: Deuce . . .

DEUCE: Sis, you're back.

Deuce and Bigs sit down under the tree.

You look so good in your makeup.

BIGS: Is everyone well at home?

DEUCE: Yeah . . .

BIGS: Deuce, you have to take care of Dad and Mom when I'm not around.

DEUCE: I will. Sis, is it tough working there?

Bigs brings out a bag of cash and hands it over to Deuce.

BIGS: Mom wants to add a second story to the house. This should do it . . . plus all these things.

Bigs shows Deuce some jewelry, then stands to leave. Deuce stops her.

DEUCE: Aren't you going home to see Mom and Dad?

BIGS: Next time.

DEUCE: Sis, take me with you. I can leave with you now!

BIGS: *(firmly)* No, Deuce. It's not for you.

DEUCE: Sis . . .

BIGS: Be good.

Bigs exits. Deuce sits back down and takes out another cigarette. Cart enters.

CART: What are you doing, Deuce? Smoking? *(taking the cigarette)*

DEUCE: Hey, that's expensive!

CART: I'm confiscating it! When did you turn into a delinquent?

DEUCE: So smoking means I've turned into a delinquent?

CART: You've been hanging out with those outsiders. Did you pick it up from them?

DEUCE: None of your business!

CART: Damn it. Where are they? I'll beat them all up.

DEUCE: Where are they? You can't find them, because they live in the real world.

CART: What are you talking about?

DEUCE: Everything within these walls is fake! The real world is outside!

CART: What's wrong with you lately?

DEUCE: What's wrong with me? *(loudly)* Don't I have the right to feel like shit? These houses have been so run down for so many years, and no one has done anything to improve them!

CART: On the day we recover the mainland, you'll get it straight.

DEUCE: Cart, your mind is permanently screwed up! You'll never be able to get out of this place! NO ONE HERE IS GOING TO GET OUT OF THIS PLACE!

CART: Shut up! Or you're going to be arrested, like your dad!

Granny Lu and her Attendant walk slowly across the stage, toward them.

DEUCE: My dad? He's been the model citizen all his life, always helping others. And they take him away! You aren't any better. You didn't stop your brother from leaving, and see where my sister has ended up? Selling her body in Taichung! Dammit! That's the real world! Look at this giant slogan on the wall here: "Defeat the Communists! Recover the Mainland!" The bigger the words, the bigger the lie! The slogan is supersized because it's never going to happen!

CART: Shhhh!

Cart looks around to make sure nobody has heard her.
Granny Lu approaches them.

CART: Hello, Granny Lu!

GRANNY LU: Having a nice chat?

Pause. They don't know how to answer her.

    Smoking?

Pause. They don't know how to answer her.

    You have cigarettes?

Deuce and Cart are apprehensive.

    May I have one?

Granny Lu sits. Cart hands her a cigarette. Before she lights up, she suddenly sits upright, tensely.

    My god . . . what's happening? I'm so tense that I'm shivering . . .

DEUCE: Granny Lu, are you okay?

CART: Do you want to see the doctor?

GRANNY LU: It should rain now.

Granny Lu gets up, and exits with the Attendant. They watch her go.

DEUCE: What was that about rain?

CART: What did she mean? Not a cloud in the sky.

Rain suddenly comes in a downpour, as it historically did that evening.

Shit! It's really raining!! Let's split!

Cart and Deuce run away.

Scene 12: The End of an Era

The morning after. Under the tree. Everyone is wailing and mourning. Hanbin is holding a newspaper with a somber front page reporting the death of Chiang Kai-shek.

HANBIN: *(wailing)* Generalissimo!

NING: *(in tears)* President Chiang! I can't believe you are gone!

CHU: *(in disbelief)* The rain last night just suddenly came pouring down! So it was at that moment that he actually . . . ?!

Mrs. Chu, Smalls, and Yen enter.

MRS. CHU: Is it true?

YEN: Can it be true?

She sees the newspaper and stops in her tracks, falling to her knees.

Chiang Kai-shek is dead! We can never return to our homeland!

HANBIN: How could you abandon us? You said you were going to lead us back!

Mrs. Tsui and Ruyun enter, in tears, followed by other villagers.

CHU: What can we do now that he's gone?

YEN: We can't go home! We can't go home!

MRS. TSUI: We can't go home!

HANBIN: President Chiang! . . .

YEN: Generalissimo! . . .

The wailing becomes a dirge.
Lights fade out.

ACT FOUR, 1982–2006

Scene 1: Far Away from the Village

A pop song from the 1980s plays. Lights fade in. Smalls speaks to the audience. He is nearing middle age. His tone is more somber.

SMALLS: We grew up. We left that village where we were raised. After a few years of working in Taichung, my big sister Bigs went to the United States with an American soldier. My second sister, Deuce, suddenly sorted herself out, started to work hard on her studies, and got admitted to a college in Taipei to study journalism. I also went to college in Taipei, while working part-time. I told my folks everything was fine and dandy in Taipei, even though I didn't even have enough money to rent a room, and had to take turns sleeping in a bed— "time-sharing"—with others.

A pedestrian underpass of Taipei Train Station. Pedestrians walk to and fro. The busy life of a big city: vendors, people passing out flyers. Chu and Mrs. Chu are older. They are lost in the crowd. They carry a lot of miscellaneous pieces of baggage.

One day Uncle and Auntie Chu came to Taipei. It was their first time in the big city.

CHU: *(to Mrs. Chu)* There!

MRS. CHU: Where?

SMALLS: *(to the audience)* I met them at the train station. I played a trick on them, telling them they had to buy tickets to cross the underpass.

Smalls sees that the two of them are afraid to cross the underpass. They search for where to pay. Smalls waves to them from the other side.

Hey! Uncle and Auntie Chu, over here! Hurry!

Chu and Mrs. Chu see Smalls, but are confused. Mrs. Chu approaches a passing pedestrian.

MRS. CHU: Excuse me . . .

CHU: Where do we pay?

PEDESTRIAN: *(pointing)* You buy your train ticket at the windows over there.

MRS. CHU: I mean, where do we buy tickets for the underpass?

Pause. The Pedestrian exits.

CHU: What's wrong with this guy? No response.

Smalls leaps in the air, waving at them.

SMALLS: *(shouting)* BUY YOUR TICKETS HERE! GIVE YOUR MONEY TO
ME!

MRS. CHU: *(to Chu)* What does he mean?

CHU: The dirty brat! He's fooled us!

MRS. CHU: Oh, Smalls, what a rascal!

SMALLS: WELCOME TO TAIPEI, UNCLE AND AUNTIE CHU!

The two chase Smalls. They exit.

Deuce enters, and addresses the audience. She is also approaching middle age.

While she speaks, Hanbin crosses the stage slowly. He is older, and frail. He carries a simple travel bag and walks slowly. He stops at times, and smiles.

DEUCE: Occasionally, Dad would come to visit us in Taipei. Once he
made a trip to Green Lake, to visit the Air Force Cemetery there,
where many of his buddies were buried. He also wanted to pay his
respects to the graves of over 1,000 fighter pilots who had died in
action.

Dad had aged, but he kept his sunny disposition. He was always busy
helping others. I knew he was going through a lot, because Mom was
in poor mental health.

Hanbin exits slowly into a dim light. The stage seems to have gotten colder.

Time flew by. We graduated, and entered the workforce. Taiwan was
evolving at breakneck speed, politically, economically, culturally.
Change was everywhere. Though the country was still ruled by a
one-party dictatorship, the opposition had formed, and a push was
on toward democracy. Smalls made a name for himself as an idea
man at an ad agency. He always had those crazy inventive ideas. Me,
I became a journalist, and started to meet many people from the
opposition. I fell in love with one of them.

Life was hectic in Taipei. Everything was moving so fast. We seldom had the chance to go home to the Village . . .

Scene 2: Buying a Coffin (2)

Huang's carpentry workshop in Chiayi town. It's the same as in Act 1, but Huang has grown old, too. It is 1986.
  Smalls enters. He is dressed smartly, befitting an ad agency man.

SMALLS: Uncle Huang!

Huang looks up.

HUANG: Look what we have here! It's Smalls! Haven't seen you for such a long time! Come in, sit down. Hey, Mutt! Make some tea!

SMALLS: I've brought you something from Taipei.

HUANG: You shouldn't have! I'm just glad to see you.

Smalls gives Huang a gift. The assistant Mutt enters with a teapot. He is old, too.

SMALLS: *(Taiwanese)* So how are you?

HUANG: *(Taiwanese)* Ah, business is tough! Those new windows don't break. When did you get back?

SMALLS: Yesterday. Came back to have a look.

HUANG: Time flies. You know? You weren't even born when I first met your dad.

SMALLS: Yeah. When we were young, Dad often told me this story . . . about asking you to make a coffin for him when he couldn't afford one.

HUANG: Right you are! Your dad was a riot. He came into the shop with 10 dollars and asked me to make a coffin! How could anyone make a coffin for 10 dollars? The cost itself was more than 100! He wanted me to make one for 10!

SMALLS: You're a kind man, Uncle Huang. That's why you became such good friends with my dad.

HUANG: Well, your dad is a good man.

Smalls suddenly turns serious.

SMALLS: Uncle Huang, I'm here to discuss something with you.

HUANG: What is it?

SMALLS: Can you help me make another coffin?

Huang laughs, thinking he is joking.

HUANG: Hey, we don't make coffins! You should know that! You must be joking! We . . . *(pause)* What happened?

SMALLS: *(slowly)* Dad—passed yesterday.

Silence.

We've heard the 10-dollar coffin story since we were kids, so I thought we should ask you to make his for him. Of course, we can afford a proper one now, but we would like to request that you do this for us. I think Dad would feel better if you did it.

Silence.
Huang nods, stands, and silently shakes Smalls's hand.

Thank you, Uncle Huang.

Scene 3: The Funeral (2)

The three houses. The setting is similar to the first funeral scene in Act 1. But there is a long line of people waiting to pay their respects to Hanbin. Granny Lu slowly crosses the stage.
Bigs addresses the audience. She is middle aged, dressed plainly.

BIGS: I regret that I couldn't return from America for Dad's funeral. My siblings told me it was a grand affair. The whole village showed up, and Uncle Huang brought many important people from the town to pay their respects. He outdid himself by making the most beautiful coffin anyone had ever seen. And everyone bowed deeply before it. Finally, everyone got to eat Auntie Chu's specially made Tianjin buns.

Yen sits in the same mourning position as when her mother passed in Act 1. Chu stands at the door in suit and tie, greeting the solemn mourners. The mourners enter Hanbin's house one by one and bow at the altar, and as they leave, Mrs. Chu hands out steaming buns to each of them.

Scene 4: Return to the Homeland

BIGS: It was a pity my dad died before the start of the new era, after martial law was lifted in late 1987, when people from Taiwan were finally allowed to revisit their families on the mainland of China, after almost 40 years of separation. This was the moment my parents had waited for all their lives. Almost everyone in the Village returned to their homes in China to visit. That included my brother, who flew to Beijing to visit our grandma, as representative of our parents. He told me that the roads in Beijing looked so odd. But strangely, they also seemed so familiar.

Even stranger was the fact that back home, Smalls learned that no one's last name was Chao. Everyone's last name was Yang.

Empty stage with three pools of light to suggest three different locales. There is one chair facing stage left in each lighting area. A woman sits in each chair, in each pool of light, waiting. The woman stage right is very old, with three family members standing next to her. The woman in the middle is also old, but younger than the one on the right. There are two family members standing around her, one of them holding a baby. The elderly woman on stage left sits alone.

It is around 1990. A Tour Guide leads Smalls on. Smalls has a lot of gifts and bags and looks around the street, in a daze. It is Beijing, China, his father's hometown, which he never thought he would be able to visit.

GUIDE: Come on this way, Tai-sheng! Your ancestral home is straight ahead, in the Shuidayuan alley. Your grandma woke up very early this morning to wait for you. Come! Taisheng, come in.

SMALLS: Thank you . . .

Smalls stops and looks around.

Granny Yang sits stage right, on an antique Chinese chair, like some ancestor in a painting. Relatives stand behind her. The Tour Guide enters the lit area.

GUIDE: GRANDMA, YOUR GRANDSON IS HERE TO VISIT YOU! Tai-sheng, come in. Come closer.

The Tour Guide beckons Smalls to enter. Smalls enters, sees Granny Yang, and instinctively falls on his knees, suddenly overcome with tears.

SMALLS: Grandma, your grandson is here to visit you.

GRANNY YANG: Come closer.

SMALLS: Dad wanted to . . . Dad wanted to come back so bad, but he couldn't make it, so I'm here in his place.

Smalls edges toward Granny Yang. Granny embraces his head.
Still overcome, he remembers his gifts, and starts pulling them out of his bag.

These gifts are for you.

UNCLE: *(loudly)* FOR YOU!

Smalls takes out a photo album from the bag, opens it, and points for Granny Yang.

SMALLS: This photo was taken in Taiwan. *(turning pages and pointing)* This is Dad when he first arrived in Taiwan. This is my mom. We weren't even born yet. This is our family portrait in Taiwan . . .

Granny Yang suddenly slaps Smalls in the face. Utter surprise.
Pause.

GRANNY YANG: That was for your father. When he left this room, he told me he was going out, on a short trip to Taiwan to have a look around. That look lasted over 40 years!

SMALLS: Grandma . . .

Granny Yang brings Smalls into her arms. They embrace emotionally.
The Tour Guide leads Chu and Mrs. Chu on. They are well dressed, carry gifts and bags, and wander toward the center lighted space.
Chu looks nostalgic as he wanders down this familiar street. Yet he also looks perturbed. Mrs. Chu is exuberant, smiling all the way.

GUIDE: *(to Chu)* Mr. Chu, over here!

The Guide exits. Chu gathers himself.

CHU: *(to his wife)* We're here.

MRS. CHU: *(exuberantly)* So this is your home?

Slight pause.

CHU: No, this is not my home.

MRS. CHU: So who are we visiting then?

CHU: Someone who is older than you. So you need to call her "elder sister."

MRS. CHU: Oh, I get it. We're visiting your elder sister?

Pause.

CHU: *(slowly and clearly)* No. Um, she's not MY elder sister, she's YOUR elder sister.

MRS. CHU: You're not making sense, Chu!

CHU: Come on in, come on in.

Chu enters. On seeing the old woman sitting there, he immediately falls to his knees. The woman is clearly Chu's First Wife, a secret he never told anybody, as was the case with many soldiers who went to Taiwan in 1949 by themselves. Without any means of communicating with their loved ones, many married and started new homes in Taiwan. Chu and his First Wife embrace each other and cry loudly.

(weeping openly) AHHH—!!

CHU'S FIRST WIFE: *(weeping openly)* AHHH—!!

CHU: *(muffled words that seep through the wailing)* I didn't want to go! They forced me onto the boat . . .

CHU'S FIRST WIFE: *(while wailing)* Let me have a look at you . . .

Mrs. Chu, who has followed Chu in, drops all the bags she is carrying in surprise, and stares at everyone in utter shock. The loud wailing persists throughout.

CHU'S FIRST WIFE: *(to the middle-aged man standing behind her)* Pay respects to your father!

CHU'S ELDER SON: *(almost hysterically)* Father . . . !

CHU: *(hysterical)* MY SON! MY SON!

Mrs. Chu watches with growing horror as she realizes what is happening.
Chu's First Wife points at the baby, which is being held by Chu's daughter-in-law.

CHU'S FIRST WIFE: Your grandson.

CHU: OH MY GOD! . . .

Mrs. Chu, who was never told about any of this, feels sick to her stomach. Her knees buckle. She runs out of the house.

    Inside, Chu and his first family continue to wail and embrace each other. Outside, Mrs. Chu is all alone, on the verge of panic. Her first instinct is to leave, so she rushes off, but then stops in her tracks.

    She takes a deep breath to calm herself down. She gathers herself and assesses the situation. The sounds of the bittersweet reunion continue to pour out from within, a constant howling sound.

    She composes herself, and after pumping her fist, she reenters the house, and picks up the gifts scattered on the ground. She is her normal buoyant self as she starts distributing the gifts.

MRS. CHU: Hello, Elder Sister, how nice to meet you! I brought gifts for all of you!

She hands a small box of jewelry to Chu's First Wife.

    This is from Chiayi's most famous goldsmith! It's pure gold.

CHU: *(while still crying)* IT'S THE BEST!

CHU'S FIRST WIFE: I can't accept something so expensive!

Mrs. Chu takes out a big gift box.

MRS. CHU: And this is Chiayi's most famous dessert . . . pastry squares!

Chu's First Wife beckons to her son.

CHU'S FIRST WIFE: Come and greet your second mom.

CHU: *(authoritatively)* HURRY UP!

CHU'S ELDER SON: Hello, Second Mom.

An awkward pause. Mrs. Chu is dumbfounded at hearing this new title of hers.

MRS. CHU: *(suddenly loud)* GREAT! Uh . . . YES! No problem! Everything is just GREAT! I have something for you, too!

She gives him a golden necklace.

CHU: There's something for everyone! Something for everyone!

Mrs. Chu points at the baby. She is both joyful and cynical.

    MRS. CHU: *(to Chu)* Oh, so this is your grandson! Wow, you're a grandpa!

Silence. Mrs. Chu slaps Chu on the back.

    I had no idea you were so . . . prolific!

She pushes Chu away, walks toward the baby.

    Let me by! *(to the Daughter-in-Law)* Oh, isn't he cute! May I?

Mrs. Chu cuddles the baby, as the wailing subsides.
Ning's Nephew leads Ning in toward the left lighting area, where a solitary woman sits waiting. The Nephew carries Ning's baggage. The usually spritely Ning looks pensive.

    NING'S NEPHEW: Uncle, we've arrived . . .

Ning looks around. He is strangely detached. The Nephew takes the baggage inside.
Ning enters. The woman stands.

    NING'S SISTER: *(Shanghai dialect)* Ning!

    NING: *(Shanghai dialect)* Sis . . .

Ning's Sister breaks down in tears.

    NING'S SISTER: Where, oh where have you been, my brother?

The two embrace.
Ning's Sister calms down as Ning looks around the room.

    How's your life?

    NING: I'm fine, sis.

    NING'S SISTER: That's good. Welcome back. They returned this old house of ours to us after they confiscated it in the Cultural Revolution. We only got it back because of those letters you wrote. Ning, it's time to come home now.

    NING: No thanks, sis. I guess I've gotten used to life in Taiwan. Sis, you've suffered so much all these years, beyond my imagination, I'm sure, because you had a brother in Taiwan. You can tell me: were Mom and Pop killed because of my going to Taiwan?

Ning's Sister doesn't answer.

> Sis, can you take me to their graves?

Ning's Sister nods. They exit the left area to another space downstage. The Nephew follows. They stop in front of the grave.
> *Pause.*

> NING'S SISTER: *(pointing)* We've restored the graves according to your wishes.

Ning falls to his knees, overcome.

> NING: Mom . . . Pops . . .

Bigs speaks to the audience.

> BIGS: Uncle Ning's sister took him to a cemetery on the outskirts of Shanghai. After paying his respects at his parents' graves, he asked his sister a question. While restoring their ancestral graves, he had also asked her to restore the grave of an old friend.

The two help Ning up. The Nephew takes a picture for Ning and Ning's Sister in front of their ancestral grave.
> *Ning turns to his sister.*

> NING: Sis, can you take me to the other grave?

Pause. Ning's Sister needs to think.

> NING'S SISTER: Oh sure. Who was that friend? Oh, Lu Han, was that his name? I know, he was from your class at the Air Force Academy. A tall, handsome man. I remember he often came over for dinner. His plane crashed soon before you left for Taiwan, right? Is that the one?

Ning nods. Ning's Sister and the Nephew lead him to another grave downstage. Ning motions for them to leave him alone for a moment. They step aside.
> *Ning looks at the grave alone.*

> NING: *(reading the tombstone)* "Lu Han. Born May 19, 1928. Died September 16, 1949."

Pause. Ning speaks quietly to the grave.

> Han, after I flew the plane to Taiwan, I never flew again. On the day you went down, I died, too. So how come I am still living today? It

was something you said to me once: "We must live life with joy. Even if one is all alone, one must find joy . . ."

Ning breaks down, falls on his knees, and weeps in front of the grave. His Sister and the Nephew come and pull him up.

NING'S NEPHEW: Uncle . . .

NING'S SISTER: Let's go, Brother . . .

The three exit.

Scene 5: Under the Big Tree (3)

Deuce speaks to the audience. Everything has turned a shade darker, colder.

DEUCE: Time passed. But many things remained unchanged. The current affairs panel continued their debate under the tree. They even kept my dad's seat for him . . .

Under the big tree. Chu, Ning, and Weird. Hanbin's rattan chair is still there in his honor. A jet plane flies over. Ning salutes the sky.

CHU: What have the times come to? Who is this current president, that little bastard Lee Teng-hui? What was Chiang's son thinking? Why did he allow him to become president? It's unfathomable! Am I right, Hanbin?

Chu pats Hanbin's empty chair.

WEIRD: Hoonboon loosten, sachergoo oster foon!

CHU: Yeah?

NING: *(intently, to the rattan chair)* Think about it, Hanbin. Chiang Junior is dead. He would turn in his grave if he knew what's going on in the president's office.

CHU: *(to Ning)* Sir, all these years I've considered you a knowledgeable person.

NING: Did I say something wrong?

CHU: Do you really think that's Chiang Kai Shek's body lying in state there in the coffin at Tz'i-hu?

NING: Oh, come on! You can't STILL be in denial! You have to accept that

Chiang Kai Shek and Chiang Junior are dead! If you don't believe me, you can ask Hanbin!

CHU: Right. Now Hanbin's the only guy among us who can answer that question. They're all gone. Those who have disappeared are all together, right?

NING: What bull! If President Chiang were still alive, how old would he be?

Cart enters with his mother's vending cart. He is now the one making and selling buns. He joins in the conversation.

CHU: How old is Madame Chiang this year?

CART: One hundred and one.

CHU: Right!

WEIRD: Nooner beetoonoot!

NING: What betel nut? Weird, we're talking serious business here, don't butt in!

CHU: Ning, you are REALLY screwed up if you don't believe what I say!

NING: Think about this: Chiang Junior has passed away, but before his death, why would he let this ex-Commie, this Japanese bastard Lee Teng-hui be our president? Behind such absolute madness, there must be a master plan that goes beyond our collective minds' power to reason. Consider carefully. Am I right? Am I right? You betcha!

CHU: And so what are you inferring?

NING: *(triumphantly)* GENERAL DAI LI!

CHU: Dead centuries ago!

NING: No way! He couldn't have died!

CHU: You're full of it!

NING: This is all part of his master plan! WHAT OTHER PLAUSIBLE EXPLANATION CAN THERE BE FOR EVERYTHING?

Chu and Weird shake their heads vigorously while Ning holds out his arms and nods in affirmation.

CHU: How many centuries has it been, and you still aren't over with General Dai?!

Smalls enters, back from Taipei. He wears a sharp suit. He stands at attention and salutes.

SMALLS: Salute! Uncle Chu, Uncle Ning, Uncle Weird.

CHU: Smalls, you're back!

Ning pats Hanbin's empty chair and talks to the air.

Hanbin, your son is back.

Smalls takes out a bottle of wine from his bag.

SMALLS: *(to Chu)* Here's some wine for you.

Ning intercepts the wine and clutches it.

NING: Don't give it to him, he can't drink it. I'll take it.

CHU: Well, Smalls, you should come back more often to visit your mom. Don't be like that guy who went to America and never came back.

WEIRD: Woogo?

Ning is piqued.

CHU: Sorry, that's not what I meant . . .

CART: My dad is referring to Fats.

CHU: No . . . I'm referring to my own son, Ox . . .

CART: Dad, stop pretending. Ox will come back. Just wait and see. But Fats! I'm sorry, Uncle Ning, but this has bothered me for many years. So what if he holds a PhD? All these years, he hasn't come back even once to visit the two of you!

CHU: What do you care?

NING: It's fine, he's busy.

CART: It's fine?! Tell you what we should do. He's in America, so we'll get my brother to nab him, and we'll forcibly repatriate him! The fuck!

NING: Watch your mouth.

WEIRD: Choonamtook. Poopelocher vooroosboose!

CART: Damn right you are!

Pause. Ning loses it.

NING: AND WHAT EXACTLY IS HE DAMN RIGHT ABOUT? ARE YOU
TELLING ME YOU UNDERSTOOD WHAT HE JUST SAID? WE'VE
BEEN LISTENING TO HIM FOR HALF A CENTURY, AND NO ONE
HAS EVER UNDERSTOOD A SINGLE WORD!

Pause.
   A while.
   *They all look at one another. Ning acts guilty, as if he's just let out a long
dark secret.*

WEIRD: *(extremely upset)* FOOKSMOOSE USOOPER MOOSTER
FOOKSMOOSE!

CHU: Now don't be upset, Weird, please, he didn't mean, I mean he
meant . . . I mean . . .

WEIRD: FOOKSMOOSE!

Weird grabs his stool in a fury, and exits.
   Silence.

NING: That's called "Exit from the Political Arena"!

Everyone chuckles and relaxes.

CHU: *(to Smalls)* Okay, Smalls, go home and see your mom. She hasn't
spoken to anyone for a long time.

Cart gives Smalls a bun.

SMALLS: Okay, I'll come and see you later! *(to Cart)* Thanks, Cart!

Smalls exits. Cart follows with the cart. Only Chu and Ning remain.
   Pause. Chu looks at Ning.

CHU: *(pointing at Ning)* My good sir . . . Are you saying that you, too,
never understood a word of what he says?

Ning shakes his head. They look at each other in astonishment.
   Chu pats Hanbin's chair, and sighs.

Scene 6: Memories of Spring

Hanbin's house. Yen sits by the window downstage, staring into space. Deuce, back from Taipei and smartly dressed like the professional journalist she is, sets up a CD player. She speaks to Yen without expecting answers.

> DEUCE: Mom, remember your old gramophone? I remember you brought some old records from the mainland when you first came to Taiwan. Today is your birthday, and I found the same CD in Taipei. I'll play it for you.

Deuce plays the opera aria "Amor ti vieta." Smalls enters with a shopping bag.

> SMALLS: Happy birthday, Mom! I've brought you authentic Beijing snacks from this Taipei shop that makes good ones! Let's break out the osmanthus sweetcakes. *(to Deuce)* How is she?

> DEUCE: Still not talking.

Smalls gives his mom a hug.
The music plays. As the aria progresses, Yen seems to awaken slowly, like ice melting.

> YEN: Melting.

Deuce and Smalls look at each other, surprised. They stop what they are doing and turn to Yen.

> SMALLS: What?

> YEN: The ice on the pond by the Forbidden City is melting. I only got to skate there once all winter.

Deuce and Smalls stand by Yen and listen to her intently.

> The buds on the willows are sprouting. They glitter in the sun. That tells me that spring is here. Oh, look, Old Xia's rickshaw is waiting for me. I hop onto his squeaking rickshaw, and arrive at Goldfish Alley. I raise my head, and see the beautiful sign: Fortune Restaurant!

Yen is lost in the music.

> Every time Uncle De saw me, he would put everything aside and sauté a special plate of soy sauce fried rice for me.

Pause. Yen savors the flavor.

Soy sauce fried rice . . . how could it be SOOO delicious?!

SMALLS: Delicious.

Mrs. Chu enters. She is old and moves slowly.

MRS. CHU: Mrs. Chao . . .

DEUCE AND SMALLS: Hello, Auntie Chu.

MRS. CHU: Oh! Deuce and Smalls, you're back! I was just going to make dinner for your mom.

YEN: Fried rice with soy sauce. Make sure the cabbage is sliced extra thin.

MRS. CHU: What? Mrs. Chao, you're . . . ?

SMALLS: Mom is talking again! Auntie Chu, we're going out to eat. Please join us.

MRS. CHU: Sure thing. You both must come home more often to see your mom. Look, once you're home, she's talking!

DEUCE: Thank you, Auntie Chu. We can all go in my car.

They prepare to go out.

Scene 7: Reunion

A room in a Shanghai-style restaurant in Chiayi town. Seated at a large round banquet table are the first-generation elders, including General Wu, Mrs. Wu, Chu, Mrs. Chu, Ruyun, Ning, Yen, and Mrs. Tsui. A Waitress brings a new dish to a large lazy Susan filled with food.

MRS. TSUI: Who ordered this fatty pork? I'm full already!

MRS. WU: This is their signature dish, you must try it.

General Wu serves the dish for everyone.

NING: Wu, go ahead and serve the dish, but don't eat it. It's pure cholesterol.

YEN: What terrible service. Uncle De, how come the staff is not serving?

WU: This is a joyful occasion. Let's not talk about cholesterol.

YEN: What are we celebrating today?

MRS. CHU: *(cheerfully pointing at Ruyun)* Ning's son has been promoted to full professor in America!

YEN: *(to Wu)* Then why are you hosting tonight?

WU: I'm the one who invited everyone, of course I'm hosting!

CHU: Whatever, thank you kindly!

NING: No, it should be on us!

CHU: Whatever, thank you kindly!

YEN: *(patting the table)* This meal is on Fortune Restaurant.

Ruyun takes out a photo of Fats. Everybody looks at it. Wu's Attendant enters, and whispers to Wu.

WU: *(to Mrs. Wu)* The car is here. You two can go home now.

MRS. WU: *(standing up)* Take your time, sorry we have to go.

MRS. TSUI: Please excuse us, there are two people waiting for us at the mahjong table.

NING: Fine. Ruyun will bring some food back for a late snack.

Mrs. Wu and Mrs. Tsui exit.
   Wu stands up rather solemnly and clears his throat. The atmosphere becomes formal. Everyone is quiet.

WU: I've organized this dinner today to make an important announcement. An old friend of ours from the academy, whom we've not seen for many years, is back today.

CHU: Who?

Li Tzu-kang, the Air Force hero who purportedly defected in Act One, enters, standing at the doorway. He looks very different from the dashing hero of years past. Now he is a humpbacked old man whose spirit seems to have been long broken.
   Everyone is astonished to see Li, particularly his former wife, Ruyun.

NING: Li . . . ?

CHU: Li Tzu-kang? Can it be true?

Silence. Ning stands up and approaches Li. Ning gives Li a military salute, then embraces him.

NING: *(emotionally)* How many years has it been?

LI: *(likewise, in a soft voice)* More than half a century.

NING: You . . . ?

LI: Ning, I must thank you.

NING: I insisted to Ruyun then, you couldn't possibly have . . .

WU: Please take a seat.

NING: *(to the Waitress, with nervous energy)* Waitress, another setting!
Let's all drink a toast to Li . . .

Ning and Li come to the table. Ning raises his glass. The others follow.

WU: All together!

*The Waitress brings another place setting. Everybody stands up and toasts Li.
Ruyun eyes Li with extremely mixed emotions.*

LI: We meet again.

YEN: Pilot Li! What happened to you after that New Year's dinner?

NING: Yes, what exactly happened?

WU: Sit down, everyone. Li just arrived from Hong Kong. He's been there
for seven, eight years now. He was severely wronged. His plane
crashed in China. They claimed that he was a defector from our Air
Force, and used him for propaganda, but then they imprisoned him,
for many, many years. Li has really suffered.

Silence.

LI: *(softly)* Later I had the opportunity to go to Hong Kong.

CHU: So why didn't you contact us? Write a letter or make a phone call
to . . . *(pointing to Ruyun)* let her know?!

LI: I did. I wrote to Wu. Wu has been helping all the way. He's a true
friend. I made it back today because of his help.

Li turns to Ning and Ruyun.

I hear your son has done well in the US.

YEN: He's a professor in America! The pride of our village!

MRS. CHU: Yes, he is!

LI: What's his name?

YEN: Fats!

All laugh.

RUYUN: Niankang. His name is Niankang.

Ruyun shows the picture to Li. Li looks at the picture.

LI: "Nian-kang"?

YEN: He peeped at Deuce while she was in the shower. Smalls beat the hell out of him!

All chuckle, then pause.

LI: Congratulations! Let me drink a toast to all of you!

WU: Together, everyone!

They all stand up to drink.

YEN: I need to use the restroom.

MRS. CHU: Let me go with you.

CHU: *(to General Wu)* Sir, shall we go outside?

WU: What? Sure.

CHU: For a smoke.

YEN: *(singing, while exiting)* My home is on the Songhua River . . .

Everyone exits, leaving Li and Ruyun at the big round table. Ruyun shows Li the photos.

RUYUN: *(points to a photo)* This is his wife. *(another)* That's where he works.

LI: "Nian-kang." Did you name him?

RUYUN: I did. "In memory of Tzu-kang." He's yours.

Pause.

LI: What?

RUYUN: He's your son.

Silence.

LI: Ruyun . . . Your life . . . how has it been?

RUYUN: *(smiling)* It's almost over.

Pause.

And you?

LI: Time passes easily when you're alone.

RUYUN: You never remarried?

LI: I always was married.

Silence.

Niankang . . . does he know about me?

RUYUN: He . . . He doesn't know about a lot of things. Because I didn't know about a lot of things. What could I tell him? Everything was a big fog, just like my brain, nothing in it was clear. But he learned one thing from you, and that is to go out the door and never come back.

I remember that day, after breakfast, I watched your silhouette as you went out the door, a 20-something, handsome, dashing young man. Now it's dinnertime. The door opens. An old man walks in. What's it all supposed to mean? *What's it all supposed to mean?* You're home for dinner?

Long silence.

LI: Ruyun, life played the cruelest trick on us. The only word I can think of now is—sorry. Sorry . . . sorry . . .

RUYUN: No, no, Tzu-kang, don't be, you can't be.

Ruyun touches Li's cheeks.
Wu enters with Ning and Chu, looking at them quietly.

LI: I've got to go. Wu has arranged everything. I'm going to Taipei to meet up with some old classmates. This photo . . . May I keep it?

RUYUN: His address is on the back.

Wu tugs gently at Li. They exit.

NING: Ruyun, I'll see him off.

Ning exits.
  Ruyun is alone.
  The Waitress enters with a bucket, which she places loudly on the table.

WAITRESS: *(loud and gratuitously)* Excuse me, do you need doggie bags
  for any of this?

The Waitress gathers the glasses and plates noisily into the bucket.

Scene 8: Blackjack (2)

*A casino in Las Vegas. It is three o'clock in the morning. Bigs is dealing cards
to the only gambler at her blackjack table. Casino Waitress brings a glass of
scotch to the Gambler.*

GAMBLER: Sixteen again. Should I hit?

BIGS: Hard to say.

GAMBLER: Hit.

Bigs deals a card. The Gambler loses. Bigs rakes the chips off the table.

Las Vegas can really do you in.

*Ox enters with carry-on luggage. He is a middle-aged businessman, very dapper, well dressed in an expensive suit. Ox sees it is Bigs dealing. He stares at her
in silence.*

BIGS: Sometimes one's lucky, sometimes not. That's the way it is.

The Gambler stands up, tips Bigs, and exits.

Thank you, good night.

Bigs shuffles the cards. Ox sits down, but Bigs doesn't notice him.
  Bigs raises her head, sees Ox, and is surprised.
  They look at each other.
  A long moment.
  The Pit Boss comes over.

PIT BOSS: What's going on here?

BIGS: *(to Pit Boss)* Nothing. *(to Ox)* Place a bet.

Ox places a bet. Bigs deals. The Pit Boss goes away. Silence.

OX: Hey, Bigs.

BIGS: Hey, Ox.

OX: How's it going?

BIGS: Good. I've lived in Vegas for over 10 years now.

OX: I know.

They play cards mechanically.

BIGS: I hear that you've been very, very successful.

OX: Thank you. When do you get off?

BIGS: Six.

OX: My flight is at six.

Silence.

BIGS: How many children do you have?

OX: Three. You?

BIGS: None.

Ox's son Andy, a teenager, enters, wearing hip-hop-style clothing and listening to his headphones. Ox spots him. He speaks with his son in English.

OX: Hey, what are you doing here? Come here!

OX'S SON: I thought you went to the airport!

OX: *(to Bigs)* My eldest son, Andy. Andy, say hello to my ... old friend.

OX'S SON: *(to Bigs)* Hey, what's up?

BIGS: Hi!

OX: *(to his son, sternly)* Why aren't you upstairs? Go upstairs. It's the middle of the night! Go to bed ...

OX'S SON: Are you kidding? This is Vegas, man! Sheesh!

Andy exits, reluctantly.

BIGS: So you brought your family to Vegas for a vacation?

OX: It's the first time. I never bring them along when I travel, but they were clamoring to come. I'm flying to LA, in transit to Shanghai. I have a factory in Suzhou.

BIGS: You're the big boss, why do you travel alone? Don't you have assistants to carry your bags?

OX: That's the Village streak in me, I guess. Sometimes I pass through 300 cities a year. My record is sleeping in 300 different beds in a year.

BIGS: That's a tough life. Ox, what are you doing?

OX: Searching for you. I guess.

Silence.

BIGS: That ship left long ago.

OX: What?

BIGS: We didn't make it on. Period. What else to say?

They look at each other. The Pit Boss passes by and glances at them.

Do you want another card?

OX: *(viewing his cards)* What do you say?

BIGS: Going by the laws of probability, stay.

OX: But it's a feeling. Hit.

Bigs deals.

BIGS: Twenty-one. Ox, you are so lucky!

OX: Bigs, I am so unlucky.

Bigs is finally emotional. Ox stands up.

I'm going.

Ox walks away.

BIGS: Hey Ox . . . My brother told me the Village is going to be demolished soon. He's inviting everyone back. Will you go?

OX: Sure.

They embrace. As friends, or lovers, or neither. A new Gambler sits down and takes out his chips.

> *Bigs goes back to dealing cards. Ox exits with his baggage.*

Scene 9: One Last Look

Chu's voice is heard over a loudspeaker.

> CHU: *(voice-over)* Dear neighbors, old friends, our military dependents' village, Formosa Village #1, will soon be taken down. Tonight, we're holding a farewell New Year's Eve party. Please be punctual, thank you . . .

Chinese New Year's Eve, 2006. The three houses are stripped bare, except for Hanbin's rattan chair, which has been left tattered outside. There is a platform behind the three houses, facing away from the audience. Tables are set up in front of it, receding into the darkness upstage. Smalls stands on the stage, back turned to the audience, the lights on him turning him into a silhouette. Everybody applauds.

> SMALLS: *(microphone in hand)* Dear uncles, aunties, brothers, sisters, and children, how's everybody? Welcome! We're gathered here again at our dear Formosa Village #1, to have a last New Year's dinner together. It's cold today, but our hearts are warm. Let us all together say a fond farewell to our village, which has nurtured us all these years!

Cheers.

> I see many people I haven't seen for a long time, like Uncle and Auntie Chu!

Chu and Mrs. Chu stand and bow to the crowd. Applause.

> And there's Uncle Ning! I heard he just returned from a round-the-world trip. Let's give him a big hand!

Ning stands and bows flamboyantly to the crowd. Applause.

> Look, everyone in the Chu family is here! My old neighbor Ox is back from overseas with his eldest son, Little Ox!

Ox, with Andy, waves to the crowd. Applause.

> My second sister, Deuce, her husband, and their kids are back from Taipei, too! Hey brother-in-law, say hi to everyone.

Deuce and her family wave to the crowd. Applause.

DEUCE'S HUSBAND: *(Taiwanese)* Hi everyone!

SMALLS: My brother-in-law keeps reminding me not to tell you a secret. But I have to. He's employed by the opposition party's public relations department . . .

Commotion.

Don't worry, brother-in-law. You're not going to get beat up here tonight.

CART: *(shouting)* Hard to say!

SMALLS: *(pointing at Cart)* Auntie Chu doesn't make buns anymore. My buddy Cart and his wife have taken over the business. Cart, please let us all get to know your wife!

Cart and his Wife wave to the crowd. She carries a baby in her arms. Applause.

Her name is Yuehong. She comes from Ho Chi Minh City, Vietnam! Her Mandarin is still not very fluent. This is her first New Year's in Taiwan, just like our parents were once away from home for the first time. Let's wish her all the best and hope she will receive lots of love and warmth here, just like our parents and elders did!

Everybody applauds. Bigs enters with her American husband.

BIGS: *(shouting in excitement)* Hello, everyone, long time no see!

SMALLS: Hey Sis! Everyone look, surprise! My eldest sister Bigs has come here straight from the airport. That foreign guy beside her is my brother-in-law. Come, Sis, take a seat. *(to the Husband, in broken English)* You—sit—you—eat!

Everyone laughs. All are having a good time.

The entertainment starts now! Let's give a big round of applause to the owners of the greatest piano bar in Kaohsiung, Big Spice and Li'l Spice, who have taken special leave today and come all the way from Kaohsiung . . . to sing you a song!

Big Spice and Li'l Spice ascend the stage, and sing a Western pop song oldie from their teenage years, for instance "Que Sera Sera."

During the festivities upstage, a solo figure appears downstage, walking slowly across the stage, toward the lone rattan chair. It is Hanbin.

Hanbin takes a look around his house and sits down on his rattan chair. He looks the same, but is very quiet.

As people take turns onstage singing, Smalls walks his wife and daughter through the three houses where he grew up.

Smalls's Daughter runs away; Smalls's Wife chases after her.

Alone, Smalls walks toward his old home in the crisp night air.

Smalls sees Hanbin sitting on the rattan chair. He can't believe his eyes. Hanbin raises his head.

HANBIN: Smalls . . .

SMALLS: Dad . . . ?

HANBIN: *(slowly)* I hear that the Village is going to be torn down soon. It's been more than 50 years, right?

Smalls nods.

After we came here, we put down roots, and after that . . . so fast . . . life has passed us by . . .

Silence. The festivities continue in the background.

You were all born in the Village, understand?

SMALLS: Yes, Dad.

HANBIN: This is our home, understand?

SMALLS: I understand.

HANBIN: So where will we live after the Village is gone?

SMALLS: The government is building housing at another site.

HANBIN: High-rise?

SMALLS: Yes.

HANBIN: Which floor have we got?

SMALLS: I don't know, we haven't drawn lots yet.

HANBIN: *(smiling)* Just like when we came? Draw a unit number, get your address plaque.

SMALLS: *(smiling)* I guess so.

HANBIN: So what happens here?

SMALLS: Here becomes a thoroughfare.

Hanbin smiles.

HANBIN: Smalls, I'm here to tell you something. Please go inside our house, to the spot where the column joins the beam. Reach inside. There's a hole with a letter inside. Can you get it for me?

SMALLS: A letter?

Smalls enters the house and finds the letter.

Dad. This letter . . .

HANBIN: I wrote you this letter when you were one month old. I was going to give it to you when you grew up. But I forgot. I was never good with words. Let's see what I wrote.

Smalls reads the letter. Hanbin recalls and recites what he wrote.

"Tai-sheng, you are born. We are so happy. You have two elder sisters, Li-wen and Li-ming. You are the eldest son, born in Taiwan, so we've named you Tai-sheng, which means 'born in Taiwan.'

We've been in Taiwan seven years now. We thought it would only be a temporary refuge. Nobody expected to stay on, but we did, and all too soon, seven years have passed! The house may be getting crowded with your arrival. I'll think of a way to make it bigger. When we're better off, I'd like to build a bathroom for your mom. That would be more convenient for everyone.

Smalls smiles.

Tai-sheng, how can a human being possibly envision what will happen in a human life? Your mom and I were two complete strangers. Like children playing house, we got married. Then, like in a dream, we crossed the seas and came to this strange place. We started a family, and now we have three of you. Tai-sheng, I have little education. All I can say is that life is a miracle. How fortunate I am to have all of you as companions on the journey.

Tai-sheng, today we mark your first month in this world. May you never know what it means to be displaced. May you never know what it means to be a refugee. May you never know war. May you always know peace.

Dad, November 26, 1956, at Formosa Village #1"

Hanbin leaves slowly.

SMALLS: Dad . . .

Smalls raises his head. Hanbin has already disappeared into the distance. The festivities continue. Yen wanders back to her old house.

Mom . . . Here, put on your coat.

Yen removes the address plate of the house, using a screwdriver.

YEN: *(looking at the plate)* Formosa Village #1, unit 99.

She speaks to the air.

Hanbin, we're moving. I worry that you might not be able to find your way home. So I'm bringing our old address plaque with us. I will nail it on the new door, so you can find your way home.

Smalls's Daughter runs out to look for Yen.

SMALLS'S DAUGHTER: Grandma . . .

Holding the plaque, Yen walks back with her granddaughter.
The festivities have come to an end. Deuce gathers everybody to take a group photo.

DEUCE: Uncles and aunties, my husband will get a photo for all of us together!

Ox and Cart move wooden benches in front of the three houses, just like when they all watched TV in the yard. The portrait includes three generations..

DEUCE'S HUSBAND: (*Taiwanese accent*) Okay, everybody look here . . . Happy New Year! Smile! Gotta be happy! One, two, three . . .

Deuce's Husband snaps a photo. A flash.

Epilogue

The same as at the beginning, a bulldozer razes a group of rundown shacks.
The mysterious Granny Lu crosses the stage slowly, as if she had never stopped.
The three Chao children, Bigs, Deuce and Small stand in a pool of light and speak directly to the audience.

BIGS: Just like all of the hundreds of military dependent villages in Taiwan, Formosa Village #1 finally was demolished.

DEUCE: The dirt walls and metal roofs are gone. But as long as we tell this story, the village remains.

SMALLS: And we will tell it, generation to generation. But at last, to our village, we must say, farewell.

They turn to watch as the demolition continues.
Lights fade out.

The End

Writing in Water

CHARACTERS

FRANK, a young entrepreneur in Hong Kong who has developed a personal development training called "Happyology"
FIONA, Frank's shrewd business partner and former classmate at Oxford
FORD, Fiona's boyfriend, from a wealthy Hong Kong corporate family
ENJI, an eight-year-old girl living on Peng Chau Island near Hong Kong
GROWN-UP ENJI, 25 years old
REAL ESTATE AGENT on the island
AUNT KIYO, Frank's aunt, an elegant, middle-aged Chinese woman living in Japan

Dancers, Happyology Center Assistant, Waiter, Law Firm Clerk, Fast Food Restaurant Customer, Coffee Shop Customer

SETTING

The play takes place in present-day Hong Kong and on one of its small outer islands, Peng Chau, only reachable by boat and ferry.

Writing in Water was developed at the Hong Kong Repertory Theatre in 2009, and first performed in this form on May 19, 2016, at Theatre Above, Shanghai, China, directed by Stan Lai, produced by Performance Workshop:

Cast:
He Jiong as Frank
Feng Li as Fiona and Dancer
Wu Bi as Ford
Wang Qiong as Enji and Grown-up Enji
Zhao Junyan as the Real Estate Agent and the Aunt
Zhao Weigang as Dancer, Happyology Assistant, Waiter, Customer, Law Firm Clerk

Scenic and Costume Design by Sandra Woodall
Lighting Design by Xiao Lihe
Projection Design by Ethan Wang
Music by Du Yun and Stan Lai

Produced by Nai-chu Ding
Executive Produced by Vanessa Yeo

Photo: *Writing in Water*, Theatre Above, Shanghai, 2016, Scene 22. Frank (He Jiong) and Grown-Up Enji (Wang Qiong). Photo by Gao Jianping.

Prologue

The sound of rain. Lights fade in. A large window, with raindrops running down it.

 Frank, a man in his twenties, sits in front of the window, gazing at it in wonder.

 Frank's narration is heard in voice-over. The raindrops on the glass form mysterious shapes and morph into key words that he is speaking, then disappear.

FRANK: *(voice)* Hong Kong has 261 outer islands. Had I forgotten? Or did I force myself not to remember, that one of them actually had something special to do with me.

On that island was a grand estate, where elegant guests danced the night away by the balmy South China Sea.

Lights transition, revealing the grand hall of an old mansion, where a glamorous dance party from the 1970s is underway. Couples in formal wear dance across the stage to the sound of a '70s band.

Behind the splendor was a tragic love story, of obsession, betrayal, and revenge. And passion—a passion that is long lost in the flowing tides.

The ballroom disappears. Frank stands and faces the audience.

FRANK: Sounds like poster copy for a forgettable '70s Cantonese pop film? Well, there's more. Recently I got a phone call from a law firm notifying me that I had inherited a dilapidated mansion on Peng Chau, that outer island.

Hang up immediately, right? I did. But they persisted. How dumb did they think I was? And yet one day, I suddenly remembered that yes, I *had* once heard of a house left to me by my mother, said to be by the seaside where I was born, a place my grandfather built to hide from the world, a place I'd always thought was nothing but a fiction . . .

My name is Frank Ho. Ho is one of those Chinese names that sounds like, well, you know, "Ho-ho-ho!" But you know what it means? It's actually a question mark, like "Who?" or "What?" It's a very philosophical name, or at least existential or whatever, because anybody named "Ho" means "who the hell are you?" I guess that's me for sure.

So "who" and so "what"? I never laid eyes on my father, and I never knew my mother. "Where?" I grew up in foster homes and hostels overseas, without the faintest idea of what the words "home" or "happiness" mean. I wound up studying psychology in the UK, and there I worked with a classmate to create a set of teaching materials in a new domain of learning. We thought we were on to something with definite niche start-up possibilities. And so my friend and I came back to Hong Kong and started our business, teaching personal development courses on the topic of . . .

Scene 1

Hip-hop flourish. Bright lights. The Happyology Institute classroom. The word "HAPPYOLOGY" is written on large paper mounted on a large easel. An Assistant, dressed in military camouflage rocks to the music.

Without losing a beat from the previous scene, Frank, dressed in a garish yellow jacket, addresses the auditorium with flair. His delivery is almost religiously passionate. The lecture is accompanied by loud hip-hop music with flourishes as punctuation. The Assistant bounds around accordingly in hip-hop fashion.

FRANK: THAT'S RIGHT, boys and girls, we're talking about the breakthrough science of Happyology! Now I'm sure you've never even given thought to the following essential life-changing question: is Happiness something that just comes and goes like a random, fickle breeze, and you catch it if you can, or is it something that can actually be *cultivated*, a skill that can be learned, through training? Raise your hand if you don't think that's possible. *(pointing at an audience member)* You! OUT! Get a full refund downstairs! And DON'T have a nice day!

Okay, so what use is happiness? What actual advantage do we gain by being happy? *(pointing at an audience member)* Put your hand down, that's a rhetorical question! Now get ready for a surprise: scientific research has now proven that happiness is a key component to—

Flourish. Assistant tears the current page off the easel, revealing the new page under it, which reads: "SUCCESS."

I'm glad you can read! That's right! When you're happy, your energy flows, leading to a greater chance of success in life, love, and career!

Flourish. Assistant tears off the page, revealing an emblem that reminds one of Oxford University or other higher institutions of learning.

What we're offering you in the course of the next five days is the fruit of the latest research at Oxford University. Yes, in five days, I WILL TEACH YOU HOW TO BE HAPPY, I will even FORCE YOU TO BE HAPPY! Then YOU will blaze YOUR OWN path to SUCCESS!

The Assistant tears off another page to reveal a big yellow smiley face.

So what then is this thing called happiness? A three-star Michelin meal? *(pointing to the smiley face)* And you turn into this? I'll take it! But in the end it's just sensory, a fleeting transmission of electrodes from tongue to brain that signals a sense of pleasure. That's why you need to post a picture of each dish on Instagram, or the next day you won't even remember what you ordered! Coming to work today, I waded through the sea of humanity in downtown Central. People coming out of all the hallowed financial institutions. What tortured expressions!

Assistant turns the curved mouth of the smiley face upside down, making a sad face.

How miserable everyone looked, caught in that sordid, candid moment, a snapshot of the suffering of humanity—well, the market is down today, but give me a break! That's us most of the time!! ALL OF US! Yes, I saw *(pointing)* you and you and you out there! Why are you so stressed out and troubled?! It's not just the little things in life, like fortune and fame and love and sex and groceries and lining up for coffee, there is a deeper underlying stream that colors all of our endeavors, the ur-stress if you may, which is—WE DON'T REALLY KNOW WHO WE ARE! We are not just the name, number, photo, and address on our ID card. There is a REAL YOU whom you actually have NOT YET MET! Who is he? For most of us, she is in prison somewhere deep inside! And YOU are the jailor!

Frank takes a Sharpie from the Assistant and emphatically draws prison bars around the smiley face as he talks.
    Frank shifts to a personable, sincere tone.

Look at me, now. I'm not afraid to say it, I never knew my father. My mother died at a very young age. So who am I? The tracks back to my ancestral past are hidden in mist. I float around in the present, a fragmented piece broken off of a genetic plate, with no clue as to what happiness is! No problem, at least I admit it! That's what fueled me to start the research in the first place!

The Assistant tears off the current page to reveal a picture of the planets.

Essential concept: happiness is predicated on who and what we encounter in our lives. Yes? Consider for a moment—are the encounters in your life totally random, or possibly part of some hidden pattern? Is our universe controlled by chaos or order? Is there possibly something called a chaotic order? Or orderly chaos? In physics, objects attract and repel each other for a reason. If we are governed by the laws of physics, could there be such a reason for whom and what we attract and repel in our lives?

So what do we call it? Destiny? Fortuity? Providence? How about "serendipity" for you touchy-feely ones? Whatever you want to call this mysterious force that brings people and things together and apart, did you ever think that you could stop passively accepting whatever "Desti-Fortui-Provindipity" brings to you, and *actively* seek to create, to generate the serendipity which is specifically beneficial to your personal well-being?

The Assistant tears off the current page to reveal the words: "ACTIVE PURSUIT OF SERENDIPITY."

Now we're talking! Let us learn the techniques that will draw all the beautiful things in life, all the benefits, TO US! If we can learn how to activate this energy of active attraction, through our own positive energy, we can draw in all the elements that will create our happiness and well-being.

So, that's the simple secret—the basis for happiness is THE ACTIVE PURSUIT OF SERENDIPITY! And that's it for today, kids!

The Assistant tears off the page, which reveals on the final page the word "DISMISSED!"

For those of you who signed up for the bungee jump, the bus leaves in 10 minutes. Those of you who signed up to destroy a hotel room, the police escort is waiting for you on the left. Do make sure you paid the extra fees!

Scene 2

Frank steps out of the bright light to address the audience directly.

> FRANK: How shameful was that? Teaching people about "happiness," something I myself am clueless about, and actually charging them for it? To be honest, my business partner and I never expected this kind of success, but since our first classroom opened in Causeway Bay, we've gone on to set up five branches, which leads to the depressing fact that there sure are A LOT of unhappy people around. What's even more shameless is that we started the classes before we even finished writing all the course materials! And here's the worst: if business continues to boom, there's a good chance we go public.

An office, where Fiona is working. She is an attractive, sharply dressed entrepreneur in her 20s.

> My business partner's name is Fiona. Look at her, so dedicated, so lovely, so gentle and caring.

Pause.

> In fact, she's a ruthless pragmatist-slash-opportunist. I shouldn't say such things about my old classmate, but we've known each other for too long, and she is what she is. She's from a generation born into a material world bereft of moral significance, and doing whatever it takes in exchange for success. Did I just say that?

Frank enters the office. Fiona is making coffee. Classical music is playing in the background, from a speaker: Bach's "Three-Part Inventions, No. 11 in G Minor."

> FIONA: Keep up the hard work, Frank. With a few more branch openings, and the proper funding, it's just very possible that we will be acquired by a company that needs us to go public.

> FRANK: Us?

FIONA: *(giving him a cup)* This is fine ground, 280 grams at 65 seconds. *(continuing)* I have friends in Shanghai who would kill for a company like ours: innovative, thriving, with a simple organizational structure.

FRANK: "A simple organizational structure" means there's just us two. It's a bit bitter. I would take off five seconds.

FIONA: The timing is spot on. It's your mouth that's naturally bitter. I've run the numbers. Twenty million [Hong Kong dollars, equivalent to 2.5 million US dollars] is all we need to make the deal happen.

FRANK: *(laughing)* Who's got that kind of money?

FIONA: An important potential investor is coming by for a demonstration. They were actually auditing your class just now.

FRANK: Who?

FIONA: The Wang family conglomerate.

Ford appears in an elevator outside the office. He is the young heir of the Wang family business, dressed in sort of a chic designer hipster fashion, with an awkward color combination.

FRANK: The guy you've been going out with? I hear he's going to inherit the family business. Wow, to think that one of my pals may actually become the richest person in Hong Kong—'s wife. So tell me, what's he like?

FIONA: Well, for one, we should't be playing this music of yours in his presence.

Fiona uses her phone to change the music on the speaker, to some random hip-hop.

FRANK: I see. He's into all things good and refined.

FIONA: Don't judge. He's not you.

FRANK: I guess not.

Ford steps out of the elevator, and talks to a recorder pen as a way of recording his days. His manner is always slightly off, a rich kid with a lack of confidence.

FORD: *(to the recorder pen)* 0-3-2-1-dot-1 [Ford numbers his entries according to the date]: "The Happiness Potential Development Co., Ltd." Here today to scout a new target. I mean investment target. A successful life-coaching enterprise with a catchy name. Miss Shaw, the key figure of the company, appears reliable, capable, responsible . . . *(losing control)* Damn, she's hot! *(back to normal)* Let's be professional about this! I can do this!

Ford reiterates to his recorder pen:

I CAN DO THIS!

Ford knocks on the office door. Fiona opens it.

FIONA: *(coolly)* Oh hi, Ford . . . *(checking her watch)* Didn't we say four o'clock?

FORD: Yes. I . . . uh . . . I'm a little early. *(awkward flirting)* To see you.

FIONA: Would you mind giving us a moment? We're just wrapping up our meeting.

She closes the door, after making sure Ford has seen Frank inside. Ford goes to his pen.

FORD: *(to recorder pen)* 0-3-2-1-dot 2. Mood: Blue. Technically, not a setback. She did not reject me. But that wasn't exactly a welcome, either. Collect yourself. But just to see her . . . is she hot or what?!

FRANK: *(to Fiona)* You just left the heir of the Wang conglomerate standing out there. Are we in a meeting?

FIONA: You don't get it. This is how it's done.

FRANK: How what's done? Wait a minute! You can't be dating him for . . . ? How shameless!

FIONA: What? Their company happens to be looking for projects to invest in. What's shameless about that?

FRANK: Business is business! Fiona, I'm ashamed to be associated with you.

FIONA: Trust me!

Fiona opens the door. Ford enters the office.

Come on in. Frank, this is Ford Wang.

FRANK: Pleasure.

FORD: Just call me Ford.

They shake hands. Ford shakes overaggressively.

>   *(to Fiona)* Excuse me.

He stands aside, and takes out his pen.

>   *(to recorder pen)* 0-3-2-1-dot-3: A confidante she spends time with alone. An obvious pushover, not in my league.

FRANK: *(to Fiona)* What's going on?

FIONA: *(whispering)* He's nuts. But kind of cute, isn't he? *(to Ford)* Mr. Wang, Frank will now explain our company's vision to you.

Ford gets a cup of coffee from Fiona, and gazes at her, ignoring Frank.

FRANK: All right, Mr. Wang, you've already obtained a general sense of what we do in the Lecture Hall, and the assorted activities that the students can partake in. Next, I would like to share our vision for the future . . .

FORD: *(to Fiona)* Do we have to listen to this guy babble on?

FIONA: These are features and figures you need to know to assess our company properly.

FORD: *(to Fiona)* I think your "features and figure" are more important. May I take you to high tea at the Four Seasons?

FIONA: Maybe next time.

FORD: Next time? I've got a real tight schedule. Let's go.

Fiona and Ford exit. Fiona exchanges a glance with Frank as she goes. Frank shrugs.

Scene 3

A beach on the island of Peng Chau. An old, abandoned mansion in the background.

>   *Enter Frank and the Real Estate Agent, a talkative local middle-aged woman who is not particularly polished in real estate affairs.*

REAL ESTATE AGENT: *(pointing)* There!

Frank inhales the ocean breeze and looks at the mansion. The Real Estate Agent takes out a folder.

> Congratulations, Mr. Ho. All the paperwork is here. I can explain the offer. This house has been sitting there for years, falling apart. What an eyesore!

Frank sinks into an inexplicable melancholy.

FRANK: I didn't know it was right on the beach.

REAL ESTATE AGENT: Prime waterfront. You're going to make a fortune. The buyer is offering 19 million 5.

FRANK: But I haven't decided whether to sell or not.

REAL ESTATE AGENT: What? Didn't you say over the phone . . . ?

FRANK: I need some time to think it over.

REAL ESTATE AGENT: Think what over? It's a dump! And how should I put it? It's just—not a nice place. Why keep it?

FRANK: I don't know.

REAL ESTATE AGENT: So sell while you have a good price.

Her cell phone rings.

> *(on the phone)* Hello? . . . I'm at the haunted house. Whoops. *(she turns away)* I mean . . . The owner is here . . . yeah . . .

She steps away to talk on the phone. Frank walks on the beach, taking it all in.
A little girl (Enji) enters and looks curiously at Frank and everything else. She is around eight years old. Though she is neatly dressed, her clothes are somewhat outdated. Frank looks at her.

FRANK: Hey.

ENJI: *(echoing Frank)* Hey . . .

FRANK: What's up?

ENJI: What's up?

She slowly backs off, while repeating everything Frank says. Her language and pronunciation seem to be overly proper for a kid of today.

FRANK: So, who may I ask are you?

ENJI: So, who may I ask are you?

FRANK: You live around here?

ENJI: You live around here?

FRANK: What's your name?

The girl is fascinated by the view of the sea. A big wave crashes in front of her.

ENJI: Wow! What a big wave!

FRANK: Ha! You lose!

ENJI: So this is what waves are like! I didn't know you could see the ocean from here.

FRANK: If you live here you can see the ocean anytime.

ENJI: But I can't see the ocean from my room.

FRANK: Then step out.

ENJI: But I can't.

She turns back and points at the house.

Whose house is that?

FRANK: Mine.

ENJI: Wow, your house is big, but it's . . . rather old.

FRANK: It's been deserted for a long time.

ENJI: Then where do you live?

FRANK: Hong Kong.

Pause.

You've been to Hong Kong, haven't you?

Pause.

Then where do you live?

ENJI: *(pointing)* Over there. I think.

FRANK: You think? What color is your house?

ENJI: I don't know.

FRANK: You don't what your house looks like? How are you going to go home?

ENJI: But I don't want to go home. Can you take me to your house to play?

FRANK: My house is falling apart.

ENJI: I mean Hong Kong.

FRANK: It's getting dark now. Maybe next time, okay?

ENJI: Okay!

FRANK: As long as we have permission from your parents.

The little girl doesn't respond.
The Real Estate Agent enters.

REAL ESTATE AGENT: So, have you decided, Mr. Ho? *(seeing the little girl)* Hey, what are you doing here, kid? Which house are you from?

She runs away. They watch her go.

FRANK: Sorry, Mrs. Hwong. I need more time to think about it. I don't feel ready.

REAL ESTATE AGENT: Whatever! If I were you I'd sell it this instant!

Scene 4

A fancy restaurant in Central. Fiona is sitting at a table. Frank enters.

FRANK: Why are we meeting here? I've got a couple of group trainings scheduled.

FIONA: Don't worry, he'll be right here.

A Waiter approaches them.

WAITER: What can I get you to drink?

FIONA: I'll have a glass of red wine.

FRANK: I'm taking off soon, so just water.

WAITER: Sparkling or still?

FRANK: No sparkles, no bottle. Just water.

WAITER: I'm sorry, sir, but all we have is . . .

FIONA: Just get him a bottle of sparkling.

Waiter nods and exits.

FIONA: *(to Frank)* Don't worry. He's paying.

FRANK: I hate your attitude.

FIONA: Ford's company is very interested in us. They sent their law-
yers over to do their due diligence. We gave them an impressive
spreadsheet.

FRANK: So fast?

FIONA: You should commend me. They had a meeting to discuss us
today. Ford set up dinner with me here, I'm guessing to celebrate.

FRANK: Whatever. Our real problem is the next phase of our curriculum.
You insist on starting an advanced class, but we're really thin on
materials. All we do is keep telling people to attract positive energy.

FIONA: What's your problem? You succeed, you're happy! The secret
of happiness is success! Make that the key point of our advanced
course! No need to learn happiness! Success is happiness! Going public is happiness! Louis Vuitton is happiness! A Beamer is happiness!

Frank shakes his head.

FRANK: Are you done?

FIONA: Twenty million is a piece of cake to them.

Enter Ford, distressed. He stops and stares at Frank.

What's the matter?

FORD: *(pointing at Frank)* Did I invite him?

FRANK: *(getting up)* I'm off.

FORD: Sit down.

Frank sits. Waiter pulls over a chair for Ford.

(to Fiona) Do you have to keep him constantly by your side?

FIONA: What are you talking about? How did the meeting go?

FORD: A setback, yes, but not defeat. *(taking out the recorder pen, repeating to it)* "0-3-2-8-dot-15: A setback, yes, but not defeat."

FIONA: What happened?

FORD: They're putting your case on hold.

FIONA: What? You didn't put up a fight?

FORD: They're putting me on hold, too.

FIONA: What's that supposed to mean?

FORD: They fired me. I'm no longer in charge of the company.

FIONA: What?

Pause.

I thought you were next in line.

FORD: They said I haven't been myself lately. Said I was impotent! Sorry, I mean incompetent! *(to the recorder pen)* "They say I'm im—competent. But I'll show them! I'll bounce right back and rise again!"

Waiter serves wine to Fiona. Ford snatches the wine glass from her.

FIONA: Hey, that's mine . . .

Ford downs the wine. Fiona motions for the Waiter to get another glass.

Tell us about it.

FORD: Their problem is with you.

FIONA: Me?

FORD: They think you're going out with me because of my worth.

FIONA: They can't be serious!

FRANK: *(sarcastically)* They can't be serious!

FORD: They said I must take temporary leave of the company if I don't stop seeing you.

FIONA: What?

FORD: After I told them that I planned to raise 20 million for your Happiness Potential Development Co., the board met and fired me! They said all I have to do to get my job back is raise the 20 million myself.

FIONA: What does that mean?

FORD: It's a cinch! Just give me 20 million and everything is fixed.

FIONA: Twenty million?

FORD: They don't believe that I can raise 20 million! They think you're taking me for a ride! They say as long as I'm with you I will not inherit a penny of the Wang family fortune! They treat me like a kid! Now they've exiled me, forcing a split with you, but if I split with you that means I lose, and that will never happen! *(to the recorder pen)* "That will never happen! Want me to raise 20 million? Just wait and see!"

Waiter enters with menus.

WAITER: Today we have a lobster special.

FORD: I REFUSE TO EAT LOBSTER! *(to the recorder pen)* "From today on, I only eat instant noodles! I'll show them thrift! I'll prove them wrong!"

Ford storms off.
Embarrassing pause.

FRANK: Make sure you get a receipt.

Scene 5

The hall inside the old house near the beach on Peng Chau. A dilapidated row of glass doors that have been boarded up. An easel lying on the floor. An old cane chair.
　　Frank and Fiona enter. They cover their faces, dust off their coats, and look around.

FIONA: Wow! Looks like no one's been in here for years. Do you remember this place?

Frank shakes his head. The Real Estate Agent enters with a folder.

REAL ESTATE AGENT: We got a pretty good price now.

FIONA: How much?

REAL ESTATE AGENT: Twenty million.

FIONA: Twenty million?!

REAL ESTATE AGENT: That's their latest offer. We can get them to go higher.

FIONA: Nice.

REAL ESTATE AGENT: The buyer plans to build a fancy hotel here.

FRANK: But I don't have the property rights yet.

REAL ESTATE AGENT: Then when?

FRANK: My aunt is coming from Japan next week to do the paperwork.

REAL ESTATE AGENT: That's fine, we can sign a letter of intent today.

FRANK: I'd like to take another look.

FIONA: What for? The buyer's going to tear everything down.

REAL ESTATE AGENT: That's right. Sell it, and you can buy yourself a nice big flat in Hong Kong. You should listen to your wife.

FRANK: How fortunate that she's not!

Fiona scoffs at Frank and answers her phone. She exits.

Plus, I haven't decided yet. I need another look.

REAL ESTATE AGENT: Let me tell you, 20 million after tax is serious money. This used to be THE best house in Peng Chau. Your grandpa, now that was a man with panache!

FRANK: You knew my grandfather?

REAL ESTATE AGENT: Sort of. It was a long time ago. He was this rich businessman who came from the mainland after the Chinese Civil War. He bought this beachfront, built the house, and hosted dinner parties every day. For us country folks that was sure a sight to behold. *(pointing left)* The dining room was over there. The spread had champagne and all sorts of fresh seafood. That long dining table could seat 60!

FRANK: You saw that?

REAL ESTATE AGENT: Sure did! Back then, they were often short staffed, so they would ask us to help out. I was just a kid. I would help set the tables, pour the tea. Your grandpa was one generous man!

FRANK: So what was this room?

REAL ESTATE AGENT: This room was the dance hall.

FRANK: A dance hall?

The image of dancers appears again in the distance.

REAL ESTATE AGENT: Are you kidding? Back then they'd ferry over the house band from the Hong Kong Club. The guests drank, danced, enjoyed the view of the ocean, and watched fireworks all night long. Your grandma was so young, and so pretty. That was Peng Chau's golden age. Every day there were VIPs drinking and dancing till sunrise.

The images in the distance slowly fade.

Then one day your grandma left. She never came back. There were no more dances, no more guests. The place looked so lonely. Your grandpa almost never stepped out of the house. We delivered rice and flour to him. The door was always locked, and all the windows were boarded up. Nobody went in or came out. Sometimes we thought that the house was haunted. Sorry, I shouldn't have said that.

FRANK: That's okay.

REAL ESTATE AGENT: But it's true.

Frank sits on the cane chair.

You can see the sea from here, too. Your grandpa would sit here and just gaze at the ocean. We all knew he missed your grandma. One day many years later, I don't know if he was drunk or what, he fell into the ocean and drowned.

FRANK: What? Where?

REAL ESTATE AGENT: *(pointing)* There. We thought he was all alone, with nobody to take care of his funeral, so we came to help. But when we got into the house: Whoa! We found this 17-year-old girl living inside! It turned out that your mother had been living in there all these years! We had no clue! It scared the living soul out of us!

FRANK: What?

REAL ESTATE AGENT: No one had ever seen her before! You see, when your grandma ran away from the island, we assumed she took both her children with her, because we never saw them afterwards. Well, turned out she didn't! Your grandpa kept your mother locked in the house all these years!

Pause.

You didn't know this?

FRANK: Not really.

Silence.

What about my father?

REAL ESTATE AGENT: He was an artist. Studied in France or something. One day he came here because he heard there was this young woman who had been locked inside the house all those years, so he was curious and asked to paint her portrait. Then they were together, and then you were born. And then, one day he left.

Silence.

Oh, why am I babbling about all this? The buyer already wrote a check for a 2 million deposit. I'll go get the contract. Sell it while you can, I told you it's not a nice house!

She exits. Frank opens the window. Sound of the ocean.
The little girl appears before the glass doors.

FRANK: Little girl? You here again? I came here to see you, but I didn't know where to find you.

ENJI: You came to see me?

FRANK: What's your name?

Pause.

ENJI: He calls me Enji.

FRANK: Enji. What a beautiful name. Who's "he"? Your dad?

ENJI: Can you take me to play?

FRANK: Where do you want to go?

ENJI: On the ferry! To Hong Kong!

FRANK: Well, let's ask your parents.

ENJI: No need to.

FRANK: No way! Who's going to bring you back?

ENJI: You!

FRANK: But I have a class tonight!

ENJI: What class do you have tonight?

FRANK: I'm a teacher.

ENJI: What do you teach?

FRANK: Happyology.

ENJI: What's Happyology?

FRANK: I teach people how to be happy.

ENJI: Then can you teach me how to be happy?

FRANK: You're a kid, all kids are happy! Only grown-ups are unhappy!

Enji holds Frank's hand.

ENJI: Take me with you.

FRANK: No way!

Enter the Real Estate Agent and Fiona.

FIONA: There's nothing to see, it's a hopeless wreck.

REAL ESTATE AGENT: *(seeing the little girl)* Little girl, what are you doing here again?

The little girl is frightened, and exits.

FRANK: Mrs. Hwong, I need some more time to think it over. I don't feel prepared.

REAL ESTATE AGENT: If I were you I'd sell it in a minute! The buyer won't wait forever.

Frank looks around for the little girl.

FRANK: Well, I . . . need some time to think.

Scene 6

On the ferry from Peng Chau to Hong Kong. Frank and Fiona are on the deck. Frank looks out to the sea. Fiona is on her cell phone.

FIONA: *(on her phone)* Hello . . . I'm at the office . . . What makes you so sure I'm not? . . . You've got your dogs following me? I seriously doubt that, concerning your current company status . . . Listen, I'm in no mood to talk.

Fiona hangs up her phone.

FRANK: Be nice to him.

FIONA: I can't stand it when he's in his "control" mode. What was it with that little girl back on the island?

FRANK: I have no idea.

FIONA: Where did she come from?

FRANK: Nowhere. I just turned, and there she was.

Enji approaches them on the deck.

FIONA: Like . . . THAT?

They see her.

FRANK: Hey, what are you doing here?

FIONA: You followed us onto the ferry?

ENJI: I want to see Hong Kong.

FRANK: No. I'm taking you home immediately.

FIONA: Nice try. Get the ferry to turn back.

ENJI: It's okay Really.

FRANK: *(taking out his cell phone)* Well, let's call your folks, now, and let them know you're okay. What's your phone number?

ENJI: *(repeating the phrase)* Phone number?

FRANK: Don't tell me you don't know!

Enji shakes her head.

ENJI: It's really okay, as long as you take me back later.

FRANK: I'm going to have to take you back? Did I win the lottery or what?

FIONA: When we get to Central, just hand her over to the police. They'll take care of her.

ENJI: What? Police?

FRANK: It's okay. I'll take her back.

Pause. Frank looks at Enji and feels a sort of affinity with her.

(to Enji) Hey kid, don't think I do this for everybody!

FIONA: What? You're the one who said it's important for us to focus on the curriculum, and now you're chauffeuring this little girl around from the islands to Central?

FRANK: *(to Fiona)* You're scaring her! Go away!

Fiona steps aside. She takes out her cell phone.

FIONA: Finish the transfer as soon as possible.

FRANK: What was that?

FIONA: Nothing. I just want you to finish the ownership transfer as soon as possible. *(on the phone)* Hello? . . . What now? . . .

Enji stands by the railing, eyes wide open, filled with wonder and surprise at the view of the sea.

ENJI: Wow! The sea!

FRANK: Wait a minute. You live on Peng Chau Island, and you've never taken this ferry before?

Enji shakes her head.

The first time you saw me you echoed everything I said. Why?

ENJI: Because I'm always by myself, and sometimes I won't say a word in a very, very long time. I often feel I'm just an echo.

FRANK: You know, I know that feeling. How many brothers and sisters do
  you have?

ENJI: I have a sister. But she left.

FRANK: What about your parents?

Enji is silent.

I've always been alone myself, too.

*It starts to rain. Fiona takes out an umbrella from her bag and opens it. Frank
grabs it and uses it for himself and Enji. Fiona is forced to one side, where she
takes out a plastic raincoat from her purse, and puts it on.*

ENJI: So you like rain?

FRANK: How did you know?

ENJI: What I like most is when I'm alone and it rains.

FRANK: Me, too. I watch the raindrops on the window.

ENJI: Right.

FRANK: They weave their paths together and start to form different signs.

ENJI: Like the water is writing!

FRANK: Indecipherable words. The raindrops attract and repel one
  another, as if the heavens are trying to tell us a secret.

ENJI: What is the secret?

FRANK: I don't know.

ENJI: What is it like to write in water?

FRANK: Well, the words disappear as soon as they appear, instantly.

ENJI: So nothing stays.

FRANK: Maybe that's good.

Frank notices Enji's pendant.

That's a very pretty pendant. Can I see it?

ENJI: Sure.

She takes off the pendant and hands it to Frank.

Open it.

Frank opens the pendant. It is a small music box that plays the Manchurian folk tune "Lullaby."

FRANK: And there's music! How sweet.

ENJI: My sister gave it to me.

FRANK: How come your sister had such a beautiful pendant?

ENJI: Because my mom gave it to her.

FRANK: You should wear it on the outside. It looks nifty.

ENJI: No. He'll see it.

FRANK: And why can't you let him see it?

ENJI: Because if he sees it he'll think of his wife, and he'll be sad.

Frank returns the pendant to Enji. Central looms in the distance.

Is that Hong Kong over there?

FRANK: Yes.

ENJI: All those tall things . . . are they houses?

FRANK: *(surprised)* Yes, they are. Over there, that's Central. *(pointing to the other side)* Over there is Tsim Sha Tsui.

ENJI: *(struggling with the words)* Tsim-Sha-Tsui.

FRANK: You never heard of Tsim Sha Tsui?

Enji doesn't respond. Fiona gets a text message. She reads and replies, vehemently typing with her thumbs.
Enji notices Fiona texting on her cell phone.

ENJI: What are you doing, Ma'am?

FIONA: I'm getting wet.

ENJI: I mean what are you doing to the thing in your hand?

FIONA: He's such a moron!

ENJI: *(to Frank)* She's writing on glass?

FRANK: You can't possibly never have heard of a smartphone?

Enji stares at Frank.

Scene 7

Inside a fast food restaurant with children's themes. Enji sits, looking at every-thing around her with glee and curiosity. Fiona is seated, talking on her phone.

FIONA: *(on the phone)* The problem is he doesn't want to sell! . . . That's right! I told him to sell it and consider it as a personal loan to me. I'll pay him back twice the amount! But he . . .

Frank comes with food and a souvenir plastic thermos, with the restaurant's mascot on it.

FRANK: Here we go.

ENJI: Thank you, Sir! Is it expensive?

FRANK: No. Dig in! We'll figure out how to get you home after we finish some business here.

FIONA: *(on the phone)* . . . we're meeting some prospective students at the fast food place on Des Voeux Road . . . What do you mean "I know"? Are you tracking me with a GPS? I DO NOT want to talk to you! . . . Who am I with? Your mother! *(hangs up)*

Enji is frightened.

FRANK: Enjoy!

Frank and Fiona are both absorbed in their cell phones. Enji watches them with curiosity.
Frank notices that Enji is not sure how to eat her burger.

Wait. You've never had a Double Cruncher with Cheese before?

ENJI: What does "Double Cruncher with Cheese" mean?

FRANK: It's . . . a name.

Frank points to the plastic thermos.

You see? That's Sergeant Crunch.

ENJI: Oh. Why is he smiling like that?

FRANK: Because, uh, I guess he's happy!

ENJI: I see. He's happy.

FIONA: The Devil knows whether he's happy or not. Corporate strategy strives to create the illusion that everyone in the environs of a fast food joint is happy, and therefore you feel compelled to spend more. The guise of happiness is just a ploy to get you to spend. Better get used to it, kid.

ENJI: *(to Frank)* I don't understand what she's saying.

FRANK: *(to Fiona)* Your dry brand of cynicism doesn't work on her, so stop it.

FIONA: I'm doing her a favor. The sooner she faces reality, the better. Which school do you go to, kid?

Enji doesn't respond.

> You aren't a dropout, are you? Your parents don't want you in school?

Enji is frightened. Frank holds her hand.

FRANK: *(to Fiona)* Enough. *(to Enji)* You want some ice cream?

ENJI: What's "ice-cream"?

FRANK: Are you kidding? You don't know what ice cream is? It's cool and sweet and . . . *(standing)* Okay, I'll just buy you one.

ENJI: Is it expensive?

FRANK: No worries. *(pointing at Fiona, sarcastically)* This lady's company is soon going public, and she's taking me along for the ride, so I'm going to become very rich. I don't think we need to worry about an ice cream.

Frank exits to buy ice cream.

ENJI: Thank you, Sir.

Enji turns to Fiona, about to ask a question.

FIONA: What's "going public," right? That's actually a complicated question. Let me put it this way: the stock market is an essential financial institution in a functioning capitalist society . . .

Her phone rings. She glances at it and doesn't pick up. Enji looks at her. The ringing stops.

> Lunatic! *(continuing)* But many people have discovered methods to manipulate the system and create a kind of money game, which in turn . . .

Ringing again. Fiona angrily picks up.

> *(on the phone)* LOONY! *(hangs up)*

ENJI: Are you okay, Ma'am?

FIONA: I'm fine! I was just showing you how to handle a lunatic!

ENJI: *(to Fiona)* Ma'am, what's a "lunatic"?

FIONA: Oh, my god! Are you for real?

Enji notices Ford's recorder pen hanging off Fiona's purse.

ENJI: Excuse me, Ma'am. What is this?

Enji takes the recorder pen off the purse.

> Is it a pen?

FIONA: *(stunned)* No, it's a flipping recorder pen!

ENJI: What's a flipping recorder pen?

FIONA: It can record what you say, and it looks like a pen, so . . .

Fiona looks intently at the recorder pen. Frank comes back.

FRANK: Super Cruncher Cone!

ENJI: *(eyes wide open)* How is this even possible?

FRANK: Hey, what's Ford's recorder pen doing here?

FIONA: Holy cow, it's recording. It's been going for hours!

ENJI: *(to Fiona)* He gave it to you?

FIONA: No, that's why I'm wondering how it got here.

ENJI: Can I listen to it?

FIONA: Of course!

Fiona replays the recording.

RECORDER PEN: *(voice)* "Can I listen to it? . . . of course!"

Enji is astonished.

ENJI: How amazing!

FIONA: It's yours!

ENJI: Mine?

FRANK: Isn't that Ford's "Precious"?

FIONA: Too bad for him!

ENJI: I can't accept it.

FIONA: Don't worry.

ENJI: No! He'll find out!

FIONA: He?

FRANK: Her uncle. *(to Enji)* You can put it away somewhere. There's got to be a place in your house.

ENJI: My room is very small. Wait, I have an idea! There's a little garden outside my room. I can keep it in the well!

FIONA: A well?

ENJI: No one ever draws water there anymore because it's salty!

FIONA: But you can't put this pen in water.

Enji puts the recorder pen in the plastic thermos and screws the lid on tight.

FRANK: Smart! *(raising a fist)* Yay! . . .

ENJI: Sir, what does "yay" mean?

FIONA: Oh, come on!

Enji struggles to imitate the gesture.

ENJI: *(raising her fist)* Yay! . . .

Fiona and Enji touch hands.

FRANK: *(raising his fist)* Yay! . . .

Ford enters and goes directly to the table they are sitting at.

FORD: Wow! What a heartwarming scene! A family of three at Sergeant Crunch's!

FIONA: Go away, you lunatic! I'm not talking to you.

FORD: No problem. *(to Frank)* I'm talking to you! Twenty million! Why aren't you selling?

FIONA: Why did you tap me?

FORD: Tap you?

FIONA: Don't play dumb. I found the recorder pen in my purse!

Fiona takes the recorder pen out of the plastic thermos. Ford looks astonished.

FORD: Oh, my god! What is that doing here?

FIONA: You want to know what I say when I'm away from you? Are there some dark secrets you think I'm hiding from you?

FORD: I just wanted to know what you say to him when I'm not around.

FIONA: Moron!

FORD: BUT TIME'S A-WASTING! Talk is cheap! *(to Frank)* "Active attraction!" "ACTIVE PURSUIT OF SERENDIPITY"! And boom! It worked! Twenty million dollars comes rolling straight to me!

FIONA: What has that to do with him? That's his money!

FORD: You're telling me that you have nothing to do with him?

FIONA: *(standing to leave)* I'm done talking to you!

FORD: *(stopping her)* I don't get you guys! Fate has set the eight ball right in front of the corner pocket. All you have to do is tap it in! Sell and loan me the money! Everyone wins! *(taking out another identical pen recorder)* "Number 2 pen recorder, oh-four-oh-one dot one—sell that dump fast! Everyone wins!"

ENJI: He has another one?

FORD: Little girl, I've got plenty of them! You can have number 1. *(opening his jacket)* Numbers 2, 3, and 4 are all here!

A Customer passes by and looks at them.
Enji is uncomfortable at all the arguing.

FRANK: Can you keep it down?

FIONA: Go get something to eat! I don't want her to see us fight like this!

FORD: Excuse me, I only eat instant noodles!

FIONA: For her!

FORD: Her? Whose kid is she anyway?

FIONA: Shut up already!

FORD: *(humbly)* But I don't have any cash.

Fiona gives Ford some money. Ford goes to the counter.
Frank looks at Enji, who's scared, and helps her put the pen back into the plastic thermos.

FRANK: Enji, it's OK! Try your ice cream cone, and then we'll start heading back!

ENJI: *(to Frank)* Sir, why do people argue?

FRANK: Because people are complicated.

FIONA: He's been down. His family is very powerful, and . . . He's insecure, so he's been trying to eavesdrop on me. He's unhappy.

ENJI: Unhappy. Then you will leave him?

FIONA: Maybe. It's possible. Might be better that way.

ENJI: What a scary place the world is. Now I understand why uncle won't let me go out and play. He doesn't want me to see all this.

Pause. She hands the ice cream cone back to Frank.

Sir, I don't want this anymore.

FRANK: Don't be that way. I'm sorry we're stuck in this place with all this very unhealthy food, but try to enjoy it. Everything will be fine.

Ford comes back with chicken wings.

FORD: *(suddenly very gentle)* Here you go, little girl. Sorry, I was acting horribly. Thank you for reminding me, I really am a moron.

ENJI: He's changed?

FIONA: Just ignore him.

FORD: It's certainly my insecurity welling up. Take your time. Enjoy your meal. I need to spend some time in self-reflection.

Ford stands off to the side.

FIONA: That's more like it.

ENJI: So he's now become good?

FIONA: Um . . . if that's a yes or no question, yes.

ENJI: Why is it that sometimes people are good, and sometimes they're . . . bad?

FORD: *(flaring up, shouting)* ARE YOU DONE YET? HOW LONG DO YOU EXPECT ME TO STAND HERE WAITING FOR YOU TO FINISH YOUR STUPID MEAL?

The Customer passes by again. He's startled and drops his food.

FIONA: YOU JUST TOLD US TO TAKE OUR TIME!

FORD: CAN'T YOU TELL WHEN SOMEONE IS JUST BEING CIVIL?! DON'T YOU KNOW HOW PRECIOUS MY TIME IS? I'VE GOT SO MANY APPOINTMENTS LINED UP!

FIONA: WHAT APPOINTMENTS? DIDN'T YOU GET FIRED? THEY'RE ALL CANCELED!

FORD: YOU CANNOT *(breaking down)* talk to me like that . . . You'll destroy me . . . you have no idea how much I need you . . .

Ford breaks down in Fiona's arms.

FIONA: It's okay . . . let's go for some instant noodles. *(dialing on her phone)* I'm canceling the interviews.

FORD: Can I add an egg today?

They move to exit. Ford turns back, grabs the chicken, and exits hand in hand with Fiona.

FRANK: *(to Enji)* Isn't Hong Kong a blast?

ENJI: Sir, what's a . . . ?

Scene 8

Frank and Enji on a merry-go-round, on adjacent horses. Enji is having a great time.

ENJI: Woooow!

FRANK: Having fun?

ENJI: Yes! I didn't know there was anything so much fun in the world!

FRANK: I don't know about that. This is just a temporary ride from the market fair. They're taking it down tomorrow. It happened to be here on our way to the pier. When we're done here, I'm taking you home.

Silence.

ENJI: Sir, why are you so good to me?

FRANK: Because you're such a sweetheart! And you know? I'm happy when I see you happy!

Enji is quiet.

I never had anyone take me anywhere when I was a kid. Someday if we have the chance, I'll take you to Ocean Park, or Disneyland!

ENJI: Never heard of them.

FRANK: Really? But you should be able to see the nightly fireworks from Peng Chau.

Enji doesn't respond.

Hey, I dare you to let go!

They let go of their hands.

FRANK AND ENJI: *(together)* Wheeee—!

They ride for a moment, in contentment. Enji has a big smile on her face.

ENJI: Sir, is this happiness?

FRANK: I think so.

ENJI: If this is happiness, then why won't Uncle let me experience it?

FRANK: Uncle doesn't want you to be happy?

ENJI: He says that all things end in sadness, so the best thing is not to engage at all.

FRANK: "Engage." "Experience." That's grown-up talk. He must be very unhappy.

ENJI: Maybe. His wife left him. He always tells me the world is a cruel place. No one ever treats anyone honestly. He doesn't want me to get hurt the way he did.

Pause.

Can this merry-go-round go on turning forever?

FRANK: No, it has to come to a stop at some point. But if you pay for another ticket you can have another go.

ENJI: So you can pay for happiness.

FRANK: Not really.

ENJI: Wait. When I think that the merry-go-round will stop and then I have to go back, I become unhappy. Sir, now I understand the meaning of "unhappiness."

FRANK: But you keep all the happy memories.

ENJI: But the happier the memory, the more unhappy I get. I see what uncle means. I'm sorry. I won't come out and play with you again.

FRANK: You can't refuse to want something just because you're worried you might lose it.

ENJI: I'm unhappy already.

FRANK: But you're still on the merry-go-round. It's not over yet.

ENJI: I don't want to play anymore!

FRANK: Enji! . . .

Suddenly Enji jumps off her horse and exits. Frank jumps off and runs after her.

Scene 9

Dusk. On the ferry back to Peng Chau. Enji keeps looking back at Hong Kong.

FRANK: Isn't Hong Kong beautiful?

ENJI: But it's growing smaller.

FRANK: You'll be home soon.

ENJI: It's almost dark. When night falls, my garden is dark, too.

FRANK: Your garden.

ENJI: There are a lot of beautiful flowers in it. There's a vegetable patch next to it. My uncle planted them. The well is in the middle there.

FRANK: There was a well near where my boarding school was in England. The locals there called it a wishing well.

ENJI: What does that mean?

FRANK: It means if you make a wish to the well, your dreams will come true.

ENJI: So did your dreams come true?

FRANK: Nope. I guess I wasn't devout enough. Anyway, you should try it.

ENJI: I will, Sir.

Pause.

FRANK: Will he scold you when you get back?

ENJI: It was a short time last time so he didn't notice. But I was out the whole day today, I wonder if he's found out.

Enji is suddenly anxious.

Oh no! I didn't make tea for him this afternoon! He must have already found out!

FRANK: You make tea for him every day?

ENJI: He likes tea.

FRANK: You boil the water yourself?

ENJI: Yes.

Enji turns around and looks at the sunset.

So this is what the sunset looks like on the sea! I never imagined anything could be so beautiful! I never knew the world was such a beautiful place! Such a beautiful place!

Frank looks at Enji, who is filled with joy, and reflects on what a melancholy girl she is.
They watch the sunset.

Scene 10

The reception room at a law firm. Frank's Aunt Kiyo, dressed affluently, in a contemporary Japanese style, and the Clerk are handling some paperwork.
  Raindrops spatter on the window.
  Frank enters.

FRANK: Aunt Kiyo!

They embrace. Aunt Kiyo has a good look at Frank. She speaks with a Japanese accent and has an imposing demeanor.

AUNT KIYO: How many years has it been? Look at you, all grown up. Please forgive my negligence. I should've taken care of this a long time ago.

FRANK: It's okay, Aunt Kiyo, really.

AUNT KIYO: The house is yours. Your mother left it to you.

FRANK: "Skywater Mansion."

AUNT KIYO: That's right. The same name as your ancestral home back on the mainland, in the city of Dalian. Your grandfather was a big general there during the war. When the Communists took over China in 1949, he was accused of treason or whatever, and fled to Hong Kong.

FRANK: Treason?

AUNT KIYO: It was never proved, and he always got angry when people brought up the subject, because he considered himself the ultimate patriot, one whose loyalty could never be questioned. Turned out he was cut out to be a businessman, and was very successful. But he always longed for his home on the mainland—a place he could never go back to. That's why he built this house, exactly like his old family house in Dalian. It was also by the sea, and he gave it the same name: "Skywater."

The Clerk comes in and checks the paperwork.

CLERK: That'll do. Please wait for a moment.

AUNT KIYO: Thanks.

The Clerk exits with a document.
Frank looks at Aunt Kiyo. She looks at him and is suddenly tearful.

Sorry, Frank, but seeing you reminds me of . . .

FRANK: My mother.

AUNT KIYO: And MY mother. Your grandmother. You know, I didn't get to spend much time with both of them.

FRANK: Neither did I.

AUNT KIYO: So what is the house like now?

FRANK: Someone wants to buy it.

On his cell phone, Frank shows Aunt Kiyo photos of the old house.

AUNT KIYO: It's come to this? Sell it quick.

FRANK: Aunt, you don't understand. I don't want to.

AUNT KIYO: What's the offer?

FRANK: Twenty million after tax.

AUNT KIYO: They offer 20 million and you won't take it? That house is damned.

FRANK: No, it's got all the . . .

AUNT KIYO: All the what?

FRANK: From my childhood.

AUNT KIYO: What childhood? Your father ran away before he could take a good look at you. Your mother passed away when you were three. I couldn't afford to raise you at that time. Then I moved to Japan, so I sent you abroad to live in a foster home. Forget about this old house! There's nothing in it!

FRANK: But there are so many things in that house that I know nothing about.

AUNT KIYO: That house was your mother's prison!

Frank listens with trepidation and fascination.

> Don't you understand? She was imprisoned in that house for 17 years! I escaped when I was 10. Your grandmother left before me. Your grandfather was a monster! A demon! He locked us all up. One by one we escaped, all but your mother. She was imprisoned in that house all her life.

Silence.

> Now that you're grown, it's time you knew these things. I chose to forget a long time ago.

FRANK: So it really happened. What gave him the right to do that?

AUNT KIYO: *(scoffing)* The right? Your grandfather was much older than your grandmother. He had a big, successful business and was a big spender. Your grandmother was just a dance hall girl.

FRANK: A dance hall girl?

AUNT KIYO: They met at the Oriental Dance Hall in Wan Chai. Some said the reason your grandfather spent so extravagantly was that he lost a sense of purpose after China fell and he couldn't go back. He didn't get involved with anyone until he met your grandmother. They fell in love and got married, and after that he built the beach house, as if to celebrate his rebirth. Guests flocked to the house, drinking, dining, a never-ending banquet. Your mother and I were born in that dream-like place.

> I didn't understand it back then, but I do now. Your grandfather loved your grandmother very much, but he also worried that a young, attractive woman like her might leave him someday.

> One day she danced with a young writer. The writer invited her to attend a Hong Kong salon, to meet the literati. Shortly after that, the writer disappeared, and your grandmother was confined, first to the island, then to the house. Later, she wasn't even allowed to leave her room. He forced us all in. *(distraught)* He boarded up all the

doors and windows! We were all trapped inside, living like rats, in the dark . . .

Frank consoles his Aunt. She regains her composure.

One day your grandmother couldn't take any more. That night, she quietly came to my bedside, and touched my face. Your mom was asleep next to me. Your grandmother said to me: "Forgive me, my sweetheart. Take care of your little sister. I hope one day you will understand why I need to do what I'm doing now . . ."

Aunt Kiyo gives Frank a small silk pouch.

The night she escaped, your grandmother gave this to me. I never saw her again.

Frank opens the pouch. He is astounded to find a pendant identical to Enji's.

Your grandfather used all his considerable resources to find her, without success. The heights of his happiness had become the depths of his suffering. He was so mad that he locked us two children in the back room.

Frank opens the pendant. The music box plays the Manchurian folk song "Lullaby." He is incredulous.

I couldn't keep my promise to your grandmother. I made up my mind to escape, too. I gave this pendant to your mother, and climbed over the wall. I was only 10. I had to learn to survive, alone in Wan Chai. Do you have any idea what that means?

FRANK: How can it be?

AUNT KIYO: This pendant came back into my possession when your mother passed away. It's only right that you have it.

When your mother was ill, in the final stages, I came back to Peng Chau to take care of her. On her deathbed, she told me to seal her room after she died, which I did. She passed away in that back room. I handled all the funeral affairs. Now the story of those dark days can finally be put to rest.

Silence.

FRANK: Thank you, Aunt Kiyo.

AUNT KIYO: For what? Your mother lived such a difficult life.

Frank glances at a document.

FRANK: Aunt Kiyo, my mother's name was . . . Sophora?

AUNT KIYO: That's right, Sophora.

FRANK: Sophora Ho.

AUNT KIYO: It's the name of the beautiful tree in our ancestral hometown. Your grandfather used to tell me that when the sophora blos-
somed in May, the petals looked like snowflakes when they drifted in
the breeze. And so the saying, "snow-like sophora." As a child, I was
so jealous of her beautiful name.

FRANK: *(carefully)* Was her nickname "Enji"?

AUNT KIYO: *(slowly)* En-ji . . . ?

Aunt Kiyo is suddenly emotional.

It's been so long since I heard that name, I'd almost forgotten it! How
did you know? Yes, Enji! Alas!

Aunt's face has softened. Frank is speechless.

Look at our little Enji's son, all grown up!

Aunt Kiyo is overcome with emotion.

FRANK: Aunt Kiyo, how could one person be so cruel to another?

AUNT KIYO: To the cruel, there is nothing called cruel, there is only
something called need. Your grandfather did what he did because of
his needs, and he got away with it. It was the same with your father.
Actually, that's the story of the world.

Silence. Aunt's words appear in the rain and vanish.
Aunt Kiyo and Frank embrace.

Scene 11

*The Happyology classroom. Frank addresses the students. But he is pensive,
and goes off script, so the Assistant, who waits for his cues to tear the next sheet
off the easel, is at a loss.*

FRANK: When external forces are too strong for us to resist, does "active
pursuit" still work? When order loses to chaos, when light can no

longer envelop the dark, does the entire system disintegrate? What am I saying? Am I doubting my own materials?

Assistant waves "no" to the audience.

You're damn right I am!

Assistant is befuddled.

Because I want you all to question what you are learning! The energies that we are "actively appealing to" are in fact our hidden desires. If we only look to satisfy these differing levels of needs, without questioning their legitimacy, without questioning where they come from, then what is the so-called happiness that we strive to achieve? Dismissed!

Frank exits. The Assistant smiles awkwardly at the audience.

Scene 12

In the Happyology office, Fiona is making coffee. Ford sits thinking. Frank enters.

FRANK: I need to talk to you about something really important.

FIONA: I'm actually doing something really important now: a perfect cup of coffee. I'm trying medium ground at 260 at 55 today.

FRANK: It has to do with my life, my everything.

FIONA: This also has to do with my everything. Think carefully: Frank, you're the key to the whole puzzle! Sell that old house, and all our problems are solved!

FRANK: Career, love, everything snaps into place, bonanza!

FIONA: As long as you can look at the bigger picture, everyone is happy.

FRANK: Meaning?

FIONA: You're selfish, egoistical, and narrow minded. That's what I mean!

Frank shakes his head. Fiona gives a cup of coffee to the silent Ford.

FRANK: You don't have a clue what's going on in my mind. That little girl, do you know who she is? She's . . . she's . . .

Frank is unable to explain.

> FIONA: She's what? Why are you using a little girl as an excuse to obstruct the entire transaction?

> FRANK: If the house is sold, I may never have the chance to . . .

> FIONA: To what? To stroll by the sea and ponder your long-lost childhood? To listen for whispers of bygone days in the ocean waves? How childish! Idiocy beyond imagination! Opportunities like this just don't come by every day!

> FRANK: I'm taking the day off. You sub for the class if you can. *(pointing at Ford)* Best if he goes to teach it.

Frank exits.

> FORD: *(pointing at the coffee)* Bitter.

Scene 13

Frank speaks to the audience, as the scene shifts back to the island.

> FRANK: Taking the ferry to Peng Chau became my obsession. I would sit outside the old house and gaze at the sea, hoping the waves would bring me some revelation. It often seemed so futile to "Actively Seek to Create Opportunity in Serendipity." But I refused to give up.

Frank walks on the beach at Peng Chau from the direction of the ferry.
Outside the house on Peng Chau, he sits down in the old cane chair, gazing at the sea.

> FRANK: *(softly)* Enji . . . Enji . . .

Frank checks his watch. Sound of the ferry horn.
It starts to rain. Frank gets up to go, and opens his umbrella.
Enji appears on the beach. She smiles at him.
Frank goes to hold his umbrella for Enji. They exit together in the direction of the ferry.

Scene 14

Night. Frank and Enji are sitting on a bench at a famous theme park. Enji wears a mascot hat.

ENJI: We've had so much fun today, Sir! What will we do now?

FRANK: We've got a great spot to catch the fireworks!

Enji looks confused.

You've never seen fireworks?

Enji shakes her head. Frank is suddenly sad.

ENJI: What's wrong, Sir?

FRANK: Life presents so many challenges. I've never had anyone I could really talk to. My mother . . . *(looking at Enji)* She was gone so long ago. Ever since I was a kid I've wished I could see her. And now, I'm in a dream that I might wake up from any minute. I see you! And now, just when no one knows how long this will last, I don't know what to say! I can't figure out what's important and what isn't.

Pause.

ENJI: Sir, you think very deeply about things.

FRANK: *(laughing)* No, I don't! I'm just afraid. That I won't be able to see you next time.

ENJI: Why?

FRANK: I don't understand: how do you actually get to my house?

ENJI: Here's the secret. Whenever I feel down, I put my head against the wall in the closet in my room, and I close my eyes and keep thinking: I want to get out, I want to get out—and then, I get out!

FRANK: Your closet? But . . . how do you know you can still get out next time?

ENJI: I do what you say.

FRANK: What?

ENJI: "You can't refuse to want something just because you're worried you might lose it."

The fireworks display starts.

> FRANK: Here we go!

> ENJI: Wow! I've never seen anything like this!

>> Wait, yes, I remember! I did see fireworks before! Sir, you've brought it back to me! When I was very little, still in the arms of grown-ups, there were fireworks right next to my house! They went up so high in the sky and reflected on the sea, everywhere, it was so beautiful . . .

> FRANK: It was your uncle who set them.

> ENJI: Really?

> FRANK: It was your mother who held you in her arms.

> ENJI: How do you know? (*pause*) It's true! Yes, Sir, I see her now! I don't remember her, but all of a sudden I can see her face. She's so beautiful!

Enji's eyes well up.

>> Thank you, Sir. Thank you for letting me see my mother. Mother, I'm sorry I was naughty and made you leave.

> FRANK: *(softly)* She didn't . . .

> ENJI: What?

> FRANK: She didn't leave because of you . . .

> ENJI: How do you know?

> FRANK: Enji, does Uncle ever . . . treat you badly?

> ENJI: What?

> FRANK: Does he . . . beat you?

> ENJI: No, he is very kind to me.

> FRANK: Has he ever touched you?

> ENJI: No. Why?

> FRANK: Enji, have you ever thought of leaving him?

> ENJI: No! That's impossible!

FRANK: Why not? You can climb over the wall and get out. That's what your sister did.

ENJI: No, Sir, you don't know. He'll catch me! He'll . . .

FRANK: He'll beat you?

ENJI: No, he won't beat me. He'll be sad. He'll beat himself.

FRANK: What a total—

Frank is in anguish.

ENJI: Sir?

FRANK: Enji, is your real name Sophora?

ENJI: *(surprised)* How did you know?

FRANK: So it's really you! Sophora Ho.

ENJI: I never told you that! My uncle wouldn't allow me to say it.

FRANK: Your father.

ENJI: No, my uncle.

FRANK: He's your father. He's locked you up in the house and won't let you out. What a—

Frank stops short of cursing the man.

ENJI: Who are you?

Frank is in despair.

FRANK: You wouldn't understand.

ENJI: Tell me.

FRANK: I don't even understand.

ENJI: Why are you sad, Sir? We're together. We should be happy, right?

FRANK: There are many things I know that you don't.

ENJI: Tell me.

FRANK: I don't know how! You won't believe any of it, and what will it change if you do? All I know is there will be lots of unhappiness in your life.

ENJI: Why are you telling me this? You're frightening me, Sir!

Frank takes a deep breath and calms down.

FRANK: Okay. Stop. You're right. Let's not think unhappy thoughts. Here we are, together, the fireworks are blazing in the sky. You're happy, and so am I. And you know, it's a miracle! Every second we have together, Enji, is such a miracle! Life is too short to waste on thinking about what's going to happen next.

Pause. They watch the fireworks.

Enji, life may be challenging, and it may be short, but you must know that you're not alone. There are people in the world who care about you. Every person you encounter in life, even a stranger, might have some connection with you, but you just don't know what it is. They might be connected to you in profound ways, and so you should try to treat them all well.

You'll remember that?

ENJI: I will.

Silence. Frank is overcome.

Sir, why are you crying?

FRANK: Because . . . I'm so happy.

They laugh.
The fireworks show continues.

Scene 15

Frank and Enji in the old house, late night. Frank lights the wall with his cell phone.

FRANK: Enji, where do you actually go in?

ENJI: Here, *(pointing)* and that's where I come out every time. *(pointing at the large glass window)* I go out through there to the beach.

FRANK: You don't recognize where we are?

ENJI: No. Where are we?

FRANK: This is the hall of your house. You've never been here?

ENJI: Isn't it your house?

Pause.

> I need to get back.

FRANK: Wait, Enji. If, I mean, if we never see each other again, I want you to know that you will surely see me in the future.

ENJI: How do you know?

FRANK: Because of this.

Frank wraps Enji's hand around his finger.

> This is me.

ENJI: I don't understand.

FRANK: No need to.

ENJI: I'm going.

FRANK: Enji . . .

ENJI: Huh?

FRANK: Be careful.

ENJI: I will. Thank you, Sir. Goodbye.

She puts her theme park hat on Frank, then disappears through the glass doors.

Scene 16

The office. Fiona is making coffee. Frank enters.

FIONA: I've got Guatemalan Hilltop today.

FRANK: I finished the new curriculum materials. You won't like them.

FIONA: This calls for 300 grams at three minutes. Why?

FRANK: Because they're real.

FIONA: What's real?

FRANK: They teach people about real happiness, rather than spoon-feeding them some cheesy aphorisms "for the soul."

FIONA: What did you just say?

FRANK: Feel offended? Can't take a little pinch of truth?

FIONA: Not at all. I couldn't care less what you write in the curriculum, as long we have something. We can wrap it in a bunch of flashy adjectives, and people will buy it. What really concerns me is the gap in funding.

FRANK: Stop pressuring me, will you?

FIONA: You stop pressuring me!

FRANK: What pressure can you possibly have?

FIONA: Do you have any idea that Ford is destroying his own future by being with me?! If I have even a single trace of conscience, shouldn't I leave him?

Pause.

FRANK: Listen. I feel I finally have something real to say about happiness, about the moment, about cherishing. As though every moment of life is a miracle manifesting around us. Joy, pain, or even your trace of conscience—when you truly live in that moment and embrace it, whatever it is, you've achieved a state that can only be called "flourishing," like a flower in perennial bloom.

Fiona is already on the phone.

FIONA: *(on the phone)* Hello? . . . Sure, let's do dinner . . . okay, no instant noodles today . . . my treat, no problem. *(hangs up)*

She gets up to go.

FRANK: Oh my god, he's so down and out, and look how you are standing by him! How touching. I guess I WAS wrong about you. Or does he still hold a teeny-weeny bit of surplus value you can squeeze out of him?

FIONA: Wrong. *(slowly)* Perhaps I've learned something, too—to accept everything life has in store for you, miraculous or mundane. But I wouldn't call it "flourishing." I'd call it "getting by."

She exits.
Frank takes out his phone.

FRANK: *(on the phone)* Hello, Mrs. Hwong? Are you free tomorrow? I'll be coming by Peng Chau and maybe we can get those papers signed . . .

Scene 17

In the old house, Frank sits in the old cane chair, deep in thought.
Enter Ford and Fiona. They high-five.

FIONA AND FORD: Hooray!

FORD: Frank sold the house! That's awesome! How did he come around?

FIONA: He just did!

FORD: But how?

FIONA: I have no idea! He just said he decided to sell the place and "let everything go with the ocean breeze."

FORD: What's "everything"?

FIONA: I have no idea.

Ford talks to his recorder pen.

FORD: *(to recorder pen)* 0-5-2-1-dot-2: Peng Chau. Who could imagine an old dump like this would be the source of my redemption? If all goes well, I'll get back my job within a month, and say goodbye to instant noodles. I refused to surrender. This marks a critical victory in my life, in which I have also learned the meaning of humility—to endure insult, to understand modesty—I am so goddam humble now, I'M THE GODDAM HUMBLEST PERSON IN THE WORLD!

Fiona slaps him on the back.
Enter the Real Estate Agent.

REAL ESTATE AGENT: All the paperwork is ready to go. My office?

FIONA: Here is fine.

The Real Estate Agent approaches Frank carefully.

REAL ESTATE AGENT: Someone must be giving you tips. The price went up another million! Congratulations!

FIONA: Don't talk to him. He's not in the mood.

REAL ESTATE AGENT: Why not? You just made some serious money! Laugh! You've got to laugh! You've got to be happy!

FRANK: *(shaking his head, to himself)* Enji . . . Enji . . .

Fiona pulls the Real Estate Agent aside.

REAL ESTATE AGENT: *(to Fiona)* So get him to sign here, here, and here, and we're done! I'll have everything ready right away, and you'll get the money next week!

Enji appears from under the stairs.
Frank sees her, and is ecstatic.

FRANK: Enji! I've been here so many times and didn't see you. I thought . . .

ENJI: Here I am!

REAL ESTATE AGENT: What are you doing messing around here, little girl? Run along now!

FRANK: Uh, Mrs. Hwong, listen, I'll talk to you later.

REAL ESTATE AGENT: What? You're putting me off again?

FRANK: The deal is on hold. *(to Enji)* Let's go, I'll take you to . . .

ENJI: The aquarium?

FRANK: You bet!

Frank and Enji exit. Fiona and Ford are flabbergasted.

FORD: What just happened?

REAL ESTATE AGENT: That little girl jinxed me again!

Scene 18

Frank and Enji visit a large aquarium. Enji is holding cotton candy, jumping around in excitement. Frank's mood is subdued. His words appear on the glass and then vanish, as if in water.

FRANK: *(voice-over)* I took Enji to Ocean World. We watched the dolphin show. She was so happy, but I kept worrying about the impending end. Would this be the last time? I couldn't decide what to do. I needed time . . . time . . .

Scene 19

Frank's apartment. A messy living room with a couch and coffee table. A door leads to the study. A speaker for music, same as in his office.
Enter Frank and Enji. Enji has aquarium souvenirs with her.

ENJI: That was so great, Sir! Everywhere you take me is fun! Where are we now?

FRANK: This is where I live.

ENJI: *(looking at the view outside the window)* Wow!

FRANK: Yes, you can see Victoria Harbor from here.

ENJI: Oh. Aren't you afraid, living this high up?

FRANK: No, I'm not.

ENJI: So what are we doing at your house, Sir?

Frank uses his phone to play music on the speaker: Bach's "Three-Part Inventions, No. 11 in G minor."

FRANK: Nothing. Thought we'd might just hang out for a bit.

ENJI: Sir, the music. It's so beautiful.

Enji listens to the music, and is moved.

It's like calling me from somewhere far away.

FRANK: Now I know where I got my taste.

ENJI: What?

FRANK: Nothing. Have you never heard Bach?

Enji shakes her head.

To think that someone could not have this music in their life.

ENJI: But now I do. Thank you, sir.

FRANK: No, thank YOU, Enji.

They listen quietly for a moment, watching the harbor in the twilight. Enter Fiona and Ford with bags of food.

FIONA: We're here!

Fiona takes out sushi, dim sum, and other snacks.

FRANK: Let's eat!

FIONA: This sushi is the best in Wan Chai!

ENJI: *(the name rings a bell)* Wan Chai?

FRANK: Come on! Dig in!

ENJI: But . . . I have to go back, it's getting dark.

FRANK: It's all right, just a bite, okay?

ENJI: Wow, what are these?

FORD: Sashimi. Raw fish.

ENJI: Raw? Can I eat them?

FORD: *(to Frank)* She's never seen sushi before?

Frank nods.

   (to recorder pen) 0-5-2-1-dot-8: She's never seen sushi before.

   (to Fiona) Oh, and can we change the music here?

FRANK: No, we cannot *(to Enji)*.

   Here, try some char-siu buns.

ENJI: *(eating)* Delicious!

FRANK: Enji, do you like it here?

Fiona glances at Frank, thinking his question odd.

ENJI: Yes, I do.

FRANK: Then would you like to stay here until tomorrow?

ENJI: What?

FIONA AND FORD: What?!

FIONA: What the hell are you doing, Frank?

FRANK: If you like, you can stay tomorrow, and the day after, and every day. What if you don't go back? Just live here?

ENJI: What do you mean, Sir? No, if I don't go back, what about Uncle?

FORD: Frank, that's false imprisonment!

FRANK: YOUR UNCLE CAN GO AND SHOVE IT—*(controlling himself)* Uncle can take care of himself.

FIONA: Frank, are you out of your mind?

ENJI: But I can't! I have to go back and be with Uncle. It's getting late now and he must be waiting. Please, take me back, Sir!

FRANK: Enji, don't worry, come with me.

Frank takes Enji through the doorway to the study.

ENJI: You're going to lock me up?

FRANK: Now, how can you say that? It's complicated . . . I have to figure things out . . .

Frank suddenly closes the door and locks it from outside.

ENJI: *(from inside)* Let me out, Sir!

Frank covers his ears and shouts.

FRANK: This is all for your own good! I NEED TIME TO THINK!

ENJI: *(from inside)* You've locked me up!

FIONA: Frank, STOP THIS NOW!

FRANK: Quiet! You be quiet, and we can figure something out!

ENJI: *(from inside)* But I need to go back now!

FRANK: QUIET!

Frank breaks down. He can barely stand.

(*softly*) I'm sorry . . . sorry . . .

Enji stops yelling from within.

> *Pause. Fiona and Ford have been watching, dumbstruck.*

> FORD: You can't do this!

> FIONA: Frank, you'd better have an incredibly persuasive and legitimate explanation!

> FRANK: I can't lose her again.

> FIONA: *(grabbing her phone)* I'm calling the police.

> FRANK: Trust me for a moment: I can't send her back to that prison.

> FIONA: What prison?

> FRANK: She's being kept prisoner in that old beach house, by her father!

> FIONA: What old beach house?

> FORD: The 20-million-dollar one?

> FRANK: Yes!

> FORD: What?

> FIONA: Who are you talking about?

> FRANK: How can I explain? *(suddenly)* She's my mother.

Pause.

> FIONA: Frank, you'd better have something better than that.

> FRANK: It's true. I tried to tell you over and over again, but every time you were either busy making your coffee, or basking in your millionaire pipe dream.

Ford thinks it over.

> FORD: Wait a minute. You're saying she's your mother's—reincarnation? Is that what we're talking about?

> FRANK: No, we're not talking about reincarnation. She IS my mother.

> FORD: But she's a child!

> FIONA: How's that even possible?

FRANK: I don't know, either. But don't you think she doesn't belong some-how? So many things she's never seen before, and her clothes . . .

FIONA: Pretty fashionable throwbacks.

FRANK: The first time I saw her was her first time out of the house. She'd never seen the outside world, never even been to Hong Kong. And when I found out she wasn't in school, I almost called the police. But she was prisoner in her house back in the 1970s! What kind of police could possibly come to her aid now?

FORD: Time Cop!

Fiona slaps Ford in the arm.

FIONA: Be serious!

FORD: I am being serious! I'm analyzing all the possibilities!

FIONA: *(to Frank)* She's your mother?

FRANK: I don't expect you guys to believe me.

FIONA: I wish I could, but all this is beyond reason.

FRANK: I know, but everything that's happened recently has confirmed that she's my mother. A child, trapped. We can't just take her back.

FIONA: So you're transferring her from one prison to another? Is that your idea of helping her?

FORD: Hold on a moment. If you keep her here and never let her go back, will you . . . even exist? If we lock up this child, who you claim to be your mother, thus changing the course of her life, then are you going to be like "poof!" and vanish in front of our eyes? Poof, gone! But if "poof," you don't exist, then your company won't exist, then I won't need to raise 20 million, which means I won't get kicked out by my own company, which means I won't need to live on instant noodles for two months!

Pause.

But if your company doesn't exist, then I don't get to meet Fiona. Maybe Fiona herself ceases to exist. Maybe I cease to exist, too!

Pause. Ford has succeeded in scaring himself.

Frank, let her out. She needs to go back.

Frank moves to the study door.

>FRANK: What the hell was I thinking? I've completely lost my mind! *(to the door)* Enji, don't be afraid. I would never harm you.

Frank listens. Nothing.

>Enji? Enji? . . .

Frank opens the door only to find an empty room.

>Enji . . .

>FIONA: Where could she possibly have gone?

The window curtains billow in the breeze.

Scene 20

Frank addresses the audience.

>FRANK: That was the last time I saw Enji. I spent the night on the deserted pier, gazing at the dark nothingness of the sea. I took the first ferry to Peng Chau, watching the sun rise out of the South China Sea, shining light on a new day.

>At Peng Chau, there was nothing for me to do but hang around the old house, and wait. For what?

>My life went on, but I never stopped thinking of Enji. She seemed to be everywhere. Life had delivered a mystery to me, allowing me to be a fleeting part of a miracle. But what did it all mean? I couldn't fathom.

Peng Chau. Frank paces inside the old house.

>I kept ferrying over to Peng Chau, walking around the old house, whispering her name. Enji. But I knew perfectly well I had messed up bad. She would never come again.

>Time passed. I decided to sell the house. The day the deal was to close, I sat alone at the window, watching the sea.

Frank sits on the cane chair.
The Real Estate Agent enters, carefully handing Frank the contract, apprehensively.

REAL ESTATE AGENT: *(half joking)* Mr. Ho! You can't change your mind this time! The buyer might not be able to handle the shock.

Fiona and Ford enter, looking around.

I need just three signatures: here, *(Frank signs)* here, *(Frank signs)* and . . .

Pause. The Real Estate Agent realizes in horror that she has forgotten a document.

Ha ha, forgot the most important one! Be right back!

The Real Estate Agent exits.
Frank gets up, and inspects the glass doors where he last saw Enji go in.

FRANK: *(gently)* Enji . . .

FIONA: *(sternly)* Are we done here?

FRANK: *(to himself)* This is where she would always appear . . .

FIONA: Stop babbling. I'm asking you: are we done? If we are, let's get out of here.

Ford leans on a beam and accidentally pushes it to the ground, revealing an opening behind it.

FORD: What the—?

FRANK: Look, there's a passageway here!

Frank starts tearing down the wooden bars around the glass doors.

FIONA: Listen, you guys, we need to focus.

Ford strikes the wall. Boards fall off, revealing more of the passageway. They look. Frank goes in.

What? Where are you guys going?

The Real Estate Agent enters with the document.

REAL ESTATE AGENT: What's going on?

Scene 21

Enji's small room. Frank emerges from the passageway into the room. He is amazed to see everything just as she described it. A simple bed. A portrait of the adult Enji hangs on the wall, in Fauvist style, beside an old calendar.
From the closet, enter Fiona, Ford, and the Real Estate Agent.

FORD: Whoa, a hidden chamber!

REAL ESTATE AGENT: Wait a minute. I recognize this place. This is your mother's room. We used to come in from that door on the other side where the back garden is. How come we're coming through a closet?

Ford studies the calendar on the wall.

FORD: "March 14, 1993. Peng Chau Residents' Committee . . ."

Frank looks out the window and sees the wildflowers in the small garden with weeds and vines.
Frank steps out into the garden. The others follow.

FIONA: Look, it's just the way she described it. The flowers are in bloom! It's been deserted for so long.

They explore the overgrown garden.

FRANK: *(pointing)* Over there.

FIONA: A well!

Frank goes to the well. He sees an old string, and starts pulling on it. He fishes a plastic thermos out of the well—the same one Enji had at the fast food restaurant. Frank is astonished. He opens it and takes out the recorder pen. He holds it tightly.
Ford and the Real Estate Agent come near.

REAL ESTATE AGENT: Well, Mr. Ho, just one more signature. Shall we get it over with?

Pause. Frank looks at the pen in his hand.

FRANK: Mrs. Hwong . . . I don't know how to say this. I'm not selling.

REAL ESTATE AGENT: What?

FRANK: I'm really sorry. I won't change my mind this time. Thank you.

The Real Estate Agent is stunned.

> FORD: *(recording)* 0-7-2-9-dot-1: . . . What I'm feeling at this moment is . . . is . . .

As if waking up, Ford seems to realize the absurdity of his actions.

> What the hell am I doing?

Ford throws his recording pen into the well.
The Real Estate Agent picks up all her documents and exits, ready to cry.

Scene 22

Time has passed. Enji's room has been transformed into an activity center. The portrait of Enji and the mascot hat hang on the wall. A Customer sits next to the well, drinking coffee.
Frank, in casual dress, addresses the audience.

> FRANK: Fiona and I sold the Happyology business. We used some of the profits for basic renovations to the old house.
>
> The house is now a center for adults who had traumatic childhoods, a place where they can heal. It's called "Enji's House."

Fiona serves coffee to the Customer.

> Fiona is also doing what she's passionate about—well, at least for now. She's opened her café here. She definitely makes the best coffee in Peng Chau.

Ford enters, in sunglasses. He picks up an electric guitar, and plays some unbearably esoteric hard licks. Fiona encourages him.

> Ford has also heeded the call of his heart. He practices hard every day, hoping to be discovered. Unfortunately, as you can see, he's just not very talented.
>
> About the recorder pen from the well: the batteries were, of course, dead. I put in fresh ones.

Frank turns, and is now speaking to a small gathering. He holds the recorder pen in his hand.

> So is happiness something that can really be learned? This audio clip I'm about to play comes from a person who had very little of it in her

life. It was a short life, a fleeting 25 years, most of it confined to this tiny room. Her name was Enji.

Frank plays the recording on the recorder pen. Enji's voice, the weak voice of an adult woman, comes out of the device.
During the following, the adult Enji appears in her room, while Fiona and Ford quietly drink coffee next to the well.

GROWN-UP ENJI: *(recorded voice)* "This is my 25th year in the world. Perhaps my last. I haven't been well for quite some time. I don't think I'll see the flowers in the garden bloom this year . . ."

The 25-year-old Enji wanders into the garden, speaking to the recorder pen. She is dressed modestly. She is poignant, choosing her words carefully. Bach's "Three Part Inventions" play in the background.

GROWN-UP ENJI: All my life I've lived in this tiny room. My father locked me in here when I was a girl. You may wonder why. But I choose not to. It was as if some force held us together to live out our dark hours in tortured companionship. As the years passed, I somehow got used to the dark, and used to being the only flicker in his dismal world.

One day, my father was no more, and I was free to go. But I had grown too used to the darkness, and so I stayed on.

Many would consider my life the cruelest of destinies. But looking back, there was a time in my childhood when I found a light. I discovered a passageway from this room to the outside world. There, I met a kind man who showed me life as I had never seen it before. He is the one who gave me this recording pen. He taught me that if I made a wish at my well, my dreams would come true. I tried many times, but how could someone like me have any dreams? All I could do was wish that no one in this world would have to go through what I have.

Those few days when I encountered him were the happiest of my life. I'll always remember his kindness—so pure, so unconditional, like the rays of the sun.

I don't know where you are now, Sir. But if you ever hear this recording, I want to say thank you.

Sophora Ho, winter of 1992.

Rain.

    Enji goes back to her room and closes a window.

    Frank takes out his pendant and opens it. Music plays.

    Enji seems to hear the music and comes out. They stand together in the garden, in the rain. Enji takes out her pendant and opens it. Music from the two pendants play concurrently.

    Enji and Frank seem to see each other. They approach each other, holding out their hands as if feeling in the dark.

    Before they reach each other, a strong breeze. Enji turns, and goes back into her room, closing the glass door.

    Frank gazes at the glass door.

    Raindrops gather and form words, only to wash away and vanish.

    Lights fade out.

    The End

On the Contributor to Volume 2

INTRODUCTION

Raymond Zhou (Hangzhou University, Sun Yatsen University, U.C. Berkeley) Zhou is among China's most influential film and theatre critics; media figure; prolific writer; author of 21 books, three in English; playwright. The only Chinese cultural critic whose photos have appeared in *Time* magazine, *The New York Times*, and *The Los Angeles Times*, which called him "Beijing's answer to Roger Ebert."

On Lissa Tyler Renaud

Editor and Translations Editor

Lissa Tyler Renaud earned her M.F.A. in directing and Ph.D. *summa cum laude* (1987) in theatre history and criticism, with an emphasis in art history, at U.C. Berkeley, where she also taught for four years. She is a lifelong actress, a director, dramaturg, and recitalist. Her honors and awards for acting and teaching include Ford Foundation and National Science Council grants.

Founder-director of the influential InterArts Training for the theatre, based in Oakland, California, Renaud has also been visiting professor, master teacher, invited and keynote speaker, and panelist and juror in countries east, west, north, and south. She has trained countless actors and directors, and given lectures for theatre professionals and scholars at major theatre institutions of Asia—Korea, Taiwan, China, Singapore, India—as well as around the U.S. and in England, Mexico, Sweden, and Russia. She has published widely on the early European avant-garde, and on the theoretical and practical training of the actor-scholar—including an invited chapter in the *Routledge Companion to Stanislavsky.*

Renaud is an internationally recognized, second generation editor and translations editor: co-editor of *The Politics of American Actor Training* (Routledge); a senior writer and theatre critic for *Scene4*, an international magazine of culture and arts, where she is founder-editor of the "Kandinsky Anew" series on Kandinsky's theatre works; founding editor for the Wuzhen Theatre Festival, China; and, for the International Association of Theatre Critics, she was longtime, founding English editor of its English-French *Critical Stages* (UNESCO), for which she remains a regularly contributing critic and board member.

Stan Lai, photo by Xiao Quan

On Stan Lai

Stan Lai (Lai Shengchuan) is considered "The best Chinese language play-wright and director in the world" (BBC), "The preeminent Chinese play-wright and stage director of this generation" (*China Daily*), and "Asia's top theatre director" (*Asiaweek*). His prolific and profound work has pioneered the course of modern theatre in Taiwan, China, and other Chinese-speaking regions, and includes plays that are regarded as masterpieces of the modern Chinese-language theatre such as *Secret Love in Peach Blossom Land, The Village*, and his epic 8 hour *A Dream Like A Dream*, which *China Daily* called "possibly the greatest Chinese-language play since time immemorial."

Born in Washington, D.C. in 1954, Lai grew up bilingual in America and Taiwan. After receiving a Ph.D. in dramatic art at U.C. Berkeley, he began his career in Taiwan in the 1980s, during a time of martial law, when little orga-nized theatre activity existed. He chose not to imitate Western works, instead using improvisation as a tool to build plays with his students and actors, a technique he learned from Shireen Strooker of the Amsterdam Werkteater. The results were uniquely new but accessible theatrical forms that dealt organically with the emerging issues of the day. Lai's over 40 original plays chronicle the external and internal journeys of the fast changing Chinese speaking world. Many earlier works were done with his Taipei-based Perfor-mance Workshop. Since 1998, his plays have been performed in China, influ-encing a generation of theatre artists and audiences.

Lai is also an award-winning filmmaker (*The Peach Blossom Land*, 1992) as well as an acclaimed opera and event director. He is Artistic Director of Performance Workshop, Taiwan, and Theatre Above, Shanghai, a venue ded-icated to the performance of his works, as well as co-founder and Festival Director of the Wuzhen Theatre Festival. Lai is a celebrated author on creativ-ity, and has taught extensively at Taipei National University of the Arts, U.C. Berkeley, Stanford University, and CalArts. He is married to Nai-chu Ding, who over the years has produced most of his work.